# Witnessing Bigfoot

## Flesh and Blood, Native American Legend, or the Devil Himself?

Glen S Boulier

*Pine Winds Press*

*Pine Winds Press*
An imprint of Idyll Arbor, Inc.
39129 264$^{th}$ Ave SE, Enumclaw, WA 98022
www.PineWindsPress.com

Cover Design: Curt Pliler
Pine Winds Press Editor: Autumn Conley

Photographs: Glen Boulier, except where credited on the photograph
Bigfoot cast on the cover from Christopher L. Murphy



paper ISBN 9780937663288
e-book ISBN 9780937663295

**Library of Congress Cataloging-in-Publication Data**

Boulier, Glen S.
Witnessing bigfoot : flesh and blood, Native American legend, or the devil himself? / Glen S Boulier.
pages cm
Includes bibliographical references.
ISBN 978-0-937663-28-8 -- ISBN 978-0-937663-29-5 (ebook)
1. Sasquatch. I. Title.
QL89.2.S2B69 2015
001.944--dc23

2014040738

*I believe there is something tangible to the mystery...*

*it's what a Sasquatch is that plays with my beliefs.*

*— Roman Forczek (The Bigfoot Forums)*

# Contents

## *Acknowledgments*

I would like to thank the following authors, magazines, website owners, and publishers for their generosity and permission to use the following copyrighted material. Copyright in all material remains with the original owner.

- Bigfoot Field Researchers Organization (BFRO). www.BFRO.net [BFRO1], [BFRO2], [BFRO3], [BFRO4]
- Bowman, Matthew. 2007. *Journal of Mormon History, Volume 33.* [MB1], [MB2]
- Clark, Ella E. 2003. *Indian Legends of the Pacific Northwest.* University of California Press. [EEC1]
- Clark, Jerome. 1990. UFO's: in the 1980s. *The UFO Encyclopedia, Vol. I.* Apogee Books. [JC1]
- Coleman, Loren. John A. Keel Has Died. Cryptomundo. http://www.cryptomundo.com/cryptozoo-news/keel-obit [LCJK1]
- Crowe, Ray. The International Bigfoot Society. http://bigfootology.com/?page_id=811 [RC1]
- Currie, Laurie. 1970. Sasquatch on Film Here. *The Similkameen Spotlight.*[LC1]
- Darwin, Charles. 1872. *The Expression of the Emotions in Man and Animals.* John Murray (publisher). [CD1]
- Fattig, Paul. 2006. Bigfoot Beware, *Mail Tribune — Southern Oregon's News Source*. [PF1]
- Franzoni, Henry J. 2009. *In the Spirit of Seatco.* Ste Ye Hah Publishing. [HJF1]
- Green, John. 1992. John Green Interview with Bob Gimlin. Bigfoot Encounters. http://www.bigfootencounters.com. [JG4]

- Green, John. Reward Article. Bigfoot Encounters. http://www.bigfootencounters.com [JG3]
- Green, John. Sasquatch Database. http://www.sasquatchdatabase.com [JG1] [JG2]
- Highpine, Gayle. 1992. *The Track Record #18.* [GH1]
- Keel, John A. 1970. *UFO's: Operation Trojan Horse.* Putnam. [JAK1]
- Kroeber, Alfred L. 1925. *Handbook of the Indians of California.* Washington, DC: Bureau of American Ethnology Bulletin No. 78. [ALK1]
- Mallery, Garrick. 1886. *Pictographs of the North American Indians: A Preliminary Paper.* U.S. Gov Printing Office. [GM1]
- Marcot, Bruce G. ... *around the world, they call it Sasquatch, Forest Man, Yeti, Bigfoot, Matdngdng*. [BGM1]
- Martin, Rick and Cortright, Gail. 2000. *The Spectrum Magazine.* March 2000. [RM1]
- Matthews, Gerry and Kristian, Ken. West Coast Sasquatch. http://www.westcoast-sasquatch.com [GMKK1] [GMKK2] [GMKK3]
- Morgan, Robert W. 2008. *Bigfoot Observer's Field Manual.* Pine Winds Press. [RWM1]
- Palmroth, Bill. 1992. See No Sasquatch. *Oregon Fish & Wildlife Journal*. Winter 1992 Edition. [BP1]
- Powell, Thom. Review of *In the Spirit of Seatco.* Bigfoot Encounters. http://www.bigfootencounters.com. [TP1]
- Pyle, Robert Michael. 1997. *Where Bigfoot Walks: Crossing the Dark Divide.* Houghton Mifflin Harcourt.[RMP1], [RMP2]
- Short, Bobbie. Bigfoot Encounters. http://www.bigfootencounters.com. [BS1]
- Wilson, Lycurgus A. 1900. *The Life of David W. Patten.* Salt Lake City: Desert News. [LAW1]
- Yellow Bird, Dorreen. 2004. Big Foot in North Dakota? Maybe, Just Maybe. *The Grand Forks Herald.* [DYB1]
- Yellow Bird, Dorreen. 2004. Tales of Sightings Lend Credence to Bigfoot Myth. *The Grand Forks Herald.* [DYB2] [DYB3]

# Prologue

It's all been said many times before: A race of hairy giants roam the wild lands and woodlands of North America, creatures of a strange origin seen periodically and by thousands of witnesses. These patterns continue today, with these undiscovered beings seemingly out of the reach of man.

We have looked into the dark, piercing eyes of something that most say does not exist: an evasive, self-seeking, shy creature that quickly moves away with cunning and craftiness, its unsuspected intelligence leading it along. There are many chasing the *Mystery,* the "Mountain Devil," as it has been called, one of the many names associated with this two-legged, upright-walking being. Expeditions of varying sizes, comprised of individuals from all walks of life, have tried to gather critical evidence to demonstrate the existence of these forest giants, and the search for a Sasquatch-type living and breathing humanoid is not limited to any one country.

In the 1970s and 1980s, in the small, quaint logging and mining town of Princeton, British Columbia, my two brothers and I played witness to the supposedly impossible — encountering the specter coming from the wilderness. Back in 1970, our mother may have sighted a similar creature when a mysterious forest dweller terrified her in the night.

From a "witness's" standpoint, I will try and explain the supposed reality of this legend and what else may be lurking within the shadows of this phenomenon. Through nothing more than basically dumb, blind luck, this ghostly myth of apparent flesh showed itself to us, though it has eluded mankind in general — surprisingly for generations. And strangely enough, the phenomenon may have shown itself yet again, possibly visiting the rental tower of a Lincoln County, Montana, fire lookout in the early summer of 2005. My wife and our youngest boy were present that fateful night, and our strange visitor(s) left no tracks or traces of their presence.

This is the story of the Sasquatch, the wanderings of a legendary needle in a haystack — an explanation of a growing dilemma that continues to challenge man's mind and abilities.

Because of the high degree of controversy involved with this subject, I have written this book about the many caring individuals who were kind enough to share their ideas, knowledge, and beliefs. This is all a part of the Sasquatch mystery at this present time. To all of them, I am extremely thankful.

For those new to the phenomenon, welcome to the world of Bigfoot! And for those who have been searching as long and hard as I have for answers, tighten your seatbelts! We're all riding in the same bus together on this journey, and we're in for quite a ride.

## Author's Disclaimer

I believe the creature I saw in 1974 and again in 1985 was flesh and blood, an undiscovered race of bipedal giants still roaming the forests of North America, and there is evidence to support this belief.

Also, I wish to say that I believe there is a seriously pressing spiritual side involved with the Sasquatch phenomenon. I believe there are unseen forces at work in this phenomenon. We will look at the spiritual side of the puzzle from both a First Nation/Native American and a White perspective. Many authors, researchers, and scientists do not agree with my belief; however, they do offer serious-minded input into the subject itself, the Sasquatch. Their voices will be heard in this book.

I again wish to thank everyone who has participated in this project, those who have offered their own accounts of the creature and others who have shared their knowledge and ideas on a confusing but profound mystery. This creature, real or not, has touched the lives and souls of many.

— *Glen S Boulier*

# I. Flesh and Blood Bigfoot

In Part I of this book we will look at Bigfoot as a flesh and blood creature. I'll present my sightings and the reports of many other people. The plainest form of Sasquatch would be a shy and reclusive, flesh-upon-bone creature that strolls through the forests at its leisure, picking gorgeous flowers or eating honey. This is what most hope for: a new and exciting species of giants, with pictures in *National Geographic*. But with the Sasquatch solution hopefully being that of an unidentified and unrealized wilderness species, we then come to the crossroads of shadows. There is certainly more to the picture than a gentle beast.

When we are finished with Part I, we will still be left with a mystery — why is concrete physical evidence so lacking? Parts II and III will go beyond the physical evidence to look at other possibilities that might explain all of the aspects of the mystery.

First, let's start with the story of how I began my quest to understand the Forest Giant.

# 1. Cutting to the Chase

These days, the information superhighway stretches out in every conceivable direction, hosting emails, websites, blogs, voices, and pictures of a connected and networked world. This holds true for any subject that may come to mind. This enormous tally, of course, includes the legendary Sasquatch — the woodland creature of intrigue, mystery, and scarcity.

There are rumors of a two-headed Bigfoot and even of someone marrying one of the monsters of the mountains. Some argue over who was wearing what appears to some as a loose-fitting, manufactured gorilla suit in the famous and controversial Bigfoot footage of 1967 — the Patterson/Gimlin Film. In actuality, the folk story film with a cult following may be the real thing; it is still being debated fiercely over forty-seven years later. And if all this wasn't enough for the last critic standing, others give the creature extraterrestrial roots.

But it doesn't end there. Another individual on the Bigfoot bandwagon may be having the creature's baby. Some even associate Sasquatch events with happenings in their own lives and can remember where they were and what they were doing when other people's sightings occurred. The heartfelt material inside this book will identify the Sasquatch by assertions, but also detail other possibilities for the continuously growing phenomenon involving this primate.

In the summer of 2005, I had a chance to seriously look over the issue of the fleet-footed Sasquatch from yet another perspective. We were passing through British Columbia on a family holiday, and we stopped for a short time at the Sparwood Visitors' Center in the small community on the lower east side of the province. As I was casually sitting back against the wall at the Center, taking it all in, I couldn't help but notice a large rack of books on a Hancock House rotating display in the center of

**Figure 1: The business side of the creature known as Sasquatch. The Legend of Bigfoot shop off of the Redwood Highway (Highway 101) just north of Richardson Grove State Park in California.**

the room. It featured all sorts of information about the legendary giant — everything from scientific explanations to a simple Sasquatch activity coloring book for children. Clearly, there is a genuine interest among young and old, parent and child.

Some commented on the possibility of such a mysterious and elusive creature inhabiting the forests across North America. There was even mention of the monster complex — the thought of a huge wild beast on the edge of the wilderness. It seemed to excite a few people and terrify others. I must admit that it was difficult to sit there and say nothing, holding the truth in my heart, witnessing the excitement, commotion, and uncertainty while knowing very well of the strange and untamed creature they spoke of. As I thought about it, I realized once again that there must be thousands of individuals out there who are learning about this giant for the first time. We forget this sometimes, but this book is written for them, at least in part. It was particularly fascinating to watch a middle-aged couple speak of the film of October 1967. They recalled exactly where both of them were at the time and how much simpler the world was back then.

I would like to see the Sasquatch mystery retain a trace of this romanticism, as things with the phenomenon are far too stressed at times, and a few individuals have been harmed both physically and mentally over the years. Other people love a good scare, like watching a horror flick at home with the lights down low. Still others pick up the baton and run with it, their newfound interest taking them into the forests where they pursue a legend that continues to escape. Just as families take a car ride to a country road outside of town to watch a rare meteor shower in a dark sky, so it is with those who yearn to look into the whereabouts of a haired biped known as the Sasquatch, a similar road leading them to the wilderness during the day. This is the adventurous and sentimental side behind the Sasquatch sensation — something we should never forget.

Surely I had enthusiasm on my face that day at Sparwood, because my fifteen-year-old son asked me again why I was so interested in the Sasquatch. I had thought about this often. I had to compare it to the art of astronomy. What exactly are we looking for and why? Man is reaching out to the cosmos in search of answers to a mystery, to find out where we come from. When it comes to the Sasquatch, I would say, after all that has happened to me personally, I'm in it for the adventure, for the inscrutable mystery behind what is yet to be fully discovered but should be left alone when it is found. As long as man disagrees on an issue such as this, without physical evidence to rely on, Bigfoot will remain categorized as just that — a mystery.

I am so sincere in my position on the Wildman of the Woods that, if I had a high-powered rifle trained on the elusive creature, I could not pull the trigger just to prove its existence. Their being out and about doesn't mean they deserve a bullet to prove it. Sasquatch is continuing to slowly emerge as an intelligent piece of a difficult puzzle. This is what I believed wholeheartedly in the beginning. After my research, my view has changed somewhat, as you will see, but nothing has changed in my belief that they should be left alone.

The material I offer here will not necessarily help the cause of scientific study. That has already occurred, as some have fled the boundaries I laid out in investigating the many things within the phenomenon. For all of us researching this mystery, believe me when I say it will be a long, dangerous road.

In these pages, I now start by introducing you to a portion of my past — the fateful sightings of a needle in a haystack, the nomadic wanderings of what may be the Sasquatch creature.

# 2. Personal Witnessing

Let me start the presentation of evidence by telling you what my family and I have seen. What better way could there be to explain why I want to understand everything I can about Sasquatch?

## The Face of the Sasquatch (1974)

In the lush, heavily forested western Canadian province of British Columbia, where the Similkameen and Tulameen Rivers meet along the Thompson Plateau, the historic little town of Princeton lies nestled between Manning Park and the many attractions of the Okanagan — the landscape dotted with fruit and vegetable orchards.

During the Princeton area's bustling glory years of prosperity, the small community featured two full-scale industries that drove the local economy: mining and railroads. Since that boom time, Princeton has continued to evolve, becoming somewhat of a retirement village for those seeking refuge from the ever-growing pressures of city life. The rotating beacon of light that shone brightly from an orange-colored tower to the south of the uncontrolled airport has also gone dark with time, and although the mining and railroad industries have all but vanished, the compact town still houses the Weyerhaeuser lumber mill, where I was employed for nearly nine years. I lived in the village of Princeton itself for fifteen years. It was in that little lumber and mining town, when I was still living at home in 1974, that a well-hidden mystery would first reveal itself.

Our mother was a single parent, raising three boys on her own, so there were the everyday hardships of life to address — but we were together. For my brother Alan and me, the National Football League (NFL) was the gold ring. We didn't need a bankroll to undertake our

**Figure 2: Princeton, British Columbia. A hominid giant was seen in this small town many times over the years. (photo © Tristan Nano)**

homespun training procedures. We absolutely lived the sport in those days, and football was just the incentive we needed to stay away from the drug and alcohol abuse that was becoming so prevalent among the townies. Every chance that presented itself, we were out practicing with our close friends, fine-tuning our athletic skills. The NFL was our dream, and we lived and breathed the sport, nearly day and night. Tucked away among our dreams, there was also the hope of Major League Baseball (MLB), and the Phillies (National League) allowed me into a free-agent camp in Florida in the mid 1970s. Major league sports experiences are something a person will take to their grave. I have been playing ball of one sort or another for around forty-six years and, luckily, I've managed to avoid any serious injury in all that time. (Knock on wood!)

Preceding the start of my serious interest in sports, there was another event in my life. It was a weekend excursion in the late 1960s where my two school chums and I planned to stay a couple of nights along a flat stretch that opened up near the Asp Creek (China Creek). We threw up a small canvas tent near that trickling creek in an area just north of the main part of Princeton.

During the first night, we all heard some activity outside and saw moving shadows, albeit at different times. Of course we questioned each other about it in the morning, each assuming it was a member of our group just using the outdoor facilities or maybe playing a trick to liven things up a bit. We came to find out, though, that all three of us had stayed put; a strong bladder isn't uncommon among the young.

Our most interesting discovery during the conversation that morning was that an entire loaf of bread was missing, bag and all. There was no sign of it anywhere; it was *toast,* you could say. If it had been a forest animal like a nibbling squirrel, there would have been some remnant left behind, but really, who knows what it was? One thing I do know is that over the years that entire area had a strange feel to it, and I was not alone in my thinking. That particular place just seemed to put one on his or her guard, unlike most areas around Princeton. That notwithstanding, the entire region was wonderful in the summer, something I cherished over the years, and our three boys loved the area as well.

Anyone who wants to travel or explore in that area and hopes to get a better understanding of the geographical settings for the encounters we shared should search Google Maps or Google Earth for the Princeton, British Columbia, area. Myself, I'm a stickler for researching matters a bit on my own when reading a book, so I suggest you do the same.

I mentioned 1974. On an early morning run in April of that year, my brother and I were privy to unforgettable events. It would be an awkward day that would forever etch itself into our memories. The evanescent, ape-like creature would show itself on a cold, two-lane asphalt roadway, a T-off at Princeton's wooden Brown Bridge on the town's north side. The road in question extends east to west and is known as Tulameen Avenue. We never would have known that this humble artery would play such an integral role in uncovering a legend.

During our training years in Princeton, it was common for us to walk, jog, or bike a certain stretch along the north side, since there was little traffic. This handy "circle-route," as we liked to call it, led us completely around the Princeton municipal airport. This complete path, nearly a three-mile circuit, always struck me as unique. If we started our activities by the Brown Bridge over the Tulameen River, as per our usual routine, that was exactly the same place we'd end up. Adding a stop-watch and pace-setting gadgetry helped with accuracy. Throwing in some wrist and ankle weights or a loaded weight-jacket helped with the workout.

**Figure 3: During an early morning training run in April 1974, Alan and Glen Boulier saw a large, bipedal creature crossing Tulameen Avenue at Princeton's Allison Flats. The pioneer Susan Allison wrote about this location as a place where the Big Men of the Mountains were seen.**

I never thought I would feel a piercing, cold fear envelop me on that frequently jogged trail, but a missing link, of sorts, would change all that in the blink of an eye. After that day, we would never approach that area of Princeton the same way again. There would forever linger the thought of what we had seen on that well-traveled roadway that fateful morning.

It was somewhere around five o'clock in the morning when my brother Alan and I tied up our runners and made sure we were dressed appropriately for the nippy three-mile run. We got out of bed early in those days, in spite of the weather, and drank raw eggs, took bee pollen supplements for energy, or stirred up thick, rich protein shakes with various carefully selected additives. We took so many supplements — some of them not even sold in Canada — that we were the equivalents of walking health-food stores, though we avoided steroids at all costs because we had no desire to harm ourselves for the sake of performance.

That morning, we left the house with bustling runners' spirits. It was relatively dark and overcast, with a blanket of grey clouds, but daylight would present itself on the eastern horizon within the hour. A very slight breeze that cool spring morning hinted to us that we should consider an extra layer of clothing. It looked like there might be a dusting of spring snow, but it hadn't materialized yet. Being the die-hards that we were, it would take a lot more than chilly weather to cool our spirits. Remember when you were young and thought you were invincible? Those were the days.

Nothing but the quiet, tranquil jogging pathway was ahead of us that morning, and the soothing lights of Princeton shared the experience with us. We started out slowly, as there was a hill that warmed up our cardiovascular systems and the muscles in our arms and legs. We always huffed and puffed on the lonely stretch of narrow gravel roadway that snaked its way up the side of the hill. There were trees throughout the area, and the road created another back way to the airport. After this rise, we faced nothing but level ground with a long decline at the end that led right back into town.

There were very few words spoken between us on that morning run, and before long, without much conversation at all, we found ourselves on the final leg of the pleasant, fresh air jog, nothing but a short descent to the bridge on the asphalt roadway. The little cool-down near the end, a simple, energetic walk to the bridge, was as common as the run. It was during the last 200-plus feet that our lives changed in dramatic fashion. On that final stretch, a large creature, a Wild Man, decided to make a visit to the Princeton area.

Not a word crossed our lips as Alan and I walked quietly toward the finish line. We had no idea that what we thought was the end of one small event was really just the beginning of something entirely different. Alan was just to my left, nearing the standing wooden structure. A fine filtering of snow had started to fall. Up ahead, just west of the prominent bridge, a monstrous, dark-colored figure had come up the bank — from somewhere near the river, I presumed. As he made his departure, the massive giant held us absolutely spellbound.

A creature of mysterious origin stood in front of us that frightful morning, with its chilling movements and huge presence. On its second ponderous step on the cold blacktop, it rendered us motionless, confusing our minds that searched desperately for answers, for an explanation of the impossibility our eyes were witnessing up ahead.

Crossing Tulameen Avenue toward the north with the largest strides I'd ever witnessed, the giant put a foot up onto the secondary gravel road that we had trotted up earlier, lifting itself into an upright walking position.

We were paralyzed, rooted to the ground by the sight of what we were up against. The hair on my neck and forearms rose up in terror. We were alone with a woodland ghost. *How can something like this exist?* I wondered. *And so close to civilization — actually inside town limits?*

Tears gathered in my unbelieving eyes as we stood there, awestruck at such a rare encounter. Seconds passed, and the Wild Man presented its back to us, completely unaware that we were only a stone's throw away. Up to that point, the large, primitive-looking beast thought it was all alone in leaving the area, but that was about to change. Before I could muster a sensible sentence, my younger brother did something I would never have imagined possible from him. In a rather loud voice, he blurted out a yell: "Hey!"

I couldn't speak for Alan, but I could very well speak for myself. My outlook on the wilderness changed in an instant with the creature's reaction. As the upright-walking giant turned in total surprise, searching the general direction of Alan's voice to find our position, my weight moved to my heels and my left leg began to shake and tremble. We had startled a being of massive size.

With my first observation of the woodland creature, I thought I was witnessing an eight-foot, strung-out gorilla. It seemed to take notice of us almost immediately. There was a slight tilt of its head, and then the Sasquatch offered a penetrating stare, as if it was looking right through us. But beyond that look, the tall stranger seemed to reveal a hint of nervousness as well, mixed with an apparent intelligence. I recall the dark eye area under his brow; his entire lower face gave me the creeps. Alan and I were gazing upon a creature of legend, the stuff of stories told by the indigenous peoples. Yes, Bigfoot himself was directly ahead of us, larger than life, and it was an extraordinary moment.

A short standoff ensued, as time seemed to stand still. The hairy giant watched us ever so closely, never wavering from his position. He was threatening by his sheer size and mystery. Having startled such a creature, first by our presence and then by Alan's bold yell, we stood petrified in our tracks. Safety at the Brown Bridge was a step or two away, and downtown was within easy reach on the other side of the Tulameen River, but our escape would require us to move a terrifying step closer to the man-beast — to a creature we feared, a creature that was now real to us and no longer the myth we had taken it for.

The creature looked as if he was built for mobility and feats of strength. Strong, wide shoulders supported the primate's head, and there was no neck visible under all that fur. A huge chest and ribcage supported my observations, as the hair thinned out a little in the pectoral area. Thinner hair in the facial area was very noticeable as well. The facial features themselves didn't stand out at such a distance and in the dim light of the early hour. His hulking arms hung well below his waist. *Where did it come from?* I pondered. *Where is it going?* The one thing I wasn't afraid of was the strange one's departure, though I didn't know when that would occur.

A distinct species, with an obvious superiority and untamed nature, the giant turned back in the direction it had come from. Without looking back, he retreated into the wilderness, picking up his pace. Obviously, he did not consider us any kind of threat. Sasquatch made his move toward the light forest, rounded the first bend, and disappeared into the cool morning.

What followed next, almost immediately, was a brotherly argument about what we should do. The captivating, glowing lights of downtown Princeton made my decision for me: I just wanted to leave the uncomfortable situation, and I felt that was the obvious choice. The jogging path and roadway up above were much darker, and I had no desire to tread into the dark shadows that occupied the hillside. Alan's boldness, however, continued to show through; he suggested we try and follow the legend.

Finding ourselves at the foot of the secondary road that branched northwestwardly from Tulameen Avenue, I raised my chin to the unknown. Morning had completely dawned, but I still remained hesitant about that thing that was currently lumbering around the woods. Making matters worse was the fact that the town of Princeton seemed to be overly silent. Not a vehicle could be seen coming from anywhere — not even an engine running in the distance.

I can't be sure who led, but after the first few steps, we picked up a trail in the very fine dusting of snow that hugged the cold ground. Numerous prints followed the first, and interestingly enough, they were the prints of bare feet. Even with the slight melting, it was clear that our large visitor was without footwear. The only thing we had at our disposal for preserving the tracks was a piece of rather large cardboard that Alan

**Figure 4: The Princeton Airport's west side was the departure route for a male Sasquatch in the spring on 1974. The creature was eight feet tall and weighed about 600 pounds. It's probable that the same area was an escape route for a sighting in 1985.**

placed over one of the first prints we ran into. It wouldn't suffice, however, for the ground was hard from the temperatures of a mountain spring, so applied foot pressure was the only thing we had to go by. Novice trackers as we were, we didn't think of looking between Tulameen Avenue and the river right away. Even though it was laden with rocks, perhaps the bank would have provided us some clue in our pursuit. We did find a couple of light tracks later, just off the road. It should be noted that when I discussed this with Alan in 2009, we both agreed that the prints were straight ahead of each other, not offset, when the thing moved up the gravel and dirt road.

When I placed my size 8½ running shoe in a number of slowly melting footprints, there was plenty of room on all four sides. Between the animal's steps, I had to jump slightly to keep with the creature's regular walking pace. I am five-eight, and we estimated the height of the Sasquatch at approximately eight feet. The weight of the primate must have been around 600 pounds, and he was very dark brown, almost black.

Putting the primitive procedures behind us that morning, we continued up the climbing gravel and dirt road. We never saw the animal again, though we didn't necessarily consider that a bad thing. I had the feeling of being lured away from town as I watched the Allison Flats residential area periodically from the hillside. Once Alan and I reached level ground just below the airport, we did a double take at every small tree and stump, looking at them rather critically. Clearly, we were spooked. I, for one, didn't want to get caught in the creature's environment, so we decided to take a short breather and then head back down the roadway.

I called the Princeton Forestry Service about the matter, and they quickly took my report. I really didn't need all that craziness getting around at the time, since I was in the middle of training for what I hoped would be a future in the NFL. The last thing I wanted to deal with were questions and rumors, for I had enough trouble trying to convince myself to go jogging there again.

## Plain and Simple (Investigation #1)

I put the Sasquatch sighting behind me, and the years slipped by. In 1982, I stumbled upon a paid advertisement in the pages of a local newspaper in Calgary, which was now my home. In addition to serving as my home, the Canadian prairies also gave up a special girl; I married her in 1980.

The ad I saw in 1982 was placed by a Sasquatch researcher from Alberta, a man named Thomas Steenburg. His ad in the Personals section asked for anyone who had seen Bigfoot to contact him.

As I sat at our kitchen table in southeast Calgary casting a few wandering glances out the window, a lot of sincere thought went into reading the small ad that jumped out at me from the pages of the *Calgary Sun*. I was drawn to the request, so I made a quick call to Mr. Steenburg to schedule a casual meeting at our residence to discuss what Alan and I saw on that fateful jogging trip in Princeton in 1974.

Very professional, structured, and orderly, with a tinge of outdoor woodsman to him, Thomas Steenburg was a man on a quest for information, for pieces to the Bigfoot puzzle. The Sasquatch researcher came equipped with a booklet, charts, and a plethora of knowledge pertaining to areas and accounts of possible Bigfoot sightings over the years. Clearly, he believed — and still believes — that the creature does exist. I could only reassure him that the legend was not a legend at all, but flesh and sinew, based on the testimony of what I saw. Our meeting was recorded, as Steenburg asked me a series of questions and shared his ideas about our 1974 encounter. In the end, my story was documented as research, and Steenburg had further evidence for proving the existence of the creature so few had witnessed with their own eyes.

## Again, the Four-Leaf Clover (1985)

Time passed after the Sasquatch researcher's kind visit to our home, and then the seemingly impossible happened to my youngest brother Richard and me, a providential happening so utterly surprising and fascinating that just writing about it now makes me shake my head in disbelief. It occurred during a visit to the Princeton area and, although my younger brother and I were living at least 500 miles apart at that time, fate would pitch us together for my second look at the creature known as the Sasquatch.

At that time, I was employed by the City of Calgary, and my first few years of employment with them, including 1985, were seasonal. In October of that year, we found ourselves visiting family, while the autumn weather was still in the traveler's favor. One night during our visit we were all sitting around, and Richard and I were reminiscing about the old days. Seemingly out of the blue, the subject of Bigfoot came up. Of course it wasn't the first time the topic came up, as it was a common discussion for folks in that area, and for me in particular. Our talk of the Sasquatch and all the mystery surrounding the creature seemed to trouble our mother from time to time. Nevertheless, on a whim, we quickly contrived a plan to drive to northern Princeton. Truly, there was little to do at night in such a tiny town, and it was easy to be overtaken by boredom, so we drove there hoping to witness something remarkable.

On that particular evening, Richard and I set aside a couple of hours for a casual search of points north of Tulameen Avenue. While we hadn't exactly made an appointment with Mr. Wild Man, we decided we would have a look between nine and nine-thirty p.m. It remained a cool, crisp evening, with a clear sky and a full set of autumn stars overhead. Richard persuaded me to ride in his Pinto station wagon.

Our trek began with the narrow side road that moved along the hillside from Tulameen Avenue — the very same gravel and dirt road where the Sasquatch had turned its back on Alan and me eleven years earlier.

Where we would go from there was anyone's guess. This night, I aimed to be nothing more than a casual observer, a person on an extended holiday. The escape from the pathetic Alberta weather was simply a bonus.

Jacobson Road, going from east to west, was a dusty gravel road, visible once we crested the hill. It was never a part of my earlier training route, and it wasn't that long of a stretch. However, it could be a lonely patch of real estate. Just to the south was a huge embankment, with the town below. A little hill section was along the north side of the road, and the Princeton airport was directly above. The interesting thing about Jacobson Road was that even though it seemed to be in a populated area, it still felt like the wilderness, as if it was in the middle of nowhere. It was very deceiving, to say the least. At the time of the 1985 sighting, three or four families resided along that quiet stretch of road, and it was at one of those cozy, tucked-away properties that the stuff of folklore would reveal himself once again.

We were eastbound on the dusty road. With darkness filling the night and a pronounced nip in the air, our drive was no more than five to ten minutes from the house, even going only twenty to twenty-five miles per hour. As we neared the property of a local family, their fence was just outside my window, and there was a wide gate up ahead. The Pinto headlights led the way in the darkness, and the edge of their beam caught a large, dark figure leaving the property. It seemed to be standing still. I was not sure what it was, but the thing seemed to be reaching for a railing or something on the fence. It was also using the gate, intelligently at that. Whatever the upright biped that I caught out of the corner of my eye was, I could tell instantly that it didn't like the position it was presently in. By now, I was sure it was Sasquatch, and with us closing in, he clearly did not want to be on that side of the road. Without any warning whatsoever, the dark, upright animal made a break for the other side of the roadway. Our approximate position was about 100 feet from the creature, and when he darted across the road in front of us, he quickly left the illumination of our headlights.

In all the excitement, Richard caught his own view of the creature. He braked immediately and reached for the gearshift to throw the car into reverse. In a dust cloud, he quickly maneuvered the Pinto at an angle, halfway on and halfway off the road so that we could again spot the massive giant in the beam of our headlights. By this time, Sasquatch was about halfway up the short hill, stopped on the hillside just looking at us.

**Figure 5: A view of the road Richard and Glen Boulier were on in 1985 when Sasquatch came through an open gate to the right and ran up the hill to the left.**

The Wild Man's breaths came quickly, escaping his mouth rapidly and forming little smoky clouds in the night air as he slightly shifted his weight from foot to foot. It was as if the thing was waiting to see what we were going to do next, and he was visibly nervous. There was an eerie calm amidst the engine noise, in spite of the utter strangeness of the whole experience.

With this view, my mind brought up images of the past. I was overcome with the same frightened feeling that had enveloped me before, as if I was looking at something as threatening as the thing I'd seen many years earlier. It was like a video recording of that morning over a decade ago. Those dark, menacing eyes still terrified me, and they were even brighter and more intimidating with the lights shining on the creature. The sheer size was overwhelming, the bipedal giant above us on the hillside, positioned there like some villainous monster in a drive-in movie. As I considered both primates — this one and the one I'd seen before — I realized that this one looked a bit heavier. The body compo-

**Figure 6: A Bigfoot's escape route while on the dead run in October 1985 took it to the top of this hill. The creature used a deer trail as part of its hurried departure.**

sition was very similar, but the other creature I'd seen had moved less swiftly. In the mere eight to ten seconds that we had to witness the creature, a pudgy nose could be seen, and the being never took his eyes off us. I also remember his coarse, grainy hair, which appeared dirty and matted, as if the Sasquatch was in dire need of a shower and brushing. His arms remained close to his side, and no neck or ears were visible.

The mountain dweller initiated the next move, running the rest of the way up the short hillside, cresting it. Then, we were suddenly alone again in the night. It was a sight to behold, watching a creature of that size on the move like that. I felt so weak and inferior by comparison. The distance between each forceful step was enormous. I had to consider the intelligence that motivated the creature's actions. It was almost incomprehensible that something that size was on a mission of escape from two insignificant human beings.

With a verbal cue from me, Richard responded to Bigfoot's hasty departure. He tore off down the road, heading east. I had to chuckle to myself, for finally my little brother had seen the myth for himself — with his own eyes instead of his imaginings spawned by my stories of 1974 — and both of us were somewhat traumatized by the chance encounter. *Been there, done that,* I thought, though, having experienced it before. We made a beeline for the other side of the airport, which was approximately two miles away the long way around. Richard was on a mission to try and intercept the big runner.

I don't remember much being said on that short, high-speed journey, but I think we both had the same idea; it was downright crazy. We knew that damn thing was going to jump over — no, easily step over — the low barbed-wire fence at the airport property and duplicate the venturous task on the north side. It was the shortest route to freedom, and our pursuit would be slowed, especially considering our vehicle had no chance of crossing those barriers.

When we did arrive at the location, Richard swung the car around lightning fast and killed the lights, allowing complete darkness to swallow us. I didn't check my brother's pulse, but I knew mine was racing, and my heart was again in my throat. As I looked out on the blackness of night, scanning the runway area, it was nerve-racking, to say the least. I thought we were a bit crazy to be sitting there like that in the dark. We had the windows rolled up all the way for our protection, but really, that was just silly. If that creature wanted to get at us, those thin glass partitions were not going to stop him. Fate was kind to us that evening, though, and we managed to keep our sanity in check. The Sasquatch was nowhere to be seen, and to this day, I think that was a good thing.

Upon the conclusion of that October evening, Richard and I talked about the odds of it all. Mind you, we'd taken drives around that very region many times before, and I'd been there with others as well. Two of our boys and I even pushed north on the Thompson Plateau a couple years prior on an early morning drive and look-see before moving on to Vancouver for the holidays. The encounter in autumn of 1985 lasted approximately forty-five seconds, but it was part of the second longest minute of my life. I found out from Richard in 2007, twenty-two years after that night, that he had gone up to the sighting location the very next day with friends. Where the road meets the hillside, they located a partial print on the hill. Other disturbed and indented ground was also found, but there was nothing definitive. Both of us did follow up on this over time, and it was noted that the Sasquatch had actually used a deer trail to amble up the hill that night and make his escape. *This creature seems to have a plan,* I thought, almost unable to fathom it.

## Going Full Circle (Investigation #2)

At the dawn of a new millennium, 2000, it was a time for change. Up to that time, I was utterly computer illiterate, having no knowledge of the technology. My wife, Rosemarie, did persuade me somehow — bless her heart — and by the spring of 2000, we were up and running with a Compaq Presario that had all the bells and whistles. This, of course, led to battling another monster: the Internet. Inevitably, the World Wide Web, modern man's answer to all curiosities, led me to a search for Bigfoot. And, lo and behold, with Google showing the way, I happened upon the Bigfoot Field Researchers Organization (BFRO). I felt it was high time the Bigfoot monkey was thrown from my back, for there was actual *research* being done on the species. For the life of me, I couldn't remember Thomas Steenburg's last name at that time, and of course I had lost his phone number somewhere in all those passing years. So, my only option was to check out the BFRO.

The fact that there was scientific research being conducted on the large primate was warmly received by me. On the Internet — as is par for the course — I also found numerous websites that were nothing but clever works of colorful garbage. These are a disgrace to actual scientific fact-finding and discredit the creature itself. Is it any wonder that eccentric researcher René Dahinden spent as much time investigating the investigators as he did looking for Sasquatch? Nowadays, he'd have plenty to investigate, as there is a viral infection of nonsensical garbage and unfounded speculation on just about every topic imaginable on the Internet, Sasquatch being just one of them.

Wanting to have my two sightings filed into the archives and off my chest, I addressed my first letter to Dr. John Bindernagel. Shortly thereafter, I came in contact with Richard Noll. My first sighting went into the books, and the second would at a later date. Little did I know, though, that the BFRO would contact the Sasquatch researcher I'd lost track of, Thomas Steenburg.

When I heard from him, he seemed to be as surprised as I was about the odd coincidence of it all. We scheduled a reunion visit for September 2000. Before noon that day, we met at my residence. Again, there was a tape-recorded session, with plenty of questions. I felt a little embarrassed reporting the second sighting in its entirety. It had occurred so long ago, and his advice from the first sighting rang in my ears. He had told me, "When you go anywhere, take your camera." He never let me forget that — and I haven't.

It was as if lightning had struck twice in the same place, and both sightings were documented.

## On a Dark Road

When it comes to being a magnet for strange events, it often involves being at the right place at the right time. I know this firsthand, and I can say this has happened to me, though it is risky to mention too many sightings because it might reduce my credibility. Seth Evanoff and I once sat at his dining room table in 2009, discussing what the frequency of strange occurrences does to a fellow's reputation. Nevertheless, I want to tell you what happened in the summer of 1979. This encounter was not as clear-cut as the ones with my brothers because the road was dark and the creature was very difficult to distinguish from the road it was lying on.

The timing of this occurrence on a highway north of Princeton is the most certain part. The year itself could not be forgotten, for I had picked up a new blue Mazda RX-7 sports car and, just two months later, I met my wife of now of over thirty-seven years.

The story of the summer of 1979 was seldom mentioned over the years because of the bizarre conditions surrounding it. I didn't know who would listen anyway. Enough had gone on already, as far as I was concerned. What I wasn't aware of was that there was more yet to come.

Behind the wheel that year, the lure of a lively mainstream band playing a concert in Kamloops, British Columbia, was the backdrop to the story. A meeting took place in the Nicola Valley that night, on the way back from the pleasurable outing. Before the high-speed Coquihalla thoroughfare was constructed between Hope and Kamloops, it was old two-lane Highway 5A that carried most of the traffic between Princeton and Kamloops. From what I can tell, including a little bit of speculation, this strange encounter happened in the same region where Tim Martindale witnessed two upright, hairy creatures along the newer Coquihalla Highway, give or take a few miles. I wasn't really paying much attention to the location, to tell you the truth; I seldom did on that lonely stretch of two-lane Highway 5A. If I were to make an educated guess, I'd have to say it was north of Quilchena.

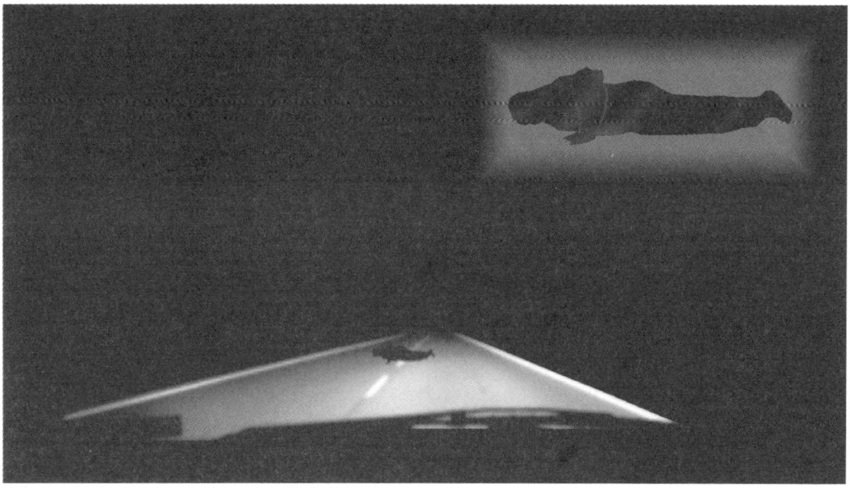

**Figure 7: Author's rendition of how the creature looked as it dragged itself across Highway 5A between Merritt and Kamloops, British Columbia, in the summer of 1979.**

Around midnight, my passenger Greg Fritz and I slowed for something still alive but hardly moving in our lane. It was well up the highway, and the vehicle headlights just barely caught it in otherwise complete darkness. I began gearing down the five-speed, thinking I was slowing for a stretched-out, bowing-down deer licking the roadway for salt — something normal. But as we closed in on it, I realized it was sprawled low, struggling over the centerline in an awkward fashion, with what looked like arms doing all the work, dragging its large, manlike frame along.

What I noticed while closing slowly were the raised elbows of the forest creature, which actually were above the body itself. There was a full extension of the arms that seemed to be going along painstakingly, and the animal's feet were being dragged. I must add that the creature was face down on the ground in a lowered push-up position, its entire body blending in with the colors of the night. Even though we couldn't see it, I could sense the entire locomotion behind the movement.

In seconds, we were beside the mysterious creature. My window was open most of the way, and the thing was just outside the driver door. I could hear it moving, laboring extensively. From what I recall, Greg was leaned over a bit, half-awake, trying to identify the subject, though he said nothing at the time. We crept along past it, moving down the highway maybe fifty yards or so, constantly checking the rearview mirrors and seeing only blackness. I hoped another driver would come along, but of course that didn't happen. I swung the car around in the middle of the highway, stopped, took a look back down into the darkness, and felt the cool night air coming through the car. Greg asked me if I'd seen the thing, and I told him I had. We decided to go back for another quick look.

By the time we approached again, the creature had entered the ditch off of the wide gravel shoulder, and both Greg and I caught the very end of its exit off the highway. It produced a terrible feeling, knowing that the creature — which I had assumed was critically injured — was out there in the darkness, lurking.

We turned around and faced southward, then both took one final look as we passed, briefly studying the surrounding conditions in the headlights and headed for home. The whole thing left us dumbfounded, and Greg and I never spoke of it again. Whatever crossed Highway 5A that night in 1979 made our flesh crawl.

## Our Mother's Encounter

I've been told once or twice that everything in life is about timing — that it is all about being in the right place at the right time to cross paths with the woodland being. I had to wonder because that winding, weaving path of chance seemed to also include our mother.

The year was 1970, if I remember correctly, but I know we were living west of Princeton's Bridge Street, near the end of Harold Avenue. I am not sure about the time of year, but I will assume it was the month of June because I know summer holidays were approaching. The weather was hot, and I was about to visit my aunt and uncle in North Vancouver. They were two very special people, a gifted duo of love and compassion for others.

Being fifteen years old at the time and the oldest of my brothers, I was in charge of the household one evening while our mother was out. We were awakened from our sleep by our terrified mother, who was pounding frantically at the locked door with her tiny fists. Sometime around one a.m., she showed up at the front door, screaming hysterically, not even able to use her key. In the midst of all the banging and commotion, we quickly undid both locks that secured the door. She shoved it open and, in her panicky, crazy state, literally fell forward into the house, toppling to the floor in the living room, screaming all sorts of weird

**Figure 8: While walking along Princeton's Harold Avenue one night in 1970, Carol Boulier came within 50 feet of a creature she described as being half-man, half-animal. The animal was probably scouting out gardens in the town.**

things, including the fact that she was going to die. She scrambled fearfully on all fours across the room.

Sadly, my mother passed away over 16 years ago, and we can no longer ask her about some of the other things she said that night. What she did say once or twice throughout the years, though, was that on that frightful night, just across the street, she saw a hideous creature — half-man and half-animal. Something was out there that night, and whatever it was had our mother hiding shamelessly behind a large armchair, scared out of her wits, with a look of insanity on her face. She cringed when I cracked the curtain on the window for a look outside.

The creature our mother saw was a large, upright-walking, ape-like man, almost fully haired from head to toe. Standing incredibly tall, the charcoal-colored thing was just across the street, less than fifty feet away, according to the measurements we took in 2005. About 4' 10" and under 100 pounds, our mother was not a large woman at all, and adult or not, she was pretty much overshadowed by what she feared. It was a giant of a monster to someone of her stature, and thinking back now, I realize just how dire her situation was and how threatening that must have been. She was encountering a Goliath in the middle of the night, a legend from a stretch of woods that faced the street.

Her very brief observation of what may have been a Sasquatch was that the animal was about to walk into the yard of a neighbor, an elderly Chinese fellow. The animal had his hand on a closed gate, attempting to open it. Although the end of the street looks very different today, the forest that lines it still winds its way westward from there. Our mother would never really talk about the face of the creature she encountered, but she did tell us that the thing stopped and watched her with interest. The animal turned its head, keeping an eye on her, with only the street-light separating them, just before my mother fled up the front steps. The mad pounding on the door followed immediately, and her sanity was most definitely put to the test.

In the days that followed, the poor woman would sit at the kitchen table, sometimes with a stunned look on her face. This subject was off-limits for months. She never got over being scared, as long as we lived near the end of Harold Avenue. The thick woods emptied out at our back fence, just as it did behind other houses on the south side of the block. In her opinion, there was a monster running loose on the street wherever and whenever it liked, hiding in the nearby forest when it didn't want to be seen. While I'm not sure that I would agree with her about it being a monster, I have seen the creature she was talking about with my very own eyes.

## The Maybe Encounter

This report also involves our residence near the end of Harold Avenue. As best I can, recollect my brother Alan and I had this hair-raising experience in 1970 as well, certainly no later than early 1971.

I had no exact solutions or final answers to the perplexing encounter, so before including it in this book, my family and I visited with Alan's clan in 2005 in Maple Ridge, British Columbia. I know my wife and boys found it very interesting, because the occurrence was being explained by Alan who was with me that night in the backyard of our old place in Princeton. When I added my knowledge to his side of it, everyone finally knew what we truly faced that bleak, dark evening. That's why I'm writing about it here.

The basement area of our old house was primitive, with a musty-smelling dirt floor. The whole arrangement was rather gloomy at best. There were two unlocked food freezers that sat to the west side, stationed on a raised mound of hard-packed ground. In the rankings for unfinished basements, this would have been rated right up there at the top.

To enter the medieval place, one had to exit from the back of the house, step down from a small open porch, and come in from underneath a small veranda. The actual basement door was a large piece of painted plywood on two hinges, with a metal hook-latch for securing it in a closed position. The basement itself was one single room below the house, and I recall little lighting. It was approximately five feet high, and the whole area was unheated; how the pipes didn't freeze in the winter was beyond me. The yard outside was rather small, with a thickly forested area about twenty-five feet from the house.

That fateful evening, we were all at home. Our mother requested something from the freezer, and two of us went to retrieve it. It seemed like every time we went down there, it resembled a rescue mission. Only that time around, little did we know there would be an unknown intruder prowling around the dungeon.

As Alan and I left the house through the back door, he held the flash-light to guide us through the unwelcoming, dismal place. We stood outside the closed plywood door, and I noticed that the hook-latch was opened.

As my younger brother shone the light straight ahead at waist level, I proceeded to open the wooden door. Immediately, the flashlight caught movement in the darkness, near the north wall; something was leaving the area of the freezer furthest from us. Standing upright in the crowded area, something on two legs was looking for escape, moving toward the far corner of the basement. In the slender beam of light, we could see it stirring up dust as it moved along the ground, though it blended so well into the back that we couldn't make it out completely. The thing was less than twenty feet away. Alan mentioned throughout the years that it was not some kind of cast shadow, as the creature passed behind a narrow pillar that stood there as part of the foundation. The light caught the vertical structure in front of the biped.

Alan describes the stranger as moving hastily on two legs, never glancing our way, and being dark brown in color. In such close proximity to what we believed was a living creature, I didn't catch a particular color, but I could tell it was dark. I couldn't make out an identifying outline, though I considered it an animal, of sorts. I thought about it several times and found it strangely puzzling that whatever it was didn't look at us as it tried to flee. It didn't have a well-defined form, but the color was consistent head to toe, though that could have just been the darkness blending in with the dark color of the creature.

The encounter lasted only a few seconds. Our fear of the unknown had us making a quick departure. Alan dropped the flashlight, and both of us ran in a panic for the backdoor. Richard, who was just inside the door, had locked it due to his own fear, induced by us screaming up a storm. During that time of uncertainty, I didn't see anything come from the basement doorway or exit the property.

The door was closed the next morning, but from what I remember, that door always closed on its own, swinging back slowly. The flashlight was there as well, sitting at the entrance. And as far as I can recall, I don't think we ever went down there again at night.

I wondered if the strange visitor could have been responsible for some of the foodstuffs that came up missing. If so, I hope he enjoyed the peanut butter cookies, because someone had caught crap for supposedly overindulging a number of times. Sure, I can joke about it now, but it wasn't funny at the time. All I know is that it wasn't a youngster in a fur suit. In those days, we would have kicked his ass if it were.

# 3. More from the Princeton Area

Our family members weren't the only ones in the area who were having Bigfoot sightings. Having only heard an odd story of the creature now and then over the years since my move to Calgary, I was surprised to hear that the Sasquatch may still be in the Princeton region. I shouldn't have been surprised, though, since the species roamed freely for over 125 years. I wonder if the ole boy I met is still alive.

Let's look at some other stories from the area.

## Coalmont, British Columbia

In my 2000 meeting with Thomas Steenburg, he told me the following story. Just eight months after Richard and I had our run-in with the living giant in 1985, the Sasquatch was seen by another Princeton fellow — around a cabin he owned near the small town of Coalmont, approximately twelve miles to the northwest. Thomas learned of this encounter in 1991, which just goes to show again how crucial timing is. He was actually traveling through the Princeton area in 1986, having a look-see near where Alan and I had seen the animal at the Brown Bridge back in 1974. He wanted pictures of the area for his files. If only he had known what was being experienced in the Coalmont region in the summer of 1986. The researcher was only a few miles away.

Then Thomas received a letter dated July 2 that same summer. A creature was stirring, visiting cabins over a five-week period, approximately five and a half miles from the town of Coalmont. I knew the area well, for our oldest boy had gold-panned there a few times. The area was full of rugged terrain, with millions upon millions of places for a forest dweller to hide. The place also had a rich mining history, and we had all visited the old ruins of Granite City.

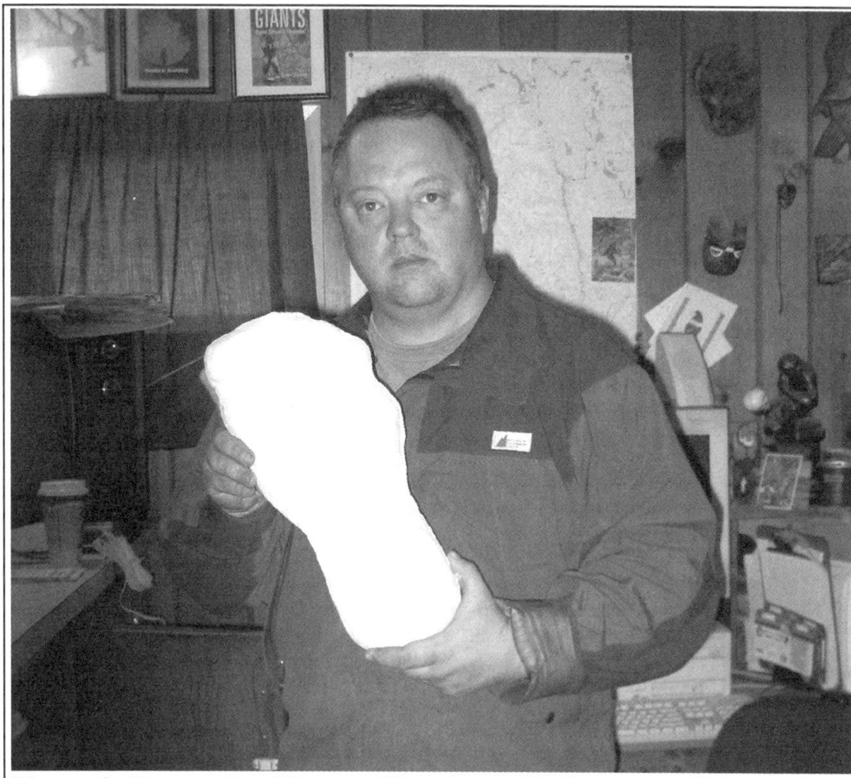

**Figure 9: Researcher Thomas Steenburg displays one of his castings. He has been on the trail of the elusive and mysterious Bigfoot creature for years.**

During those weeks, a number of tracks were found, measuring seventeen by six inches. The prints were more than one and a quarter inches deep in an area where men didn't leave much of a track, and they were clearly made by a bipedal creature. These facts were proven over that five-week stretch, and one individual even drew an illustration of the creature he had seen. Others identified the Sasquatch as well. One cabin owner who wrote to the researcher claimed to have spotted a female with hairy, saggy breasts. The specimen was reported to be seven and a half feet tall. The witnesses also reported hearing chattering and a type of whistling and the sounds of what seemed like small trees being broken up.

## Elkridge, British Columbia

Learning about the Coalmont area incident added fuel to the fire and proved once again that the Sasquatch might still be calling the Similkameen region home. Passing through the Princeton area again in 2005, we had the opportunity to stay near Elkridge, west of town, where we shared a cabin with our three boys and two deerhounds. One evening, one of the owners told us of a friend of his, a woman who had traveled the dangerously narrow road to Tulameen via Princeton. In the general area of the hazardous bluffs, and slowly negotiating the winding passageway at night, the woman was stopped dead in her tracks for a Sasquatch that came up on the roadway. It seemed to be in a hurry. To say the least, the creature frightened her. It watched her continuously as it made its way across the road in front of the vehicle headlights. She described the being as the one so many are looking for, the ever-evasive Sasquatch. Hairy from top to bottom, the huge specimen disappeared into the waiting woods after its presence intimidated and awed her. From that time forward, the woman was a nervous wreck whenever she had to travel the dark stretches of that road at night.

## Coquihalla Highway

Something was on the wind in 2004, nineteen years after our sighting of 1985. A gentleman from Merritt spotted the elusive Sasquatch north of Princeton — not just one of the animals, but two of them. A news team, CTV Vancouver, interviewed Tim Martindale on location, including at his home in Merritt. Thomas Steenburg was also present during the activities, providing his expertise in the Bigfoot phenomenon.

I initially contacted Tim Martindale through email, and this brief message led to a number of written communications and a couple of lengthy phone calls, highlighting his sighting, follow-up, and my past experiences with this ghost of the woods. Since his highway meeting with the Sasquatch species, he opted to learn more about the primate that interrupted his life, and he now investigates the phenomena. This is his story, much like the stories of so many others who have witnessed these giants:

## The Tim Martindale Encounter Story

On May 10, 2004, I was driving east on the Coquihalla Highway, approximately thirty-eight kilometers east of the city of Merritt, British Columbia. On this day, I was running very late in picking up my wife and daughter from the hospital in Kamloops, where my little one had [had] some dental surgery done. The day was cloudy and dismal up on the mountain road.

While driving along, I noticed off to the left of the highway, approximately 200 feet in, two figures standing beside a small pond. Looking back at it now, all it was was a scum pond of sorts, and not really what we'd consider a pond.

I saw two figures standing up that day, which I immediately thought were father and son human beings, because the one was much bigger than the other. I thought they may be out fishing, and it looked like they were wearing black outerwear. All of a sudden, the bigger of the two bent down to get what looked like a drink of water. At this time I was much closer, and I thought to myself, Okay… these obviously aren't people, so they must be bears because of their color. But as soon as the big one bent down, I could see clearly the shape of the left femur, the upper leg bone, [bent] at the hip and at the knee. It was down on one leg, just as humans do when we bend down to pick something up. Straightaway, the thought of these being bears just wasn't possible anymore, and I knew 110 percent [that] what I was looking at were, in fact, two Sasquatch, standing right there out in the open.

They didn't appear to be even remotely afraid of anything. Please keep in mind that this all happened in about ten [to] twelve seconds that day, and I know this time frame because I've been back and driven by the area time and time again, making sure I knew exactly how long it took me to slow down a bit and drive by the sighting area. It was as if time stood still.

As I was passing by that day, my eyes shifted toward the smaller one, which was about six feet tall, and around 250-300 pounds — hardly small, but still smaller than the big one, which was around seven feet tall. Full of muscles; I am thinking this animal was close to 500 pounds in weight.

Anyway, when I looked at the smaller of the two, it stared at me the whole time with an almost evil glare in its eyes, arms straight down by its side. Ya know, till my dying day, I will always believe that if I had been within arm's reach of that smaller one, I would have been in grave danger, just because of how it was glaring at me. If anything can describe evil, it's the eyes and fierce stare of this smaller creature.

The two Sasquatch creatures had black hair that looked maybe around three inches long, and they seemed to be almost uniformed. I didn't notice any shape of a neck on the two, and it was almost as if their heads just sat on top of their shoulders. The smaller of the two had lighter shades of hair on its face, with the face dark in color. Their eyes seemed to be just black holes, but I was too far away to see any definite color to them if there was any. The arms of both Sasquatch were considerably longer than a human's and were below the kneecap for sure. They were very bulky in nature, the big one's muscles sticking out as plain as day. Even though the smaller Bigfoot was a lot lower in stature [than] its counterpart, I'm certain that an animal of this magnitude could and would easily tear a person limb from limb and probably haul you away and just dump your body somewhere.

The younger Sasquatch also gave me the impression that he was calculating something and maybe waiting to see if I was going to stop and get out of my car, but there was no chance of that happening — No *thank* you! I sometimes wonder if the smaller creature was some sort of a protector for the older Sasquatch that [might have been in its] last stages of life. I don't know. [It was just] a thought, but I'm thankful I was in the safety of my moving car, and not face to face with this one, that's for sure.

As I was going past them, the big one never even once looked in my direction, so he wasn't concerned about anything which, now [that I think] about it, was quite daring. Was he just used to seeing people and smart enough to know that we puny humans would be no physical match for him? Or was he old and maybe losing his mind? Nonetheless, I didn't stick around to answer any of my questions. Ten or twelve seconds passed, and then I was out of sight of the two.

[Upon] arriving [at the hospital], I told my wife what I had just witnessed, and she believed me. I didn't think she would, to tell you the truth, but she did and now supports my ventures off into the forest once in a while, looking for this thing again. I don't go out on foot because of fear, so I usually stay in the car, hidden as best I can. But one of these days when I have some other people with me, I'd like to be outside and away from the vehicle to hopefully catch one of these things off guard.

After my sighting, I placed ads in as many newspapers as I could, hoping and praying that someone else would come forward to tell me about their sightings or encounters. I've also been on a four-minute slot with CTV — re-interviewed with them again on a follow-up of what's been happening. I've been on a few small expeditions on my own and have found small amounts of evidence, but nothing that would support their existence 100 percent.

As the snow is starting to fall, this will have been, of course, the second winter that I've been involved with the search for the Sasquatch, and I'm really curious to see if the sightings taper off or if they'll continue just as strong as they seem to be in the summer months. If they taper off, it could mean one of two things: Number one, the Sasquatch may actually hibernate like bears do or something to that effect; and number two, they may migrate south for a better food supply. These two very important questions are something that needs to be answered, so I can't wait for a real good snowfall somewhere around the end of December to see. Personally, I think they probably head south, so we'll see, I guess. I hope I'm wrong, in a way. If the sightings south of the Canadian border don't increase by much, then it could mean these guys are staying here and could be just stockpiling food for the winter, or they're hibernating, like I said is possible.

One thing is for sure: When I go out to look, I won't be on my own ever, because even though I'm extremely curious, I'm also extremely frightened in a hard-to-explain sort of way. I wonder if I see one again, [will] I have the nerve to follow it?

## Red Lake

Another story would surface over discussions of the Sasquatch, this one in 2005, with a friend of mine from Mission, British Columbia. I didn't know it at the time, but years ago, north of Princeton, he encountered something strange and different in the realm of hunting — something he would hold onto for many years. This was revived during our conversation of the wilderness giant. I found the tale helpful, as it was another indication of possible Bigfoot whereabouts on the Thompson Plateau. I had heard him tell this story to others once before and asked if he'd like to present it, as there are many puzzle pieces to the mystery of the Sasquatch. This is his account of those events; Ken Kristian is a researcher as well.

## Ken Kristian's encounter on British Columbia's Red Lake

During the fall of 1977, a few friends and I decided to make a duck-hunting trip to Red Lake, up in the Kamloops region. We packed a couple of camouflaged boats, fifty or sixty rubber mallard decoys, grub, [and] guns and headed for the high country.

Once we reached Red Lake, high on the Kamloops plateau, my friend Randy and I decided to hunt a marshy area on the lake that we knew well from our eastern brook trout ice-fishing trips during the winter. At the time, the closest ranch or building was a good ten miles away, over bush roads.

We had our boat loaded before first light and made for the marsh. Once there, we set out our decoys and slipped the boat back into the high weeds and grass about sixty feet from open water.

Hunting was slow due to warm weather and little wind. We would blow our mallard calls once in a while, hoping to entice a duck from the far end of the lake, but nothing was moving. A few hours had passed, and we had not fired a single shot.

Randy [and I] were both bored and staring out over our decoys on Red Lake when something suddenly but quietly surfaced just outside the edge of our flock of decoys. What came up appeared to us to be a human-type head, covered in long, wet hair — what a person with long hair would look like if they surfaced while swimming. The skin under the hair, as well as the eyes, appeared dark brown in color. Our view of this strange head [indicated that it] was about even with the shoulders, although they did not break the surface of the water. The eyes (what [we] could see of them under the hair) looked dark (no white), like an animal's. The face had no expression or movement. It seemed to look at our decoys and us for maybe ten or fifteen seconds and then slipped silently under the surface with a slight swirl or wake, and it was gone. Nothing else was seen or heard.

When we returned to Cliff Tuscon's ranch, where we were staying, I asked him if he had ever seen anything like what we [had] witnessed on Red Lake that morning. I'll never forget the look he gave me. I think he figured I was either piss drunk or on the verge of going crazy. In any case, old Cliff [had] never [seen] anything like what I described in his forty years up in that country.

Afterthoughts on my possible Red Lake Sasquatch encounter… First, I would like to state that I honestly did not know I had possibly witnessed a Sasquatch on British Columbia's Red Lake until many years after the incident had taken place. Second, since Red Lake was considered fairly remote at that time, I doubt whether any duck hunters had ever hunted over decoys like we had that day. At the time, it was simply too much work for the rewards, but we were young, foolish, and still fairly green.

To tell you the truth, neither I nor [my] good friend Randy had the foggiest idea of what the hair- or fur-covered head we saw outside our flock of decoys could have belonged to.

Thinking back, I firmly believe the creature (possibly a Sasquatch) was swimming underwater to grab a meal of fresh duck. Upon reaching the decoys, it likely saw no feet from the ducks and then the strings leading to anchor weights and knew something was wrong and badly out of place. After surfacing just beyond the edge of our decoys, the possible Sasquatch most probably saw our heads that were now inquisitively poking out above the weeds and quickly decided a long, underwater swim was required to get the heck out of the country and away from us as fast as possible.

I would also like to say that the swirl or wake I witnessed when the creature departed was far too big to have been [caused by] a beaver or any other aquatic animal or bird that I know of in British Columbia.

In closing, I have often pondered the thought that it may be possible to fool Sasquatch with a decoy that would either stir its curiosity or perhaps mimic a key food source.

## Hedley, British Columbia

Sometimes the timing of things is just plain funny. I lived in the town of Princeton for fifteen years, and not once during that time did I ever hear of the Sasquatch around the Hedley area — nowhere down the south corridor at all, to tell you the truth. It would materialize in 2005, however, when the First Nation's Upper Similkameen Indian Band opened a new interpretive center that included a place I used to freely visit when I was younger: the historic mining shacks on the side of a mountain overlooking Twenty-Mile Creek, above Hedley. The shacks stood there, begging to be explored, clinging to Nickel Plate Mountain. Upgraded and protected, they are now shown on tours, but it was the beginning of the tour that I found interesting, all of us present looking at each other with healthy grins as we watched a little film in the interpretive center. After all, research was one of the reasons we were in British Columbia, and my family knew this and smiled.

The Similkameen Indians of the past named the colorful striped cliffs on both sides of the canyon *Sna'zaist* meaning the "Striped Rock Place." Those scratches in the landscape were put there by the creature known as the legendary Sasquatch, according to Native beliefs in the area. Even in Hedley, the Sasquatch is bigger than life these days, and that was what the film in the center started with that early morning.

As the situation would have it, Ken Kristian had a story available, posted on the West Coast Sasquatch Internet site. I happened to pick it out, as the Hedley area again popped up during a search. His description of the events is as follows.

## Ken Kristian about Hedley

About 1973 or 1974, I was down by the Fraser River, talking with some of my old hand-logger commercial fishermen friends, and the subject of Sasquatch happened to come up in the conversation. During this talk, it was the first time I had ever heard that, at times, these beasts might make some form of nest or bed.

Old Bob was a local shake-splitter who had just returned that same day from a deer-hunting trip up in Hedley country. He somewhat shyly explained to the group that he'd found a large animal bed located on a perfect vantage point, with six inches of fresh evergreen tree boughs laid carefully in the bottom. He went on to explain he had also found quite a few piles of huge, human-type droppings that no man or animal he knew of could make.

**Figure 10: Hedley, British Columbia, approximately 23 miles south of Princeton, has also seen visits from a strange creature over the years.**

Apparently, these droppings were located about seventy-five feet from the bed and concentrated in one general area. Old Bob also went on to seriously explain that the bed he'd found had plenty of dark-colored hair in the bottom of it and that it stunk like hell.

Now, if I remember right, about six people burst out laughing. At that, old Bob became extremely angry and remarked he would take any one of us assholes (excuse the language) back up to Hedley at that very minute and show us the bloody Sasquatch bed he'd found. Seeing that old Bob was seriously mad with the ridicule, the entire group said they were sorry and jokingly believed him. Sadly, nobody took Bob up on his offer. I wish to this day that I would have. [GMKK1]

## Keremeos, British Columbia

It's a funny thing, what happens when you lay in wait and wait and still wait. Being Mr. Pleasant many times when it came to getting a possible reply to messages that were left on community and town forums, the whole ordeal made me feel like a mail sorter at the plant. I had to expect the cranks, humorists, and comedians, and also the everyday busybodies who either didn't want to understand the question or wanted to lambaste a person out of plain ignorance. (Water off a mallard duck's back was how I addressed it mostly.)

I was bold in my placement of these written invitations but still polite, asking about a giant species of creatures that called the hills home. I knew there were a few people who held knowledge in their hearts, jeering and sarcasm their probable reason for never coming forward.

In response to my invitation, a woman from Keremeos, British Columbia, did come forward. The woman talked about her parents, an elderly couple who had grown fruit in the Keremeos/Cawston area for years. This couple had a dark secret: a wandering, dark-colored species that came to their property over the years for appetizing fruit and leftovers. The story was told by the daughter, whom we shall refer to as "Julie." The woman herself had not seen the creature as a young child, but her parents had seen it regularly, while making fruit growing their livelihood in that section of the Similkameen Valley.

### Julie's Story

My folks were in the growing belt for years, starting out briefly in the Okanagan Falls/Oliver region. I was very young at the time. Before long, we were your average family around Keremeos, working hard for what [we] had, the reward, a living. My dad would tell me about the orchard fields, the dust, rodents,

**Figure 11: A fruit orchard in the small town of Keremeos, British Columbia, saw visits from a number of Bigfoot over the years. (photo © Sean McCann)**

and the pestilence of insects that were like fine rains on a summer evening when the sun went down. Later on, he would also tell me about a race of giants that visited after the twilight hours, a harmless bunch that were only interested in feeding their bellies, going about their way as a pet dog would roam freely in the yard. My father was the first to believe in such… mountain men and women coming from nearby. This was the same simple man who told me where freckles came from, and I would honestly think he was joking.

He was a hardworking man, but his humor broke down the walls of life. I was young, and he didn't want to scare me. He would humor both [Mom and I, and she was] fearful at the start. When he was serious, [we] could take it to the bank. This was serious.

Dad had wondered what was evading his flashlight the first year in Keremeos and otherwise setting off the dog at times. It

> wasn't long after that that he would see a "mountain man" for himself, a strange animal picking up loose fruit off the ground and doing a really good job of it with hands that worked. He felt this creature had seen him around before, because it sure wasn't scattering later on — I think, getting accustomed to our being there. The animal would go about its way, selecting whatever it wanted. I'm glad now that my folks never filled me in entirely earlier on, because I don't know what I would have done, a "real" big monster in our big backyard. My parents said these mountain people seemed harmless enough, but were always aware of their surroundings. They were really watchful. They didn't have to look at you to know you were present. That, and they must have seen my folks a million and one times. I did not see the mountain people myself; I wasn't out at night. "They [aren't] about to introduce themselves," my mom would say, but as far as she was concerned, the Bigfoot were becoming tame. Both my mother and father would see these manifested creatures about thirteen to fourteen times throughout the years.

Before continuing with Julie's story, I want to set the scene a little bit more. Cathedral Park is just southwest of the town of Keremeos. Hedley is just to the northwest. The Sasquatch (actually a number of them) were seen near Keremeos, according to a 2005 report by the Bigfoot Field Researchers Organization (hereafter referred to as BFRO). If you look at the geographical setting around Keremeos, you can ponder the Sasquatch giants being a part of the Similkameen River Valley. An aboriginal fellow by the name of Lester pointed out to me that these creatures were "spirits hiding in the woods." A spirit family had come down from the reaches of Cathedral and also from the direction of the Chuckuwayha 2 First Nations Reserve (the Hedley area). For inquiring minds, the indigenous population density was less than three people per square kilometer in 2006 — plenty of room for haired giants to roam freely. That could also be the reason why the Sasquatch is seldom seen in the valley. Keremeos, as an example, is populated by less than 1,500 people. How much of this village's citizenry do you think is up after midnight?

Still on the topographical setting of this territory, Lester pointed out an interesting thing that he and his family had seen firsthand, the rock formation in Cathedral Park that went by the name of Grimface. In addition to his understanding of it, a few others talked about this high

**Figure 12: What the First Nations people describe as the face of the Sasquatch portrayed in rock on Grimface Mountain in Cathedral Park, British Columbia. (photo © Richard Teszka)**

rock resembling one of the spirits of the woods. You're seeing this photograph as I first saw it.

As with most things, it depends on how you look at it. One individual can take meaning from nature's sculptured rock, while someone else may think it just a piece of stone. I've found this many times with pictographs and petroglyphs. You have to be careful in your speculation of things: Bigfoot from one voice, centipede from another.

While on this topic, I would like to add that one of the areas at Keremeos where these creatures were dropping from ran practically into the town landfill, giving the Sasquatch options for sustenance. I would also like to comment on the number of sighting opportunities that Julie's parents had.

Our oldest son, Brandon, asked me immediately about this when I was researching the story. He asked, "Why didn't her parents take a picture of the visitors on one of the [over a dozen] occasions that they witnessed such creatures?" The daughter would say that her mom and dad never gave it a thought. Julie felt it may have also been a publicity thing, and they wouldn't have any part of that. They were set in their ways and asked for nothing from such encounters. Her dad especially, in everything, said that he would take a hand up but never a handout. She would ask me if these creatures could sense the innocence of her parents approach to the giants. I told Julie that her guess was as good as mine. This wasn't something I had seen in the 1974 and 1985 encounters. The creatures I saw were more on the go, departing.

Julie's story continues:

> Yes, Mom and Dad didn't do much of the camera idea of it — mostly family-oriented stuff. That didn't stop them, though, from describing that on one of the social calls, there were two of the mountain men on the property. They seemed to know each other, although they weren't together at the start. The other thing my folks took notice of was that each of the mountain people had come from the opposite direction that day — one from the east, the other from the west, both between three and four in the morning one summer day. They didn't stay long. Dad talked about this visit a few times. The company watched the skyline like a hawk looking for rodents. The two cradled fruit in their arms as you'd carry a baby. And, for being large animals, they all had finesse in gathering the stuff that covered the ground some days.
>
> Dad was usually the one to see these creatures, while he was near the house or looking down between the rows of fruit trees. He said it was always a male doing the roundup, picking fruit up off the ground. Father never [saw] one of these creatures strip a branch or rattle a tree. He never did, but he would have found a way to shoo them away if this [had been] the case. Dad cherished being half the boss and making a living when things were much simpler. These mountain visitors never complicated things, and were mainly around on hot summer evenings, after dark. Mom would say, "Who [knows] what [goes] on before morning?"
>
> There were seldom tracks around either, not that they paid attention or cared. She didn't like to think about squashed fruit between the toes or under the toenails if they had them. Mom was a stickler for hygiene. Combining this all together, both of them would agree that the mountain people were between seven,

eight, and nine feet tall consistently — and from what my folks could tell, they were of the male variety usually. Speaking about the female, she would have been less than eight feet tall. If these animals had children or little ones, they were never visible. The bunch didn't like lighting, but the creatures seemed to tolerate Dad's flashlight or lantern. He would cover the flashlight with his hand, [and] the odd ones [were] full of curiosity about this. Dad would also dim the lantern in slow motion — nothing quick. The visitor or visitors would continue on with what they were doing then, not as cautious as before. Dad would say because of the settling in of night around him — literally a monster-sized animal in the darkness before him — he always felt intimidated and uneasy. He wanted to make that perfectly clear. There was a common respect between both, never getting too close to each other. Mom was more apprehensive, watchful of the giants. She admitted not liking being alone in their presence. She also agreed with Dad that the world would and will not understand such animals out in the open. These mountain people slip right under you, right under your nose. Everything in nature (what there was around Keremeos) went silent when this creature was [present].

My father was convinced that these well-natured mountain giants could feel what type of a person you were and responded accordingly. They didn't hang around like a cow grazing or a canine licking his testicles; these creatures were always focused, with an agenda, like there was no time to be wasted. Dad figured maybe it was like that because he was an unpopular guest in a dangerous predicament.

Mom would say they did things with persistence and that the creatures were good at what they were up to. Other times, she would say she felt as though she was being watched, [even] with no creature present. Dad was there to reassure her — to tell her this was normal and not to worry. When a person knows of these animals' [existence], you can get ahead of yourself sometimes. You never know when they [are] going to pay you a visit, [so] every noise and banging brings out the worst in you — well, your nerves anyway. Although Mom was a strong woman in many ways, she did yabber a few times that the animals' presence did make her and Dad feel like prisoners, but their upbringing was what kept them going. Both of them had stood shoulder to shoulder, looking out on the mountains at times, trying to understand who these creatures were. I do remember some of this, standing between them as a youngster, holding each of their hands.

Later on, my folks would tell me that much of it after that was plainly pigeonholed — a lot like what you hear about in stories of the Bigfoot today. They asked if that would be all right, sufficient for the story.

I don't want to be long-winded and a bore, but these are the things that were told to me and my husband over long periods of time. My folks are much older now and have been retired for years. We are all still residents of British Columbia.

I thanked her and told her it was fine, explaining the story to this extent. Once or twice in this book, I will mention that I didn't always want to go into the stereotyping of the Sasquatch — size this, weight that, torso this, facial features that, etc. Rather, I wanted to get away from the norm. Many authors have done a fine job of describing the features of Sasquatch. I will discuss later why I feel there is more to the phenomenon than mere physical description.

# 4. Bigfoot Characteristics

This chapter is for those of you who have a healthy interest in the strengths and weaknesses of a creature that places first in all the races it enters.

We humans have a basic shortcoming concerning the woodland beast that leaves the wilderness to visit the doorstep of mankind. It isn't always about sagittal crests, dermal-ridged prints, vocalizations, and all of the other possible proofs of the primate's existence. Long hours have been spent addressing those.

It is an amazing thing to build profiles of something that most people claim does not exist. In a number of scientific conversations about Bigfoot, I heard that this bipedal giant is of high intellect and is possibly North America's Great Ape. Maybe that is so. I have no credentials other than witnessing the creature. That said, we have seen a few pieces of the puzzle beyond physical descriptions that need to be recorded. Let's look at them here.

## The Art of Escape

Harry Houdini was one of the greatest American stage magicians of all time, specializing in the art of escape. To successfully complete his stunts, he had to plan the course and direction he would undertake to free himself.

Though not quite as extreme or dramatic, and definitely not trying to perform for an audience, the Sasquatch may also plan its various escape routes. There are certainly many people looking for patterns in the creature's behavior. It would seem that this animal differentiates between certain escape courses, depending on whether it is day or night or whether or not they are frightened or hurried. Let's face it: The night is one of any animal's biggest allies. I believe the bipedal creature thinks it can flee and dodge anything on strength and speed alone, and it may be correct. So far, the Bigfoot track record for escapes is perfect.

During our meeting with the giant in 1985, the Sasquatch moved much more quickly during the final part of its departure, with the last few strides an unbelievable sight. The woodland sprinter crested the hill in a flash.

Over the years, very little was said about the species by those who resided in Princeton. They certainly never talked of the creature happening by for a visit. Those restrictions have loosened a bit, it seems, for some are willing to speak of such things now that they are older, even if only in a passing reference. Those casual remarks have included the Asp Creek (China Creek) area, a general feeling of uneasiness, fast-moving bulky shadows, and other hints that something is out of place near that trickling creek that heads north of Princeton. I'm almost certain that in both my encounters with this primate, the biped ultimately made his way to Asp, north through the vegetation that paralleled the creek on both sides.

During the 1974 sighting, the creature had to take a certain pathway because of daybreak. Just beyond the west end of the airport's restricted area, on a descending sloping bank, there is a beaten trail that leads down to the tiny creek. I believe this may also have been the escape route the creature took in 1985. It is quick and convenient for a creature to lose itself in the shadows of Asp, and I must add that this weaving creek gets only a little sun at certain periods of the day — even less when the sun is lower in the sky during the fall and early spring.

Of course, escape routes could vary somewhat, allowing the Sasquatch more room to operate to the north. The cover of Asp Creek is still available with only a few large steps either way. The reason I didn't really document along the roadway is because of the houses located there. Added to that is the fact that over the years some of these homesteads have had a canine presence. The Sasquatch will stick to an unobstructed passage it feels comfortable with. Going through the populated course risks their exposure and shrinks their comfort zone.

The Asp Creek behavior has worked for the species for well over fifty years. I arrive at such a number because earlier on the area was more remote and less populated. The creature could roam to its heart's content in the old days.

In those times, there were more encounters between the woodland giant and the aboriginal community and pioneers who crossed its path. There was a laid-back, live-and-let-live approach. Nowadays, there are hunters with rifles and a different frame of mind. Is it possible that the Sasquatch, as a species, can identify change? As an example of the firearms issue, Princeton had hefty mountain lion problems years ago, and the large cats began making their way into town. The temperamental felines were removed from the area. The Sasquatch still remains a mystery to the town, for this creature that is much bigger than the lion goes almost totally unnoticed. What Alan and I saw that morning was a monstrous giant that looked like he had walked the designated path before, crossing Tulameen Avenue nonchalantly — at least until it was surprised.

Taking this one step further, our mother's fateful adventure allowed her to see the visitor taking one of two main escape routes to freedom. The first escape is that vein of timbered landscape that borders Harold Avenue and also leads to an extension of the avenue, known as Pumphouse Road. The second escape route borders along the wooded stretch's northern side, the corridor running east and west with the Tulameen River. It allows a creature of such mass to move freely at night, with no one around, dodging into the trees anytime it wishes.

Phillip, a man in his early forties, retrieved his irate dog from the river in 1982 and spotted a hairy, upright creature standing approximately seven and a half feet tall. On that secluded road, the dog owner was a bit cautious, quite understandably. As is often the case with these stories, the man stated that it was the first time his hound barked at but refused to chase after a forest creature. It was totally out of character for his dog. This road ends at the Municipal Depot along the river, and guess what sits across the Tulameen River from the Depot: Asp Creek, where it empties out. How convenient for a mystery to stay intact!

Concerning the second route I spoke of, Bigfoot would just continue on past the Municipal Yard. This would provide the creature with practically instant avenues to the Coalmont area. I wish to point out here that Princeton's tunnel area to the south is just that: a long, straight tunnel through the mountain. The town sits on one side, and there is wilderness on the other. These days it is used primarily as a bike trail, for the railway is long gone. Geographically speaking, Princeton is the perfect setup for such a creature to come and go as it pleases. How else could a bipedal giant stay hidden all these years?

**Figure 13: What has been referred to as Princeton's Pumphouse Road could have been used as an easy pathway for the Sasquatch in the 1970s and 1980s.**

We'll see other evidence of Bigfoot's skill in escaping in stories later in the book. It's easy to believe, with all that evidence, that the Sasquatch is perfectly able to plan what it is going to do in many different contingencies.

## Size and Age

In regard to the scary basement scenario and what may have been an adolescent Sasquatch, I would like to discuss some other events that played out in the Princeton area around those years. This information was garnered from researcher John Green's online database. I'll focus on two particular reports related to the size of creatures being seen in the Similkameen Valley area.

As I scanned John's reports of the British Columbia area, I came across documented information that led me to one of the witnesses who had encountered the creature. The man's name was Stuart Syme, and he was an outdoor writer with the *Kelowna Courier*. While he was hunting north of Princeton, he gained new knowledge of the legendary woodland giant.

I exchanged some emails and a phone conversation with Stuart to discuss what was posted about him on John Green's site. Through these discussions, the columnist/hunter provided me with a Google Maps location of where he met up with the creature between the areas of Dry Lake and Mackenzie Lake, approximately twelve or thirteen miles north of the town of Princeton and just west of Highway 5A.

The outdoorsman's encounter took place about four miles from the northern reaches of Asp Creek (China Creek), a place I consider to be one of the creatures' main escape routes from town. His sighting was also approximately ten miles from the Coalmont area, where researcher Thomas Steenburg followed up on an aggressive female Sasquatch who taunted cabin owners for a number of weeks. This location is about five miles west of Asp Creek — and on it goes. Everything is extremely easy pickings for a swift-footed bipedal creature.

Now, the coincidence in all this was the creature's size; there seemed to be a younger group of the things running around at the time, possibly a large number of them in the areas surrounding Princeton. Our mother's ordeal was within the same timeframe as Stuart Syme's contact with a member of the Sasquatch species, only a few months separating them, as the resident of Kelowna came into contact with an adolescent (or perhaps a dwarf adult) creature in November of 1970. Our mother's sighting was a grown adult in my understanding. One of the points I'm trying to relay here is that the basement creature was around the same height as the smaller one the hunter saw.

In the spring of 2010, Stuart and I discussed his introduction to the Sasquatch phenomenon. As I mentioned, I found his story on Green's website, which reports the following:

> Stuart Syme, writing an outdoors column, said that while grouse hunting in the hills west of Allison Lake, he saw at the bottom of a gully, a creature five feet tall, covered with long, straight, cinnamon-brown hair. It had a small, round head, sloping shoulders, arms dangling loosely.
>
> He put a slug in his shotgun and aimed it at the creature, but gazing in its reddish-brown eyes; he had a feeling of tranquility and lowered the gun. His dog whimpered, hair standing on end from nose to tail, pressed against his leg. He bent down to the dog, lost sight of the creature — went down gully but did not see

> it again. He did not look for tracks. Dog tried to climb a tree — he didn't try to find out why. (Bird-dog stuck close to owner, hair standing on end from nose to tail, whimpered. The dog then went down to where creature had been without hesitation, and there, tried to climb a tree.) [JG1]

In a discussion with Stuart Syme, he pointed out to me that the encounter took place between the two lakes previously mentioned, all south of trout-stocked Allison Lake.

Another report on John Green's site pointed to the species having what we would call "youngsters" in the area, this time west of Princeton, approximately five years later.

> October 1975, before 3:00 a.m., southwest of Princeton… Frederick Kirkwood and his wife Millie were traveling east on the Hope-Princeton Highway at 2:30 a.m. — two miles west of the Allison Pass works yard when they rounded a curve and saw a dark figure come up on the road 100 yards ahead. They slowed almost to a stop while the creature crossed the road, angling toward the car. It came within twelve feet, looking straight ahead, and kept going. Eyes looked black and did not reflect. Face was light brown — looked human, hair-covered. The hair was light colored, one and a half inches long, like a dark golden retriever. No prominent ears visible. Hair on back of hands but not on feet, which were shiny black and looked wet. Creature was about five feet eight inches tall and very heavy, thicker from back to front than a man. Arms were normal length. Head hair same length as body hair and down on forehead but not on face. Nose like a human's. Neck short but not exceedingly so. [JG1]

Sasquatch seem to come in different sizes. While we can't be sure, we can guess that these are young Sasquatch. Others, such as Sali Sheppard Wolford in *Valley of the Skookum*, have reported seeing whole families. That they have a family structure is an important characteristic to note.

## Curiosity and Food

Let's combine the three sightings of 1970, 1974, and 1985, and we'll also throw in what we believe to be a young Sasquatch in our basement in 1970 or 1971. Is there a possible contributing factor that has brought

**Figure 14: Princeton's Brown Bridge where a Sasquatch may have made a river crossing in 1974.**

the giant from the hills north of Princeton? A hungry belly may have initially started the activity, but the months of April, June, and October are hardly feeding-frenzy months related to gardens. On the footsteps of Sasquatch, our observations of the past, including researching the circumstances of those events, led us to a weakness of the haired primate. That inborn fault is curiosity, and we can vouch for its relationship to the habits that the animal possesses.

During the years of those sightings, we believe that our witnessing was partly due to the animal scouting out interests, or perhaps following up on its earlier desires. By this, we can presume that the creature bases its actions on a good memory. Focusing on the fact that the Sasquatch came up from the area of the Tulameen River as in 1974, there is one component that has not yet been discussed and remains an option to illustrate how such a giant thinks and operates.

In her last few years, our mother lived at an apartment complex that sat just southwest of the area where Alan and I encountered the beast. At the east side of the building, closest to the pathway the Sasquatch had taken, sat the area where the tenants dropped off their garbage. It was easily accessible, with one of those simple latches and everything on the outside of the building. I knew a few other tenants who lived there, and at times, they wondered who was making such a big mess of the place. Young offenders or maybe the odd bottle collector took the blame for the garbage being scattered about. Or was it a black bear, though there was never a scratch on the plywood? You understand, of course, who would never ever get the blame. I wonder if the damn things are aware of that, too.

This particular scenario involved the north side of the river, but now for the south side. Suppose the Sasquatch species crosses the river, using the Brown Bridge as a shadowing ally. Many months of the year, the Tulameen River does not come up high enough to touch the ankles of Bigfoot. Therefore, once across, the creature had access along the riverbank to the end of Harold Avenue. The animal could come in one way and depart another.

There is also an honorable mention to this. Years ago, the first building that sat across the river on the south side, along Bridge Street, was a supermarket, the Amos Red & White. The grocery store had a loading dock and perishable trash was housed there week in and week out. The Sasquatch could check on this treasure trove whenever necessary. The crafty species has many talents, but they haven't mastered their inherent curiosity. Furthermore, taking into account our span of encountering the beast, the Sasquatch was willing to come and go for at least fifteen years in our immediate area alone.

## Garden Connections

As we've previously hinted, it should be asked: Could the fruit and veggie yield in the Princeton area be part of the draw for this ambitious creature? An older Chinese fellow lived across the street from us at the time of our mother's confrontation with the giant, the very residence where the forest dweller had a hand up on the gate, holding it, about to walk through. The single gentleman who lived there planted tall, plentiful gardens every year, the food plants easily standing out in season. Also, from what I remember, roots and other nutritious items sat around for a period after being harvested. What more could a species of such great size want from such a property?

The time of year seems to play an integral role when it comes to Sasquatch visits to gardens and fields. Do the primates scout out their

**Figure 15: This property, overlooking Princeton, was where Richard and Glen Boulier spotted a large primate in 1985. Were gardens in the area what the creature was after?**

pursuits ahead of time, and do their mental capabilities allow them this luxury? In the surrounding area, including Princeton's Allison Flats, a number of local people take pride in the gardens they grow. Due to this, a roaming Sasquatch would have no problem complementing its diet a little at a time. Of course the deer population — an animal everyone believes in — was blamed for the nibbling and making messes, but who did the pulling, roots and all? Surely that could not be accomplished by a four-legged ruminant.

The garden topic becomes a little more mysterious when we consider the 1985 encounter and its location. The property just below the airport featured a garden for years. Again, was this what the Sasquatch wanted? With my very own eyes, I saw the animal using the gate. The geographical setting has a major drop-off to the south of the residences along the shelf, so it isn't a transportation route for the species. It was early October at the time, so I have to wonder, was Bigfoot checking out the end of the harvest in the Princeton area?

I interviewed a number of property owners in the summer of 2005, as I had others in the past. They claimed they'd never seen a creature of that sort, but they did mention that vegetables and other produce had gone missing over the years at a number of homesteads. The roots also have food value, and they are available in the late fall, as reported to me by an aboriginal lady and fellow when discussing the creature's needs.

The following are findings of other possible encounters with this species in the garden:

> In 1937, Mrs. Jane Patterson, a British Columbia resident, observed a Sasquatch sitting in an abandoned garden. Another sighting saw the creature frequently stealing food from gardens and sheds.
>
> Pearlington, Mississippi, Hancock County: A woman saw nothing as she looked toward the woods. Hearing chewing sounds near the house, she looked down to where her grandparents' vegetable garden was and saw what she thought was a man squatting down, eating from a row of tomato plants. Only twenty feet from the house, she soon realized that the being was covered with shaggy fur, dark brown in color. The next day, they found a few footprints in the garden where the creature had walked in dirt.
>
> Whatcom County, Washington State: A person mentioned that her friends who lived in Maple Falls have had problems with Sasquatch at times. They report that they hear screams, and their gardens are raided.
>
> Near Flagstaff, Arizona: Two women walking to a vegetable garden on their ranch witnessed a seven-foot giant in the garden with one armload of corn and the other arm pulling up turnips. Covered with light-colored hair, it went through a wheat field, jumping a rail fence.
>
> In an area in Oregon, near Applegate Lake and the Applegate River (where the Sasquatch-Bigfoot trap was built), a miner by the name of Perry Lovell came across eighteen-inch tracks in his garden. The one that made those manlike footsteps had a step span of six feet.

Another convincing report about the garden situation and Sasquatch comes from Linda Coil-Suchy in her book, *Who's Watching You?* In the book, the author's grandmother talks about a Bigfoot including the woman's plentiful garden as part of its eating habits. It was by no means a deer or other creature that would just nibble away at the produce selection.

Finishing this out in the Hedley, British Columbia, area comes George Douglas, an aboriginal gentleman whose mother Adeline related a story from her childhood:

> Where they lived, in a cabin near an old mine around Nickel Plate Lake, there was a fence at the cabin where they placed fruit and vegetables when they heard the Sasquatch scream. The children were all gathered into the wooded shelter they called home, and the creatures would come down and take the food.

These are just a few of the examples of the primate possibly using human gardens as a food source to supplement its forest diet.

## The Meat of the Matter

Another facet of sustenance leads us to the meat of the matter — a brief and somewhat rushed investigation spinning off from the garden search of Princeton. This involved unlocked sheds in the district that hosted hanging kills of skinned deer, moose, and whatever else was in season. Unexplained, sketchy events hinted at a predatory animal scouting out the curing meat — the stuff of things-going-bump-in-the-night stories. The whodunits ended without being completed; the humans involved wanted to remain anonymous when relating their similar tales of a huge, shady character sometimes leaving their properties at a quick walking pace. Not one of these witnesses wishes to be associated with the likes of the creature, and I will respect their wishes. This subject concluded with one individual actually firing a number of rounds into his wooden shed one night in the fall somewhere around 1987. They were willing to take that risk.

There has also been talk of the Princeton Dumpsite and the smorgasbord that lay there for the neighboring animal kingdom. Situated just east of town, about a mile as the crow flies from my 1985 encounter, the sanitary landfill lies wide open and is unmonitored during the night. Years ago, Richard rode along with the local garbage man as a helper. During a late run one evening, they came across black bears feeding on the waste in the darkness. Could there be another scavenger that pays visits to this convenient out-of-the-way location? I recall taking garbage to the landfill, giving someone a hand here and there over the years. During hunting season, it wasn't uncommon to see animal remains such as deer entrails tossed out, even the odd ribcage and such from who-knew-what. Coming down from the hills, it would be nothing for a Sasquatch to stay completely hidden.

Years ago, a Princeton business merchant found herself, as she puts it, "in the wrong place at the wrong time," sometime around 1989-90. We will call her "Dorothy" here. Well before normal business hours, she was alone, making a casual trip to the local dumpsite to discard odds and ends from her home and store. Dorothy had heard the stories of frequent black bear sightings at the secluded site and was cautious during the times when she made garbage runs, typically in early morning hours. The woman was especially fond of completing this chore on mornings when there wasn't a cloud in the sky.

On one such smelly visit, there were no ravens present, no morning birds singing, and no one else to give a nod to as she was about to swing the truck around for the quick drop-off before she returned to her business for the day. The Princeton resident hadn't tossed out more than one or two items when the garbage — including cardboard items — began to "come to life" near the other side of the open pit. Dorothy stopped in her tracks, monitoring the site for bear activity. It seemed the scavenger was rummaging through the refuse, noisy enough to wake the dead. She dared not turn her back to the movement, which lasted a while. Suddenly, a head much larger than that of any black bear rose from the area of the moving garbage. Something was watching her cautiously. The creature did not exhibit the straight, long muzzle of a bear, and Dorothy had the jitters even as she recounted the tale.

Her nervousness turned into a full-fledged nightmare. She'd seen the strange-looking creature show more of itself as it prepared to leave the area. The witness felt that the animal was somehow stooped over, picking at the garbage. It did have grotesque-looking pieces of some kind of waste clinging to it. A number of these things caught the sunlight, producing a reflection. Others did not.

At a hurried pace, the tall one never dropped to all fours. It made its way up out of the small hollow. Dorothy indicated that she felt as though the presence of the haired being made the hole in the ground seem smaller, as the creature was so much larger than an average man. It was at the top of the pit in a flash and watched her briefly from beside a tree. In seconds, it was gone. Without knowing it, Dorothy had backed herself up against her open truck door and was trying to get her wits about her.

What she recalls of the animal itself was an ape-like face with a human side to it. The long arms (forearms) came in contact with the outsides of the upper thighs when the creature left the pit. It did not watch her at all while it departed the actual cavity. Once the creature reached level ground, it looked her way a couple of times before stopping at the tree for a better study of the startled woman, even though it was for a short time. The skin seemed to cling to the animal, and there were many things going on within the beast's entire framework while it was mobile. There didn't appear to be large fat deposits anywhere on the creature. According to Dorothy, it rolled along like a machine well suited for the environment.

I asked Dorothy an innocent question: "At any time, did you think it may have been a bear of some kind?"

The woman laughed such a possibility off. "That's impossible — silly," she stated. "Impossible!" was all she had to say to such an absurd notion.

After that day, she refused to go to the landfill site again and opted to pay someone else to handle the errand or disposed of her garbage by crushing it and cutting it up small enough for the local garbage collector to handle. No matter what, the business merchant refused to go there again.

She left Princeton years later, still giving her head a shake when she thought about what she had seen on her visit to the dump. During the last month of her stay in the area, she took a nervous drive past the site, to the nearby Princeton Fairgrounds where she turned around, checking the old pit much more slowly on the second pass.

I'll leave you with this, questions that were asked by others pertaining to the garden situation: Can the Sasquatch eat just enough out of a garden at one time, so as not to bring attention to itself? Do they have the knowledge and mental capacity to make such a distinction? Would they be smart enough to take a little here and a little there? I can only wonder.

## Fire

In the past, supposedly the Sasquatch people had fire, though maintaining flame could be a problem. What would change this way of living? What would make them relinquish the use of such a tool? Can they distinguish the dangers of fire in this day and age, giving up their use of fire in the interests of safety and remaining undiscovered?

It makes one wonder. You'd think there would be Sasquatch-oriented campfires all over North America. Another mystery to a complicated puzzle of what Sasquatch really is, wouldn't you agree?

## Step and Stride

Step and stride aren't characteristics unique to Bigfoot, but measuring them correctly is essential in creating accurate reports about Bigfoot sightings. Everywhere I look, there are discrepancies on how these two things are measured. Many were willing to argue for their point of view until they were blue in the face. I wasn't an expert, but I did manage to find someone who had the credentials.

Bruce G. Marcot is a Research Wildlife Ecologist with the Ecosystems Processes Research Program, USDA Forest Service, in Portland, Oregon. He holds a BS and MS in natural resources from Humboldt State University, California, and a Ph.D. in wildlife science from Oregon State University. He participates in projects dealing with analysis of wildlife population viability, assessment of biodiversity, and ecologically sustainable land-use planning. He has worked or traveled in Russia, China, India, Mexico, Costa Rica, Ecuador, Bolivia, Germany, the Bahamas, the Virgin Islands, New Zealand, sub-Antarctica, Australia, Africa, Canada, the continental U.S., Alaska, Hawaii, and elsewhere, and much of his information can be found on the World Wide Web. The information can be used to measure any prints you may encounter, so you can better realize if and when you may be facing something out of the ordinary.

Bruce writes about Bigfoot in general, step and stride in particular:

> **… around the world, they call it Sasquatch, Forest Man, Yeti, Bigfoot, Matdngdng.**
>
> Does some nonhuman anthropoid really stalk the dark woods and hinterlands of the world?
>
> Evidence includes strings of hair, nest beds on the forest floor, foul odors, visual encounters, fuzzy photos, taped calls, and… footprints.
>
> I'm a professional wildlife biologist. I've worked in the field in many parts of the world, especially the conifer forests of the Pacific Northwest, the supposed heart of Bigfoot country. I've worked with Native Americans whose legends of Bigfoot-like

creatures [mirror those] in far corners of the globe told by other indigenous peoples.

What might this be? From a wildlife biology perspective, it seems incredible that so wide-ranging, so large a creature would remain undiscovered by science and escape scientific scrutiny. Stories of only recently discovered species of ungulate in the deep jungles of Vietnam, or cryptic oceanic life forms such as the coelacanth and giant squid, are often raised as supposed evidence that Bigfoot exists or could exist. In one sense, this is so; absence of evidence is not evidence of absence. No one would be more excited, more delighted than would I, if this were the case… and, at least in the wildlife management profession, we truly don't yet know. As we must take care not to let possibilities be taken as evidence of probabilities, we should approach the available evidence with some scientific care.

**What about the Footprints?**

But as for those tracks… of big feet that started it all… I can hazard an explanation. Here is a critical examination and explanation of Bigfoot tracks.

Evidence of tracks takes three main forms: recounted direct sightings, photos of tracks, and plaster casts. Remember, though, that most of the evidence you can really weigh is what someone wrote of theirs or another's sightings or someone's photographs of supposed tracks or of supposed plaster casts. So remember to keep on the *skeptical glasses* and not believe everything you read or see in photos.

I'll break this little treatise into several chewable sections. Please take these in sequence, or they may not make much sense:

**What to Measure**

So what can be told from a brief survey of prints and casts? I myself have made many photos, sketches, and plaster casts of wildlife tracks ranging from cranes to grouse to raccoons to mountain lions… and have tracked a wide variety of mammals, including carnivores and even primates, and other animals, in North and South America, India, Asia, and elsewhere.

My experience tells me several things about making accurate casts and scientific measurements of tracks:

**Block out the Casts**

When you take casts, you should block out a rectangular area well beyond the edge of the impression itself and fill the entire volume with plaster. Otherwise, you cannot tell if the shape of the cast was manipulated — deliberately or inadvertently. Virtually none of the Bigfoot track casts I've ever seen have done this correctly.

**Align Photos with Scale**

When photographing a track, at least some of the pictures should be taken directly above the track to avoid problems with parallax and perspective (however, photographing a track series may necessitate taking the photo at an oblique angle to capture multiple tracks in one image.) Also, something recognizable — usually a pen or a ruler, with known length — should be placed next to the track for scale.

**Inspect Multiple Tracks**

One print tells you little. You really need a sequence of tracks, because individual imprints can vary quite widely, even from the same foot. It depends on the moistness of the soil or mud, the stance of the animal, the slope and the relative direction of travel, the speed the animal was traveling, and other factors.

Some individual tracks may not show all toes (this is common with larger carnivores such as bears) or dewclaws (commonly missing in most ungulate tracks,) or the full foot pad (if the animal is resting its weight on the toes and forepart of the foot, which happens with some big cats, bears, and others, and which varies by type and speed of gait.) Other tracks in the same track sequence might reveal details and lead you to a very different conclusion about its maker.

**Take Multiple Measurements from Each Track**

For mammal tracks, you need to take multiple measurements at each imprint, be they from live tracks or from plaster casts, including: overall length from the hind edge of the pad to the front of the toes; length of just the pad; overall width including the toe imprints; width of just the pad; and length, width, and perhaps spacing of the individual toe imprints. Again, none of the reports I have seen on Bigfoot tracks or casts offers this kind of information.

Also, you should inspect the variation in the depth of the imprint. In most mammals, the arch of the pad and the part of the foot between the pad and the toes should appear the least deep in direct tracks (so the deepest in the negative image of a plaster cast.) I have seen photos of supposed Bigfoot tracks that are uniform in depth from heel to toe tip — a sure sign of a hoax. (But remember that variable depth does not mean it is not a hoax.)

**Measure the Stride**

This includes the distance between front and hind feet tracks on quadrupeds, and also front foot to front foot stride (or hind foot to hind foot.) This tells more about the pace of the animal than it does the size (a typical misconception in Bigfoot track-hunters.)

And measure this stride between as many consecutive tracks as possible, not just one set. Report the average and variation in stride length. Few if any Bigfoot track reports offer such data, at least that I have seen. Occasionally you hear reports of Bigfoot strides (such as the stride of the Matdngdng tracks reported by my researcher colleague in India) but with no actual data presented or information on how it was determined, other than measuring between only two tracks.

**Inspect the Variation in Pattern**

Does the front foot always appear just behind the hind foot? Does this pattern vary? Are the tracks in a straight line with every fourth track slightly offset, like foxes and other canids? Do they alternate from a line such as with the third track offset, like some big cats? Do they regularly alternate back and forth from a line with individual tracks slightly pointing outwards, such as by us bipedal hominids?

**Report on the Environment**

This includes many things:

- the condition of the substrate — wet mud, sand, friable soil, track partially obscured by leaf litter, etc, which tells you how impressionable the track would be
- the general habitat or vegetation type
- recent rainfall or precipitation, which may melt tracks to larger sizes or make them unrecognizable
- recent warm days, to interpret tracks in snow, which may grow when snow sublimates or melts, even if it refreezes.[BGM1]

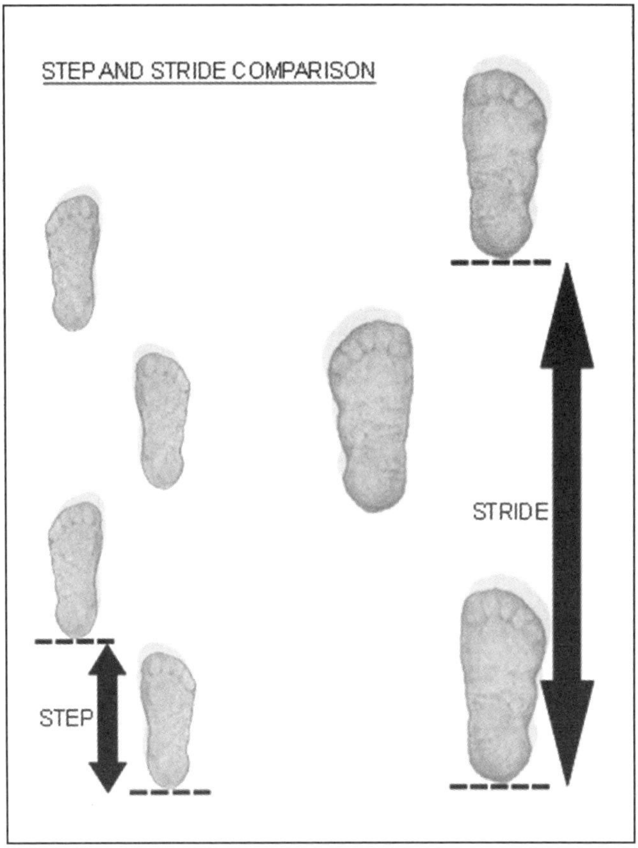


**Figure 16: The difference between step and stride.**

Given what Bruce says, I'm sure you can see that Bigfoot researchers have a long way to go before we reach the level of detail required to effectively use the evidence of Bigfoot tracks. And the hoaxers will be doing their best to keep ahead of the game. One inventive jokester, let's call him the Pumpkin Man, tried this scheme. With a little in-house carving, the artist produced a set of Bigfoot sandals out of a pumpkin. The gifted person obviously did his homework, keeping up to date with scientific research methods concerning the creature. His carvings included their own set of dermal ridges, with an imaginative pattern on the outsides of the fabricated shoes. One problem: pumpkin particles were left in the tracks.

Bottom line? Implementing as much of Bruce's procedure as possible will make faking tracks much more difficult. We can be surer of many things being discussed about the Bigfoot of North America, through the prints being found, if we researchers are more diligent in recording our findings.

## Sasquatch and the High Places

The Sasquatch people seem to defy logic, and the world seems to be baffled by thoughts of some giant, ape-like wild man running free in our technologically advancing world. I want to look at one more trait that seems logical and may even help us understand why the Sasquatch has a chance to remain uncaptured after many sightings, encounters, and investigative follow-ups.

The Bigfoot seems to know where it's going all the time, evidently intelligent in the path it follows, which often seems to be the path of least resistance until something comes along to force the issue. This changes rapidly when the primate is threatened, and this is where we come to high places. Certainly, Sasquatch who live in the mountains have a friend in elevation.

Whether or not this bipedal creature constructs bedding areas or nests is still an open question. Many of these supposed resting areas are found in high places that may give Bigfoot the chance to observe without being seen. These areas, in most cases, allow the Sasquatch to watch at least two directions at once; this is yet another sign of the woodland giant's intelligence, for that would mean there is planning involved.

When it comes to height advantages, it would seem that the species uses it for a number of reasons. In the 1924 prospectors' story about Ape Canyon, the creature was seen on the cabin roof. Coincidentally — or maybe not — in Thomas Steenburg's writings of the 1986 Coalmont incident, the Sasquatch was also on a cabin roof. Though not everyone is a gifted artist, there is a drawing supplied by witnesses of the giant in such a position. But height usage doesn't end with these examples.

This species has been known to move uphill when someone is knowingly tracking them. In one report, the Sasquatch, when fired upon by an outdoorsman, moved immediately higher. Along those same lines, another encounter featured a twofold, apparently thought-out departure. The Sasquatch, walking on the side of a roadway, went directly up a bank as a family approached by car. When the vehicle stopped, the Sasquatch stopped as well, walking a few level steps on the mountainside. When the individuals exited their car, along with their accompanying hounds, the Sasquatch made a beeline straight up the rocky slope and was never seen again.

In the 1941 Ruby Creek story involving the Chapman family, the creature's tracks were investigated by two men. Crossing the railroad, the trail of footprints continued to go straight up a mountain that was near the property.

It seems the native guides of the past were aware that the Sasquatch uses inclines as a frequent means of escape. On many occasions when men searched for the bipedal giant, guides would often abandon them when the mountains came into view. This can also be said of other tracking expeditions. When the tracks were fresh and they seemed to be whittling down the distance between them and the quarry, some found themselves in fear of what lay hidden ahead. They really did not want to find what was producing those large prints that sank so deep into the ground.

The mysterious giants also show their preference for going up in the oral tradition of the aboriginal people around Harrison Lake, British Columbia. There is a story of an Indian woman being carried away, an ape-like man heading up a steep mountainside with his kidnapped victim.

In the general vicinity of the Harrison River, another example of Sasquatch departure antics was recorded. There, researcher Thomas Steenburg was investigating the theft of some trout from a couple of American campers. The track of the Sasquatch followed the creek for a bit, then suddenly ascended a hillside, an old slide area bordering the waterway. It was up that gravel slope that the fish thief disappeared. When there are a number of routes the woodland legend could take, many times the Sasquatch chooses the most difficult one. Such things limit the pursuer and can also decrease the possibility of tracks being left, thanks to the hard ground and difficult terrain.

A number of reports detail such escapes — the giant fleeing by way of the high ground. A frightened woman in Idaho watched such a thing with disbelieving eyes, thinking it was a large animal down on all fours. It was actually crouching and finally stood up tall and looked right back at her. The Sasquatch then walked up the hill, remaining upright the entire time. In our 1985 encounter in Princeton, the creature darted for an available pathway on the hillside, stopping halfway to monitor our movement before hurriedly carrying on. This species knows its surroundings, is suited to the environment, and understands where it wants to be and how to get there.

An investigative organization conducting a field study in New Mexico experienced a similar situation with a Bigfoot that presented itself in the daylight, when they least expected it. As the story was told to me, they had just completed a 35 mm photo shoot, expending the last frame on the roll, documenting a previously reported encounter. As they headed back to the car to leave the area, contact was made with something in the brush beside one of the cars. One of the crew threw his empty camera through an open window of the vehicle and began pursuing the guest at a dead run for approximately 350 yards up a 40-degree slope at the 7,200-foot level. Physical exhaustion made further pursuit impossible, but the individual provided a more detailed observation than the person who saw the subject through the brush near the vehicle.

There was a slight twist to the uphill direction in a story that came from a fellow I work with. He's in management and wishes to remain anonymous, but he wanted me to share this story, as he found it as humorous as it was surprising. It all took place not that long ago in the Takakkaw Falls area of Yoho National Park, near Field, British Columbia. The area also boasts Point Lace Falls, Laughing Falls, Twin Falls, and Angel's Staircase.

While on a day trip to enjoy the majestic Rockies, my coworker trekked a raised hillside just south of the highway, where he could take in nature's splendor. From that vantage point, on the outskirts of that section of woods, he thought he saw hikers across the highway, well up the mountainside opposite him, a small group walking up a trail. He then witnessed a large, lone hiker approximately 200 yards behind the larger group. He assumed it was a grossly overweight straggler, but something didn't seem right, for the individual was abnormally tall as well. Neither party could see the other from what he could tell, and no one seemed to be waiting up for the big one. That inspired him to have a look-see through his binoculars.

Through those lenses, he could make out what looked like four well-content hikers, enjoying their surroundings. They gradually left his field of view, moving behind foliage or rocks. Then, a single individual a ways back from the hikers flabbergasted him. It was an ape-like giant, walking the same path, with shorthaired arms swinging gently. The creature was on a steady, slow walk, but it covered a fair amount of ground rather quickly, and it never looked off the mountainside, from what he could tell. In time, it also disappeared from view, continuing in the same direction as the unsuspecting hikers.

He waited patiently, scouting the area for some kind of sign, but he didn't see any terrified hikers running along the mountain or jumping off, so he was sure they never met up with each other. Nevertheless, he feared for the safety of the hiking party, being that close to a following monster without even knowing it. It reminded him of a bear stalking a human being. He packed up hastily, uneasy with his own position and looking into the wilderness behind him. Until now he never mentioned it to anyone.

What we can glean from all of this is simple: The Sasquatch likes to take the high road and seems to be sure-footed, quick-witted, and physically fit. Enough information has been documented in the annals of the phenomenon to more than adequately demonstrate this fact.

# 5. Legends from the White Settlers

In Part II we'll look at legends from Native Americans and First Nations, but there are legends from White settlers, too. Here's a look at some of those stories.

## The Big Men of the Okanagan

So, where did the Big Men of the Mountains come from originally? This is what the Sasquatch creature has been called in parts of British Columbia's Okanagan Valley — the land of famous vineyards, fruit orchards, and semi-desert climate, amongst a wealth of forests and other natural beauty.

As with Hedley and Keremeos, I had never heard of a single story of the Sasquatch anywhere near the Okanagan region. It was around the year 2000 that my investigations began to uncover a picture of what Bigfoot has left behind as indications of its presence. Up until that point, there seemed to be little room for the Big Men, when the emphasis was on the Ogopogo of Lake Okanagan — another mystery that remains unresolved. This creature of the waters has modeled carvings, souvenir trinkets, and who knows what else. A reward is even being offered for the serpent's capture. But what about the Sasquatch? (What Sasquatch?) Again, the creature is passed over and discounted, dismissed like a leaf blown in the wind, a figment of someone's imagination.

Many of the indigenous people of the 1800s and early 1900s knew stories about these seldom-seen beings. In those days, both the Big Men and the Ogopogo were equally notable — somewhat feared by some and nothing more than myths to others. The Sasquatch is seldom talked about in open conversation these days, and very few associate the Okanagan with the massive forest giant. The number of documented reports is considerably lower than other areas in British Columbia.

I knew they were there, though. With a little perseverance and honesty, I found some who came forward to add insight into the mystery of the forest dweller. This was in a tiny communication with a member of the native band that calls the Penticton area home. In 2005, two of the aboriginal tribe members found large tracks, with heavy indentations in the soil, leading them to believe that the animal had passed by there. Both tribe members were familiar with game tracks and impressions made in the wilderness. This led me to look for further evidence, and I found some in the history of the region.

Several years earlier, one spring and summer in the early 1970s, I had done some volunteer work on the Dewdney Trail south of Princeton. There, I was also introduced to that little British Columbia varmint, the wood tick, as I found twenty-three of the little buggers on me in just one day. It is toward the west end of this famous trail though, at Hope, where we will begin with this historical look at the mystery of the Big Men.

A pioneer woman, Susan Allison, was about to set off on a journey from what was Fort Hope in the Fraser Valley. By chance, I had gone to school with grandchildren of the mother of the Similkameen, and it was rather ironic that Allison Flats at Princeton was where the 1974 encounter took place. If the pioneer lady had only known that her assumptions (the stories told to her by First Nations) were true! Susan, a feisty woman, even penned her complete memoirs about her experiences in the Similkameen. During the 1860s, she pressed through the wilderness, riding horseback to what would be Vermilion Forks, present-day Princeton. Susan was also the pioneering woman who would sit numerous times with Indian scouts and guides, sometimes talking about the Stenwyken, the Big Men of the Okanagan.

The pioneer family, along with the native population, endured one of the Similkameen's worst winters on record, 1879-80. After a dump of nearly three feet of snow, extreme low temperatures followed, crusting the snow pack, freezing rain sealing the deal. I have seen brutal winters in Princeton, but nothing like that — not even close. According to stories, due to food shortages and everyday life slowing to a death crawl, the Sasquatch species ventured down from the mountains to beg for sustenance during the extremely tough times. They were prone to begging from the natives, who likely better understood such creatures. If that was the case, it would have been a sight to behold. Information that I found from the locals, relating to their predecessors, seemed to support the possibility of such a cruel winter and visits from the hungry Big Men. The biped panhandling was also rumored to occur near Lumby and the Okanagan Valley, though it could not be confirmed whether it only happened in the winter in those areas.

At some stage, the primates turned to thievery. This was evident at Vermilion Forks (Princeton) in the era of pioneers A. E. Howse and John Fall Allison, in an area now known as Vermilion Avenue, where it intersects Highway 3. A natural formation of colored sandstone banks was the stopover point for pioneers, miners, and occasional First Nations peoples, thanks to events such as the Gold Rush. Conveniently situated for travelers was the Vermilion Cave, a massive hollow opening. Pioneer merchant A. E. Howse stored goods there, as did many others over time, until the building of the Hope-Princeton Highway during the late 1940s practically destroyed the cave. The huge hole in the earth could hold just over twenty loaded railway cars at one time. This was proven by Princeton's Caribou Brewing Company many years ago, when they used it for their goods. If only sandstone walls could speak.

The First Nations people knew of the ones who visited the impressive cave. Over time, those visitors became known as the Tall Stenwyken, or Big Men. When necessary, the mysterious creatures helped themselves to the supplies that were periodically placed there for safekeeping; an educated guess makes it rather clear who to blame for the supplies that seemed to be hitting the wind. The aboriginal population was blamed for much of this, but they knew better, for they knew of the ones who stood motionless and walked in the colored shadows.

According to words spoken on such things, when the cave ceased to hold perishables, the Big Men then moved their focus north of Vermilion Forks. Did Bigfoot then watch a part of British Columbia's Similkameen history unfold — the Gold Rush around Coalmont, Tulameen, and the ghost town of Granite City — near the area where Thomas Steenburg investigated sightings of this creature in 1986? It seems the Sasquatch knows a thing or two, particularly when to stick to a certain region. Even Blakeburn in the 1920s and 1930s, now a ghost town, was within easy reach of the creature. The coal-mining town produced much waste, and the Sasquatch were very close by, in their element. While it is mere speculation, I propose that before the Sasquatch came to Princeton, a much easier first stop along the way would have been Blakeburn, the

**Figure 17: What remains of Vermilion Cave near Princeton. The Hope-Princeton Highway took out parts when it was built in the 1940s. Traveling merchants, gold miners, and pioneers stored goods in the cave. Bigfoot took some of those goods out for their own use.**

place high on the mountain just southwest of Coalmont (in those days, practically the middle of nowhere).

In 1868, pioneer Susan Allison and her husband blazed the Dewdney Trail into the mountain ranges of the Cascades. On her first night around a warm campfire, the woman's ears were filled with the stories of mystery, the realm of aboriginal consciousness, since there were three native guides also in camp. Of course, stories of the haired, massive giants were whispered around that fire.

Once they were situated in the interior of British Columbia, Mrs. Allison was told a story about a young aboriginal boy who had helped his father with fish traps. Those traps began to be mysteriously raided, so the brave youngster opted to keep a lookout one night in an attempt to solve the mystery of where their catch was disappearing to. The moon was nowhere to be seen that night, and with the thick cloud cover over the region, it was extremely dark. Out of utter boredom, the boy fell asleep, but a while later, a whistle in the woods jolted him to attention. In the seconds that followed, the young boy was picked up, blanket and all, until he was able to look into the monstrous face. After scooping up the boy, the Big Man moved back into the mountains with him. Story has it that the boy was taken to a cave, where he watched the creature line fish on a stick. He also witnessed the appearance of a second Big Man, who brought venison to accompany the pilfered fish. The two creatures chatted. With perseverance, the talented boy finally managed to escape, and he reached his family again only after months of travel through the forests.

Concerning the Okanagan and the Similkameen, there would be other tales of things similar to those Susan Allison heard and documented. These were mostly passed down to family when it came to legends of mystery.

With the help of museums in a number of places in the region, as well as the proverbial grapevine, I was able to discover something more — something that resembled stories of the Big Men. A native Okanagan storyteller relied upon a British Columbian author to translate stories of native background. That author, however, didn't seem to understand the significance of the Sasquatch presence, as they focused on many subjects spoken about by the spinner of folklore yarns. One tale centered around Hedley, somewhere around present-day Nickel Bridge Road, which was nothing but a dusty old trail at the time.

Three native hunters were nearly finished field dressing their kill. They had agreed that one of the youngest among them, a boy, would transport the fallen animal to camp while the others attempted to build on their good luck.

On his journey, the lad thought he heard a squirrel just inside the timberline. Naturally curious like young boys are, he wanted to catch a glimpse of the little creature, so he looked for it briefly. This, however, was no small forest rodent. Instead, what the boy discovered with his own wide eyes was a big, tall man covered with hair. The storyteller referred to it as a gorilla. The child was abducted by the creature. Trackers followed the barefoot prints of the bipedal giant to the top of a mountain. For reasons unknown, the boy was released near a lake in the area and picked up by another indigenous tribe. In that way, the Big Man actually changed the course of that particular young person's life.

In what seems to be a very small world, that Okanagan storyteller also shared a tale he supposedly learned from a white man. The Allisons were specifically mentioned, their obvious hindsight being applied to what they knew of the Big Men of the Okanagan and Similkameen Valley. The aboriginal storyteller learned of this story through Albert (Bert) Allison, a descendant of John Fall Allison's first wife, native Nora Yakumtekum. The narration included Similkameen ranch country. There was a knock at someone's door. There, standing on the stoop, was a man, described as a bear but taller, more like a gorilla. He was covered with hair and seemed to be capable of killing anyone he pleased. He was asked if he was, indeed, one of the Big Men of legend.

Now, it must be said that one must be careful when such a phenomenon crosses over, especially when it is something few of us believe in or understand. As the story goes, the creature spoke not one word. He was able to shape-shift into a human being, then a mouse, which was then eaten by the host. I told this account to those educated in such things in the Okanagan, as this was the example of folkloristic native storytelling. In response to the bizarre ending, I was told that the meaning might include the continuation of white settlers to the valley, which ultimately forced the Big Men to distance themselves from the humans flooding into the area. They would do just that, becoming mainly a thought in the minds of men. One aboriginal man even said the strange giant would shy away from fallen snow if it could, when the creature's shadow was cast on a moonlit night.

But the Big Men stayed nearby. In the winter of 1969, just over a hundred years later, a party of three individuals was driving the winding, slow-going Hope-Princeton Highway. At approximately 3:00 a.m., they happened upon a large, upright-walking creature crossing the road. Another report thirty years later in 1999, again along the highway at Nicolum Creek six miles east of Hope, claimed that a motorist confronted a giant that was standing on two legs.

# 6. The Cathedral Park Incident

Have you ever had a hunch about something? Something so obvious that it jumped off the page at you? Well, Cathedral Provincial Park in lower British Columbia, bordering Washington State, was one of those hunches.

The page this hunch jumped off of was a Rand McNally road atlas. I was following up on another issue that had nothing to do with the Sasquatch at the time. However, since I have always been mindful of the animal, an area just over twenty-five miles southeast of Princeton as the crow flies caught my attention. I wondered, *Why is there no evidence, no reports from such a secluded place as Cathedral Park?* It had to be because very few people were there.

The Provincial Park has five turquoise-blue lakes above the 6,500-foot level. Cathedral Mountain itself sits at 9,184 feet, with other jagged peaks reaching up to 8,622 feet above sea level. The British Columbia park is 81,500 acres of mountain wilderness. The surrounding areas include Snowy Crater and Manning Parks and the Pasayten Wilderness to the south in Washington State's Okanagan National Forest.

Private vehicles are restricted from traveling into the core area of Cathedral Park. Park visitors leave from a parking lot ten miles away, either backpacking in or using the Cathedral Lakes Lodge Jeep shuttle service. With rock formations such as the Devil's Woodpile, Stone City, and Smokey the Bear, the twenty-plus miles of hiking trails make for a soulful experience. As high as they are, these pathways are susceptible to snowfall in any month of the year. Even to the south in the Pasayten Wilderness, the trails are often above the 7,000-foot level. There are more than 600 miles of trails snaking throughout the landscape.

Research shows that the Similkameen Valley aborigine groups hunted in the alpine areas, including quests for the prized hoary marmot.

While doing the research, I found two words that I'd never heard of before, Kwi-kwiyai and St'iyahama. Both seemed to be alternative names for Sasquatch.

First Nations individuals talked about Okanagan vision quests. They believed a remnant of the Kwi-kwiyai took up residence in and around Cathedral Basin after taking an overland journey for reasons unknown. Could they have been Susan Allison's Big Men of the mountains? Was this the clan I witnessed at least twice in the Princeton area?

The other name was St'iyahama. These are the tall, monstrous creatures that reside in the high mountains. These creatures are talked about in the Whistler area where it is said they sleep during the day but move about freely in the night. Sunset to sunrise is their time to prowl.

I believe both of these creatures are the forest-dwelling Sasquatch or Bigfoot, the thing that owns and masters the wilderness. Information from the past convinced me to move on with my quest in Cathedral Basin and surrounding areas.

I proceeded to make a request for information on the trails of those two neighboring parks, Cathedral and Pasayten. It was not that I was on a schedule of any kind, but I did limit myself to approximately eighteen months to research this area. I decided to concentrate on people who walked the trails because there was a good possibility that the Sasquatch might use the available trail systems.

I began with an advertising barrage to raise public awareness. I hoped a number of phone calls, emails, advertisements on corkboards, and other measures would produce responses from skeptical and bashful hikers. Beyond the skepticism about the existence of the ape-like species in the North American wilderness, there was also the challenge of embarrassment. Too many times the response to talking about seeing a Sasquatch is that the person who had the sighting should see a shrink.

Fortunately there were some responses. Once the crackpots and jokers were eliminated, we got to research what we intended to. We could check out the possible trail use by the Sasquatch in the two parks and just outside Cathedral Park.

## Short Stories

Some informants were hikers, with no actual views of the creatures and possible tracks only. There was also a duo who witnessed the actual creature. The individuals came from varying backgrounds and tried to explain their findings as best they could. Following are the short stories of those who came forward, and I thank them.

**First Story**

In 1999, a group of us were on a long hike toward Manning Park, leaving Cathedral Park. We were on a rest period at the Ashnola River near a footbridge that is part of the Wall Creek Trail. We'd been footing it all day under cloud cover.

Stocking up on water to boil later, a member of the group found tracks leading away from the river that looked big and just plain unnatural. Summoning us all over, we were all unnerved seeing them on the ground. It was as if a very large man (the biggest man we knew of) was walking in the woods barefoot, the toes grabbing away at the soil.

**Second Story**

While backpacking the Boundary Trail route in the Pasayten Wilderness of the Okanagan Forest in July of 2001, we encountered footprints that intersected our path along the trail, around Horseshoe Basin, near Louden Lake. They sat very noticeable in soft ground to both sides of us.

Comparing shoe prints, the biggest size an eleven, we estimated the found prints to be a whopping fifteen inches. The distance between them looked to be groin pulling. You could not miss these steps, my friend, and the whole works of them sank in the ground.

When on Boundary, if you ever hike there, please take maps, or they'll be selling your truck from the parking lot when you fail to return.

**Third Story**

Hiking Quiniscoe Lake in lovely Cathedral Park in 2003, two of us were on the trail with the snow falling in July, as my husband recalls. Over from Europe visiting Canada, we are accustomed to rain at this time of the year, not snow.

There were large, rather huge-spaced footprints beside us on the walkway. This person went off the given path, and without shoe. As we moved along, I tried in vain to match the unusual distance between the steps to my left and could not do it. The footsteps remained a mystery to us as we continued in their direction. We are sorry they were destroyed in our negligence. We did manage to show others the odd-looking tracks, as passersby became curious.

Whatever made these markings continued to do so along one side of the lake. Hopefully this helps with the study you are producing.

### Fourth Story

On a week of holidays in 2004, part of the time two of us spent leisure time in the high country at Cathedral Provincial Park. Unusual tracks [were] found in snow-pockets as both of us hiked along the Ewart Creek-Centennial Trail, the hike almost killing us. The tracks were kinda interesting. [We] have no idea what made them. I showed another couple a dozen or so footprints when they passed. They stopped for a moment.

Measured to my walking stick, which I'm sure is five feet, there was almost a foot past that for the steps this animal took (no less).

Both women there, including my wife, were a little apprehensive about sticking around. I don't know how the other fellow felt, but he looked surprised. He said he had lots of experience in the outdoors. I thought I knew quite a bit about the woods. I couldn't identify the animal's prints; they had me stumped. And do you want to know what the strangest thing was with these continuous steps? They ended suddenly and surely, right out in the open snow before our very eyes, vanishing with the thinner air up there. (My wife has asthma.)

This struck a really weird feeling. We looked around for about ten minutes while my wife caught her breath. We thought maybe heavy snow accumulation had fallen from a large tree limb a skip away, possibly burying another sign of the animal's steps up ahead. That tree hadn't been disturbed, I'm telling you!

### Fifth Story

I'm quite hesitant about relating this story to anyone. I don't think a phone call will hurt, as my girlfriend and I discussed this beforehand.

Our off-road vehicle was not allowed on the road up to Cathedral, of course. We would use the transportation supplied by the lodge. It was a one-time thing, so we went along with it, though a bit pricey for our liking.

This all took place in 2008, during early summer. We're sure the driver didn't see anything, as he was busy with the uphill climb and [had] his eyes on the road. Others were caught up with whatever they were doing at the time. I remember looking at them. I don't think they saw what we experienced that day.

The journey took around an hour. We were situated on the right side of the vehicle, casually looking out on the scenery, trying to get our money's worth. If this strange animal wouldn't have moved around, we might never have spotted it.

About a good 175 feet away, a huggermugger of an animal stood out in a thinning of trees that were slightly off and below us. My girlfriend would like to stipulate that it stood the entire time, never going down on all fours as other animals do. She got excited, but nobody really paid attention to her, as I tried to fill the experience with it just being the wilderness. I figured that by the time I showed someone and they reacted, the creature would be gone out of view. (Then I'd be the idiot.)

Everything going around and around in our heads, we didn't think to notify anyone else afterward at the lodge. We couldn't believe our eyes! [Even after] running the bush in our 4X4 numerous times, sometimes almost recklessly, we have never gotten a sniff of anything even close to something as crazy as that. We spend as much time in the wild as we can, many times with others, and we've never seen anything as disturbing as this.

Discussing this with her during our vacation time up there, we agreed that the animal was off-brown in color, entirely hairy, and what felt like half as wide at the shoulders as it was tall, the bottom half of the animal a bit longer than the top. [The] arms were very long. We questioned ourselves (each other) during our eventual visit up at the Provincial Park. The animal walked off like a man, but not with the same approach. It is sketched in my mind forever, yes sir. The animal would have to be seven to eight feet, anywhere in there. It was standing and moving around in the sun at the time, seemingly enjoying it.

> Please feel free to jot this down for your investigation. We would like to stay out of this otherwise, if you don't mind. My buddies would roast me for such a tale.

There were other reports. Either they resembled these observers or they didn't quite measure up. Possibly another animal or maybe tracks belonging to such an animal had been sighted. These were the best. I was particularly interested in the impressions made on just soft ground, under relatively ideal conditions.

Before moving on to more reports, I want to look at things from a hoaxer's perspective. Can tracks like the ones described here be easily faked? If track depth is to be faked, the individual would have to add weight to himself — and a lot of it — to create proper track depth. The individuals in the second report stated that they didn't sink into the soil like the prints in question. They and others also said it was not an animal walking in its own footsteps, front leg and hind leg, like so many people mistake it for.

I asked a very skilled independent researcher I know to try and duplicate tracks by adding over 200 pounds to him. The added weight, although secured over his body, still shifted, affecting the researcher's tracks. It could not be completely controlled, especially in landing. Takeoff, of course, also affected the step-to-step length, and that was only 200 pounds strapped and secured to the man. When we tried it with more, matters only got worse. The researcher compared it to a big-busted woman jogging without a tight-fitting sports bra.

If large strides are to be faked, the key to a staged print would be movement. With the extra distance of the gait of the Sasquatch, stride comes into play in a unique way. Picture a hoaxer making a jump from step to step. The individual would push down toward the toes of the footstep in an unnatural takeoff, leaving a deeper imprint than the rest of the foot. With the other foot coming down mostly heel first on the awkward jump, the fake print would show depth discrepancies again, as well as signs of a slide forward. The footprint would become distorted, especially around the toes. The hoaxer has no hope in snow, slipping and sliding around. There is no casualness to a continuous set of faked prints; they are usually rushed and forced because the hoaxer needs to keep up speed to make the jumps between footprints.

My conclusion is that the tracks described in these reports are probably genuine. The distance between prints, the depth of the prints, the remote location, and the large number of prints all suggest that they are beyond the abilities of hoaxers.

## The Area around Cathedral Park

The story in and around Cathedral doesn't end with these reports. Certain areas of the provincial park show habitual use and Bigfoot's roaming presence. The outskirts tell us a story, as well, with observations over the years adding to the entire mystery.

Here I want to describe Sasquatch activities around the Crowsnest Highway where it comes relatively close to Cathedral Park to the east and west, and also the entire stretch between. Reports west of Manning Park, where it dips down close to the U.S. border, and all the encounters at Princeton and Hedley, will be covered elsewhere in the book.

The encounters begin in 1908, with a sighting of large footprints found by Gordon Haim near the shore of Trapper Lake in the Pasayten Valley. Just west of Cathedral Park, these tracks — several of them — measured seventeen to eighteen inches.

A report came in to researcher John Green in 1971 of a man having witnessed an eight-foot Sasquatch moving across a lighted highway department yard in the early morning hours of a September day. This took place in Manning Park, west of the town site.

In 1976, a landowner along the Hope-Princeton (Crowsnest) Highway came in contact with a large, mysterious creature on his property. The creature rose up from one knee and was watching his every movement. The landowner would never forget how small the creature made him feel. He remembered that as the Sasquatch rose, he saw pine needles and dry forest debris falling from the previously planted knee. The sight of this upright stranger made him want to vomit, since he was alone at the time. He said nothing more about this, except that it happened between Deep Gulch Creek and Nine Mile Hill.

The next sighting was on the Hope-Princeton Highway, this time in 1981. Two people in a car on the highway spotted the elusive creature along the winding road as they traveled toward Princeton during the evening hours. The slow going in that area gave them time to see an upright animal cross the highway. Both occupants of the vehicle agreed that it was fully covered in black hair. The arms swung quickly, the animal noticeably glancing at them twice from what they both recall.

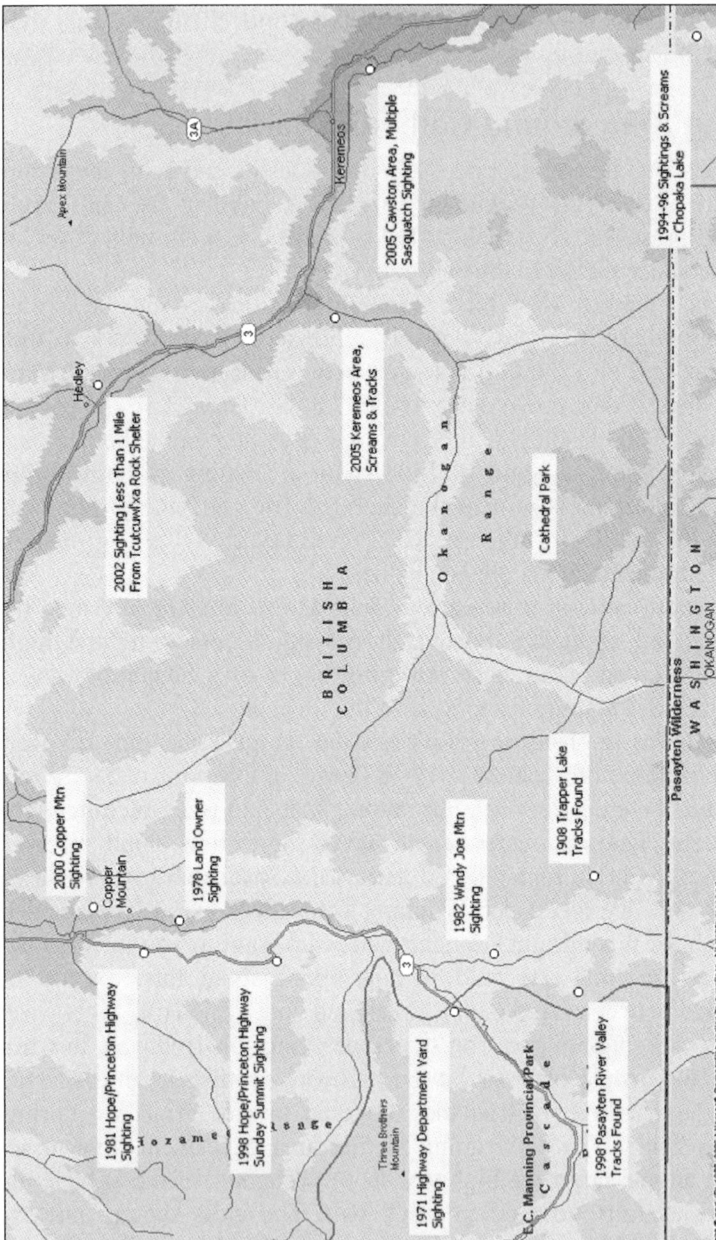


**Figure 18: Sightings and encounters near Cathedral Park, BC**

In reference to Manning Park being a visiting hiker's ideal location, they spoke briefly of their sighting around the Windy Joe Mountain area in 1982. They remembered a fire lookout with interpretive panels being there and the sighting taking place about a half-hour from the cupola-style cabin. The ape-like being moved agilely through the trees to flee. The person feels this was due to a large group of people in the area.

The next sighting is a good hour's Sasquatch pace from Cathedral to the southeast, just inside Washington State in the Chopaka Lake area. Trails through a mountain wilderness study area, through to the Okanagan highlands, intersect at Chopaka. During 1994-96, sightings and high-pitched screams were seen and heard around this area, including a controversial video, the Memorial Day Weekend footage. I'm not an expert on blurry films, so I won't comment on this.

Back to the west side of Cathedral Park and below Manning, a hunter would possibly enter the world of Sasquatch in 1996. His story about this mystery is as follows, with thanks for these segments taken from the West Coast Sasquatch site.

> October 1996 — I made a hunting trip for mule deer in the Pasayten Valley. I towed a sixteen-foot trailer into the area with my truck and decided to make camp at a favorite spot of mine in a clearing along Peeve Creek.
>
> A crisp, clear dawn found me slowly hiking in toward Trapper Lake, high in the hills above and east of the creek. I hadn't gone too far, when suddenly I cut across a fresh trail of huge, five-toed, barefoot, manlike tracks made in an inch or so of freshly fallen snow. I couldn't believe what I was seeing. Upon careful examination, these manlike tracks did not appear to have any type of claw or nail marks ahead of the toes like that of a grizzly or black bear. These manlike tracks were an estimated sixteen to seventeen inches long by seven to eight inches wide, with a step of about four to five feet — much further than I could possibly step, even stretching my legs out.
>
> I followed this reasonably straight line of giant manlike tracks for several hundred yards until they entered a thicket. These barefoot tracks seemed strange in that they did not wander about like the tracks of most wild animals would and showed little or no straddle from an imaginary line through their center. Thinking back, it almost seemed like the maker of those tracks was heading for a place with a purpose in mind.

> After looking into the thicket and envisioning all sorts of strange scenarios — I decided I didn't want to meet the maker of those tracks and rapidly hightailed it out of that country for the season.
>
> Over my last forty or so years of hunting big game in the wilds of British Columbia, I have, at times, been far too close to big bears. I have smelled, seen, and tracked both the grizzly and the black bear. The tracks I found in the Pasayten River Valley during October of 1996 were not the tracks of a bear or any other animal I am familiar with. [GMKK2]

Again along the Hope-Princeton Highway, this time near Sunday Summit, an individual living in the Princeton area met up with the Sasquatch in 1998. He was returning from the Manning Park area. A little embarrassed about the speed he was traveling, the area resident saw a brownish-black giant walking upright near the highway, haired from sole to crown. As he passed it, the creature immediately headed in the direction of the trees. He then asked himself, *Would a bear do this? Walk?* He said he was sure he'd encountered the Sasquatch, the one people were talking about. This occurred during the early afternoon.

The possible sightings and dealings with the forest creature didn't stop there. A short story came into my hands from the gentlemen at West Coast Sasquatch and their informative Internet site. Segments used from the following account by Ken Kristian are the possible findings of a hunter in the fall of 2000, south of Princeton.

> In brief, the witness who reported this incident claims to be an avid big game hunter, woodsman, amateur prospector, and skilled survivalist. He also stated that he regularly hunts much of the southern portion of the province. He enjoys backpack hunting in remote areas for four- or five-day stints. In other words, he wanted to make it clear that he was not your typical road hunter.
>
> On this particular trip, he was hunting mule deer in British Columbia's Princeton area, close to the Washington State border. To be more precise, the witness was hunting in the Copper Mountain-Flat Top Mountain area, just outside of Princeton, to the south of Highway 3.
>
> The witness said he had made his way through a farmer's property, then around a swampy area, and finally proceeded uphill toward the summit of Copper Mountain. He stated he was

> climbing up toward a cresting knob of rocks when he suddenly caught about a three-second glimpse of something big and black on two feet, quickly moving off the knob and into the cover of some thick willows.
>
> Upon reaching the top of the rock outcropping, the hunter discovered two piles of extremely large-diameter human-type excrement (not coiled, but rope-like), with one pile on either side of the rock outcropping. Looking closely at the excrement, he saw what appeared to be some amount of fibrous material that he took to be either squirrel or rabbit fur. He said that because of the amount of droppings or scat present at the site, it looked like whatever was using the area had used the rocks as a lookout and spent a great deal of time there, squatting down facing in two general directions. Those two directions offered what he thought were the best lookout-type views of the valley below.
>
> On further inspection of the area, the witness found the remnants of a crude fire (no rock fire-ring) that appeared to be fueled by long strands of old-man's-hair tree moss and small sticks with snapped ends. In, around, and on top of the fire area were what looked like remnants of small animals (thought to belong to either rabbit or squirrel) and grouse breastbones that looked like they had been sucked clean. The witness stated that after closely examining the bones, there were no tooth, gnaw, or chew marks he could see. [GMKK3]

Dropping down south a bit and a tad to the east, we come to the Hedley area. Just south of the little community lies a thing of the past, the Tcutcuwl'xa Rock Shelter, hosting Native pictograph drawings. It was a mile south from there that the Sasquatch shared the landscape in 2002. A motorist from the Okanagan Interior, as he describes it, played second fiddle to such a creature.

Mountain sheep live in the region. He drove out west that morning looking for them, his roving eyes scanning the nooks and crannies of the mountains for the goat-like mammals. He saw what he thought at first to be a black bear on a hillside to the right of him. He soon realized it was a creature on only two legs, climbing off at an angle. This got his curiosity boiling.

Pulling off the highway, he saw the animal approximately 400 feet from where he was. With the general slope to the hillside, he found it peculiar that the thing never once went down on all fours; the giant stepped very well on the incline. A car passed by as he watched the creature climb. The other motorist didn't stop or even slow down and remained oblivious to the whole thing. The climber soon topped the hill and was out of sight. The man looked to the larger hills and mountains for the next few minutes and saw nothing more.

With a level of uncertainty to all this, he found himself a ways from his vehicle. There was something strange about the whole thing that he didn't like. He had unknowingly moved up onto the hillside himself, looking at the climber. The man was intrigued.

He estimated the size of the rambler to be over seven feet tall, weighing in excess of 400-500 pounds. It did not struggle on the elevation gain or show signs of strain, and it never stopped to rest. The being never looked back toward the highway once. He felt the biped was heavyset but still built for the task. He was sure he would never see anything like it again.

Rounding out our observations, we conclude with the year 2005 and a report on the Internet pages of the BFRO. This encounter occurred east of Cathedral Park, near Cawston, British Columbia. Segments of this report are as follows:

> My family and I were on another family outing in the Cawston, British Columbia, area. Finishing a small walk, we were coming back to the truck, and I noticed four black objects standing in the Similkameen River. Two were standing, and it looked as though the other two were bent over drinking. The rest of my family and I watched these things move around in the water. The only thing we could say for sure due to the distance (roughly 300 meters) was that they were all completely black, and they looked huge. We wanted to get a better look, so we hopped in the truck to drive around for a better view. We couldn't find a spot, so we turned around and returned to our original location. They were gone.

## Follow-up by the BFRO Investigator

> He and his family watched the subject group for about five minutes. He described to me what appeared to be a group of four Sasquatch.
>
> All four individuals were black in color, and they were standing nearby in the river. The witness observed that the two

> Sasquatch who appeared to be drinking did not use their hands to scoop water; rather, they simply slurped water from the surface of the river. The witness believes the water depth was about three feet, halfway up their thighs. The witness informed me that the largest of the group shuffled around in the water but did not appear to be maintaining a lookout position. The creatures were about 400 yards away. [BFRO1]

Figure 18 suggests there might be a pattern to these sightings. There is evidence that the Sasquatch may be using the intricate trail systems that span the region. And why not? The species could get from Point A to Point B quickly that way. At least three-quarters of the reports listed were in close proximity to a hiking trail or pathway. I was sure there were other accounts out there; they were just not confirmed.

## Cathedral Lakes Lodge

A strange set of circumstances would cross my desk however — a story of the creature's possible presence around the Cathedral Lakes Lodge. The Bavarian-style lodge has been in operation since 1972, operating at 6,800 feet, entertaining guests with British Columbia's hospitality, creative meal planning, and superb accommodations. It was around the lodge, in 2002, that a different type of entertainer brazenly arrived in camp, unnerving owner Richard Padmos and his staff. This is his description of events at the secluded lodge in British Columbia's high country:

> This all took place over a period of three months in 2002 — July, August, and September. Since then, we have not noticed anything. It started with a few of the staff members saying they [were] awakened by what sounded like someone banging on the metal fuel tanks near the generator. This happened often, and at two to three in the morning. The generator is located some 300 meters from the main lodge. The staff also mentioned that they heard footsteps near their tents at night and felt there was some animal walking around at night. Everyone felt a little uneasy.
>
> My personal experience happened one night. I shut the generator off at eleven p.m., then went for a walk using my headlamp, up to Glacier Lake about thirty minutes away. I felt I was being followed the whole time; heard noises but did not see anything. I slept that night out in the open at Glacier Lake. At

> approximately two a.m. I was awakened by what sounded like someone (or something) pounding the ground with a large stick. I could not figure what animal would make that kind of noise. I went back to sleep, then it happened again around four a.m.
>
> The strangest thing that happened was at our pigpen. We keep two pigs here each year to eat all the food scraps. The pigs are kept in a five-foot-high wire fence enclosure near the generator. The pigs do not eat eggshells, and there are always lots in their pen. One morning we noticed that something had pushed the fence down, stepped over the fence, and eaten the eggshells. We also found scat that looked like large human excrement, full of eggshells.
>
> The same year, one guest, while hiking, heard a strange noise that he said was not a bear or cat. He then smelled something and saw a pair of red eyes from inside a small cave. My son also heard something one night and saw red eyes in the trees.
>
> Since these events in 2002, we have not had any other strange occurrences. Hope this is of some help.

So there we have it, Cathedral Park's initiation into the documented world of the Sasquatch — yet another region to ponder. If there's one thing I would like to stress in all this, it is the fact that if there is this much activity actually going on in just one region, how much activity is there in total throughout North America?

# 7. The Fire Lookout Stories

One of the richest set of stories that I have found comes from fire lookouts. There are stories from the professionals who work in the towers, but the number of these is limited by concerns about reporting unusual sightings. Another source is from people who stay at decommissioned towers. My family has done that, as you will see in the first story about the Webb Mountain Fire Lookout. People who have stayed in this lookout and others have their own reports of encounters, which we will look at in this chapter.

## Webb Mountain Fire Lookout — Montana, 2005

For ten years, whatever family members were available for a long weekend or holiday would use the U.S. Forest Service rental fire towers. Because our trips were family-oriented, we always chose the towers we could drive directly up to. We went for rest and relaxation. However, at a Montana fire lookout in the summer of 2005, things would not end up very restful. Something strange paid us a visit in the middle of a Friday night.

The forty-one-foot wooden stilted structures made the whole visit relatively safe. There were hatchways and trapdoors to prevent intruders from getting up on the decks. Another structure, a concrete jewel of the forest, overlooked the Montana town of Superior. This included electricity for a stove, heater, fridge, etc. From there, guests can do their mountain-biking, etc. This decommissioned fire lookout has a steel door at the bottom as protection. At all of the towers we visited, there were metal forestry gates that swung free once they were unlocked with a key or the right combination. We liked that idea, as with some of those gates miles

**Figure 19: In the summer of 2005, Glen, Rosemarie, and Adrian Boulier may have had a visit from Sasquatch at Lincoln County's Webb Mountain Fire Lookout in northern Montana.**

down the road, we didn't have to worry about unwanted guests coming up — an added feature to insure security and seclusion.

The concrete structure we stayed in during these events was situated in Lincoln County, in the northwest corner of Montana. This particular four-day, three-night stay took place over a long weekend in August, and I was accompanied by my wife Rosemarie and my son Adrian.

The rental fire lookout is approximately twelve miles from the Canadian border as the crow flies, this same bird looking to the town of Eureka, about fourteen miles to the east. We crossed into the United States at the Port of Roosville. Lake Koocanusa sits well below the tower just to the east.

The whole thing began on Friday evening around six p.m., after we settled in. When I ventured out to take an initial photograph just west of the lookout, I heard a single loud knock, perhaps on a tree, coming from the south. Two minutes later, a second knock came from the same general area. At the time, the skies were clear, the weather hot but cooling, and there was a gentle breeze coming up from the southwest. A knock was just a knock.

Proceeding back toward the tower, I began to smell something different, some foul odor in the air. It wasn't like a skunk; rather, it was a smell akin to the stench of rotting eggs. During that same walk, I happened to see Adrian standing out on the west side of the tower, on the catwalk, pondering this piece of God's creation. Before I said a word to him, he asked me if I happened to smell something funny coming up from down below. I found it interesting that he was catching a whiff of something as well.

A few minutes later, Adrian and I went to explore a ridge west of the tower. It seemed to be an excellent place for a predator, such as a bear or mountain cat, to sit and wait for prey. Deer and other prey ventured there every day, just below the ridge. Adrian was near the edge, and I was about forty feet away with my back to him. At that point, I heard the tail end of something screaming, a vocalization coming up from the south. A few seconds later, Adrian told me he'd heard the whole thing. When I reached him, he had goose bumps on his arms, and there were terrified tears in his eyes. He asked me if I'd heard it too, and I asked him what it sounded like. "Like a woman's high-pitched shriek or scream," he said. We both felt a little uneasy, so we walked immediately back to the tower.

Adrian suggested putting a large metal fire screen at the bottom of the stairs in front of the walkway, and I thought it was a great idea. The last thing we needed was a hungry mountain cat coming up the open stairway.

As every day at Webb Mountain, the deer were there the next morning, a buck keeping an eye on everything. After a pleasant jaunt down to Kalispell for the day, we were back at the lookout, and we crashed into bed sometime around midnight. It was very dark that night, with a clear sky, the stars seemingly just out of reach from the deck outside. A light breeze was present as well, a welcome change from the gale-force winds one might expect in such a place.

At approximately 2:10 a.m., I awoke to the beeping of my wife's cell phone, alerting us that her battery was low. When I sat up to tell her to turn it off, I heard an unsettling noise below us. Someone or something was tampering with the padlock. From what I had gathered earlier, the room below us was meant only for storing firewood, and the only entrance to it was through the steel door. To get inside, one would have to walk up two concrete stairs on the outside and stand on a concrete

**Figure 20: The creatures visiting Webb Mountain spent almost two hours at the location, including over an hour at the south side of the tower shown in this photo.**

walk, then reach up and tinker with the lock on the bolted door. The sound could be heard easily, as I had my head near a small opening in the center of the room. It was pitch black down below, and I wasn't happy, sitting there in the darkness, trying to rule out all the things that couldn't possibly be trying to gain entry. Then I heard something moving around down below on the rocks, making much more of a racket in the stones that surrounded the lookout.

I immediately woke Adrian up and asked him quietly to listen carefully. I had noticed a beer bottle just to the east of the tower during the day. Whatever was out there came in contact with the bottle, noisily moving it aside with a clanging against the rocks. Then we both heard the visitor wandering around outside, seemingly systematically, on the rock surface.

While all this was going on, my wife had woken up briefly, but she was asleep again. I'm sure glad she felt safe enough to simply doze off again, because we didn't. In truth, our hearts were in our throats. Adrian and I watched the catwalk like a couple of hawks, quietly debating about what we should do since we couldn't see anything. We actually put a couple of large, heavy items against the door, just in case whatever was out there decided it wanted in.

To the south of the tower, something began moving around quite a bit on the rocks. Whatever visited that night spent a fair amount of time there. During the day, my wife had noticed that the deer, one buck in particular, liked to lick the rocks. They practiced that odd behavior every morning. Putting two and two together, we found that other lookout renters were throwing their wastewater and grease off the south side of the deck, so that explained the deer behavior. We could only assume that whatever was out there might also enjoy licking a rock or two, in search of something edible and tasty.

From that location, approximately ten feet from the tower, everything was deadly quiet for a few seconds. Very quickly, however, something seemed to jump from one level of ground to the next, about four feet high, coming up toward Webb. We knew where it was: a small drop-off on the south side. The strange jump bothered both Adrian and me, as the creature came down with a huge, solid *thump.* It was such a hard landing that we could feel a slight vibration inside the lookout every time it pounced, and the building we were in was resting on a concrete foundation. The creature then continued to move around outside.

After a while, Adrian also fell back to sleep. At that point, I heard what I thought to be a type of gargle from the throat of something out in the darkness. I woke Adrian up again after he'd caught about five minutes of shut-eye. The rocks were still being stepped on outside, all around us. We both heard something that we couldn't understand: a whistle coming from the east side, down below us. Both Adrian and I looked at each other, wondering if there were more than one out there.

At that point, we opened the window and considered going outside on the deck for a better look. We didn't know what we were up against, though, and I did not want to risk the lives of my loved ones. I tried to assure Adrian that those outside didn't know how many of us there were, and I hoped that was true. By this time, I was relatively certain we weren't dealing with human intruders, because of the sheer weight that had come down during their earlier jump, which we'd felt even in the tower. It would have taken three or four 200-pound men jumping in unison to produce such a vibration. I tried it the next day, just to be sure, and I couldn't even jump upward the four feet on short takeoff; I could jump down, of course, but my wife and son felt nothing during my attempt, even when I stomped around.

The night of these events was illuminated only by a quarter-moon, and the whole ordeal lasted around an hour and forty-five minutes. When a hint of morning light came up on the eastern horizon, it (or they) disappeared into what was left of the night, walking off to the west. What struck me as funny was that whatever it was seemed to use the rock surfaces most of the time to walk on. We found no tracks that morning — no human tracks other than our own and no tracks from large animals. Clearly, it hadn't been a bear.

That morning, my wife read some of the visitors' notes and short stories in the logbooks, and I left one of my own — something not a lot of visitors actually do. I began to read some that were there, and I found three that could have related to my own experiences there:

> July 19-20, 2003: The dogs barked in the window in the middle of the night. Something was down there, but I didn't see it.
>
> July 31, 2003: Went to the outhouse about twelve at night, when an animal blew and thumped away. There was a scared woman. Next morning, a muley [mule deer] lingered around — so that's probably what it was.
>
> July 9, 2005: We came souped up for war, yet ran in fear of two shiny eyes in the dark that reflected off our flashlights.

On Sunday, Adrian and I laid out cantaloupe in eight different locations, placing it on the rocks so the little wilderness critters couldn't reach it. In three of those places, I gently smoothed dirt areas, hoping to make a place to see tracks. Dark night was coming, and I hoped the creatures wouldn't be able to tell the difference in the dirt, though I was sure our human scents lingering around for those uncanny wilderness noses wouldn't help matters. Booby traps were set up, in hopes that they might at least slow the animals down. We timed ourselves in the tower: we could get outside and look over the south side of the catwalk with lighting and a camera in just three and a half seconds. The night before, we'd been quite unaware of everything, so now we were truly focused. Not being lucky like Americans who can carry guns, we only had hunting knives and bear spray.

Five large, circular log pieces were placed at the top of the stairs, and we allowed the fire screen to stay in place to block the entryway below. We did what we could to hinder anything coming back, even going so far

**Figure 21: Glen Boulier looking for evidence below the fire tower at Webb Mountain.**

as trying to knock down a key escape route to the south. We figured it might try to use that area if we turned on our lights and tried to take its picture. The area directly south of the tower was a bit unnerving, and there was something about it that made us uneasy.

On Sunday afternoon, Adrian and I were out briefly exploring where our visitors might have gone, a certain area about fifteen to twenty feet south of Webb. It funnels down into a squeezed-off area, where anyone or anything could step down, but in our investigation just to the south and slightly east, we found a tucked-away ledge that would have been capable of hiding practically anything of an animal nature — even an intelligent giant. Its face was mostly rock and included an indentation where someone or something could hole up and still be within twenty-five feet of the tower. Moving along the east, one could possibly remain hidden and could also jump down to open forest and disappear into the night in seconds. A really crafty creature could follow that forest wall and remain out of sight. The whole area is hardly visible during the day, never mind at night.

Although the area had a spooky atmosphere to it, the eerie ambiance was not what bothered us most. In the indentation of the rock, I saw what I called a little "soap dish," a natural part of the face, and there really were no loose rocks or stones around the area. Inside that soap dish formation were five shale-like, sharp objects of thin rock; clearly, they'd been purposely placed there, for they did not match any of the other stony material around the area. Both Adrian and I looked for clues — initials scratched into the nearby rock, digging at the base, cuts or scrapes or anything else that may indicate the objects' use — but we found nothing, *nada*, zilch! Nevertheless, it was very clear to us that someone or something had placed them there, and for a reason that we couldn't grasp.

Each of the strange objects was similar in size, approximately five and a half inches long and two and a half inches wide. The thickness remained constant as well at about a quarter-inch. They were impossible to overlook, unique as they were and placed in such a way. They had obviously been put there on purpose. They sat about four feet off the ground, if I remember correctly. As intriguing and mysterious as they were, we left the five pieces out of our initial report, assuming visitors who had booked the lookout in the past had planted them there, left them by accident, or maybe even used them for defense. We really wanted to believe that mankind was responsible, because it was a bit unnerving to ponder that the Sasquatch could be so intelligent. It wasn't as if such a species would have no other means of defense. Its size alone would be menacing enough.

Nervous as I was, I grabbed all of them and tossed the pieces down the hillside. I wouldn't think about the possibilities until weeks later, when I considered scientific studies of gorillas and chimpanzees. Those animals are capable of using mathematical solutions to find food and achieve other goals, including creating tools. They can also pick out what they need from a number of things purposely left in bunches. I had to wonder what kind of creative thinking a creature like the Sasquatch might possess.

In spite of our planning and the great efforts we'd taken, the evening turned out to be quite uneventful. That is the way such things usually go, so we were not in the least bit surprised that the creatures did not come back when we were at least somewhat ready to learn more about them.

Daylight was our alarm clock the next morning, Adrian and I checked on our traps. The deer had gone for two of them, as their prints led right up to the places where the food had been. After everything was said and done, Adrian — the smart kid that he is — actually asked me if something from the tree line might have been watching us set our traps. We'll never know if that was the case.

We arrived back in Calgary on Monday afternoon, and I was still in search of answers to the lookout puzzle. I went to the BFRO site on the Internet, hoping to find some audio clips that we might compare to what we'd encountered at Webb Mountain, something similar to the strange scream the boy had heard the first night. We found a 1973 Puyallup, Washington, recording that was at least in the ballpark. The piece struck a close resemblance to what Adrian had heard that evening as the sun was setting on the Montana/Idaho mountain ranges.

Continuing on, I began looking for other possible sightings and encounters in the Lincoln County area. On the BFRO site, I came across the 1978 report of a happening near Libby, Montana, about twenty-five miles from Webb Mountain lookout. Further examination of the available information found Sasquatch sightings between Moyie Springs, Idaho, and Libby, Montana, some thirty-five miles away from the tower. Forty-five miles away from Webb, near Bonner's Ferry, a hunter felt he had a Sasquatch walking parallel to him amidst the thick timber.

We stayed at the Webb Mountain lookout again in the summer of 2009 and researched the area somewhat. That was a more peaceful visit, with no strange feelings or out-of-the-ordinary happenings to bother us. Just as in 2005, the deer ventured up on our final night; this time, early the next morning, I found their tracks. It still puzzled me that during our first visit to Webb, we couldn't find any evidence of what had visited us for almost two hours that summer night. It was even odder because in 2009 we had no problem seeing the three or four paths the deer could have taken, and the prints were easy to see, clearly standing out in the morning sun. Whatever had visited us before had been far more inconspicuous. During the 2009 visit, I checked through the logbook again and found this entry:

> June 16, 2006: Many strange occurrences last night. I know what caused them. Are you brave enough to find out for yourself?

## What Visited Webb Mountain Fire Tower?

Once we were settled safely back in Calgary after the uneasiness we'd endured at Webb Mountain in 2005, we started to categorize what might be responsible for the visitation.

I came up with four potential creatures that might have fit the profile, although three would be easily cast aside over the course of the investigation. Initially, though, bear, mountain lion, human being, and Sasquatch were the major suspects. Right off the bat, I want to stipulate that at no time did any two of these species spend time together in that almost two-hour stretch. No one would have seen any combination of the four (bear, lion, human being, and Sasquatch) working together or sharing the ground at Webb — not unless it was a Sasquatch researcher trailing the beast, both of them circling the lookout over and over again like a comedy skit.

That said, the bears are the first up for elimination. Although the bear is known to be intelligent, such an animal could not have made an upward jump or come down with its feet solidly planted together and then walked like a man. Also, it is highly unlikely that a bear would remain quiet for almost two hours, without even grunting or groaning. Also, bears do not whistle Dixie or anything else.

Other evidence for elimination was the movement of the rock on the south side of the tower: the stones seemed to be lifted and placed aside, not scraped, pawed, or handled in any clumsy manner. It is notable that this would eliminate the lion, too, for the rock seemed to be moved, rather than the animal sliding or maneuvering around it. I've watched deer and their ruminant counterparts numerous times over the years, shifting rock and such around. The sound was completely different that night at Webb Mountain.

My friend Seth Evanoff spotted a grizzly through binoculars to the east of the fire lookout that same summer, *Ursus arctos horribilis,* digging and scrounging a certain area for over an hour. Seth placed this account in the visitors' logbook less than twenty-four hours before we visited Webb that year.

I had seen clawings made by grizzlies, both on the ground and on tree trunks. There was even a note left on a tree, a warning to passersby at Alberta's Kananaskis Country. As with any other type of bear near Webb Mountain, there were *no* signs of grizzly activity up there in 2005 — at least not during the four-day extended weekend when we visited.

Just like the black and brown bears, the grizzly was written off as our secret visitor.

In the grand scheme of things, the bear has been the animal most frequently mistaken for a Bigfoot, with many sightings throughout North America. This is understandable, for many encounters last only for a second or two and often occur in poor lighting or thick foliage where visibility is not 100 percent. However, on Thursday, August 12, 2010, our oldest boy saw no less than four grizzlies in Alberta's Kananaskis country while he was hiking. One of the rangers in that area told him, "You seem to be having quite the day." Brandon expressed to me that it might have been the perfect time to buy a lottery ticket. Since he'd witnessed so many grizzlies in the wild that day, I asked him if, in his opinion, the grizzly could have been mistaken for a Sasquatch. He reported that it would have been almost impossible under most conditions to misidentify the two.

I refuse to blatantly bash anyone who claims to be an eyewitness to a Sasquatch. Unfortunately, in encounters lasting only a few seconds, many incorrectly identify (albeit inadvertently) the bear as one of the bipedal giants. I guess my almost one-minute encounters in the past pretty well clinched it for me. I saw something else. A bear is a bear, and the Sasquatch is a *mystery*.

We also had to consider the mountain cat when thinking about our Webb Mountain visitor. Such a stealthy feline would most likely not have been heard during the night. A lion would also be an unlikely suspect to make the jump and landing. On top of that, I don't feel that the cougar/catamount could have possibly been fiddling with the lock on the door and pulling at it in such a way, nor would a cat whistle. I'm positive no such animal would pick up a beer bottle and place it between two rocks almost six feet away. I've been told over and over again that cats are stealthy operators, but combining these factors makes me almost 100 percent certain that neither the bears nor the cats had anything to do with that fateful Friday evening.

So, we come to our own kind, the human being, one of the distinct species that cannot always be trusted. It's sad in a way to put it like this, but that is one of the outstanding reasons we wouldn't open the door to the tower that night and look over the railing. Chances are, a cat, a Sasquatch, or maybe even a bear would have fled the scene. One or two men, on the other hand, could have been armed with high-powered rifles and might have been more than happy to get in our faces. However, due to the forestry gate down the road, a three-mile hike in the dark would have been required — not to mention that the metal gate was designed to keep humankind out (and only humankind, mind you).

Nevertheless, I did check the road around the area for footprints, and I found none. Any man who attempted to come up there would have been *loco* — downright crazy. He wouldn't have known how many of us were in the tower, and he'd have had no idea whether or not we were armed. Many individuals who rent the fire lookouts come equipped, and few would dare bother someone at close range like that without knowing what they were getting into — especially since they'd be quite literally backed into a corner. I suppose if someone had a death wish or was half-baked or pie-eyed, they might brave such a foolish excursion. After all, man is the strangest species of all. Nevertheless, human visitors were likely not the case.

A human being could not have performed such a foundation-rattling jump. Also, there would be no reason for even the craziest of fools to dig in the rocks south of the lookout, even if they'd lost a watch or something. I can say I have seen a man lick a rock, but that is another story.

So, that leaves one possible culprit from our original four: Bigfoot. Putting it all together, that animal would be entirely capable of everything that unfolded that night and possibly Friday evening as well. Independent researcher Bobbie Short, from California, seemed to think so as well. Our story is posted on her Bigfoot Encounters Internet site. Bobbie, who sadly died in 2013, put her time and commitment into sharing relevant information about the phenomenon, including the historical background of such a creature, and many happily supplied information for her site. The woman herself purported to having crossed paths with a female Sasquatch during a backpacking outing in northern California in 1985. The creature she witnessed was scarred and sickly looking.

At this point, I would like to summarize all four suspects, particularly focusing on the ground around the fire tower and any evidence of tracks. Of all the species discussed, only the Sasquatch would have had the aptness to keep his or her footing on the rocky surface without leaving evidence of its presence. On Sunday, I went over the ground in that area fairly well. Unless the visitor had been trying to hide its footsteps, there would have been no way of walking about without leaving any tracks. I easily found all our shoe prints. I could even tell the difference in the patterns in the dusty dirt, when available. But we didn't spend two hours around the base of the lookout — not until Sunday anyway. I also documented the three deer, our only visitors other than our mystery guest(s), and their tracks were found in a snap. Interestingly enough, those deer never ventured close to the tower.

Something heavy had been there, but whatever or whoever it was, it left no tracks behind — not around our vehicle or near the lookout. There was nothing left anywhere. We searched very carefully, and we could not tell what or who had visited us. The most unsettling thing about it was that the visitor didn't just stop by briefly. It was not a one-time pass by the lookout to offer a wave. No, whatever visited us there stayed for almost two full hours and left no evidence of itself behind.

A while after our stay at the fire lookout near Eureka, someone commented on the logbook entry that we'd left up at Webb. Seth Evanoff was with his brother up at the fire tower in 2006. In the middle of the night, they believe they were also subjected to an interesting and thought-provoking vocalization — what the men called a "whistle."

Intrigued, Seth spent many outings at Webb Mountain, along with his wife Jennifer and their two children, Morgan and Hudson, focusing a little more on the possibility that a mysterious species was visiting the area. He attempted to make an audio recording and to use a camcorder with infrared night vision to catch the creature on film, though he thought the infrared spectrum might look like a flashlight beam to such a creature. Other researchers have also commented similarly on infrared.

Seth mentioned a journal entry that caught his attention in July, one signed by the name of "Wilson":

> A guy spoke of being awakened at two in the morning to a lady screaming for help. He went out looking for her, but she would move further into the woods. He said she screamed from six different locations and that he never found her. The man said he was going to alert the authorities in the morning. Funny thing is, I think the screams stopped just before dawn.

Wilson also said in his log entry that he went out again at 6:00 a.m. to try and locate what he thought to be a missing woman, because he was concerned. The man found nothing.

Seth Evanoff relayed this logbook entry to me and also mentioned some possible tracks he'd come across in the past in northern Montana. He also explained a photograph he took of the area:

**Figure 22: Tracks found near Tally Lake northwest of Kalispell, Montana. (photo © Seth Evanoff)**

I found the tracks up a road called Rhoades Draw, leading into the mountains behind Tally Lake and Star Meadow by Kalispell.

I went to this location because I got a strange feeling there once when I was riding my dirt bike. I felt like someone was watching me and that I wasn't welcome. Well, I later found out that a lot of people who are around the Sasquatch get this very same feeling.

I went back in the winter. It's in the mountains, so it was slow going forward. I made it to a gated Forest Service road and decided to take a walk. The snow was about a foot deep. I made it up the road about 100 yards, when I crossed by these strange tracks meandering down the road. I followed them, thinking maybe it was a bobcat or mountain lion that had pounced in the snow, but I never found any track of the sort. There were none — only these strange impressions about eighteen inches long. Well, soon they took a turn off the road, toward the middle of a meadow. They went behind a ten-foot pine tree and stopped. From the safety of the small pine tree, I could see up and down the road and also the main road, where my truck was parked, but anyone in those locations would have had a hard time seeing me. That was where it got weird. There was an elk trail right in front of that tree with a ton of tracks, but the big ones just disappeared.

As you can see from the picture, these tracks were about eighteen inches long with the stride consistently offset — not directly in line. The step was almost six feet long. I've been in the woods since I was three years old. I've never seen anything that could explain this.

## Big Creek Baldy Fire Lookout

You've got to love the technological age — well, some of it. Technology would help a couple from Lewiston, Idaho, reach me after their ordeal one night at Montana's Big Creek Baldy fire tower, southwest of the Webb Mountain lookout where we'd experienced strange events back in 2005. Theirs would be a little more significant however: a visual sighting of a strange creature with an overly active curiosity. It would confirm, as well, what contributed to the sightings in Montana's Lincoln County and our first stay at Webb.

This courageous couple was braver than we were during their encounter. I'd worried that our visitors that night were disturbed rednecks with high-powered rifles. This couple wasn't as frightened or disturbed because they were thinking what they heard were four-legged "varmints."

The Lewiston couple's story is as follows, as told by C.M.

This involves geocaching [a treasure hunting game where you use a GPS to search for containers placed by other geocaching participants] and the coordinates N 48° 38.040/W 115° 32.711 waypoint GCJKDP (Big Creek Baldy Mountain, Montana). It was late in the season (2007), and there was no one at the tall tower, to our knowledge. We had walked in from a gate that was locked and secured, taking a little day trip. This was the second fire lookout my husband and I would pay a visit to with a geocache at a nearby structure. The first was at Quartz Mountain Lookout, Montana, as well. The story, though, centers on our mini-stay at Big Creek.

**Figure 23: The Big Creek Baldy Fire Lookout in Montana where C.M. and R.M. spotted one Sasquatch and possibly two more in 2008.**

We instigated a search into this whole area after our caching, and we found a small number of interesting things, including Garver Mountain, McGuire Mountain, Yaak Mountain, Webb Mountain, and Big Creek Baldy lookout rentals — all for the outdoor enthusiast. We had vacationed in the Koocanusa region for years and knew nothing of the tower rentals that lay hidden there; those had escaped us completely. Previously, we figured them all to be manned by the forestry. There are Idaho rentals as well, not that far from us. All of this was a lovely find. We looked so forward to the year 2008, the adventures to come, thanks to geocaching.

I will make an attempt to keep the events in order as they happened, although just one episode is significant to what you are researching. This would involve the wooden tower that has been generously done up nicely for visitors, thanks to the USFS, Big Creek Baldy fire lookout.

The same place we'd geocached was where my husband and I would stay first in 2008, a four-night restful, romantic stay overlooking the mountains. Just being us, we do not leave replies in the books that are left conveniently available for visitors to share their thoughts, disappointments, hard luck, or thankfulness. Both of us do read them, however, mostly together; we have always been interested in people, and many of these personal entries are the cheerful side of things. There were many years' worth.

This is what unfolded at recreation Baldy: On our third night, the evening was anything but restful. It all began after midnight, creaking lower stairs letting us know that something was up (coming up). We both heard it on the otherwise quiet night, and the frequency wound down to a minimum. We watched out the rectangular windows, which we'd cleaned, on the east side of the tower rental — stargazing, with our hands behind our heads on the pillows and two glasses of cooled red wine nearby. There was little voice of nature (wind) to be heard as we gawked out at the stars. This was a new experience, us blending in as a part of the night sky.

We got up and calmly walked out the open door, addressing what we thought must have been one of the heavier varmints that tend to invade these towers, according to the notes that had been left. Some kind of thing did an about-face, walking down the stairs. That was all I could tell from over three levels away, our reasoning going beyond a "chewer." My husband didn't say a word, surely agreeing that it wasn't your average mole or badger — the return of the ghost porcupine that had plagued the tower and visitors and families some time ago.

This was repeated less than an hour later, the visitor to the stairs. The only difference this time was that we didn't respond. Maybe an animal was interested in our offensive, stinky socks hanging over the deck outside. That might have explained it — a repulsive odor. We chuckled, and I must say now that we were in no way fearful.

With the third visit, we weren't sure if we should be irritated, amused, or beginning to take notice of the nuisance that was down below, exercising its freedom. This attempt included us out on the deck, lantern in hand, sticking it out way over the railing and hopefully sticking it to the culprit. My husband leaned over the railing very precariously; I reprimanded him afterward. And this was where I was stunned, not understanding such things as I'm discussing and sharing this with you now. Both he and I caught a bothersome glimpse of an upright, tall, black animal, with its back to us, leaving the stairs and heading for the darkness. Now I was fearful and visibly shaken. The thing had its right hand/paw on the end stair railing before it left. We returned to the main cabin and discussed it, very frightened.

Glen, I hope all this makes sense somewhat, this completely dark-haired figure. This insistent visitor was not alone. What I would describe with no imagination were two shadows moving around the immediate area, with tree cover somewhat available to the left only, perhaps thirty to forty feet away from the exhibitionists. From what my husband and I saw of them, they were much larger than their bold and unashamed friend. The larger visitors moved as a blur in the night. The two of them never stepped close enough to be identified completely as the other that pressed us.

There was a "smartness" to them, an intelligence in the shadows. They were in cahoots with each other. The boldest of the three was, to the best of my judgment, over six feet tall. It filled the width of the stairs and more, or at least the top half of the animal did. The larger two creatures scattered like scared rabbits when you tried to put them under the lantern. They moved quickly ahead of the glow from the Coleman lantern, as my husband swung it outward over the deck and railing toward them below.

There was a welcome quiet interval for over ninety minutes, but there was a fourth attempt made of the lower stairs after that. My man didn't say a word about that. He was spellbound by it all at that point, though he wouldn't admit it. I was just plain bewildered, fearful for us both. I felt now as if we were being studied — played with. (Did you feel like this yourself? Your wife and your boy?) I held my bladder after those visitations were over. There was no way in hell that the outhouse was going to see my rear end during the night. I'd tinkle off the deck before going down there. I couldn't convince myself to raise the rather heavy and awkward trapdoor, even if I changed my mind about

**Figure 24: Area to the east side of Big Creek Baldy Fire Lookout. In 2008 rental visitors encountered a mysterious creature during their stay.**

> the toilet. Old wood was the only thing separating us from what roamed below.
>
> Concluding that we were experiencing a very "thinking" creature(s) changed the complexion of things for both of us, our intellects being challenged by mere forest creatures. They also had some sort of communication between them at given times.

Our encounter at Webb Mountain had included a night free of wind, unusual for the area since the prevailing westerlies blow hard and continuously in the region. The couple at Big Creek Baldy also experienced no wind or only a light breeze when they encountered the creatures in 2008. This part of their story had a very familiar ring to it for me, and others have experienced the same: little to no wind blowing during sightings involving the Sasquatch around a fire lookout. I had to wonder if it were just a coincidence or some kind of trait of the creatures.

Backtracking a bit on my research, I asked this question to personnel who worked the towers and had come forward about sightings. They mostly agreed, thinking back, that there was no air motion when they had sighted a creature; they could have heard a pin drop. Also, if I remember correctly, a few of the kidnapping escapades featured a quiet evening or day. The Sasquatch was clearly somehow reading the environment when it came to clouds, moon, and wind. Those creatures were not like some rogue bear, stumbling around, claiming its ownership of sections of wilderness by brute force.

The other thing that would be agreed upon was the intelligence of the strangers at Big Creek lookout. The Lewiston couple mentioned that they figured the smallest of the lot had been elected to negotiate the stairs, as if the biped giants realized their weight difference was an issue — that and their sheer size. Of course, I am in no position to argue with C.M.'s and R.M.'s observations, nor the Idaho couple's speculations about what they saw. They'd seen enough to make that judgment, and it was their turn to have a kick of the can.

Her story continued:

> Glen, as for my recollection of the encounter, this still humongous/smaller animal would try the stairway another three times. I'm almost sure of it. Our ears strained to feel out the sounds being created, and we felt that it got no farther than the first flight of stairs. The thing couldn't get to the observation deck unless it wanted to monkey its way around it. Closing the door to the lookout loudly, and also walking heavy footed just outside, seemed to be enough to back off the attempts. I manned the door every time, making sure my husband wasn't far away while he attempted to look over the upper railing, light in hand, my hand grasping his belt from behind, steadying him. Near the end, I was fearful of the aggression toward us. I can't stress this enough. I don't like the idea of a monster somehow looking in our window. It was creepy enough just knowing what was moving around out there. What they were after, we will never know. You should have seen us when we came down off the tower — like small, scared rabbits caught out in the open with a bald eagle circling overhead. We hurried up in our leaving, and that was it for that visit.
>
> After long, patient talks back home, a welcome shared glass (a bottle actually) of sweet red wine, and a time or two out caching, we finally spent two whole nights at Webb Mountain in 2009, in the middle of the summer. I must say, we weren't overly

impressed with the paperwork involved with the rental, especially after what the two of us had endured in the south. There were a few mentions of possibly strange things that had occurred around this lookout as well, and you were the first person to single out the "Bigfoot" word — the one responsible for what may have happened to your family. You used the actual name associated with this being. There was no forwarding address made in your log representation, so I computer-searched your family name. That gave me your user name on the Web, and that, in turn, allowed us to contact you with a little work on our part. We would not place our confidence with anyone else about our sighting of that strange thing back in 2008. It is not our place to be involved with this uncomfortable subject. My husband spent one evening addressing the idea of this on the World Wide Web. It was puzzling, phony, and foolhardy, what we mostly saw before our eyes. We will not be made fun of anytime in the future. None of our friends or family will know of this — not directly anyway; they don't read Bigfoot books.

That will be our only story on this, and we'll stick to it. There is something "intelligent" living out in those woods.

## Near Libby, Montana

While researching many possibilities about Sasquatch in mid-January 2010, I left a private message for Thomas Steenburg through the West Coast Sasquatch forum, asking for his contribution to what we hoped was a flesh-and-blood creature.

In that forum, I focused on a thread highlighted by two others. It seemed that in late 2009, John Green had generously posted his accumulated database of years of research and investigation reports on the Internet. I must admit, I sat back and thought about that detailed work and all that had gone on. The gentleman, who was along in his years, found it a little tougher to get out into the field, but he shared his knowledge, time, and insight with so many of us.

I wondered if John's reports would include extra knowledge on places like the area around Big Creek Baldy tower in Lincoln County.

Here are some of the reports I found. Pipe Creek Road, which we had traveled northwest from the small town of Libby, Montana, to the Big Creek Baldy lookout, was the same road where a large upright creature had been spotted over the years. It was a generally wooded area with a sparse population.

In the case of Lincoln County and the proximity of the Lewiston couple's encounter with the giants at Big Creek Baldy, John Green's database revealed that biped creatures were scattered throughout the area. This upped the ante, so to speak. I pulled the following reports from Mr. Green's database, specifically focusing on the center point of Libby, Montana:

> 1962: South of Libby, Montana. Paul John Lindstrom quoted Myran Haugen, who told him that he'd seen a Sasquatch near Cherry Creek, in the Snowshoe area, at the Libby Audangle Silver Tip mine. It was flat-nosed, burnt brown in color, and about eight feet tall, with broad shoulders and long arms. He could see male genitals. It had a foul odor and was eating thimbleberries.
>
> August 1978: Early morning near Libby, Montana, north of the town. Jim Hewkin, the interviewer, was told by Ernest Fritz, a former rancher, that while Fritz was fishing at around five thirty a.m. at his ranch in the Yaak River area, he paused at the edge of a meadow, hoping to see a moose. A deer burst out of the timber into the meadow and stopped about a hundred feet from him. He heard a terrific scream in the woods where the deer had come from. The deer froze, and a huge bipedal creature appeared. It took about six strides, grabbed the deer by its antlers, picked it up, and bit its neck, and the deer offered no resistance. The creature then stood for a moment, looking around and growling, then grabbed the deer by the muzzle with one hand, threw it over his shoulder, and walked back into the woods. The creature was very large and heavy, but also quick and agile. It was very dark but not black in color. Hair covered the hands and feet, but there was not much on the face. Its head appeared to be gorilla- or ape-like.
>
> About 1979: West of Libby, Montana. Interviewer Robert S. Wilson, Ph.D., a clinical psychologist from the Washington State Department of Social Services in Medical Lake, Washington, spoke with Larry Davis. Driving toward Libby at one thirty a.m., Larry Davis turned up Pipe Creek Road, a mile before town, and saw what he took for a brown garbage bag on the road. As the car neared, the object raised a head with bright yellow eyes,

squatted like a man at the edge of the road, and then stood up at eight to eight and a half feet tall, with its long arms hanging down. It looked at Davis for three or four seconds, then turned its head sideways, lifted a leg up, and made a long step. It was in the woods about twenty feet, and its height was judged by comparison to a nearby signpost.

November 1983: Northwest of Libby, Montana. Interviewer Bob Wilson video spoke with Donna Davis about the sighting of a large creature. Donna, while driving from her home on Copper Mountain at about four p.m. on Pipe Creek Road, saw something at a distance — something very tall and dark. Whatever it was, it walked like a man across the road, taking only about five steps.

1985: Northwest of Libby, Montana. Bob Wilson offered a video of Larry Davis quoting Chris Doty, saying that he and Jason Fleming had seen an eight-foot brown creature with long arms and legs, some fifty feet away, in the bush. They ran. [JG2]

And spinning off slightly from the reports of the database, a small message came across my laptop around the same time, from Libby, Montana. Another helpful soul issuing a small find:

> I just spoke with an archaeologist from the forest service here. He remembers reading an account of a Bigfoot sighting in the West Fisher area around the time of World War I. He said he will try to find the resource and let me know. He wasn't aware of one in the Big Creek area.

## Update upon Update

In the summer of 2010, I wanted to roll the dice again and see if a strange flesh-and-blood creature might again grace us with its presence. We booked the fire lookouts of Webb and Big Creek for mid-July. I had remained hopeful over the years that the creature was just the luckiest son-of-a-bitch going, the ultimate *National Geographic*-type brute, sidestepping everything that hounded it.

Before we left for our stay, I discussed the situation with my Montana friend Seth Evanoff. We figured that putting ourselves out there again might stir things up. Something to that effect had materialized in the 1985 sighting at Princeton, as we continued the crapshoot, going for one of many drives over the years. In that instance, the Sasquatch had been there, so I wasn't writing anything off.

Seth agreed to join us up at Webb Mountain, hoping for a late-night adventure. Unfortunately, my trip out of town was canceled due to a problem with our youngest son's GMC. The leaking transmission caused an environmental issue on our residential street in Calgary. It's a very long story, and in the end, it set us back an entire day.

I did warn Seth about the possibilities coming his way, that he might just see something while he was all alone up there in the fire tower. Taking the suspense out of it for the reader, nothing did happen, but I do wish to say that a friend opened a doorway for my wife and me. Seth braved hurricane-force winds and pelting rain to cut through a tree that had fallen across the narrow road that led to the lookout on the final approach to Webb. Had we been on schedule, it would have been something we'd have had to deal with, but Seth Evanoff got through it without the best tools for the job. I wish to thank him for his thoughtfulness, as we were up there the very next afternoon, after he had to return to Kalispell.

The only reward he reaped for his heroic efforts was a clearing sky, lifting freezing temperatures for a July evening, and that same crisp sky filled with stars that seemed to be touchable from high in the mountains. At least his night was peaceful. I also wish to add that his pickle included the tricky place where he couldn't turn around; his only option was to back down a rain-soaked, narrow, sloped dirt road for almost a mile. Seth Evanoff didn't have much of a choice besides maybe walking to the tower and dealing with the fallen tree the next morning.

During our short stay at Webb Mountain, I did have the opportunity to watch something in action. This event proved that deer had not, in fact, been the culprits in 2005, as some researchers felt was the case. Of course I always knew differently, but this put the icing on the cake. I patiently watched four deer operate around the tower that night and five the next morning, going through their daily routines. At no time throughout their endeavors did the does and bucks make the noises and scuffling that had been produced on that fateful night in 2005. I carefully watched the everyday forest creatures operate around the fire lookout in the daytime and the evenings, and their behavior and noise were certainly different from what I'd witnessed before.

After that, we visited Big Creek Baldy Fire Lookout to the south. We were as comfy and as snug as bugs in a rug and spent almost a full day up at the second tower. I again wanted to review the visitors' logs that had been left there, writings from 1986 on, from almost every year. The page-by-page, book-by-book search offered dividends to the Sasquatch efforts. My wife and I located a particularly intriguing two-page story left by visitors (whom we presumed to be five or so men) at Big Creek Baldy in the summer of 2004. In uncanny fashion, their entry was from July 14, six years earlier to the day from when we were reading their entry in the Big Creek logbook. Those visitors to that tall, wooden-stilt tower had this to say about the legend they witnessed during their jaunt there:

> We arrived at the tower two days ago. The sky was clear, and the sun was high. We enjoyed the view, went on hikes, and had a couple of crazy games of poker.
>
> But the real excitement started during the first night. During a poker game, our friend Matt had to slay the brown knight. It was during his trip to the toilet that we heard him scream, and we booked it down the tower. We called out to Matt for what seemed like ages, but we got no reply. Then suddenly, Matt appeared, one sandal missing, with a look of fright on his face that silenced the group. As soon as he calmed down, Matt told us the story of a beast with a white face, on two legs, that had scared him out of the toilet.
>
> Everyone was reluctant to believe that the creature was anything but a bear — that was, until our second trip down the tower in the dark once again. Matt was separated from the group and again encountered the beast. As we searched for the place where we'd last heard Matt, eerie noises that sounded like a screaming child arose from the hillside on the east cliff. We cautiously approached the noise, fearing the worst for Matt, and then we saw it: a beast with a white face and white claws and fur as dark as the night, just fifty feet from our position. At that, we turned and ran toward the tower until we realized we had not found Matt yet. As we ventured back to the area of the beast, Matt emerged, now shirtless, telling us of how the beast had thrown rocks at him and us while he was in a tree. After that we called it a night. Needless to say, we didn't rest soundly until the sun came up the next morning.
>
> The next night, we decided to capture the beast on film and go looking for it this time. It was about twelve thirty a.m. when

we went out with our flashlights. Two remained at the tower, one with a spotlight and the other with a camera. It was not until Sean went off alone toward the forest north of the tower that the beast came out. It appeared right next to Sean, whereupon he screamed, "It's over here!" and took off. TJ and I took off toward the direction of the scream where we shined the spotlight. And there it was, a figure covered in black fur and hunched over, moving like a baboon. It was only in our sights for a little over ten seconds, but we were able to get it on camera. After the sighting, we went as a whole party and searched the area around the tower but found nothing more.

After consulting amongst ourselves, we are convinced that there is more than just one of those beasts out there, because the one we saw the first night was different from the one we got on film. These creatures are definitely nocturnal because we hiked around the entire mountain and more, yet found no signs of the beasts during the daylight. The creatures don't seem to be aggressive either, because every time a lone person encounters the creatures, they always seem to be just as afraid of us as we are of them.

We also looked back in the journals to find other records of the beast and found one other collaborating story. It is within the 2001-04 book — written by a young girl on July 13, 2003, on the very first page of the book.

Whether anyone reading this story believes it or not, we know what we saw and are determined to come back and capture the beast. Enjoy your stay at Big Creek Baldy and keep your eyes open at night.

The July 13, 2003 entry was, in fact, made by a young girl named Ashley Logan, who visited Big Creek Baldy with her family:

Hi. My name is Ashley, and I'm twelve. I was shining my flashlight from the outpost last night. I saw three wolves by the table, looking for scraps. Then something spooked them. It was rocks. Somebody was throwing rocks! I looked, and all my family were snug in their beds. Then I heard a clatter at the table. I aimed my light and saw not a man or a bear, but what appeared to be a man-bear! I saw its back for the majority, as it walked away, but it took one last gaze at me as it entered the woods. There was a white face and teeth. What was it?

## Wilderness Fire Tower

The happenings at Webb Mountain and Baldy Mountain introduced a whole new avenue of research for the Sasquatch mystery. I could check for fire tower personnel who'd addressed such things. It would be a touchy subject for them, as their credibility and possibly their employment would be at stake.

I was well received by the United States Forest Service, and a key spokesman explained that reports such as these would not be publicized at a national level. I was also told that it would be up to the individual districts to address the issue, should a certain report come in.

Forestry logbooks might hold information about encounters, but it seemed more likely that they would be documented in personal notes by the individual workers. Putting Sasquatch in official reports could damage a worker's credibility. Someone compared it to an airline pilot reporting a UFO. Even though the reports might be limited, I decided to dig into them to see what I could find.

The Sasquatch, it seems, is on the minds of many people these days, at least according to a woman working a fire lookout in Idaho's Frank Church Wilderness. She is frequently asked, "Have you ever seen a Bigfoot out here?" Another fire lookout woman, Mary Verbeke, with fifteen years experience on the towers, was also commonly asked the same question.

The question didn't even have to be asked of a young man working a fire tower in Clackamas County, Oregon, in 1970, around the Timothy Lake area, because he actually witnessed a Sasquatch walking up the road that led to the tower.

Bolan Lake, Oregon, in the Rogue River-Siskiyou National Forest, sits just below a rental tower. We had the opportunity to stay at that fire tower in 2008, though I wasn't aware that the lookout and the Bolan Lake area had seen Sasquatch activity in the past. An individual from the Internet's Bigfoot Forums offered an interesting tidbit concerning the Bolan Lake region, beyond what I found out post-visit. It seems a large creature had been seen in the immediate area of the lake. Ace (his user name) posted this on the forum:

> … I met an OSP officer who was checking fishing licenses. He stated that he is related to a federal employee who worked for twenty-seven years in this area. In his twenty-sixth year, he saw Bigfoot cross the road in front of him while driving near this location. I didn't ask any follow-up questions about when this was, but this same officer was very familiar with the Oregon Caves incident [that had occurred] several years prior.

A retiree that I have had several conversations with has much to say about the fire lookouts. In 1966-67, she was stationed at Horse Ridge Tower in the Mad River District of Six Rivers National Forest in California. She mentioned a man who visited the lookout a couple of times. He claimed to have plaster casts of Sasquatch footprints piled up under his bed, and he was full of stories, though he seemed very sincere. She recalls the gentleman being from somewhere around the Trinity National Forest in the Hayfork or Weaverville area.

Another straightforward fire tower individual spotted three of the Sasquatch people near the Washington State Nestor Peak fire lookout in the 1980s. The tower sitting on the highest peak was destroyed in 1995.

An Oregon fire lookout watchman contacted me about something he had to address in the coastal state. The lookout called himself "Oregon," as he wanted to otherwise remain anonymous. The man had thought about asking for a web weather cam at the tower, but he settled for his own camcorder, figuring it would be somewhat difficult to review any footage other than that he captured himself. Over a period of six months, he'd witnessed a strange creature through his binoculars a number of times. The forestry employee wanted to get the biped on film. He attached his camcorder to the railing with a clamp, training the photographic device in the direction where it spent most of its time, and then he waited.

After a generous amount of time, the guy tallied up what he'd captured on film. Not a damn thing in the way of an upright being! The sequence was repeated, to the point where he would walk, on his own time, down into the view of the camera. Of course spotted himself in the footage, and on closer examination of the film, he also spotted an occasional animal. However, there was no Bigfoot creature. It wasn't until ten days later, when the forester pulled down his video contraption, that he again spotted the savage-looking creature. He had again wasted his time, and he refused to play cat-and-mouse any longer. Nevertheless, in time, he posted the evidence of something going on in the wilderness where he spent half his time.

A young South Seattle woman visits a number of these towers as a part of her involvement with the Forest Fire Lookout Association (FFLA). We had several conversations about the fire lookout connection. She relayed a story to me of a lookout ranger who worked on a tower on the Spokane Indian Reservation in 2002. He'd claimed to have seen a Sasquatch below the tower one morning, banging rocks together. He mentioned to her, as well, that another worker had seen something similar in 2003: rocks being struck together several times just off the immediate tower area.

For those who work in the forest every day, it would make sense that there would be a greater probability of encountering the Sasquatch. It doesn't happen at all to many out there in the forests, and their careers remain uninterrupted by unusual things, but the next watchman had a taste of what shared the timberland with him over a few seasons out of the seventeen he was there. He prefers to remain anonymous, but he explained his dealings with the creature as follows:

> Well, Glen, it's nice to see that you and your family have used the tower recreation program over the years. You understand the reclusive atmosphere behind the lookout life.
>
> It seems we also share something else in common, both of us having witnessed a Bigfoot creature in our separate journeys. I was like most who witness this forest giant: It doesn't exist until you've run across it. I'll be the first to admit this now. Only three or four times over the years did I actually think about the subject, and half the time it was only because a visitor brought it up.
>
> I reported smoke as a USFS employee for seventeen seasons, mostly in the Pacific Northwest. A number of these fire seasons included Montana in the mix. I was in Big Sky Country when I caught a brief glimpse of the creature.
>
> I'm almost sure I was being watched first in this, as I was up one early morning, scanning the sky for a red-tailed hawk I had seen the day before. My focus was shared on the lower landscape as well, just a casual observation of things.
>
> Binoculars in hand, on a horizontal scan of the forest area to the east side of the tower, I stopped rather dumbfounded — or, for a better word, I was astonished. There was a large animal stopped dead, looking directly at me from a distance of approxi-

mately 275 yards. I confirmed this distance after my shift one evening, taking a walk. There was no evidence left in the area where the creature stood.

The creature I saw that morning was standing and continued to do so, then walked off under the same intention. I believe this departure was due to me observing it. This was interesting in a sense, as the animal's eyesight would have had to be sharp. When I placed myself at the creature's position, I took a good look at the tower. I could have been easily seen on the catwalk, although I hadn't moved around much during those minutes previous to the sighting. The creature moved away, as if it did not want to be watched or monitored.

A visual on this animal lasted for only eight to ten seconds, as it pivoted to walk away into timber that would shield it, strutting something like a man. It was a brownish color in the morning sun. I'm thinking somewhere around the nine-foot mark for height, maybe a little less, but not much. It had an extreme presence about it, something I wouldn't soon forget. That one was an older variety, I would expect, at that given height. The hairy man was completely covered with a thick coat of hair, different lengths throughout.

After witnessing such a creature, I heard the odd story from other tower personnel, including some in Idaho. I'd hint at the subject, and a few individuals would open up inquisitively, but not as many as I would expect.

On my interest alone in the off-season one year, I pursued a few things in relation to the high density of wilderness in Montana. One would think there would be more activity there. I continuously proved myself wrong. With time on my hands, I found there weren't that many documented sightings in Montana as compared to other western states. And what was even stranger, there were states in the east that furnished three to four times as many reports. Then I began to answer a few of my own questions. The population of Montana is minuscule in comparison to many of the other U.S. At times, there are more visitors and tourists in the state of Montana than there are residents — I'm sure of it. So it would make sense that this animal could move around more freely throughout the territory. I also find that Montanans

> are more loud or vocal, to put it politely. Such a shy creature would not be around long in that kind of boisterous environment.
>
> Another thing to consider is what you stated about your visits to our rentals here in Montana and that you come from hundreds of miles away in Alberta for pleasure. Many locals living in their respective areas here in the state know very little about their surroundings, including the fire towers nearby, right at their doorsteps. I guess you'd have to have an interest to appreciate the fact. Add everything to this, and a person can soon see why the Bigfoot is seldom encountered locally.
>
> These are my ideas on the subject, and now I am also an observer of the creature. It would seem that the local native population knows more about the subject as well.

Another forestry lookout worker wasn't so keen on sharing information he'd obtained. He saw the Bigfoot creature with his own eyes, near the bottom of the first flight of stairs that led up the fire tower. He didn't even share his isolated experience with the watchman who relieved him. He only decided to talk about it years later, when he was no longer working there. His reports were never written in any logbooks. He likened it to a bad dream, looking through the hatchway from two stories up, seeing an ape-like giant almost one level closer to him simply because of its monstrous size. Sometimes these perplexing encounters leave one completely spellbound. From that day forward, he felt he had to be somewhat on his guard, as he worked periodically on one of three towers during his time in the mountains. What we faced up at Webb Mountain lasted only two of three nights, and we had each other for company. This individual, like so many others, faced continuous nights alone at the towers.

Adding segments of a BFRO report to the list of fire lookouts in relationship with the Sasquatch, the next experience pointed to an encounter that happened in 1970 to a Forest Service employee on Mt. Emily, about ten miles as the crow flies from Brookings, Oregon. He had a black Labrador named Bucky, his canine companion at the fire tower, which was twenty-five feet from ground to the catwalk. This is the BFRO report:

> Leaving one evening for a doctor's appointment and needing groceries, he locked Bucky on the tower with the intention of being back on the mountain early the next morning. His dog did

not like being alone and apparently jumped off the catwalk. When the man returned the next morning, his canine friend was gone. He looked for tracks and called for the dog but found nothing. He gave up hope.

About ten days later, the lookout heard noise in the late evening sunset, down off the hill. Sure enough, it was Bucky. The dog was very tired and worn out. He carried man's best friend up the tower and into the chart room, then laid him on the bed.

Now, Bucky was the type of dog that never barked or growled. He just did not. The dog was so mild and good-natured; he just did not carry on like most dogs. That was why he was such a great companion to this fellow.

After the incident, he never left the lookout's side. He stuck to him like glue. The dog did not want to be left alone. He was scared — very scared. He took to sleeping under the bunk, something the dog had never done before. He also took to barking in the early and late evenings. He would stand there on the catwalk, looking down at the mountain to the southwest, and bark and bark and bark — something else the dog had never done before.

About two weeks later, in the early evening, the gentleman was scanning the woods with his binoculars, when he heard a ripping, tearing sound — the kind of sound a dead tree makes. It sounded like the sound you would hear ripping up a dead, rotting tree. He knew it wasn't a bear opening up a dead tree looking for grubs, because there were no bears on that mountain. In fact, the only animals he ever saw up there in the two years he spent on the mountain were a few rats and a couple of chipmunks. Occasionally there was a human visitor; otherwise, he was practically alone. He went down the tower and walked in the direction of the sound and searched for quite some time, while Bucky stayed on the tower and barked. The dog was really frightened. The lookout had his rifle with him but never found where the sound came from nor saw any sign of what made the noise.

Several days later, late in the evening, about ten thirty or so, they were both trying to sleep. The full moon was sitting on the horizon, and the whole tower was lit up. It was very warm, as the temperatures had been in the high nineties for several days. As he lay out on the bunk, there was a huge boom, and the whole tower shook. It felt like a car had run into the tower or perhaps a sonic boom, but the tower shook first. Something had hit the structure.

> He crawled out the window to the catwalk and belly-crawled around the tower deck, looking to see if anyone might be down below. Bucky was under the bed with every hair on his body standing straight up, growling deep in his throat. The lookout had never in his life seen an animal so scared. The dog actually evacuated poop and urine right there on the floor under the bed. His eyes were actually drained of all color; the iris was actually white. He was scared to death. It took the lookout hours to coax his friend out from under the bed.
>
> The lookout remembers not seeing any car lights approaching the mountain, and since the last two miles of road could only be traveled by foot, four-wheel drive, or mountain bike, they would have been nuts to make that climb in the dark, let alone during daylight. The boulders were big enough to rip wheels off or oil pans out, unless great care and skill were used, even during the day.
>
> Whatever it was that had slammed the tower had disappeared. [BFRO2]

Here is another confirmation of the possibilities of finding information in forest service files.

> [Department of Fish and Game] used to keep a Bigfoot file because we would get regular reports/calls and folks wanted them logged with the State. Some of the more recent years' reports were from deer hunters on the eastside above Bridgeport. (Eric, Current Chief, California Department of Fish and Game, Wildlife Branch)

Continuing on this topic, I had a personal phone conversation with a fellow who works as a lookout in the Tonto National Forest area of Arizona. He is presently looking into the idea that tower logbooks may hold encounters of something like the Sasquatch. Not only is he using his position to follow up on this, but he has also watched the giant creature through binoculars while standing on guard for fires, much like the man from Oregon. In his spare time, he's hiked down to the place in question, looking for clues. It seems the Sasquatch is using a narrow ravine in the valley well below the lookout tower. Unlike most tower personnel who fall prey to the Sasquatch phenomenon and just write such things off as unusual, this individual is willing to steer his experience in the general direction of a newfound hobby: the quest to solve the mystery of the Sasquatch. He, like me and so many others, yearns to get to the bottom of it.

Here's an interesting tidbit for us all to consider: The U.S. Forest Service, Umatilla National Forest, Walla Walla Ranger District, has listed the following on their front page on the Internet:

> Rumored to live in the district, but not yet proven, are northern lynx, wolverines, and even the elusive Sasquatch.

Our final entry, from someone by the name of Dini, is likely the way many men and women who work at these structures address this issue:

> Perhaps it may be wily enough to recognize and avoid Forest Service and National Park Service personnel and our green rigs as well! And hence, it has rarely, if ever, been spotted by one of us. For that I am grateful. I'd prefer not to have a chance encounter with one, no matter how gentle the giants may be.
>
> And who knows? If they *have* been sighted by one of us, we may value our jobs too much to talk about it for fear of being considered unstable. Or, if an employee has reported such a sighting to his supervisor, it may have been kept hush-hush to avoid causing panic amongst other personnel.
>
> If these creatures do, in fact, exist — and I'm not doubting your word — how can we be so sure they aren't above causing harm, just as some humans are not?
>
> I'd like to learn more about the creatures for the purpose of either avoiding them or knowing what to do in case I happen to encounter one.

# 8. Logging Stories

You would think that, along with forest rangers, loggers would also be likely to have encounters with Bigfoot. The stories were sometimes hard to uncover for the usual reasons, but here are some that shed more light onto the mystery of Sasquatch.

## Accident of Gigantic Proportion

In April of 2009, a story finally fell directly in my lap — one that had gone practically unnoticed. Over time, this rather sad tale ended up possibly being the real McCoy, seen through the eyes of one man in the wilderness of lower British Columbia near the United States border.

Over five years ago, traveling through Princeton and on to Maple Ridge lap — the family visitation gig lap — we were again down at the coast in the Vancouver area. During one of our family conversations around the dinner table, a certain Princeton fellow was brought up. I don't know what originated the discussion, but I wanted to know what happened to that logger many years ago out in the bush. His case seemed to be somewhat different from practically all the others when it came to loggers being injured in the forests around the Similkameen Valley. I knew some of those individuals and went to school with others, and a few did not survive. Logging and truck driving for a living can be dangerous jobs.

### The Bob Mervin Story

My brother and his wife did not know what happened to Bob Mervin. A name was given to me of another logger. When I contacted him, he seemed to know very little; he was actually quite obnoxious when I asked questions about Bob Mervin's injuries. I never once mentioned the Sasquatch in my conversation with the grouch, and I let the entire thing slide for quite some time after that. At that time, it was no big deal, and I was busy writing up a storm anyway.

Lisa Carleton, an associate publisher with the *Similkameen Spotlight* was instrumental in bringing this sketchy tale to the foreground. At the time, she knew as much as I did. The unfortunate accident had occurred many years earlier, southwest of Princeton in the Pasayten Valley.

I originally emailed Ms. Carleton to ask for help with a mystery. I wanted to know what had happened to that man out west. I communicated with her at the newspaper, and she graciously started a search for anything related to my request. At first, there was nothing. I had actually tried both papers in Princeton, and the answer was the same. Eventually, the *Spotlight* was able to illuminate some things for me.

In December 2008, the associate publisher contacted me on the subject. She asked if there was a date that would help with the search. We had to leave it for the time being, as I didn't have a clue. After all, I was looking into it from 500 miles away. Nevertheless, I did leave her with all the information I knew.

In late March of 2009, Lisa Carleton reached me via IncrediMail. She hadn't forgotten me or my request, and she was eager to share what she'd found out:

> Hi, Glen.
>
> I have made contact with extended family members. Mr. Mervin is still alive, although quite unwell at this time. What I've been able to find out for you is that the incident happened about twenty to twenty-five years ago. When I inquired about Mr. Mervin's accident, I was told he'd been whomped on the back of his head. And it seems, Glen, that Mr. Mervin is quite sure the creature you speak of is exactly what hit him. The story I was told also included the statement that a day or two prior to the incident, Mr. Mervin had heard a very horrible-sounding scream. It scared him so badly that he left the area for the remainder of the day. I have been given the name of a person who worked with Mr. Mervin at the time. I am working on tracking him down and will contact you again when I find him.
>
> Hope this is helpful.

As strange as it may sound, this story began to fit well with another — a man possibly injured by a Sasquatch creature southwest of Princeton. One day, as I was looking around on the Internet, I happened upon a website owned by a Princeton man named Hank Rabe. He included historical pictures of Princeton, as well as the names of old trucking firms and such — mementos of long ago, many of which I recognized. Truly, I had come across Hank by cyber-accident, but believe it or not, he was acquainted with Bob Mervin! He gave me the man's phone number and told me to give Bob a call. I was having quite a bit of good luck and wouldn't hesitate to press it.

Still, it wasn't an easy thing to pursue. I wasn't exactly sure where to begin. The man had gone through many serious hardships concerning his health, including the recent amputation of one of his legs. I was saddened by that, and when we did speak, I never asked how much of that limb he'd lost. I wanted to take my time in speaking to him.

I had actually mentioned the injured logger to Seth Evanoff of Montana, since I happened to be in touch with him at the time, and he suggested that I might want to tape my conversation with Mr. Mervin. My son Christopher had found a micro-cassette recorder and my wife grabbed a pack of tapes from a dollar store, and we were in business. The thing actually worked flawlessly, so a taped interview was soon underway. It was technically my first interview, if you could call it that, because I sounded terrible on tape, partly from being so nervous.

The interview lasted almost an hour, as he spoke freely of his encounter with a legend.

Bob Mervin mentioned almost immediately that he considered himself a fair-sized individual, but nothing compared to the Big Men that were there with him some days in the Pasayten area this side of the U.S. border.

He had seen the creatures over time. No one would believe him at the start, so he kept quiet about seeing such things. This would only change sometimes, when the odd individual happened to come along and encountered the primate with his own eyes. Bob would just laugh while the visitor or worker would almost shit their drawers. He said, "They wouldn't ever believe me if I'd have just told them." The odd person who did witness the Sasquatch would never talk, and according to the logger, there were few people who knew the truth about it.

There was talk of the ape-like creature being spotted between Merritt and Princeton as well. The conversation was held between workers. As I interviewed the man, I asked him a number of times what animal or creature we were talking about, just to be sure — really sure. He never missed a beat in responding. It was the Sasquatch, and not just one. Talking with witnesses and those who know Bob Mervin, his story was mostly consistent throughout. The man could be trusted, after everything was investigated.

In his trials in the bush with the giants, both male and female, the logger did mention that when he dropped trees, there were times when the creatures would scream with the commotion and destruction. He noticed five big ones, including three girls at a time when this occurred, as an example. Bob Mervin also noticed that the more he clear-cut, the more the creatures seemed to push back into the woods. Also included in his observation is that he couldn't possibly outrun such a species. They could kill you before you could turn around: his impression of the giants. He stated that he could see the creatures rather close, and in the next second, they were gone. Bob said, "How they can do things like that, you can't even dream it."

On another day, Bob Mervin saw three Sasquatch, including two females, as the childbearing creatures were always smaller than the adult males. The logger felt they mostly defecated as they walked, and the buggers crapped quite a bit. He also seemed to realize that when the creatures were all dirtied up, they could better blend in with their surroundings, and they understood that concept. The Sasquatch demonstrated such things, looking over the situation behind them or when it involved each other.

During this interview with the retired logger, he spoke of a well-known, reputable researcher who had made the trek to Princeton to investigate the encounter. I heard the name mentioned while Bob Mervin was conferring with his son on the issue, and I planned to contact the investigator in the next two or three days, after a little homework on my end. I have no idea if the researcher ultimately placed the information into the stream of things. It had been quite a few years.

With Bob Mervin logging, one day something would go terribly wrong. Except for the noise at times, the haired giants would gradually become complacent, getting too close to the logging job. Bob Mervin did much the same, getting closer and closer.

Then came the day that changed the Princeton logger's life. My understanding of this was that there were at least three large males, one smaller female, and one other that was of unknown gender, though it was much smaller, what Bob Mervin called "the baby."

Bob Mervin felled a tree that came into direct contact with the youngest of the Sasquatch gathered there. The man figured for sure that he had killed the small creature and called out, "Oh, my God!" That set off terrible screams and howling from the young female, as she moved all over in panic. The frenzy that was created by the unfortunate accident instantly roused the males, one of which attacked the logger in seconds, hitting the man on the back of his head. Bob Mervin felt he was hit more than once, but that was all he could remember, for he went in and out of consciousness. Two men who worked with and around him showed up later. Leading up to the strike, it was all a blur.

Robert W. Morgan is a Bigfoot researcher from Montana and also the head of The American Anthropological Research Foundation. He also authored the book, *Bigfoot Observer's Field Manual* by Pine Winds Press. In his material, including his ideas of the forest giant people, he said the following about their possible behavior:

> These giants only respond to violence. They don't initiate it. If attacked, shot at, or wounded, the forest giants have a history of wreaking quick revenge. [RWM1]

This is what I believe happened to Bob Mervin, a result of violence in the forest. One of the Sasquatch was grossly injured, and another of these creatures responded immediately and defensively. The jury is still out, though, as the bipedal giant is considered an animal by many. There was even talk of different breeds, one of which was menacing. I haven't seen such a thing during my encounters with the giants.

The Princeton logger's story continued:

After everything was said and done, both these individuals told Bob that they had found nothing near him that could have struck the man. They didn't completely know what they were looking for at the time. Of course, the logger knew the truth about the ordeal.

There was no investigation that I know of by the Royal Canadian Mounted Police, based on what Bob and others have said. Bob Mervin spent quite some time in the hospital in the Interior, related to his head injuries, and, according to my findings, he was near death for a time. From what many have told me, he has never been the same since.

Concerning the Sasquatch that were there in the forest that day, they had obviously taken care of their own. Though there'd possibly been a death of one of the creatures, no body was ever found. If anyone was interested in this, it wasn't looked into until much later, and any evidence had vanished with the passing of time or tampering by the Sasquatch themselves, possibly dragging the dead body off. The aboriginal population and the Forest Giants seem to be good at that.

Soon after Bob Mervin's taped interview, Lisa Carleton contacted me again. I owed the associate publisher a big thank you. She replied as follows:

> Hello, Glen.
>
> I'm glad you got to speak with Mr. Mervin. Due to his health, I was not too sure if that would be a possibility for you. Although I am a *newspaper girl,* I give you my word that I will not pursue this extremely touchy subject.
>
> I will be here to assist you if I can. Also, I did find out that there is a former co-worker of Bob's who is supposedly a Pastor who lives in…

I thanked Lisa and took her advice again. Using the Internet and the phone, I tracked down the individuals who were essential to establishing Bob Mervin's credibility, as well as others I happened across.

The pastor was found in Osoyoos and was previously from Parksville, British Columbia. He had worked alongside the logger for many years in the Pasayten Valley. He mentioned that Bob was just an average guy doing a job he'd been asked to do. He also said the man had a good head on his shoulders. I found the same to be true about Bob, for he was a man in good spirits, especially considering everything that had happened to him. This was also discussed briefly with the researcher who knew of the encounter long ago. He and I seemed to agree that it was a random attack, a defensive situation by the species, reacting to what they considered a hostile act. I have no idea if the Sasquatch is an actual killer. There are many ideas being tossed around about this, most of the research leading to dead ends. Many like to remind us that it is an animal; sometimes I tend to agree with this, but not always. When I encountered the Sasquatch myself, I did not see one piece of evidence that we were about to be attacked. The creatures I saw wanted nothing more than to get away, as quickly as possible, from us vile humans.

Investigating the idea that there might have been some other Similkameen Valley loggers out there who had shared such experiences of witnessing an unfamiliar giant in the hills surrounding Princeton, the search was on. I tied this into others possibly knowing Bob Mervin, or perhaps they'd run across the Bigfoot on their own.

After a few days researching this, I found two others who knew the injured logger; they'd had their eyes opened to a mammoth giant that toured the woods. Both of these gentlemen were retired. One lived in the Princeton area, but the other had moved out of town. They both mentioned that there were still others out there who had seen these creatures over the years. One even referred to an Illuminati group — something that was as hush-hush then as it still is now, considering the embarrassment one might be subjected to when coming forward with such an announcement, particularly in a logging community. Interestingly enough, no one thought of getting those beings on camera, including Bob Mervin. He had mentioned it a time or two, but that never did materialize. Trying to film the creature would have been scorned and dangerous, so the creature managed to escape proof for all those years, in spite of all those who'd seen them.

Both ex-loggers agreed that Bob Mervin could be a credible witness, but there were others who had other things to say. Some individuals hadn't seen the Sasquatch, but they did have some input to offer. Most of them agreed that there was a button-lip agenda, for mention of the Sasquatch could have had negative effects on the stability of logging in the region. The mine had closed years earlier, and the forest industry had become the staple of the downsized British Columbia town. First of all, no one wanted to become a laughingstock in the small number of coffee shops in and around Princeton. Loggers are mostly rugged individuals and do not take kindly to folklore, hauntings, and monstrous creatures living in the woods. Some had a fear of what might occur if the Sasquatch was ever discovered. They worried that the being's existence could take food from their tables and clothes off their backs.

The two men I spoke with talked about their fears if the existence of Sasquatch was proven. Environmentalists would rush in to protect the creature and logging would be in serious danger. There would be migration and nomadic behavior to worry about, and what if there were a breeding season? Then we have things like sacred ground proceedings, where the creature walks and spends its time, and an Endangered Species Act lying out there on the horizon. Even Bob Mervin had mentioned that there were certain types of trees that the Sasquatch preferred over others, hanging around them more often. The animal seemed to know that the color of their body hair blended in with the selected timber.

Skilled outdoorsman Ken Kristian mentioned something related to this issue, as it was told to him:

> I was told by loggers many years ago (and mention it in my Pitt Lake reports) that they were told by the boss to shut up about the Sasquatch. The whispers about Sasquatch being in the bush along with the loggers slowly filtered back down to us kids because we heard what was being said in camp when the boss was not around.

These kinds of things didn't stop there, as more began to surface on the idea of a diversion being executed when needed, depending upon the geographical location that felt pressured by a Sasquatch that supposedly didn't exist.

I found similarities in the Similkameen Valley region. Ranchers who seemed on the cusp of speaking about it sat back and thought about the possible repercussions of such a species traveling freely along the open range and the whole world knowing about it. Governments would surely react. When I thought about it, I couldn't blame the ranchers at all. From my end of researching the bipedal being, though, the truth was still the truth. The Sasquatch creature had still visited Princeton over the years, and there were at least four of us who were living eyewitnesses to the fact that something was walking the area. This book will likely make no difference with the Sasquatch realm overall. Only a specimen will really matter.

Another logger's voice echoes the say-nothing sentiment. "See No Sasquatch," written by Bill Palmroth, appeared in the Winter 1992 edition of the *Oregon Fish & Wildlife Journal (OFWJ)*. Below are some segments from Mr. Palmroth's writing:

> I know many of you OFWJ readers are loggers and you have seen some amazing things in the woods: single-antlered cow elk, as well as lightning-fast, stiff-legged deer, visible to the human eye only when they stop running and lean against a tree to rest or sleep…
>
> Thus, it only stands to reason that it will be a logger who makes the next significant Bigfoot sighting…
>
> Now, if you do happen to sight a Sasquatch sometime in the future, what are you going to do about it? Are you going to report the sighting to authorities or keep quiet about it? If you were to report it, there's always the chance that the federal gov-

> ernment could suddenly become interested in Bigfoot. If so, your logging operation probably would be suspended indefinitely while the feds take time to study the creature's habitat requirements. That would leave you in a real fix. What's more, any habitat study by the government would very likely lead to a Bigfoot recovery program, necessitating additional forest be set aside. In this case, perhaps second-growth timber would be targeted.
>
> Your smartest option is to keep any future Bigfoot sightings under your hat, especially if you're on public land. As my grandfather used to say, "Say nothing and saw wood!" [BP1]

I found a few other fragments of possible information on the online Bigfoot Forums. The first discussion was related to a thread on the Bigfoot subject written by a person who writes articles for a number of newspapers on a variety of topics. One response from someone named 911 Guy was fitting to the logging situation. He would like to point out, though, that this is a story passed on by others. If it is true, it is the frame of mind that warrants continued secrecy amongst so many who wish the creature would remain just a mythological fable:

> I did hear from a friend once that he had a friend who was a logger, in northern California, and a memo was attached to the paychecks saying that if anyone spoke to a Bigfoot researcher in town, they would be terminated.

Although this could not be confirmed, as 911 Guy stated, it was quite likely to be true, from what I'd discovered anyway. All I could do was trudge on in my research, trying to separate the possible from the impossible.

Another anonymous post on the Bigfoot Forums mentioned the hush-hush protocol about possible Bigfoot presence, in light of a person's character and position and what is ultimately at stake:

> I work with an old-timer who spent thirty years in logging and working for the railroad. He told me lots of loggers and railroad guys have Bigfoot stories to tell. He told me in all his years in the woods, he never saw one hint of anything Bigfoot related, but then he had one cut through his front yard. He thinks it is very ironic. He also told me how in the early nineties, he was working as a tender for a water-dropping helicopter. The pilot

told him about dropping water and coming around the back side of a mountain, and there were two Bigfoot making their way across a ridge away from the fire. Later, the pilot told him not to repeat it to anyone. This old guy said he would never report anything like that to the authorities or anything because it would damage his reputation in the business. So stories over beers are okay, but officially swearing you saw it? Not okay.

Another party shed some light on the situation only days later. I happened upon *Where Bigfoot Walks: Crossing the Dark Divide*, authored by Robert Michael Pyle. His work complemented everything I was researching along the line of logging and the Sasquatch sharing the same wilderness. Below are segments from a number of pages from his book that was published in 1997:

> Have the United States Forest Service and certain timber companies collaborated to suppress Bigfoot sightings?
>
> In fact, the Trout Lake Forest Service camp was in total disarray over this modest spotty lump of a bird. With the federal listing of *Strix occidentalis* as an endangered species and Judge William Dwyer's ruling that the USFS was in violation of federal law until they took the owl fully into account, chaos reigned. Most timber sales had been shut down until the owl populations were surveyed and a new plan approved for their protection…
>
> Ray Wallace had told me about his road-building contracts with the Gifford Pinchot National Forest; the contracts said, in effect, "If you see Bigfoot, don't tell, or we will cancel your contract." [RMP1]

It might be worthy to note that Mr. Wallace was a man of many tales and suspect stories, and his shenanigans were closely followed by the media, accepting his misinformation as fact at times.

Robert Michael Pyle's writings continued:

> Al said he had heard the story of the Bigfoot contract clause, but he couldn't say if it was true. An old-timer told him he had worked under similar restrictions…
>
> Later, I heard other rumors and whispers about Bigfoot clauses in forestry contracts but never saw one…
>
> Grover told me that the rumor mill consistently turned out stories of forestry workers, both government and private, being

instructed by their superiors not to reveal any Bigfoot evidence or intimations they came across in their work. I have heard such accounts also…

So think what a big ape might do. Sasquatch would make the spotted owl look like a gnat…

Suppose an unrecognized species of anthropoid ape was discovered on a national forest… or a hominoid, which would raise questions of our evolutionary singularity and perhaps even call up issues of human (or near subhuman) rights. Even if the beast were an ape along the lines of chimps and gorillas, its animal rights position would be volatile…

If the Forest Plan had a new overlay for its maps, showing the suspected range of Bigfoot, it would not be a whole new ballgame. It would be completely out of the park… [RMP2]

What a large reality pill that would be to swallow!

# 9. Sasquatch and the Railroad

We've touched on loggers and forest services, so why not railroads? There may be a number of reasons why the Sasquatch travels the railway lines and has done so for many decades. We begin this journey by rail at a place where the Sasquatch may have been hit by a steam locomotive. This report is courtesy of Rita Swift, from the International Bigfoot Society:

> 1880s, Colorado, Wyoming Line RR
> U.S./Canadian Border to Eads, Colorado
>
> My name is Rita Swift. I live in Orange County, California. In 1945, my great-grandfather, George Kuhn, told me a story about the time his train hit a large ape creature and bent the cowcatcher on his train.
>
> This was in the 1880s, and he was the engineer on a train that ran along the borders of the U.S. and Canada. It was night, and all of a sudden, their train hit something. They stopped the train because the cowcatcher was dragging on the tracks. At first they thought it was a moose, but when they all got out with their lanterns, they discovered this huge, smelly ape, hung up in the catcher. They had only lanterns for light, and they were in a forest, basically in the middle of nowhere. It took most of the crew to pick it up and lift it into an open flat-car. They noticed it was structured differently from a gorilla or ape and smelled so bad; the crew got the smell on them. They left it in the flat-car, because it took at least two hours to straighten out the cowcatcher.
>
> Good thing my great-grandfather was also a blacksmith. They were at least two hours from the next water tower and

station of sorts. The brakeman noticed Indians sneaking around in the forest, but he thought they had disappeared. When they were ready to go, the crew checked on their smelly passenger, but he was gone. They looked for tracks and decided the Indians had dragged it away into the forest and across a stream. They found the tracks and pieces of hair and, of course, the smell. They washed up in the stream and were glad to get rid of it. The smell had even remained in the flat-car. My great-grandfather took pieces of the hair back and gave it to a doctor he knew in Michigan. They all decided the creature had escaped from a circus or sideshow. Great-grandfather thought it was 8 feet tall and weighed at least 500 pounds. It took six men to carry it off the tracks.

My great-grandfather said the ape had a different face than what he remembered of a gorilla. He said the teeth were like humans', but extremely wide and large.

The body hair was thick, dark brown with light tipping, and the eyes were large and dark. He said they agreed it was male because of its genitalia.

Grandfather continued as a railroad engineer on the Colorado Wyoming Line until he retired in 1925. He fought off outlaws with his six-shooters from the cab. I have a photo of Grandfather with the crew, stopped in Eads, Colorado, with a large cannon hole in the side of the engine. This was in 1898, when some outlaws on horses pulled up an old Confederate cannon along the tracks and fired at the engine. The crew chased them away but they damaged the train. The train was on its way to Durango carrying bank money from Denver. Grandfather would never tell stories that were not true. He was a devout Methodist and said his prayers so loud every night that the whole house could hear him. He had originally come from Amish in Mercer County, Pennsylvania, but left to fight for the Union in the Civil War. His father did not accept his decision, and he never returned to Mercer County. He was born in 1845 and died in 1947, in Claremont, California.

It is fine with me if you publish the story. Great-grandfather said this BF was extremely large. It took all of the crew, six men to carry it. Of course I am sure a young BF is extremely large too. I have heard these large, hairy creatures have been reported

> all over the world. Maybe they are that missing link, when man came down from the trees four million years ago.
>
> We are discovering things all the time that we had no knowledge of. I know after the story, I didn't sleep too well that night. I was six years old. I remember the next morning, I asked him how much it smelled. He said it smelled like 1,000 skunks locked in an outhouse in the dead summer. He was nearly eighty when he retired from the railroad. His sight and hearing were great, and he was as sharp as a tack. I feel fortunate I have his beautiful gold railroad watch and chain with medals he got from the Colorado Wyoming Line in 1925. He was 102 when he passed away in his sleep, in 1947. [RC1]

There have been so many Bigfoot stories, including those that have been extensively written about, such as the Jacko 1884 incident near Yale, British Columbia, and the Ruby Creek incident in 1941, also in British Columbia.

The reason I have mentioned these two stories in particular is because they have some bearing on the Sasquatch/railroad connection. The Chapman family of Ruby Creek lived with a railroad right next to their property, and Mr. Chapman even worked for the railroad company. The Sasquatch creature was right in their midst. As for Jacko, that not-so-little creature was supposedly found sleeping near the track around Tunnel No. 4, up from Yale. Whatever that was, it disappeared as well.

## Railway Personnel

Perhaps the best way to discuss the railway and creature conundrum is to speak to railroad personnel. A report filed with the BFRO involved a Union Pacific Railway conductor observing a "great ape" on the railroad track bed in the summer of 1995. This occurred in Multnomah County, Oregon, near the town of Cascade Locks:

> I am a conductor for Union Pacific Railway, working pool freight from Portland, Oregon, to Hermiston, Oregon. We were traveling westbound on a train going around curves between Bonneville, Cascade Locks, and Dodson. As we came around a curve near Milepost 36, I saw something dark between the rails. I said to the engineer, "What is that!?" He then blew the whistle. Something tall and hairy, with long arms, got up and ran into the trees and brush. Its arms swung wildly when it ran. We looked

into the spot where the animal went into cover but could not see it. Time was daybreak. We got a good look as we approached at about fifteen railcar lengths.

Also noticed: Three months earlier, a sighting at Eagle Creek by another engineer, then one sighting after mine in 1995 and another late 1999; two people sighted a large, apelike animal in 2000. All are railroad personnel.

Follow-up investigation report was done by BFRO Investigator Dr. LeRoy Fish: Kyle talked with me for several minutes about a number of sightings near Bonneville by railroad personnel in both Multnomah and Hood River Counties.

Kyle additionally described the apelike animal he saw as appearing to be interested in something on the railroad bed. The animal was sitting down between the tracks when first observed, then raised itself up to stand and ran away on two legs with its arms flailing back and forth. The creature appeared to be frightened by the train whistle. [BFRO3]

## Cascade Tunnel

So what, exactly, is the Sasquatch after, sitting between the rails? Many documented sightings confirm that the creature has some strange partnership with the railroads. Is it simply quicker passage between two points in the wilderness, as many of these stretches include native reservation lands? Do the railway bridges that span raging rivers and steep gorges also support the weight of the Sasquatch, saving the roaming creature energy and climbing time? Are hundreds of average-sized tunnels doing the same? A middle-aged couple from Bellevue, Washington, would find out the hard way that this creature uses at least one of the manmade structures.

Centered between metropolitan Seattle and the city of Wenatchee, and also less than twenty miles south of the Mt. Baker National Forest, sits Stevens Pass and the old 2.63-mile Cascade Tunnel, abandoned in 1929 after an eight-mile tunnel was built just south, all part of the Central Washington Cascades. The immediate area was also the site of the 1910 Wellington disaster where ninety-six souls lost their lives when two passenger trains were stuck in the area in a blizzard. Both of them were swept off the mountainside in a massive landslide after hours of delays.

I wouldn't find out until much later that this tunnel area has been tagged with names like "the scariest place" and "the creepiest place" in

**Figure 25: The Cascade Tunnel in Washington's Cascade Mountains where two creatures were hiding in 2007. (photo © David Shank)**

America. When I first began to delve into these mysteries by following up on a couple from Bellevue, I had no idea this was going to include haired spooks.

The husband and wife remember the day being hot and humid in the summer of 2007, not even a breeze on that particular July day, even high in the Cascades. They were very quiet on their approach to view the old, worn-down tunnel that was a part of the grim history of 1910.

Nearing the mouth of the old portal and really just taking in a bit of history, the two barely noticed movement inside the tunnel, perhaps twenty-five to thirty feet beyond the entrance. It seemed like nothing more than tree shadows at first, but they soon realized there was definite movement. Stopping, they looked around and saw nothing outside that would cause such an effect. The wife was the first to feel uneasy, and she removed her sunglasses to get a better view of what was going on. Both knew the area was notorious for grizzlies, wolves, and mountain cats, but they had not brought along bear spray or any other defense for their short hike. The couple just stood there, motionless and frightened.

Without being provoked, two enormous creatures exited the tunnel, coming out toward the man and wife, catching them off guard and in utter surprise. The woman called out her husband's name and a curse word or two as the two mountain beings lumbered toward the nearby trees, grunting all the way. The creatures moved with an ever-so-slight crouch, with noticeably bent knees and positive footing on all obstacles. The creatures actually looked at the hikers, though not like a human might. The two creatures didn't run as if they were startled, but the couple remembers that they did not appear to be happy. There was an almost human look of disgust on their faces.

The husband and wife were both white as ghosts and felt dwarfed by the two hairy giants, thanks to their incredible size. What scared the day hikers the most was the fact that everything grew deadly quiet again in an instant. The two beings were still out there and close by. They could feel their presence, as if the creatures were watching them with interest. The woman said she felt traumatized, physically sick to her stomach, and her husband didn't know what to make of any of it. There was absolutely no warning, and it was over in a matter of seconds. He didn't have time to think about possibly dying at the hands of the two rare creatures. The husband was worried about them still being in the immediate area; he feared that they hadn't left and were both lingering there, paying close attention.

It is important to mention that some of the encounters in this book may seem very similar to one another when it comes to what the Sasquatch actually looks like. When I can, I've bypassed the repetitions. These creatures were very similar to most cases.

Once the couple was back home where they felt safe, they had a chance to discuss why the creatures would have been in the tunnel in the first place. The creatures weren't that far into the cavern, and from what the couple remembers, the giants weren't moving around that much, at least not based on the shadows they saw. In reality, it seemed the creatures were simply resting. As I discussed this incident with the couple, we all came to the conclusion that the Sasquatch were cooling off, seeking solace from the blistering afternoon heat, which would be hotter for them since they were covered in hair.

I have had similar experiences regarding the coolness of tunnels. Over the years, during visits to Idaho and Montana, we had gone mountain biking on the Hiawatha Trail, located east of Wallace, Idaho, what was once the old Milwaukee Line but is now a premiere biking trail. On the start of the north side of this route, and going under the Idaho/Montana border, is the almost 1.7-mile Taft Tunnel. The day we rode through on our bikes, the temperatures were in the high nineties, just over 104 degrees when all was said and done. Inside the tunnel, it was considerably cooler, to the point of putting on a light jacket. Then, almost two miles later, we were thrown back out into the heat again. The tunnels are often susceptible to cold-water leaks and seepage, perfect for providing a cool drink to a creature like the Sasquatch when other water sources are scarce. These tunnels drain continuously from cracks and holes, the water cold and satisfying — at least for those living in the wilderness.

The Washington state couple hinted at the convenient water supply as well. After their initial shock subsided, they showed a great deal of interest in the subject. They initially described the creatures moving in their direction as a nightmare gone bad. The gentleman assumed the large beings took the initiative, seeking the quickest escape route. The other journey would have been over 2.6 miles straight through the tunnel, if it wasn't blocked. Also, there was no way to say that a person would not be in the tunnel along the way or outside on the other end.

In the region of the old Cascade Tunnel on Stevens Pass sits one of the littlest towns in the state. Skykomish is to the west, about twelve miles away. The town of Scenic lies to the south. All these locations have had possible Sasquatch vocalizations, but Skykomish, in particular, may lend some further evidence to the Sasquatch and railroad relationship, an incident discussed by a photographer:

> Last winter, Jon B. and I were up near Skykomish when I heard a sound I still can't explain to this day. We were set up to photograph an eastbound train on the Miller River Bridge. Jon elected to park the car near his chosen vantage point and wait inside the car, near the gate to the old quarry. I elected to hike off down the road to try for a different angle. I ended up near the old wooden highway bridge, adjacent to the railroad bridge. It was snowing pretty hard and starting to get dark. All was dead quiet. I got my camera set up and settled in to wait. I had been standing there for about twenty minutes when, all of a sudden, I heard a God-awful howl/roar/scream come echoing out of the quarry just to the south of my position. I have never heard anything like it before or since. It kind of made my blood run cold. With all the trees and brush around there, I couldn't actually see where the

sound had come from — just somewhere back in the quarry site. I was thinking about leaving at that point. But, moments later, the train we had been waiting for showed up. So I got my shot and headed back to the car. When I returned, I asked Jon if he had heard anything. He said he hadn't. He had been in the car the whole time with the windows rolled up. I looked around the entrance to the quarry for any sign or tracks. The gate was locked. There were no tracks in the snow or any sign that anyone had been there.

Was this a Bigfoot? Who knows? But it was a weird experience.

## Kettle Valley Railway

On the topic of abandoned railroad lines, the town of Princeton has had some events through the years. The Kettle Valley Railway cycling route was once a working railway, but now is used by biking enthusiasts, as well as others. The entire route is hundreds of miles long from start to finish, the west leg ending around Hope, British Columbia.

I had the opportunity to touch base with one of two authors of *Cycling the Kettle Valley Railway*, by Dan and Sandra Langford. Campfire stories of Sasquatch often entertained those on a bicycling excursion, and Dan was kind enough to allow a message on their *Cycling the KVR* website concerning the subject of the creature. Always on the lookout for sincere individuals out there who are not overly shy about what they may have encountered, I left my contact information.

Still, as always, I did have to put the flour through a sifter. Given the number of people who ride the KVR, including those who live on or near the line, there was little said of such a creature. A person or family could live in that region their whole life and hear or see nothing out of the ordinary. Then, out of the blue, someone who was just visiting would immediately be drawn to the Sasquatch phenomenon. Four such people tell their stories. The two couples weren't locals, just visitors passing through the valley, one duo biking and the other exploring. For them, these encounters brought a whole new meaning to "supernatural British Columbia." The couples were not originally associated with one another, but they would end up learning firsthand about a giant race of creatures that still secretly maneuver through the forests of the Tulameen and Coalmont areas.

**Figure 26: The Kettle Valley Railway corridor where a couple of bikers happened upon a Sasquatch near the old railway tunnel to the left of the pavilion in the picture. (photo © Dan Langford)**

In the late summer of 2007, a few leaves were already on the ground in the mountains. A man slowly traveled by bike through a section of the Princeton subdivision with his girlfriend. They planned to finish their trip at Merritt, where a friend with a vehicle would meet them, after initially dropping the couple off at a starting point south of Princeton. The fellow's girlfriend was very hesitant to tell her story at first. She'd gone bicycling with him that day, and she wanted nothing to do with what they saw from a distance below the Tulameen Bluffs along the KVR corridor.

The couple described what they thought was a black bear stooping over and tinkering with things on the ground not too far from the river, seemingly unaware of the pedaling riders coming to a complete halt at the sight of it. As the animal went back and forth with its pickings, there was never a balance problem even when it bent over time and time again and grabbed for things.

**Figure 27: The Tulameen Bluffs area where a holidaying couple chased a Bigfoot in 2001. (photo © Dan Langford)**

The posture and control of body were what attracted the bikers. When the creature spotted the two, it quickly abandoned its search and walked off into the woods a ways away, only to be swallowed up by the forest. The couple agreed that the size of this creature was over eight and a half feet tall, fully standing. It wasn't a pretty sight. The animal was scraggly, as if the damn thing had rolled down a mountainside, finishing that off with a run through briar bushes. "It looked beat up," the guy said, and his girlfriend chimed in, "It looked like the man in the suit years ago." At such an announcement, I had to wonder what the woman had heard or seen. They were both good sports about it, all things considered.

The second couple had a similar experience six years prior, in the summer of 2001. They had parked the car somewhere up top, though they couldn't remember the exact location, on one of the few places to pull over on the treacherous road to Tulameen, British Columbia. They saw what they at first took for a large black bear. This husband and wife were adventurers that day, their initial goal being to lodge in the Tulameen area and spend a day or two around Otter Lake, renting something afloat and maybe doing some horseback riding if they had time. They considered themselves gringos from the city, and while they ended up sore, it had nothing to do with being on horseback.

On the road that day, the two of them thought they were witnessing an upright, blackish bear pushing its luck near the roadway up ahead. They were amazed that it stood on its hind legs for that long. Their idea of the creature changed quickly when the animal moved down slope in a fully standing position. They then found themselves cautiously — or perhaps crazily — following the creature on foot from what they considered to be a safe distance. The couple mentioned that this was completely out of character for them, as few people would actually pursue a bear in its natural habitat. Yet there they were, following something even bigger. It defied logic. The woman admitted following her husband rather than the animal. She wouldn't let him go alone, and she wasn't about to stay at the car by herself. In their haste, the doors were unlocked, her purse was lying on the front seat in full view, and the windows were down. They laughed when I mentioned that the creature might have been a thief. Ultimately, they were away from their vehicle for over thirty-five minutes. They didn't even pay any mind to whether they had the car keys, as they were utterly mesmerized by what their eyes beheld.

They could hear the creature moving down the rather steep hill. Rocks and pebbles tumbled, and they could see the creature several times as it trekked away. It attacked the hill as a man would: slightly angled, long arms ready for a spill, weight poised back, but covering an incredible amount of ground for such a tall beast on a downward slope.

Once the hurrying creature hit level ground down by the river and the old railroad line that heads along that bluff, it seemed to head for a certain point at the edge of the woods. The couple was far behind, and as much as they'd tried to keep up their pursuit, it was over. They looked themselves over and saw dirt, dust, and red marks on their bodies, the reward for trying to follow a forest legend.

I asked each couple about tracks left on the variety of ground surfaces that the creatures crossed in these encounters. Both couples were so spellbound by the sight that they didn't even think to look for possible tracks left by the Sasquatch.

## More Sightings

The railroad connection with the Sasquatch involves many things. For instance, these stories have to be weighed against topographical areas and mapping systems. The ideas of waterways and water supply around the railroads were investigated, and the idea of available food supplies also played a part. The railroads provided much to the Sasquatch.

Reports of these creatures wandering many of the rail lines throughout North America have been documented from many sources, a few of which are as follows:

In the same general area as the Ruby Creek incident, a native gentleman and Adaline August confronted a Sasquatch while walking along the railroad tracks, the giant coming toward them.

In British Columbia, the creature was spotted along the Canadian National Railway line at Laidlaw, west of Hope.

Still in Canada, up in northern Ontario, three individuals investigated tracks of the Sasquatch, also beside railroad tracks, since train engineers were involved in the sightings.

Washington's Pierce County is our next brief stop, near the town of Elbe. A Sasquatch stepped out in front of an individual walking along the railroad tracks. The environment at the time hosted two sets of railroad tracks, with an abandoned boxcar on one set.

Another sighting in Washington, in Skamania County near Stevenson, saw a Sasquatch climb a railroad bed.

The Florida East Coast Railway line near St. Augustine was the location of a sighting of a creature in a semi-crouched position, located in the middle of the tracks. Two persons on horseback spotted it after they had passed.

In Canadian County, Oklahoma, on Cheyenne and Arapaho tribal land, a father and two sons stopped at a railway crossing. Using binoculars, they spotted two Sasquatch down the tracks.

In 1998, two teenagers walking along the Wisconsin Central Railroad line, near Manitowoc, heard a horrifying scream. They then saw a large creature rise behind them. When it began to move toward them, the two fled.

Continuing around the country, in Maryland, dating back to 1973, a Sasquatch was spotted by three separate individuals near railroad tracks. This took place at Sykesville, in Carroll County, behind Schoolhouse Road.

In 1988, between Mineral City and Sandyville, Ohio, four individuals had planned to visit an old collapsed train tunnel, including tracks that had been removed. In the deep brush nearby, a huge creature was observed at a fairly close range. This took place in Tuscarawas County.

At the entrance to a man's property in Pennsylvania, he stopped his vehicle at the gate and looked down the lonesome tracks, only to witness a creature with long hair, between seven and eight feet tall. Seeing the man, the animal walked into the waiting bush. Seconds later, deer were chased out across the tracks.

## Lucia Falls Road

Still stoking the fire for the case of a flesh-and-blood creature from the bowels of the forest is a gentleman's story featured on the Bigfoot Encounters Website, courtesy of researcher/writer Bobbie Short, reiterating the creature's affection for railroads:

> Clark County, Washington, August 2006
>
> My brother-in-law and I were headed east on Lucia Falls Road NE when we saw something on our left, sort of like it might have been a shooting star. It was still light outside, but barely. He thought it might have been a light airplane crashing (he was a medic), so we pulled over to the side of the road and got out of the truck and listened but heard nothing — no cries for help, no sounds of metal burning… just silence.
>
> This area is due south of the city of Yacolt and east of Lewisville, Washington, but only a stone's throw from Moulton Falls State Park proper.
>
> We had been over on Yacolt Mountain Road earlier and had come down this way via NE Kelly Road, where it intersects with Lucia Falls Road.
>
> Thinking we should help if it was a plane down, we worked our way through the brush and trees to where the railroad tracks parallel Lucia Falls Road, and I told him one of us better run back and get a flashlight in case it was a downed plane and somebody is hurt. He yelled that he was going on ahead to see if he could find the source of the flash of light and look for survivors.
>
> At this point, I stopped and turned around real quick to race back to the truck. I have a high-powered spotlight that is portable in the back, and my mind was on hoping the batteries were still good.

When I turned to make my way back to the truck, I could have sworn I saw a big man higher up on the road near the truck, just standing there, but I caught my foot, looked down for a minute to get a better grasp on where I was stepping, and when I looked up again he wasn't there. I called out to him but got no reply.

Limping a little, I finally got to the truck. The batteries were working fine, and it was almost completely dark by this time. I grabbed my wife's cell phone off the seat, tucked it into my pocket, shouldered a loop of rope just in case, and grabbed the lantern. I don't remember seeing another car on the roadway there, but I remembered wondering where this man had come from that I had seen on my way up from below the apron of road on my way up to the truck. He was nowhere in sight.

I hurried on to catch my brother-in-law and wondered where he was, because by now I was barely finding my way, and it was getting darker. I called out to him, but I got no answer.

I moved on slowly toward where I thought I had left him at the railroad tracks and looked both ways on the track but didn't see anything or my brother-in-law. I called out again and listened intently. There was no sound of anything — not wind, not crickets. So I cupped my hands around my mouth and called out my brother-in-law's name in both directions of the railroad tracks, but I heard nothing, saw nothing, and began to wonder if that man figure upon the road was him a few minutes ago, but I couldn't figure how he would have gotten there from where I left him.

I picked up a rock and placed it in a strategic spot on the rail of the tracks to mark where I should head for the road and began walking east on the railroad tracks, aiming my lantern to the left and right of me looking for him. Now I was thinking something happened to him because he wasn't answering.

Darkness fell quickly as I pressed on, uncertain that I was going in the right direction for the flash we thought we saw. I don't know how far I walked on those tracks, but my ankle was beginning to hurt, so I stopped to loosen the strings on my shoe and call out for John again.

Still no answer, and I was growing concerned. I wondered, Should I go back and wait at the truck or press on? I listened but heard nothing but the sound of my own breathing. I checked my watch; it was already after eight in the evening. I called out for John again, then turned to head back to the truck to phone home when I remembered I had my wife's cell phone in my pocket.

The lantern scanned the tracks and terrain left and right of the tracks as I came back upon the marker rock I had placed on the rails. No sign of John, but I thought maybe he went in the other direction, so I left the marker rock to the road and walked the tracks in the other direction for about fifteen minutes, calling out for him all the while. About the only thing I noticed was the quiet. Where was my damn brother-in-law?

It was roughly nine at night now and there was no sign of John, but I didn't want to leave him behind. I sat down and pulled out the cell phone and dialed home. I tried to explain where I was and what had happened, but I couldn't explain where John had wandered off to, and I told the gals that I wasn't leaving there without him. Just as I was about to hang up, I heard footsteps coming and the disturbance of gravel on the railroad ties.

I flashed the lantern around and down the tracks where I heard the footsteps and thought I saw John coming. "John?" I yelled out several times, and then I told the girls he was coming and hung up the phone.

John looked a mess.

"Where you been, buddy?" I asked.

He reached out and put his big arms around my neck and said he was glad to see me.

"I didn't know you went in this direction, bud. Where you been, and what happened to you?"

He just hung on to me and said, "Can we get me back to the truck right now?"

I asked, "Are you hurt?"

"No," John replied, "just scared shitless."

"What happened? You've been gone over an hour."

We started walking back toward where I had the marker rock on the rails John sort of leaning on me.

"Man, you're not going to believe this."

"Believe what?" I asked. "What the hell's going on with you, bud?"

"I saw something," he said, "something huge."

"Yeah? What? Is there a plane crash?" I asked.

"I gotta sit down," he groaned. "My heart's coming out of my chest, and, man, I didn't see any plane."

We walked with arms around one another's shoulders till we got back to my marker rock to the road, sat down in the gravel, and turned off the lantern.

John sat there in the dark for a few minutes with his head down between his knees, trying to collect himself. He was visibly shaken. He told me there was something out there. He said, "Something man-shaped, very tall but it looked like the thing had hair on it, and then I lost enough light to tell much other than it stood off to the side of the tracks in a hulking manner, me facing it and it facing me for a long time. I heard it breathing, I swear I heard the thing breathing and I froze. Man, I just froze stiff. My mind shut down, and I couldn't think what to do.

"I thought I was seeing things," he continued. "It was something nightmares are made out of, and I don't recall I ever saw anything or a man that big before, and I never want to see anything like that again. I started to back up and run, but I couldn't see well — kept tripping on the rails, crossties, and such and falling down. I think I'm all skinned up. Let's get home."

Back home, he recounted the same story to the girls. He was all cut up on the knees, skinned up and bleeding, with one bad place on the side of his right rib, where he said he fell on something, maybe a railroad railing or one of the ties.

My brother-in-law is a big man, tall, and he describes this thing he saw as "huge and hairy." Then I started wondering about the dark figure I saw on the road that I called out to when I went back for the flashlights.

My son and I went back to the area the next morning and walked two miles in either direction but found nothing — no sign of any plane down, no fire, no nothing. From John's description, we thought maybe he had a meeting with a Sasquatch, but we aren't sure. We never did know what the flash of light was.

Whatever it was scared him, and he's a seasoned hunter, son of a slew of seasoned hunters, and he doesn't drink. So I don't know what he saw. I didn't see or hear anything other than the

> figure on the road, but I believe my brother-in-law did, and he believes it must have been a Sasquatch.
>
> That is the story, little lady, and ma'am, you can do with it whatever you like. My name is Marshall. I've lived in this area all my life, and so has my wife. This was a first. [BS1]

And so it continued with these types of reports on the Sasquatch, one story after another about the creature being around areas of railroad ties and driven spikes.

## Finding a Sasquatch on the Rails

The Humane Society of the United States and the Urban Wildlife Research Centre arrived at a realistic figure of one million animals killed every single day on American highways — every day! I find this incredible. Just think about those numbers for a moment. Have you ever smelled a skunk at highway speed? Chances are, it wasn't living. Other creatures that are maimed and don't die on the highways right away may not be counted in the numbers. This may not include railroad strikes, where the Sasquatch seem to roam.

With those incredible numbers, it is highly possible that the Sasquatch is a creature of opportunity. We will take this one step further with the rails-to-smorgasbord idea.

The railroad system in North America is by no means infallible. From thousands upon thousands of freight cars and hopper compartment cars, food substances such as grain, wheat, canola, and fruits and vegetables spill or leak along the miles and miles of track — so much so that some cars reach their destinations empty, entirely spilled along the routes. This occurs as a result of faulty bottom latches, improper closing and loading techniques, and just plain negligence when it comes to proper maintenance and repairs. These chronic spillages sometimes last for hundreds of miles, luring unsuspecting animals to feed along the tracks, many times resulting in their deaths. When the carcasses of trackside kills lie there, this draws in other scavenging animals that are also killed for their efforts, especially by fast-moving passenger trains. The Sasquatch could definitely play a role in this train-induced feeding frenzy. Whether or not the primate is interested in the initial food droppings from the cars begs further investigation, but animal deaths along these train routes hold continuous promise for the bipedal giant. In many places animal and bird species return to the tracks on a daily basis, especially in the spring and winter, when food may be somewhat scarce in certain geographical locations. Animals rewarded once or twice with goodies like grain and wheat will certainly seek the trackside rewards, even when spills are minimal. The creatures of numerous sizes will go looking for a free meal whether it is present or not, a habit forming in their bellies. Really, it's no wonder that the Sasquatch would visit the railroads frequently to take part in the buffet.

Under seasonal reasoning, using the Canadian winter as an example, kills of animals such as deer, elk, moose, and bighorn sheep drop considerably in May, June, July, and August. The killing of scavengers and carnivores, such as the bear, coyote, wolf, cougar, and eagle, is considerably less in all those months, and also September. This would make sense, as the carnivores have an extra month in which to scavenge. Both groups spend less time on the tracks in the summer months. With the sightings of the Sasquatch reported by train personnel and others, one would assume the hobo creature uses all these avenues to hunt and feed. It would be easy pickings for such a quick giant. Coincidentally, the most common scavenging birds observed at animal kills alongside tracks were the raven and the crow. We know that the Sasquatch has been seen with these avian messengers.

During the cold season, which sometimes extends for what could be eight or nine months in these mountain regions, the plowed railroad corridors would look quite attractive for the journeys of any ground-traveling animal. With the snow deep and food sources challenged, animal behavior will dictate drastic measures in the mountains. Good or bad, animals figure out any possible solution to a problem; you can bet the thinking Sasquatch is way ahead of them. Sasquatch corpses are not among those found along the tracks — at least not as of late.

Let's look at what has been found. Wildlife identification was done by personnel from a number of different backgrounds, including the Canadian Pacific Railway. Over 525 wild animals were hit and killed by trains in just Banff and Yoho National Parks since 1981. The Canadian National Railway reports over 968 ungulates, 44 black bears, 20 wolves, 11 grizzlies, and 2 cougars killed in Jasper National Park since 1980. And in just a two-year period, between 1994 and 1996, thirteen black bears paid the price along a short nine-mile stretch in Glacier National Park on the British Columbia side. As I was reviewing this manuscript in 2010, bears were being killed on the rails in Alberta. You can imagine what the entire number would be throughout North America. Again, we must remember the many that limp away and are never seen again. These statistics also fail to include livestock that roam onto the tracks.

The kill process compounds itself. As an example, if a smaller creature is hit by a freight train, a larger animal may come along to prey on it. This animal may be hit by another passing train. Sadly, an even larger carnivore comes a-calling, only to pay the price for what should have been an easy meal. If the first or second dead animals have been thrown clear of the tracks, other predators will be lucky, but with one or two dead animals and a third animal's attention concentrating on its feeding, the Sasquatch could quickly get the notion to use these scenarios. Concerning the whole affair involving rough terrain, a heavy snow, and the mental capacity of the Sasquatch, the creature may be able to calculate the possibilities in a number of given situations.

Involving the idea of the kills themselves, I've seen a mother black bear dead along the tracks in Alberta, her cubs remaining at her side. The bears were there because of grain dropped along the line.

One last note about food spoilage in regard to the railroads, and we shall again focus on the Kettle Valley Railway line as a part of the Princeton area. The 1,063-foot tunnel at Princeton, built by Vancouver, Victoria, and Eastern (VV&E) Railway in 1910, sat just west of what was Princeton's rail yards years ago. Much has changed since then, and that stretch of the KVR track was permanently shut down around 1962. The next interesting thing to note was that more than 14,000 train cars carrying fruit left the Okanagan every year, working these railway lines to the West Coast. Leaking, damaged, and malfunctioning railcars were a problem then as today, so perishable goods may have fallen through the cracks — literally. Aboriginal influence in the area talked of relatives knowing of such things — of the spoilage and loss on the KVR track. Once that was exhausted, the Sasquatch may have continued to use the system to get close to town. Our mother's encounter with the Sasquatch was just over a mile and a half from the KVR line. The creature could have easily stuck to that tract of heavily treed land that went practically to our doorstep at Harold Avenue.

# *10. Seeing Would Be Believing*

We must have compassion for researchers in a field without a specimen, either living or deceased. The Sasquatch phenomenon is this kind of research. Bigfoot is evidently almost everywhere throughout Canada and the United States, yet there are no examples to prove that they exist. Still, thousands of sane individuals trust in what's available, the slowly mounting evidence of the Sasquatch's ability to hide. The creature continues to remain as untouchable as the wind.

As I've already described, I personally stood in the tracks of *something* that cold April morning, those steps (not stride) between five and six feet apart. Still there are those who claim misidentification or, even worse, wishful thinking, imagination, and outright lies. And this comes from presumably open-minded individuals. All I can do is report what my brother and I saw and provide more reports from others who have witnessed the same sort of creature.

## Keith Foster's Reports

Here are reports gathered by another individual who had a view of what is secretly moving around in the forest. While his life seems to be led by logic, the track of the Sasquatch defies such thoughts. Keith Foster has stood next to the footprints of a wilderness giant and found reports from others who have done the same.

> I am a bowhunter of thirty years' big-game experiences. I love wilderness areas and places few other humans ever wander, especially when seeking places to fish for big trout in timberline lakes. I found a set of a couple dozen seventeen-inch-long Sasquatch tracks in the South San Juan Wilderness, across a dirt slide that piqued my interest in the possibilities. Who would fake

seventeen-inch, humanlike tracks in such a remote area? So, in spite of how ridiculous the notion of Sasquatch seemed to me and others, I started collecting sightings from other bowhunters and eventually got six sightings and track find reports from Colorado hunting guides and outfitters. Some of these sightings by guides were long-term daytime sightings, one of which was from less than thirty yards' distance in broad daylight while the hunting guide was bugling for elk. He said the animal stepped in full view before detecting its mistake.

Another guide in Colorado watched a Sasquatch sunning itself by a beaver pool for over ten minutes through binoculars at a range of approximately 125 yards — long enough and close enough to see details of the face. JD's descriptions generally indicated that it had a gorilla face, but with nostrils lower down closer to the mouth and not flared — kind of like a squished-down human nose. His sighting took place near Raspberry Mountain. JD was very serious and straightforward about the encounter.

Another bowhunter contacted me and said he found some odd scat that appeared to have been latrined over a period of time. The very outsized scat he described, all in one area, did not fit the norm for any other creature, so perhaps he had accidentally happened upon a Sasquatch latrine. Other theories are that since Sasquatch is a predator, it buries its feces like a cat or covers it somehow with deadfall or something. It may even defecate in running water.

I get a little tingle up the spine when sitting alone at night in the quiet forest on a cold north slope of dense forest far from any other human. My senses are at their highest, and I am keen to every forest sound. Step falls of animals become louder, so much bigger than they are in daylight. I feel very alive but also out of place. I feel like I belong there but also like an intruder. I didn't feel that way until after I found those huge tracks that fit the Sasquatch mold in that beloved, remote, deep forest habitat. Now I live in a world with something that makes huge, humanlike tracks in a place where before I only found elk and deer tracks and an occasional bear track. If a 1,000 pound, nine-foot-tall ape comes walking into your Colorado wilderness world some night, it will make the forest nights more interesting from then on.

In regard to Sasquatch vocalizations, my sons and I heard what may have been a Sasquatch screaming at us in the South San Juan Wilderness. The sound was different than any other animal sound I have ever heard and much louder. The source seemed to be about 100 yards from us, with willows between us and the sound maker. It's hard to describe the very loud sound, but it sounded kind of like car tires peeling out on dry concrete, with kind of a gravelly nature to it — a really scary-sounding noise to hear in the forest at close range. It also had a resounding nature to it, which we could feel as well as hear, similar to the way you can actually feel an African lion's roar when it is close by. Since we did not see what was screaming, we can't really say it was a Sasquatch, but I have no idea what else it could have been. Some of the recordings of supposed Sasquatch noises sound very similar to what we heard, and others don't.

AH, of *Traditional Bowhunter Magazine*, had a similar incident of a screamer south of Silverton. South of there is where four bowhunters reported catching a Sasquatch out in the open in the Twin Sisters area. They all reported the same well-furred, heavily muscled, manlike creature that ran in full view of them for some 200 yards across open ground while they were there elk hunting.

I have talked to at least a couple dozen hunters in Colorado, both hunters and bowhunters, who have reported seeing Sasquatch in that state. Most times, the Sasquatch was in firearm range and in several cases, the Sasquatch was within bow range. None of these hunters even began to think about shooting such a manlike creature.

I think back still to the article from the 1880s Leadville, Colorado, newspaper and how miners were very scared of a Sasquatch in a stream drainage in what is now the Holy Cross Wilderness. A good, experienced hunter went into the area to put an end to the monster and was unsuccessful in his hunt.

The Jemez Pueblo Indians came into the area of southern Colorado and northern New Mexico in the early fourteenth century and have plenty of tales and myths of giant hairy beasts encountered in the high ponderosa forests in the very areas where I found just such tracks in 1993. They even named at least one pueblo city after the man-creature. My research in that area found that a government bear hunter named Willford had encountered a huge, upright-walking bear of some sort in that same area in the 1870s. He also had stories of how the native Indians would not go into certain areas because of the creature.

Two Wyoming biologists that have reported seeing Sasquatch themselves in Wyoming had their personal experiences in the 1970s and 1980s. One of the biologists, recently retired from the Wyoming Game Department, has gone partially public with his experience. He was their bighorn sheep field biologist and spent time in tents at timberline areas doing field study. The other biologist, who saw a Sasquatch in open ground and somewhat chased it with his vehicle, causing it to break through a split-rail fence and leave behind tracks and hair samples, still works for the state of Wyoming and has not gone public.

If the Patterson film is genuine, then that musculature depiction indicates that it can possibly walk all day long, uphill and downhill, at over five miles per hour.

One sighting on the Colorado/New Mexico border was by a professional veterinarian from the Chama area, who said he watched a huge Sasquatch walk up a rockslide just off Highway 17. He said it rarely touched the rocks with its hands and walked steadily up the rockslide without stopping once. It ascended the slide in less than ten minutes. The veterinarian went back to the location the next day to try and find any tracks below and above the slide on the creature's route. He said it took him about an hour, with several rest breaks, to climb the same rockslide. He was just as impressed, excited really, with the creature's physical ability as he was with the creature itself.

When we look at the tracks, there are also many indications of extreme flexibility lengthwise. They can evidently bend their feet more than we can — similar, I suppose, to how we can bend our hands, only not quite so extreme because of the thickness of the pad evident on the bottom of the Sasquatch foot.

A few years ago, I investigated a set of nineteen-inch tracks along the Eagle River that were found by fishermen. Another set had been found by fishermen near Gypsum, about seven miles from the set I investigated in the same time frame. The local Colorado Division of Wildlife biologist, local law enforcement, and I came to the conclusion that that set of tracks was genuine and not hoaxed. Several foot-expert anthropologists also came to that conclusion.

Track finds and sightings indicate that there are three main areas in Colorado that host the Sasquatch. They are the South San Juan wilderness and adjacent national forests, the Holy Cross Wilderness and adjacent forests, and the Lost Creek wilderness and forest areas, especially where elk densities are highest in those three given areas. Tracks of the Sasquatch have been found and recorded in sizes up to twenty-two inches.

The Sasquatch likes to spend its days in cool or cold environments and hates the heat. It will stick to deep forest, where elk are going or returning from bedding areas. The creature knows many human habits and also elk habits. In summer, it likes heavily forested north slope exposures because they are up to ten degrees cooler than other places in the mountains. Streams seem to be part of their travel routes.

In spite of the creature's size and weight, they sometimes only make tracks about as deep as barefooted human or bear tracks in any type of soil, simply because their feet are so big. Some of the tracks I have investigated were every bit as deep as human tracks, yet so much larger, that if they were faked, the hoaxer would have had to be wearing a 700-pound backpack and taking steps over forty-eight inches long while walking uphill. Tracks even showed flexibility in the toes and such.

I hope someday that some law enforcement officer finds good, fresh tracks and has the gumption to try and use some resources to follow them to the end. Officer JTJ almost did just that with two sets of Sasquatch tracks in snow and mud about fourteen years ago, southwest of Antonito, Colorado. He was on his own and in unofficial capacity. What he picked up was video of the tracks available, along with a lot of exercise. Those tracks were nineteen and twenty-one inches long, respectively. That is huge for tracks, and it can be pretty scary looking. No wonder officer JTJ eventually gave up following those two sets of tracks, as he was probably afraid of finding the things that made them. I'm not sure I want to come face to face with one of them either, but curiosity would push me on, I think. In the officer's case, the tracks were found at the edge of the forest, on the backside of a woman's pasture, while she was out trying to photograph mule deer. She was the officer's niece, so she called him to look at the tracks on the property. He described them as having a step of over forty-eight inches even while walking slightly uphill. The deputy said that in the better tracks in the mud, he could even see where the tracks showed chisel-like toenail imprints — the Sasquatch evidently curling the toes downward into the mud to get a grip when walking uphill in slippery conditions.

Sasquatch may hunt cooperatively with each other at times as well. In the winter of 1993, a rancher living near San Antonio Peak in northern New Mexico reported watching two Sasquatch hunting a herd of elk together. The elk were grazing in an open sage area adjacent to the forest edge near the rancher's house. He noticed a Sasquatch stalking up on the herd and another Sasquatch on the opposite side of the herd waiting, unmoving. The rancher had enough time to grab binoculars and watch from the house. Both these creatures, according to the rancher, were bulkier in size than the elk they were attempting to catch. As the stalking Sasquatch approached the herd, the elk bolted in the direction of the hiding companion, but they failed in catching one of the animals, and eventually both moved off into the woods. This event occurred within a week or so, and in the same general area where the deputy had recorded the sets of tracks — which may lend credibility to the rancher's story.

How would a Sasquatch catch an elk? They are not as quick out of the starting block as, say, smaller deer. I have sat within a few feet of the downwind side of an elk trail and had whole herds trickle past without the least knowledge that I was there. With the size, strength, and agility of the Sasquatch, it would be a rather simple task at times to take two quick steps and grab a passing elk, snap the neck, or break the back legs.

Because Sasquatch intelligence is partly geared around pattern of movement, it would naturally be very good at patterning the natural movements of humans who travel its territory. The same would go for animals. Sasquatch also knows where man hates to travel mostly, such as timber heavily strewn with deadfalls. That is where Sasquatch likely spend their rest time: in the horrible stuff, with heavy cover.

> Concerning the human element, several different motorists reported a Sasquatch walking near the edge of the highway during a heavy snowstorm, right on Kenosha Pass, as reported to me by a sheriff's deputy who responded to the numerous calls. Tracks were found by a coyote hunter nine miles southeast of Kenosha Pass on Long Gulch.

These kinds of experiences happen on a regular basis, it would seem, and many of these stories are very informative, deepening the controversy.

## Chris Hegg's Story

Chris Hegg, from Nevada, offered a tracking story that took place in the area of Pilot Mountain, near Hawthorne. The western Nevada man wrote the following two emails to his California friend.

> May 9, 2010: We just had snow prints at the local mine, with photos. I almost went with my friends to check them out but didn't. When I was a kid, some geologist friends of mine got a print and photos of snow prints going up and over the top of Pilot Mountain. I'm trying to get those now.
>
> May 10, 2010: I'll forward the picture. They followed the tracks past a steep wash, and it maintained the same stride around trees, flat, up, or down. They could not jump the same stride except going downhill! In the snow, jumping the stride was impossible.
>
> Four more tracks, including one young one's prints, about a size 8 in men's shoes, stepped over the barbed-wire fence and continued through the mine, heading uphill east, just south of Lucky Boy Pass Road. My friend and his son saw where the trails separated. The one they followed turned right beside the road, going around the mine fence, followed a deer track, and continued to where my friend and his son turned back. It went some distance into the forest and uphill. They followed a mile uphill in three-foot-deep snow and ran out of energy. They could see them going east up the mountain, at least another 500 feet, and keep going. They figured if someone was faking it, they would have run out of energy far earlier. They saw no evidence of stilts, tripping, or other identifying marks in the snow. The mine geologist who told us about it that morning followed the

> other tracks through the mine until the road stopped and the footprints kept going; the prints remained for some weeks. I hunted a week before, about a mile from there, with my snow poles and snowshoes, and I could not keep even a normal pace due to the snow being so powdery.

Two months later, Chris Hegg contacted me again to inform me that the creature he was trying to locate in western Nevada, southwest of Hawthorne, was still hanging around. Below is what he had to say about his findings in July of 2010:

> July 14, 2010: Wow! Hold the presses! Have I got much more info for you on the Bigfoot here! I have two more stories and possibly some more snow photos of those last tracks. One addition is the same: Mine, where the photo was taken, has tons of animals running all over it, and they won't leave to go back into the mountains. Mountain lions, deer, antelope, and such are inside the fence, and nobody has ever seen anything like it!
>
> Better yet, on our property only a mile from there, my friend is protecting some Bigfoot tracks by his pond. Beyond that, those tracks were put down after a rain eroded older tracks still in place at the time. On top of that, my co-worker, V.L., with several friends hunting at the same time as those first tracks were spotted, saw a super fast-moving, darker brown, streamlined, hair-covered, massive shape moving over a ridgeline just two miles due north of the track spot I'd completely forgot about. They said it was just shy of a bear's size, and it moved around thirty MPH, on what looked like all four legs, due to the slick, smooth, wavy motion of its back, but they are unsure if it was on all fours. We'll be in the area and have print photos Friday. I will be back to make a cast Sunday or so.
>
> July 18, 2010: Pretty exciting if they are hanging around. To me, it was worth dismissing as a one-time thing I'd never see again, but now this! I'm putting my trail-cam at the ponds as well. Maybe I'll get something. I'm home and heading up.

## Peter Antonick's Story

Peter Antonick saw something strange many years earlier around 1958, when he was just a youngster at Camp Latona, British Columbia, on the north end of Gambier Island in Howe Sound. I also happened to know Peter when we both worked for Weyerhaeuser Lumber. He'd been a millwright in those days.

Peter attended the Catholic camp for ten to thirteen-year-old boys and girls. He remembered leaving from Horseshoe Bay by ferry to get to the isolated camp. Once situated at Latona, approximately twenty-six individuals went on a small boating day trip to what would be a guided hike, after the half-hour boat ride from home base to what Peter thinks might have been part of the mainland.

He remembers being on a wide trail that day, then walking across a creek. A few youngsters spent time on some fallen trees. They ran across some boughs that they took notice of and figured they might have been some kind of shelter. Some thought the previous kids from camp had constructed it.

Then, without warning, they all heard a loud, weird noise coming from above them. The hairy-armed creatures began throwing rocks and small logs, ten feet or smaller, freaking everyone out. Even their guiding instructor was nervous, and for safety reasons, he ushered them out of there. Peter remembers an unusual smell in the air.

One thirteen-year-old boy went back up, surmising that it was some kind of phony bologna that the camp was putting on. The instructor tried to get them all safely back to the boat, but that stubborn boy went back up the trail. He returned shortly with a bloody leg, having been hit by a thrown rock. Peter Antonick remembers that there wasn't much said about any of it back at camp, not by the priest or anyone else.

Peter is a good-natured, avid outdoorsman. He has hunted for years in the Princeton area and studies tracks. He admits he has never seen large footprints like those of the Sasquatch, but he has heard of the giant. His neighbor, Stan, stated that there'd been a Sasquatch up in the Whipsaw Creek area over the years, west of Princeton. Peter talked about two men who went missing; neither was ever found, even after an extensive search of the Whipsaw. Whether that was related to the Sasquatch or not, we'll likely never know.

Another person had heard of huge barefoot prints being found in regions of this untamed area where I had found fossil specimens of bugs, leaves, and fish with a friend when I was younger. The tracker, who had witnessed the sixteen-inch footprints, commented on a third individual who'd gone missing in the Whipsaw region, never to be seen again. He enjoyed a good mystery, but mentioned that he didn't want to become a statistic.

## More Personal Stories

If the Sasquatch is ever captured, dead or alive, or even a piece of such a primate is displayed, this would set off a barrage of media that would spread faster than a tsunami. It would also allow people to come forward to share their experiences concerning the forest dweller. There would no longer be the problem of embarrassment. Below are the tales of four more individuals who were willing to come forward before a capture, finished off with an honorable mention.

### Story One

I decided to go to the Shenandoah National Forest in the Blue Ridge Mountains. I turned and found my way up to the Thornton Gap. I put on my pack and started down the trail with the sun blazing high and hot and not a cloud in the blue sky, which helped make my pack not seem so heavy. I walked for about a one and a half hours, up and down through the mountains, looking for a campsite, until I came to an area where a great forest fire had run rampant. I was perspiring and needed to take a break, so I decided to skirt off the path. I found this excellent area just a little bigger than my tent, with a beautiful view of the mountains. The ground was nice and soft, and I started to think maybe it might be a good place to make camp for the night, as I hadn't seen a soul. I stayed there, but on one night, I had a particular scary encounter.

On that night at dusk, a raven took up residence in a nearby tree and cawed for around an hour. I was lying in bed looking up at the night glow. At night, the animals who found my campsite looked for food at dusk, so I could hear them every night. I recognized them as owls, raccoons, and such, but on that night, it suddenly got very quiet. I heard claws or hands grasping at my sack of food that was high in the tree, and I thought an owl must have investigated.

But my heart started to race; I could sense something was wrong. I became afraid, for I was truly alone, and nobody in the world cared. Suddenly, I saw something race up to my tent door, completely silent, in some sort of super-fast motion — a dark shadow, just hovering there, waiting. It was about five feet tall and lean but roughly humanoid. I thought it might be a person or bear, but it didn't make any sound, and I couldn't hear breathing. I was going to take a peek out of my tent door, which was closed up against the cold, but a voice in my head said, "Don't do it! It's a Windigo." I thought it a very odd reference because I'd only heard Native Americans using that term once or twice before, and I didn't really know what it meant. I closed my eyes and tried not to feed the fear. When I opened my eyes again, everything was back to normal, so I did manage to get to sleep.

I woke up the next morning at dawn. It was time to go. I guess it must have been a dream or something because there were no tracks by my tent, whereas the other animals on previous nights had left tracks. I have a special method for keeping the food animal-proof, so it was fine, though there were lots of smudged prints on the pack.

## Story Two

You know, I have a story, but I don't like to tell it because it is always followed by the same, "What were you smoking?" "Yeah, right," and calls of B.S. But a group of Boy Scouts and I all saw something on a cliff overlooking us on a river during a fifty-mile raft trip in the late 1980s in Oregon.

We were rafting the Grande Ronde River in northeast Oregon, southwest Idaho. There was a group of about fifteen Scouts and four adults along on the trip. I and five others were in the last raft of a three-raft train going through an S-curve canyon, when the Scout leader in our raft pointed up at the cliffs and said, "What's that?" What I saw on that cliff was a large biped animal standing upright, with reddish-brown hair that covered its entire body. It stood approximately eight to ten feet tall, and it also appeared to have breasts or no hair at all on its chest. The first thing that ran through my mind was that I was looking at the biggest black bear I had ever seen. Then the thing turned its upper body and looked over its shoulder, something I have never seen a bear do, and I have seen plenty of bears in my life. It looked back over its shoulder and then back at us, then turned around and walked upright into the timber.

Now, first of all, I hate telling this story because I am forever ridiculed by whoever I tell it to. Second, I am not 100 percent sure I saw a Bigfoot. What I am sure of is that I've spent years in the woods of Oregon, Washington, and Alaska, and I have never seen anything out there that could explain what I saw that clear, sunny day on the Grande Ronde River. It was neither bear nor a refugee from the movie *Deliverance*. Only the five of us in the last raft saw it. And, of course, being on a whitewater raft trip, all of our cameras were in watertight bags and not readily on hand for a Kodak moment such as that.

I do not consider myself a believer nor a full-blown skeptic. I saw something that did not have an explanation. I would liked to have had a camera so some disbeliever could look at the pics inside and out and say it was nothing more than a man in a suit, but that was not the case. I do think a large mammal could be out there without us knowing about it. Hopefully some day, someone will either prove or disprove this myth once and for all.

You are right about people and their good-natured ribbing after I tell this story. Over the years, I have only told a handful of people. Unfortunately, I have lost contact with all of the others who were in the raft with me that day. While around the campfire that night, as we recalled our story to the other members of our party, one of our Scout leaders told us of a run-in he and his brother had had while horseback riding. According to him, the thing had come down a hill and stopped on the trail in front of them for a couple of seconds, then continued downhill. He said this all had happened in the dark, and he was pretty sure it was not a bear walking upright downhill. I know this is a secondhand story coming from me, but it is further testimony from another party who has had an encounter.

As for using the story in your book, I don't have a problem with that. As I said, I am not sure if it was a Bigfoot that I saw. I do know that it was not a known indigenous species to the Oregon or Idaho forests, and it gave us the creeps to camp only a few miles downriver from where we saw it. I don't think I would want my name to be used, however. There is a certain stigma that goes along with people who claim to have seen something out of the ordinary, such as a Bigfoot or a UFO. A person seems to be cast into a different light by others, almost as if it might be a mental illness to believe that you saw such a thing. The only reason I am able to share my story here is because it is being done under different circumstances. I'm sure you understand, as well others who have had an encounter, that the story of a run-in with such an animal does not go over well with the general public. You are forever seen as a person with no credibility. However, as you stated, more people have seen this than have come forward for whatever reasons.

There is another source of information you might want to research if you are looking for firsthand accounts. I remember going to a small restaurant in Oregon, in the town of Tollgate, in the same geographical area where I had my encounter. The owner of the restaurant had a handful of plaster cast prints that had been collected from the area. It seems that the locals have been finding these for years, or something to that effect. I'm not sure if the same people own the place or if it still exists. It is a small community of fewer than 500 people, so someone would have to know what happened to the owners if they aren't still there. I hope this is of some help. I'm not a 100 percent believer in Bigfoot, but I believe 100 percent that I saw something that defies logical explanation. (Alaska Hunter)

## Story Three

Saw your website posting about Bigfoot. Interesting subject, to say the least. I'm sure many skilled and even unskilled people in the woods have had sightings, and no doubt some have even reported it. I reported a cougar sighting to Vermont Fish and Wildlife back in like 1985. They told me I'd no doubt seen a deer. I've been a hunting guide for many years and moved to Vermont in 1984 from Alaska. I think I know the difference between a deer and a large feline. Those in official positions won't believe a cougar sighting. Would they ever believe a Bigfoot sighting?

Anyway, back to your subject. Back in the mid-1970s (mid-November), while deer hunting a remote mountain in southern Vermont, I saw an injured doe limp by, about 200 yards from my stand. There was a little fresh snow, and the deer passed through several clearings in the mostly open hardwood section where I was watching. This was a bucks-only season, by the way. I had a scoped rifle and could clearly make out that it was a doe.

About one and a half hours later, I again saw movement near where I had first seen the doe appear. A very large, upright critter came along. It was dark brown, nearly black in color. It was not a bear. Bear season was still open, and it was a good two-mile hike back to the four-wheel-drive-only logging road I'd walked in on. It walked like a man but appeared HUGE! I got a pretty darn good look at it in my scope for about three minutes in total. It was carrying either a long bone or a gray stick in one hand. It appeared to be able to do that, as if it had a thumb. Its arms seemed longer than necessary. It was very furry. Its head was very large. The face appeared to be not totally furred. It made a couple easy, short leaps across a small, winding creek; I later judged those leaps to be over ten feet.

I later walked down to where I'd seen it. There were huge, manlike footprints, here and there, where there was snow. It was barefoot. The rest of the ground was frozen, so there were no tracks there — just depressions in the leaves. I was convinced I'd seen something unlike anything I had ever seen before. This animal was RIGHT on the doe track, by the way, obviously following it. Oddly, I twice saw the animal squat and appear to sniff the track of the deer. At one spot, I saw a partial handprint, even in the snow. The finger seemed to be the width of an Italian sausage! It was a bit scary, to be right honest. I didn't even CONSIDER trying to track it. I told very few people of my encounter.

In the mid 1990s, this time in northern Vermont, while bear hunting with a friend on a remote mountain, I again came upon a large, upright animal — easily eight feet tall and reddish brown in color. I never saw its face. It stood behind a large tree in thick, low conifers. I thought it was a moose at first, until it turned and strode away, making a huffing sound. I could then see that it was manlike, upright, and HUGE! It was between nine and ten feet tall! I was only twenty yards from it or so.

When it left, it went up a hillside that I could not climb. My friend and I both later examined its huge tracks in soft soil and mud, where it had crossed an overgrown logging road, near where I'd seen it. We were both also able to still smell it (musk-like) and even hear it above us. We talked over whether to track and kill it and decided against it. We both carried high-powered rifles, by the way. We knew that by doing so, we'd risk our safety. We also knew we'd be somewhat rich but probably hated by over half the world for killing it. We both also felt it would be morally wrong to do so. We don't shoot other animals when hunting that are not in season either, by the way. We are ethical hunters. By the way, we have never gone back to that area to hunt, and it is just now that I realize that. Odd, huh? My friend, by the way, was oddly nicknamed "The Sasquatch" long before our sighting, for he wore size 14 hunting boots! The tracks left by the animal I saw that day were longer and wider than Rick's boot print! Rick is a very big guy, not just tall and big-footed, and even he was visibly shaken that day, as was I. We discussed whether to track it or not for about five minutes. When we decided not to, we immediately left that area and hiked back the three or so miles to the truck straightaway, making no stops at all.

I think many people who encounter this species feel as we did: at odds with what to do next, if anything. This is why you don't see the photos or videotapes that probably do exist. They simply keep it to themselves. I'm semi-retired now and no longer hunt as much or get as far back into the woods. But when I was younger, I spent more time in the woods than anyone else I ever knew. I've always kept my eye out, since that first sighting, for a sign of such an animal, and I've never found any — until that second sighting. To say these critters are uncommon would be a huge understatement. But I know what I saw, and I know that these animals do exist. I'm not of a mind to think they are in any way human. The ones I saw did not look human or even seem closely related. They looked like some sort of upright ape, and their upper bodies, especially, looked in larger proportions than a man. Their arms were longer in proportion too, and they had very short, thick necks. A very large, broad head was also noticeable.

Part of why the public will not accept this is due to the nitwits who are out there studying it. I've seen these types on TV shows, and most are so obsessed that every stick in the woods that breaks is a Sasquatch to them! They are so busy trying to convince others that they have lost their open-mindedness. It's like the UFO nuts. To them, every light in the sky is a craft from another world. They come off as unbelievable, frankly; as such, they hurt their own cause. I've seen a lot more UFOs than Bigfoots, that's for sure. That's not to say I know what the heck they are, but when you spend as much time outside and at night as I have, you'll see lights you can't identify from time to time — some in the daylight, too. But I'm not prepared to say they were aliens pressing for abduction. Who knows what they were?

I'm sure some will agree: Give me enough money to do it and enough trail cameras (100-200 or so) and a good helicopter pilot and about two years, and I could no doubt get the photos that would prove Bigfoot's existence. You put enough of these cameras (placed six feet high) in enough remote locations, where no person ever walks, and you'll eventually capture one on film. No one is doing it to that extent though. They all want to be there to get the film or photo. That's not how they'll find one. These creatures obviously do their darnedest to AVOID people — and with good reason! Both my encounters, not so strangely, were nearly at the tops of very remote mountains, where few people ever go. I could nail a twenty-dollar bill at eye level on a tree in these spots, and I bet it'd still be there five years from now, unless it rotted away to nothing by then. Good luck to you in your quest and study. (Jim)

## Story Four

Just this past weekend, I was out hunting with a friend in a semi-remote area of the Sierra National Forest in central California. We pulled over to take some pictures of the scenery. As soon as we got out of the truck, we heard an eerie moaning/howling sound coming from the ridge above us. It was about 600 yards up the ridge, right at snow line. I have never heard anything like it before, and I am very familiar with the sounds that animals in this area make. It was not a mountain lion or a bear. My friend and I just looked at each other, wondering what the hell it was. We listened for about five minutes, and then I blew on a predator call, to see if I could coax whatever it was down the mountain. Shortly after I blew the call, we could tell there were two creatures up there, as they began to talk back and forth to each other in different tones of the moaning/howling.

> Once they started to talk, we could tell they began to move away from us and eventually up and over the ridge, calling back and forth the whole way. It was as if one was leading the other away from us. This whole incident lasted about fifteen minutes. I'm not saying it was Bigfoot, but I have no other explanation as to what would make that type of sound. We considered going after it but were too scared. I did, however, take a picture of the ridge that the sounds were coming from and remember exactly where it is. I'm thinking about going back up to where I heard the noises to look for footprints or other evidence. I'll be taking my camera and rifle of course. I'll let you know what I turn up. (PP)

The last short story is secondhand and has not been substantiated, according to the fellow who relayed the message. Nevertheless, its genuineness places it as a significant entry.

> A friend was camping at Stringer Lake above Allison Lake in Princeton a few years back and heard some weird shrieking howls, definitely not cougar, just outside the ring of light from their camp one night. He let fly with his shotgun in the air, and whatever it was took off through the bush around the lake and joined up with other somethings at the other end of the lake, where they had a great old howling and shrieking session.
>
> He took off out of there at first light and has never been back to the area. Apparently, there have been a few others who have had the same experience there. (Anonymous)

# 11. David Cleaver and the Texas Bigfoot

Another mysterious chapter in the Sasquatch story opened for me when I ran across a man who had, as it would appear, literally run into the creature. This individual's story is unfinished, as he continues to research the southern United States.

Our paths crossed in the sweltering summer of 2009. Over a number of weeks, I had many conversations with Texan David Cleaver out of Lago Vista. Some people seem to be a magnet for the creatures. It is impossible to explain the reasons behind this, but it does happen to some. David Cleaver is one of those people, finding himself at a particular location with another person along for the ride. I have often wondered, *Why us? Why them?* He has also shared this story on the BFRO website.

In 1969, the creature began to affect his life, in an area accessible only by water. Palo Pinto County set the stage, Mineral Wells being the closest town:

> I was at summer camp at age fourteen, one of about twenty campers including two counselors that were involved with a three-day, two-night canoe/camping trip down the Brazos River.
>
> We put in just below the dam at Possum Kingdom Lake. The first night we camped near the Highway 4 bridge. We set up our tents on a section of open, flat grass next to the river. There was a thirty-foot cliff set back from the river around thirty yards, and that ran in both directions for quite a ways.
>
> As we were setting up the rest of camp and securing the canoes for the night, several campers noticed some type of unknown animal peering down on us from the cliff, only a glimpse of the head being seen. The animal was in a different

**Figure 28: The location where David Cleaver literally ran into a Bigfoot in Palo Pinto County, Texas. (photo © David Cleaver)**

> location each time. No one was really concerned or thought much about it.
>
> The night was uneventful, and we all slept well. The next morning, we were up eating breakfast and then loading the canoes. As I came back for another load, my tent/canoe buddy said he'd seen the animal. I asked if he knew what it was, and he said it was a fox.

I asked David how someone could ultimately label the creature as a fox, but it only serves to show how easy it is to misidentify the Sasquatch, especially for a younger, less experienced person.

David went on to say:

> The creature had apparently been curious about us since the day before. It must have been hanging around, because its head was seen at least three or four times from different locations. Around eighteen other campers, including two counselors, heard the commotion related to the encounter.

> I had found a way to get up the cliff face, and the two of us were on top in no time. As we made the last push to the top, we could hear something running off through the woods. We immediately gave chase, and I was in the lead. There were some very large boulders scattered about, and I ran around one of the larger ones. As I came flying around the edge of this boulder, I ran smack into a rather large tree, which knocked me back flat on my rump. I was crumpled at the base of the tree and dazed. When my eyes focused again, I noticed the tree had hair. I looked up. It screamed, and I literally peed my pants. My friend screamed, I screamed, it screamed again, and all of this happened in quick, but distorted time. We ran fast from that position and right off the edge of the cliff, forgetting it was there. We were in a blind panic.
>
> At the time, no one around there had even heard of a Bigfoot that we knew of, so it was hard to explain. We said it was a giant gorilla, but that didn't go over too well with anybody, including all the other campers and counselors who'd heard the screams and witnessed our fall — from grace, as it turned out. They thought we were crazy and had made the whole thing up. But why would we risk death if we were faking it? I only say that because the fall we took over that cliff shoulda killed or seriously injured us. We were very lucky that we landed in one of the few areas that offered survival: heavy brush. In retrospect, the creature was not aggressive and must have been very curious about us.

David made more than one entry on the Bigfoot Field Researchers Organization website, which he gladly explained:

> I have made two reports to the BFRO and illustrate the difference between a so-called friendly Bigfoot visit, where they initiate the encounter out of curiosity, and is non-threatening (Report #14,376, Texas, Palo Pinto County) and another with myself and a friend as the curiosity seekers, and a threatening response (Report #3,585, Washington, Snohomish County). You certainly have my permission to use either or both stories.
>
> Also, I have had two more threatening encounters, both times at the exact location where my initial sighting took place, which is the location described in the BFRO Report #14,376.

When asked about the Washington State story, David had the following to say:

> This took place in August of 2001, as mentioned, in Snohomish County. A dear friend bought several hundred acres of land in Washington State, in the mountains near Monroe. While building a road and house over time, he has had many strange occurrences — too many to discuss here. This is second-growth forest, and it is virtually untouched.
>
> To make a long story short, while hiking in a very dense gorge between two mountains, we came across a nest. If you have never been to the wilderness of the Pacific Northwest, let me tell you that it is dense! I mean, there could be 100 Bigfoot within 20 yards of you, and you wouldn't see them. Ferns and other undergrowth grow anywhere from waist to shoulder height, with absolutely towering trees every few feet. It's truly amazing.
>
> The nest was completely concealed, and if I hadn't walked directly in front of the opening, I never would have noticed it. The construction was unbelievable; the undergrowth was woven to form about a seven-foot tunnel leading to a larger domed inner room, about the size of a mid-sized car. We went inside to look for evidence or smell there but couldn't find anything.
>
> While investigating inside, we both looked at each other for no reason, and both of us suddenly became very spooked. We didn't see or hear anything. We just knew we had to get the hell out of there and did. We were going to go back later, but the weather went to hell and began pouring down rain. We had tried to find some caves down in the gorge but never found them. My buddy, who owns the place, knows a native who lives nearby, and he can take us to the caves, even though he himself won't go near them. He will however, point us in the right direction.

It's funny that David mentioned the creatures possibly constructing nests, because another fellow I talked to over the years also stumbled upon such things, after a small number of off-path witnesses (hikers) told him about a haired giant coming and going from something similar in northern Oregon. Of course, this is where it once again gets very strange. Once he mounted his arsenal of technology at some distance away, with the camera lens still able to capture pictures through the trees, the quarry never returned to this complex nest in the middle of nowhere. As long as there was a chance of being photographed, the creature stayed away. Once the camera was removed, hikers again spotted the tall visitor.

This toying around frustrated the researcher a second time, though he was still drawn to the mystery. Still, the no-show eventually embarrassed the man again on a personal level. Hikers and mountain men were eliminated as culprits. He'd spent sixteen months and two summers observing, ultimately producing nothing more than small, common critters — nothing even close to a Sasquatch. Other researchers have suffered the same fate and maybe worse.

Concerning David's 1969 brush with the Wilderness Being, there were possibly others who'd been exposed to the creature in a similar way. Boy Scouts at the Worth Ranch Summer Camp north of Palo Pinto had spotted an upright forest giant in 1988. That story was featured also on the BFRO website and happened in the same general area, nineteen years after David Cleaver's experience.

Over the years, the list has grown. David went on about the other instances and possible situations — also in the vicinity of the original sighting of 1969:

> The plan, after studying the location, the 200-year history of sightings in the area, Hugo's Monster and the Brazos Ape-man, all centering in and around Kyle Mountain, I made my future campsites right near the base of the mountain and on the Brazos River.
>
> What I noticed was that anyone coming down the Brazos River could be seen for miles from Kyle Mountain, and with all the people doing river trips, you would think some kind of lookout would be employed to see them coming. My plan was to paddle upriver, against the current, hug the cliff face, and remain totally out of view from any vantage point. I also have a kayak that is camo-colored. Canoes are slow and make noise; it is hard to paddle a canoe without hitting your paddle on the sides, and this makes noise, especially the aluminum canoes. The kayak is very swift and quiet. This place is not accessible by roads either. I have always believed that your best shot to see a Bigfoot is by water, as you can't get to normally inaccessible places by road. Quickly and quietly in a kayak will suffice.
>
> So there I was, on my first stealth trip, set up in a fairly hidden camp, taking great care not to make any noise. I waited for darkness.

> At around nine thirty p.m., I made three loud yells, trying my best to imitate some of the recorded screams I'd heard. I received no responses of any kind. I decided to just remain quiet and eventually went into my tent to escape the bugs.
>
> Around eleven thirty p.m., I could hear something big coming through the brush, heading in my direction. In fact, I had fallen asleep, and the noise woke me up. It was bipedal for sure. My tent was hidden pretty well, and when the thing got to within maybe twenty yards of my tent, it must have seen it. The beast let out a string of very loud and angry gibberish, for lack of a better word. He or she then turned around and headed the way it came, breaking branches and making all kinds of pissed-off verbal noise. I could almost feel what it was saying: It was pissed it had come all the way down from the mountain to find me as the source of the earlier screams — ME! And it would take them about the same amount of time to get to where they were before. Also, I had two kinds of cameras ready inside my tent, but there was no way I was getting out of the tent. They were very pissed, and I felt threatened enough just being there. I waited for them to get a ways off, and then I got out of the tent and made a nice fire.

The idea that we can get pictures by using a camera seems simple, so the lack of pictures has always amazed me. David's experience here, where he is afraid to get out of his tent is one of the reasons why. We are really no closer to solving the mystery. Much of it is wishful thinking now, because there is more to this than anyone can imagine.

David went on to describe his other encounter:

> The second aggressive encounter took place in the same spot, two years later, in 2004. It was the same deal, using the kayak stealth approach and quietly setting up a hidden camp. I had a new plan though. There had always been a large cattle ranch across the river from my camp, and I had a device that would closely mimic the sounds of a calf in distress. I started around eight thirty p.m., just before dark, and must have been doing a pretty good job, as a female cow started coming aggressively toward me from across the river; I immediately stopped. Anyway, about eleven thirty p.m., I decided to try one of my screams. Within an instant of my yell, I got a frightening response. A roar came from across the river from an animal that

had massive lungs. It was similar to the roar of an African male lion, a little different though, but with as much power behind it — and it was pissed right off! As a footnote, I have been involved with a nonprofit organization for many years that rescues big cats from people who buy them, thinking they can make them into pets. There are eighty-plus now at the sanctuary, so I am very familiar with the sounds these big cats make.

Almost immediately after its roar, it started mimicking a screech owl call, only much louder and more powerful. The creature was across the river from me, about fifty yards away and slightly off to my left. Within seconds of the initial owl call, two others answered in succession, from my side of the river. They were about thirty-five yards out, one to my right, and the other to my left. I was in the middle of a triangle, and it wasn't love. They kept the owl calls going back and forth for maybe ten more seconds, and then there was silence. About five minutes later, I heard the sounds of a calf being attacked and killed. This took maybe eight seconds, and the death sounds that the calf made, especially toward the end, were extremely unnerving. I'd never heard such a horrible noise. Then there was dead silence again. Yep, I got another BIG fire going! I couldn't hear anything from the two on my side, so I got out my parabolic dish and could hear them creeping around for another forty-five minutes.

What I figured happened was this: They heard my calf calls and decided to check it out, and at least three of them took the bait. There is a low spot in the river just to the right of my location. I figured the one across the river approached the herd from my left, with the other two to my right — in waiting on my side — and in close proximity to the low spot in the river where the cattle would flee if panicked. The creatures were setting up the perfect ambush! This wasn't needed, as the one across the river made his kill undetected by the cattle. As a footnote, the mother cow wandered all over the area looking and crying for her calf for the rest of the night and well into the next day when I left around eleven a.m. Her voice was completely hoarse from the frantic calling by the time I left.

Certainly, it had to be a scary experience for David, being caught in the middle of something like that.

What these two experiences have shown me is that Bigfoot is capable of being tricked or fooled but is not amused in any way by it. In fact, he gets rather upset and aggressive! The key is to do things to drive them crazy with curiosity and then to proceed with caution. They just might show up, and you'd better be ready!

Timing is very important too. All animals live in their own time line. I guess the easiest way to explain this is a human glance versus a stare. If you look at someone, there is a point where the casual glance becomes an intimidating stare. Most animals, with their short lifespan as compared to humans, interpret their world and surroundings much faster than humans do. Therefore, the old wildlife saying, "Don't look at their eyes or stare," is really true.

What we would consider a glance is aggression in the animal world. A fleeting glance is all that is allowed in the animal world, as the stare-down is usually reserved for predators. This probably doesn't apply to Bigfoot because of his longer lifespan, but living in the wild, he must certainly be aware of it and live by it to a certain degree.

Hopefully, you are beginning to understand that I try to notice everything in nature to the smallest detail. Bigfoot must certainly do this, too, and I'm hoping it will give me better insight into his world and habits. I know they migrate through this area, as I've seen plenty of signs — even twice in my own yard. There is a major power line that cuts through my town and the surrounding woods. They seem to be using the power lines to migrate, which are kept clear and free for miles and miles. It sure beats bushwhacking!

I've heard of both the migration possibility and also a hibernation issue: heat in the southern United States and the freezing cold regions of Canada, forcing the creatures to adapt or react within the two extremes. David elaborated on these factors and how they might affect the creature's habits.

After just about keeling over yesterday (July 16, 2009) hiking in the 100+ heat, it affirmed my belief that the Big Guy heads north from the southern states during the summer months. The few that might hang around must spend a lot of time

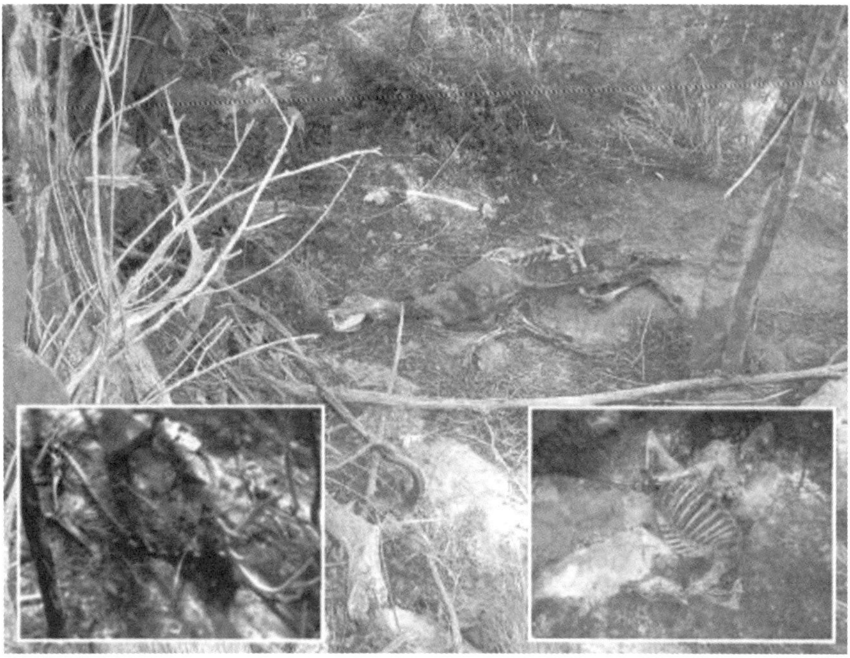

**Figure 29: David Cleaver came across this Killing Zone in 2008 near Lago Vista, Texas. There were 35-40 dead animals at the site. (photo © David Cleaver)**

> underground in caves, caverns, and the like. The heat must be miserable for them. This year, I believe there is some type of migratory activity going on in the area, especially with the drought.

David was also dealing with another extremely puzzling situation, which some refer to as the "Killing Zone." Here is what he had to say:

> There are probably thirty-five to forty animals, mostly deer, anywhere from a few days old to over a year, and all within a fairly small area. I hesitate to mention the dead animal place, as I am perplexed as to what other type of animals could do something like this. I always try to think of anything else that could do this. It's too easy for a Bigfoot guy to say, "Bigfoot did it." I am not that way and want to explain the phenomenon another way if possible.

> Some are fresh and some older. What seems strange to me is that the animals are being mostly consumed without the normal dismemberment that I am used to seeing. Only after the carcasses are mostly consumed do the smaller scavengers come in and start spreading things around. The whole scene is just plain weird.
>
> There aren't hardly any teeth marks on these, and they show more signs of being twisted and broken: snapped necks and other dislocations. On one in particular, the shoulder blade didn't have marks. It was as if the meat was pulled off and the skull was shattered. It had taken a very heavy blow, not a bite. I meant to comment more on this one. The legs were horribly twisted around and broken, as if the deer was caught in midair, swung around, and slammed to the ground. I have seen hundreds, if not thousands, of predator kill sites, and these are just different than what I normally see. They aren't just being killed with teeth and aren't being chewed on.

David was then asked, "Can you rule out man's involvement? Are there signs of weapon usage — the animals being shot, poisoned, and hunted?"

> No sign of gunshots at all, and I looked pretty good. One thing I do find occasionally on my hikes are arrows. Any poaching done in this area would have to be with a bow or crossbow, and there was no sign of this either.
>
> Considering poachers, there are many more reasons for this not to be the case than for it.

An ex-poacher I spoke to on this issue agreed, saying that the killings there didn't quite fit the profile. As far as government involvement, David had this to say:

> Remember, this is Texas, and I don't think the authorities, i.e. the local cop who handles animal control, really cares. He is a friend, however, and I did mention it to him back in May. He expressed interest in hiking over there, but I've heard nothing so far from him. I'm not really interested in making any kind of official report by phone or anything either. That would beg the question, "Well, Mr. Cleaver, what the heck are you doing over there?" The answer would be stranger than my original question.

We discussed the possibility of some mischief-making city crew using the area as a dumpsite rather than going through the proper channels, for whatever reason. I casually contacted the Lago Vista department spokesman who would know how their road maintenance crews dispose of dead animals, and she said that the crews take the carcasses west, to city property on 1431, and use lime when necessary (though it is not exposed to the public). I could vouch for a similar process, as the city of Calgary also disposes of animals using lime. David made it clear that city crews likely had little to do with it, because there was no trace of lime use.

Next, David was asked if there'd been any new entries placed in the Killing Zone between his visits. He answered: "In late May, there were three fresh, maybe three-day-old kills." As David has mentioned to me, the killings have quieted down since the start of the scorching Texas summer, with many watering holes and water supplies drying up. Whoever or whatever is responsible, they seem to have taken a break in this investigator's neck of the woods.

Khat Hansen, a protector of a group of Bigfoot creatures who will be discussed later in the book, asked that David take the greatest degree of caution when being involved with the area he was researching. Under anonymity, two well-known mainstream researchers offered the same advice, and a paranormal and Bigfoot investigator mentioned he'd heard about it before. The Killing Zone is dangerous, and one must be prudent in his or her observations where conditions might be perilous. This is one of the few things about which a number of observers and enthusiasts actually agree. Ken Kristian also had some things to say about the Killing Zone:

> No animal I know of in the wild will drag or carry kills back to a single place or spot. Cougars and bears will generally eat their prey where the opportunity for a kill presents itself.
>
> I have also heard of (read from Ray Crowe's old site) about a trapper in northern British Columbia finding just such a killing zone. Also, some mention in *RainCoast Sasquatch* (the book) of the skin of several deer being ripped off in one single spot. I read one old report from down south of another killing zone being found on a farm. The deer were all killed in what appeared to be the same manner: caught by the leg and then necks broken, their livers neatly ripped out.
>
> Tell that fellow to be careful!

I'd also heard of such zones being found in Washington State by a northwest trapper, who referred to it as "the bone yard," a story I first found on the Bigfoot Forum; it had originally been told on Blog Talk Radio, hosted by Larry Battson.

David went on with his description of the Zone in Texas:

> There is a ravine where the Zone is. Both sides have near forty-five-degree inclines, perhaps fifty yards to the top. Further on down the same ravine, it starts getting thicker. The area is along the bottom, right next to a creek.
>
> The area up at the top is the general location where I believe these animals are being ambushed and killed. Right on the edge of a pasture, at the top and on the edge of the ravine, the opening to a creepy natural little hideout, with several good hidden views of the pasture. There is also a nice little hidden lake, not too far away. Of course, I considered if this was manmade, but there is absolutely no sign of that, and no hunting is strictly enforced in this area. It just looks and feels creepy when I am there. It's hard to explain. The Zone is right on the edge of town, and there is no farm there. The pasture is one of the old fairways for a closed golf course that went out of business several years ago.
>
> I mostly go alone and have never taken anyone to the Zone. They won't go! Besides, most of my buddies are too old for this sort of thing, and it's too hot for them!

Thankfully, in the summer of 2009, this changed for David. He put up a posting on the Bigfoot Forums, asking for assistance from another independent researcher. David needed help because the junket would involve nighttime surveillance of the Killing Zone. I don't think anyone should go it alone, especially when it comes to something like this, so it was good that David received some assistance on the investigation. James Johnson, an active-duty U.S. Marine from Montgomery County, helped David, providing a much-needed level of safety.

> The Saturday night outing was during a full moon, staking out the Killing Zone with sound and cameras. We had nothing to report this time out.
>
> The man himself, my accompanying investigator, was forty years old, with twenty-two years in the Marines, including two tours in Iraq, one during Desert Storm. We clicked immediately and trusted each other's abilities from the start.

This is what James had to say:

> I can see why he wanted someone there to watch his back. It's dangerous terrain with some dangerous wildlife, regardless of Bigfoot very likely being in the area as well. At night, it's close quarters, and you are in a world of hurt if anything goes wrong while you're alone.
>
> I do believe Bigfoot are using this area and terrain as an easy way to ambush prey, as well as conceal their own movements. These ravines and trails intersect with power and gas lines, also giving these creatures a secluded superhighway to travel upon from protected land up above — down to the lake and river miles below. There are thousands of places to lie up during the day where no one would ever find them if they didn't want to be found.

When I asked David whether or not he had found tracks near that area, he answered:

> I was over near the Zone today (August 6) and found a rather impressive footprint that wasn't there yesterday. This was a game trail about a mile from the Killing Zone, heading away from it and toward the river. My 220 pounds can't make a print like this — not even close. It's hard to see the detail in the photo; the heel is defined and ends just to the left edge of the small white rock. There was reasonable toe definition. This was a right foot.

The man's research is continuing on many different levels. The Texan has been pressing the areas of his previous sightings, seeking out clues to the creatures he had close contact with years ago as a teenager. He will never forget the day of that Bigfoot encounter in July of 1969, because, as he puts it, "they landed on the moon the next day."

I presented one final question to the Texas fellow, involving camera technology and Sasquatch, something I will touch on later as well. A number of researchers have tried to record the creature on film, yet the beings seem to evade everyone, and that is something worth touching on.

So sincere in his efforts, David Cleaver likes to step things up a notch, including when it comes to his encounter with the Sasquatch. He really wants to put the beast on film, and there are literally thousands like him across North America. When asked about the technical devices he planned to put in place, this was what he had to say:

**Figure 30: David Cleaver tries out a photo trap set for a massive giant. The wires and mat are disguised with natural vegetation to complete the installation. (photo © David Cleaver)**

Here's a test shot from one of my camera traps I put out the other night on the game trail going through the Killing Zone. This gives you an idea of just how fast my cameras fire — much faster than the store-bought kind, that's for sure. Of course, after the mats and wires are buried, they are invisible. Plus, the cameras are very well hidden as well, using natural materials from the area. I have the area rigged with cameras and a remote trigger to fire them off, with audio as well. There is no visible technology. As far as store-bought game cameras, don't use them! Bigfoot will avoid them for several reasons. First, I believe it's due to visibility; they are not stealthy and can be seen. Also, the triggering device gives off electrical impulses and/or beams.

I have built several items to address these needs and have developed what I would term "species-specific" technology. I have a pair of lens-less glasses with two hidden cameras; one I leave on is a normal 480TVL color CCD mini wide angle.

**Figure 31: One of David Cleaver's trail cameras. Many others also have cameras out trying to capture a picture of Bigfoot. (photo © David Cleaver)**

> Mounted to the side on the ear rail is a telephoto lens. Both cameras are nearly invisible and even fool my friends. They are connected under my clothing to a mini DVR 40G recorder in my pocket, good for a twenty-hour stretch. There is also a switch in my pocket where I can go from one camera to the other. I also rigged a mini mic on the glasses for sound. So many of the Bigfoot videos, especially the Patterson/Gimlin film, could have benefited from the telephoto lens, and I don't want to repeat that mistake. Chances are you will never be close enough for the wide-angle lens to get a clear shot, but the telephoto would. Wherever I look gets filmed. I also designed a pretty badass game camera. It fires multiple cameras and is really stealthy. No electrical impulse used on the triggering device either.

This sort of thing is happening all over the United States and filtering into Canada as well — the technical boom for Bigfoot. A person must remember that when an individual such as David Cleaver puts such time and effort into a mystery that has spread itself over several hundreds of years, something is going on.

The research continues like this all throughout North America, researchers and the curious always on recon missions, seeking answers to age-old questions.

# 12. The Patterson/Gimlin Film

No story of Bigfoot would be complete without a look at the Patterson/Gimlin film from 1967. There are many ways to approach this story, so I would like to present how it happened in my neck of the woods in British Columbia.

I contacted Lisa Carleton at the *Similkameen Spotlight* again in October of 2009. The traveling copy of the film had made its appearance in Princeton years earlier, and I wanted to know who had brought it to Princeton. I assumed it was Roger Patterson and Bob Gimlin. On October 20, Lisa responded with archived information and a story that accompanied the film advertisements. I realized two days later that the newspaper lady had sent those articles to me on the anniversary date of when Roger Patterson had shot the controversial film, and that actually brought a tear to my eye. Below is how the article appeared in the *Similkameen Spotlight* in the Wednesday, February 25, 1970, edition, an article entitled, "Sasquatch on Film Here," by Laurie Currie:

> In true Alberta character, those who last summer sighted the Sasquatch west of the Rocky Mountain House says ours is bigger. They are comparing the Alberta ape-man creature to the California Bigfoot that is photographed in the controversial motion picture *Sasquatch* that is being shown here in the Jubilee Auditorium.
>
> Estimates of the California Bigfoot, photographed on 16 mm, color film in October 1967 at Bluff Creek, California, are that the bulky, hair-covered creature is eight feet tall.

Similkameen Spotlight page 2, Wednesday February 25, 1970

Spotlight on

## White Paper Will Hurt Our Province

The proposed White Paper on taxation is turning slightly brown, right about now with mounting criticism across Canada, and if the small business man has his way it will completely fade away. But if the White Paper on taxation, will all but wipe out the small business man, the province of British Columbia is going to get hurt the most if it is implemented.

The White Paper takes a very healthy punch at the mining industry and this is what really concerns us. The White paper proposal hits at the three year tax free period for mining companies and from the information we have this will effect new mines far more than established mines. This means of course that exploration and development of mines in British Columbia will feel the brunt of the new legislation. It might also mean the exodus of mining capital from the province to more lucrative areas of the world.

Most people do not realize that our province has mostly low grade ore deposits which are marginal. At the moment the advent of new equipment has provided some margin, but it is our opinion that the tax incentives are still very necessary in attracting new capital.

It is our opinion that proposals in the White Paper on mining could cause a mining depression in our province if they are introduced, and would do great harm to the economy.

## Mill Rate Line Held By Village Council

It appears at this moment that the mill rate will not increase for Princeton taxpayers this year and in fact there may be a slight reduction.

The school board announced their position at a meeting last week in which the Village Alderman were present. The Board have stayed within the 110 per centum allowed by the provincial government. They are $298.00 beneath the figure, to be exact. The mill rate for the school last year was 39.6. It is estimated that it might be as low as 36 this year, due mainly to the fact that one basic unit has been added to the school this year providing an extra $12,990 and also because the Provincial Government has increased the Education unit this year.

With school costs generally in check, the Village Council are in a much better position, since they have also exercised some savings. The total mill rate last year was 69.4 for education, general and hospital and at this moment it appears that if the Village reduction comes through the mill rate could drop to the lower range of 60, which will come as good news to the over burdened Princeton taxpayer.

If there is a saving, both our school board and village council can take a bow and also receive a hearty round of applause from everyone.

**The Similkameen Spotlight**

THE SIMILKAMEEN SPOTLIGHT PUBLISHING CO. LTD.

EDITOR & PUBLISHER - LAURIE CURRIE
OFFICES IN PRINCETON AND KEREMEOS

PHONE 295-3535

Published every Wednesday at Princeton, B.C.

LETTER TO EDITOR

Sir:

Now it is spring and time to think ahead. My family and I often drive through the Interior and the lovely Okanagan, - in other words we are Tourists. I wonder why the word seems to annoy so many people. In some small towns we and our money are welcome. The towns look forward to the holiday season, and the extra dollars we leave. Foward looking town are clean, tidy, have well painted buildings, nicely kept homes, attractive stores and often some form of beautification for the main streets, - other small towns seem to look backwards instead of ahead; the tourist is a nuisance to anyone in business, he brings noise and disturbance to our Rip Van Winkle existence. Nothing is done to attract him. Do these people not realise that without his money, a lot of the stores would have to close and move to more prosperous places? Thereby making it hard for the towns - men to purchase needs without driving many miles.

Surely its worth a little paint, and effort, to make a place attractive to the eye of the passers by, a few shady trees, a campsite - by a little water, a few tables, a little volunteer labour maybe, but money to be made for the towns betterment.

J. Benson,
Tourist.

## "Sasquatch" On Film Here

In true Alberta character, those who last summer sighted the Sasquatch west of the Rocky Mountain House says ours is bigger. They are comparing the Alberta ape-man creature to the California Bigfoot that is photographed in the controversial motion picture "Sasquatch" that is being shown here in the Jubilee Auditorium.

Estimates of the California Bigfoot, photographed on 16 mm. color film in October 1967 at Bluff Creek, California, is that the bulky, hair-covered creature is eight feet tall.

Two of the five Calgary Power Big Horn Dam site construction workers who spotted the Alberta Sasquatch last August also saw Patterson's "Sasquatch" film when it was shown last November at Rocky Mountain House.

And both Stan Peterson and his son Harley of Condor - say the Big Horn Sasquatch stood close to 15 feet tall. Peterson says the estimate was made after some men went over to the ridge where the creature had been spotted as it reclined on a bank watching the dam site laborers working. The creature stood up and ambled off as the men watched, covering half to three-quarters of a mile in less than two minutes.

Peterson says when the men their fellow workers on the ridge in comparison.

The Peterson's add that the Big Horn Bigfoot was not as bulky, but more man-like in its lankiness, although it did have humped or hunched shoulders.

Patterson's Bluff Creek Bigfoot in the 25-minute "Sasquatch" color movie documentary will be narrated here by Canadian Sasquatch searcher Rene Dahinden of Lumby, B.C. "Sasquatch" will be shown as a special supplementary to the Arctic Safari Productions, Ltd. Jim Bond outdoor adventure "Yukon Safari."

Patterson's film shows a bulky muscled female Bigfoot as it makes its way through the dense bush. The creature appears wary of Patterson at all times during the filming.

The August sighting of the Sasquatch in Alberta was the first documented although the breakway band of Ermineskin Indians from Hobemma Reserve apparently have known that at least one family of four Sasquatches live in the Windy Point region of the Kootenay Plains. The Indians said little of the sightings, however, not wanting further interference of white men searchers in the wilderness retreat Chief Smallboy's band seeks.

It is said that the late Chief Walking Eagle, the famed weather forecaster of Rocky Mountain House, also sighted Sasquatches during his many years of life in the Kootenay plains, but he, too, chose not to reveal their presence to white men.

The Big Horn Sasquatch giant, however, is nearly twice as tall as any reported in B.C. or the Pacific Northwest since the first recorded sighting in 1884.

OKANAGAN COLLEGE SLOWED BY FIRE

Dr. Rowland F. Grant, Principal of Okanagan College, said today the fire at the Kelowna Centre on Raymer Road which occurred Tuesday night, February 17, represents a loss of 10,000 square feet of space.

Dr. Grant said that the situation was being evaluated both from the point of view of physical plant and the academic program.

"We don't exactly know what we can put together for the balance of the term, but we will have something organized in a few days," Dr. Grant said.

All Kelowna Centre classes are temporarily cancelled. Adult night classes will continue as scheduled at Kelowna Secondary.

St. Peter's Parish BINGO
Canadian Legion Hall
Thursday March 5, 8:00 pm.
4 - $50.00 Jackpots & Usual Cash Prizes
Next Bingo Thursday March 19

ARCTIC SAFARI PRODUCTIONS PRESENTS
FAMILY

SEE CARIBOU · MT. LION · SHEEP · GRIZZLY BEAR · MOOSE

THE "SASQUATCH"
(the only color film footage in the world actually showing you the legendary SASQUATCH!)
*You Must See It to Believe It!*
PRINCETON SCHOOL AUDITORIUM
8:00 p.m. Tuesday MARCH 10
KEREMEOS VICTORY HALL

**Figure 32: An advertisement in the *Similkameen Spotlight* for the March 10, 1970, showing of Patterson/Gimlin film.**

Two of the five Calgary Big Horn Dam site construction workers who spotted the Alberta Sasquatch last August also saw Patterson's Sasquatch film when it was shown last November at Rocky Mountain House.

As both Stan Peterson and his son Harley of Condor say, the Big Horn Sasquatch stood close to fifteen feet tall. Peterson says the estimate was made after some men went over the ridge where the creature had been spotted as it reclined on a bank watching the dam site laborers working. The creature stood up and ambled off as the men watched, covering half to three-quarters of a mile in less than two minutes. Peterson says when the men reached the edge, those who stayed back figured the Sasquatch they had seen was nearly three times the size of their fellow workers on the ridge in comparison.

The Petersons add that the Big Horn Bigfoot was not bulky, but more manlike in its lankiness, although it did have humped or hunched shoulders.

Patterson's Bluff Creek Bigfoot in the twenty-five-minute *Sasquatch* color movie documentary will be narrated here by Canadian Sasquatch searcher René Dahinden of Lumby, British Columbia. *Sasquatch* will be shown as a special supplementary to the Arctic Safari Productions, Ltd. Jim Bond outdoor adventure, *Yukon Safari*.

Patterson's film shows a bulky, muscled female Bigfoot as it makes its way through the dense bush. The creature appears wary of Patterson at all times during the filming.

The August sighting of the Sasquatch in Alberta was the first documented, although the breakaway band of Ermineskin Indians from Hobemma Reserve apparently have known that at least one family of four Sasquatches live in the Windy Point region of the Kootenay Plains. The Indians said little of the sightings, however, not wanting further interference of white men searchers in the wilderness retreat Chief Smallboy's band seeks.

It is said that the late Chief Walking Eagle, the famed weather forecaster of Rocky Mountain House, also sighted Sasquatches during his many years of life in the Kootenay plains, but he, too, chose not to reveal their presence to white men.

> The Big Horn Sasquatch giant, however, is nearly twice as tall as any reported in British Columbia or the Pacific Northwest since the first recorded sighting in 1884. [LC1]

Many reputable individuals, such as David J. Daegling, Grover Krantz, and Dmitri Donskoy have addressed the authenticity of this controversial motion picture. Some believe it is authentic. Others are convinced it is a fake. In my opinion, without wishing to insult anyone's intelligence, I do not believe folks of the 1960s would have had the mindset, knowledge, or technology to construct such an elaborate hoax and would have had trouble creating such a suit. Some have tried to reconstruct the Bluff Creek scenario, but those results were not even close to what was filmed in 1967. It is also worthwhile to mention that Roger Patterson and Bob Gimlin had no ties to Disney or any such production company, and an individual such as the supposed wearer of the alleged suit, Bob Heironimous, couldn't have possibly pulled it off without it being obvious. The tracks would have been nearly impossible to fake, especially when they were placed under such scrutiny, the microscope of reason. John Green had this to report on his database:

> It was back in 1957 that I began looking into local reports of encounters with giant, hair-covered, bipedal creatures, long known in Canada as Sasquatch. A year later, Bigfoot broke into the news in the United States, and I saw for myself, beside a creek in a California forest, enormous, humanlike footprints sunken so deep into a solid sandbar that no one who saw them could come up with a way that humans could have made them. Since then, I have been on a lifelong quest to establish what is behind the sighting reports and how those footprints come to be.

A hoaxer's mentality in those days would have been geared toward plywood impressions and the like, so it is relatively safe to rule out a manmade hoax. We'll hear later about John Green's reward for duplicating those tracks. A paranormal fabrication of enormous proportions would have to have been at the very root of things.

## Jeff Meldrum's Thoughts

One of the constructive individuals in the field of Bigfoot research who has been both criticized and praised is Dr. Jeff Meldrum, Associate Professor of Anatomy and Anthropology at Idaho State University. Dr.

Meldrum is an expert on primate anatomy and locomotion. I've had the pleasure of communicating with Dr. Meldrum three or four times. From a scientific standpoint, he has addressed the validly of the Patterson/Gimlin film.

> It has been obvious to even the casual viewer that the film subject possesses arms that are disproportionately long for its stature. John Green is a veteran researcher into the question of Sasquatch or Bigfoot. He was among the first to view the film captured by Patterson and Gimlin and has studied it intensely in the intervening years. His recognition of the significance of the inhumanly long arms of the film subject is a point that has not previously been articulated in such a straightforward manner. It is such a fundamental observation that it is considered a breakthrough in assessing the validity of this extraordinary film. Anthropologists typically express limb proportions as an intermembral index (IM), which is the ratio of combined arm and forearm skeletal length (humerus + radius) to combined thigh and leg skeletal length (femur + tibia)x100. The human IM averages 72. The intermembral index is a significant measure of a primate's locomotor adaptation. The forelimb-dominated movements of the chimp and gorilla are reflected in their high IM indices of 106 and 117, respectively. The positions of the joints on the film subject can only be approximate, and the limbs are frequently oriented obliquely to the plane of the film, rendering them foreshortened to varying degrees. However, in some frames, the limbs are nearly vertical, hence parallel to the film plane, and indicate an IM index somewhere between 80 and 90, intermediate between humans and African apes. In spite of the imprecision of this preliminary estimate, it is well beyond the mean for humans and effectively rules out a man-in-a-suit explanation for the Patterson/Gimlin film without invoking an elaborate, if not inconceivable, prosthetic contrivance to account for the appropriate positions and actions of wrist and elbow and finger flexion visible on the film. This point deserves further examination and may well rule out the probability of hoaxing.

## John Green's Interview with Bob Gimlin, 1992

Now let's look at other aspects of the Patterson/Gimlin film seen from a broader perspective. There is an article posted on the Bigfoot Encounters website (John Green's "Interview with Bob Gimlin, 1992") that even I didn't know about. I have to tell you honestly that over the years, I wasn't the type of hardcore researcher who pursued everything Bigfoot. I was clearing out my own closet of Sasquatch memorabilia — the strange things that had happened to my family over time. Only the documentation of the 1974-85 sightings occupied my attention.

When I found the interview, I was intrigued. Since many other people are unfamiliar with the interview, I will present it here.

In November 2009, researcher Bobbie Short of Bigfoot Encounters generously took her time to explain her part in the process. I knew by reading the article that she had been instrumental in pulling it all together. John Green had sent her a videotape that she'd painstakingly transcribed.

The talented, independent researcher had to take literally weeks of her life to put everything into readable dialog. John Green, as another example, had to travel to Yakima, Washington, to meet with the lone survivor of the Patterson film, Bob Gimlin. All parties worked very hard to give us a piece of history.

In reviewing this subject in the fall of 2009, I briefly talked with Mrs. Gimlin. It was difficult to pick up the phone and call the Gimlins. I knew through a number of sources that the couple had gone through a lot of strife over what he had seen in October of 1967. Another reason I wanted to call was to ask for permission to post the lengthy article in print form. John Green's name was also listed as a correspondent. After everything, including two emails with researcher and author John Green, I was allowed to post the story in its entirety. I wish to thank Bobbie Short, John Green, and the Gimlins.

### Bobbie Short's Prologue

When this videotape was sent to me in May of 1995, I couldn't believe what an incredible piece of history it represented. It didn't take long before I decided that it needed to be aired publicly, and what better place than on this California Sightings webpage? Thus began the long and arduous process of transcribing the narration, if only for posterity.

The following interview is Bob Gimlin's account, as told to John Green, concerning the events that occurred when Roger Patterson filmed the Bigfoot on the afternoon of October 20, 1967. This interview is by no means complete. The circumstances that occurred prior to this event were not recorded by Gimlin or Green; there are other significant events seen in this film, and these do require an explanation.

We should all be grateful to veteran Bigfoot researcher and author John Green for his foresight in recording Gimlin's views and his generosity in giving me this heretofore unpublished interview for this website. My sincere appreciation to John and to Bob Gimlin, as well, for these few recollections of the Bluff Creek incident. My thanks also to Peter Guttilla, who made it all come together with prodding encouragement from the wings. It is testimony to veteran Bigfoot generosities. (Bobbie Short, September 30, 1995, updated 2002 and again in 2008.)

## The Video

John Green's videotaped interview with Bob Gimlin was dated 5:42 p.m., March 29, 1992. The camera is trained on Bob Gimlin throughout the film, with John Green asking questions out of range of the camera. The interview proves to be a treasured piece of Bigfoot history, as these two gentlemen take us through the events of October 20, 1967, as seen through the eyes of the only surviving witness to the filming of the famous Patterson Bigfoot film. Gimlin is soft-spoken and extremely credible as he quietly recounts the event, dispelling myths, eliminating half-truths, and dismissing hearsay about what truthfully happened that day. Bigfoot historians and devotees should find Gimlin's account worthy of review for generations to come.

**Green:** This is John Green talking to Bob Gimlin in his home in Yakima, Washington. This is [in] regard to the movie Bob and his friend Roger Patterson made twenty-five years ago in Northern California (Bluff Creek Area), but we'll start a little further back than that. You've known Roger for a long time, haven't you?

**Gimlin:** Yes. I knew Roger in the early 1960s. I met Roger about 1958-59.

**Green:** So that was before he got interested in Bigfoot?

**Gimlin:** Yes. I can't recall just exactly when he did start talking to me about Bigfoot, but it was probably in the early 1960s.

**Green:** Did you go out with him at all, looking into this?

**Gimlin:** Yes. Roger and I had gone out many times in different areas and over in the Mt. St. Helens area and actually up in this area here, because there was a fellow who said he sighted one right up here at

Cowiche Canyon, about twenty miles from here. I went up there with Roger on that investigation. Of course, we covered as many of them as we could when they'd call or somebody would give us a report on something happening in the area. Roger and I rode [horseback] in the mountains quite a bit because I was training horses at that time. Of course I rode a lot in the mountains, and Roger would go along with me. He'd play tapes and talk to me about the creature. I was a skeptic in those days. I trusted Roger's thoughts and his knowledge, but I wasn't really convinced that they existed.

**Green:** How did you come to take this particular trip to California?

**Gimlin:** Well, Roger and I had been over in Mt. St. Helens riding the roads and just more or less going by the lava rock caves and things when we came back from there... well, let's go back a little bit here... it started raining real heavy over there. This was in the last part of August and the first part of September. When we got back to the Yakima area, somebody in California had phoned Roger's wife and left a message that there had been tracks sighted on new roads they'd been pushing back into the Bluff Creek area they were building logging roads into. That's the reason we went down into that area.

**Green:** Did Roger usually carry a movie camera with him?

**Gimlin:** Yes. Most of the time he had a camera, as far as I can recall. I wasn't much on cameras, but Roger did have one, and prior to that, he'd been working with a guy up in this area here. That was when he bought the camera. I knew he had that camera. He usually kept it in his saddlebags on his horse.

**Green:** When you went to California, did you have some definite time you were going to spend there?

**Gimlin:** Yes... well, we didn't know exactly, because I was working construction at that time and was between jobs, so I said, "Yes, I can take off and go down there." I cannot recall the exact amount of time I was going to stay down there with him, but we stayed longer than I'd planned on staying. In fact, we stayed a week longer than I'd planned.

**Green:** How long were you there?

**Gimlin:** I think we were down there [in California] a total of three weeks.

**Green:** And what were you traveling with?

**Gimlin:** I had a one-ton truck with a horse van to haul the animals and all of our equipment. Of course we took all our supplies to stay as long as we needed to stay — the hay, the grain, our own food — because once we got in there, we never went into town.

**Green:** How many horses did you have?

**Gimlin:** We had three, two saddle horses and a packhorse. I had a saddle horse, Roger had a saddle horse, and of course we had a small packhorse along.

**Green:** What was Al de Atley's role in this?

**Gimlin:** Well, Al de Atley was Roger Patterson's brother-in-law, and he backed Roger financially with whatever expenses it took Roger to go to these places. He was supposed to help me on some of the expenses, which I never did receive.

**Green:** So you provided the truck and the —

**Gimlin:** Yeah, and the fuel, my own horse, and my own food. The agreement when we left on any of those investigations was that whatever Roger spent, he would split the expenses with me, but Al de Atley was backing Roger, because Roger didn't have a job at the particular time.

**Green:** So, in fact, he only financed Roger. He didn't finance your share at all?

**Gimlin:** No, he didn't finance my part of the trip at all. I had my own horse, my own equipment, and my own food. I didn't expect somebody else to support me on that. It would have been nice if I could have gotten part of the fuel paid and expenses on the truck.

**Green:** So you went to an area where you heard [that] tracks had been seen fairly recently?

**Gimlin:** Yes. Just prior to the time we had gotten there, they had sighted tracks on that Tuesday after being off over the Labor Day weekend. It had also started raining up and down the West Coast. By the time we got down there, these tracks were supposedly three different sizes and were just globs in the mud, as far as I was concerned. We couldn't get any plaster cast definition of them at all.

**Green:** I never realized you went down there for that specific set of tracks…

**Gimlin:** Yes, that's the reason we went into that area. I wasn't real anxious to go down there because I needed to get back to work, but Roger kept saying these guys were pretty good down in that area. I can't remember the fellow's name who called up here…

**Green:** Probably Al Hodgson.

**Gimlin:** Yes! It was Al Hodgson, but there was somebody else who had talked to Roger too, a guy who worked for the Forest Service.

**Green:** Syl McCoy maybe?

**Gimlin:** Yes, I think that was his name. Yeah, McCoy… or something like that. Course, it took me a while around here to get things ready so my wife could do my chores because I had animals at that time, to be able to feed them and take care of them… to be gone that long… [reflecting]… why, I had to make provisions for her to take care of the animals.

**Green:** That's interesting, because I was there and saw those tracks you're referring to, and when I was there, Al Hodgson told me he was expecting Roger. Maybe he'd called him already by then.

**Gimlin:** May have.

**Green:** I took that to mean Roger already had a trip there planned before that…

**Gimlin:** Uh-huh. Well, I don't recall whether he had a trip planned prior to the call or not. In fact, I don't think he did. Like I said, we'd been in the Mt. St. Helens area, and when I came back here I was going to go back to work in two weeks. Then I talked to him [Roger] again. We said we were kind of between jobs, so we could take a couple weeks off, and that's mainly the reason I went down, and Roger went with me because it was my equipment.

**Green:** So what did you do when you got there?

**Gimlin:** Well, first we set up camp, of course. Then, the way we do is just ride the roads. When these guys were working on the roads with bulldozers and everything, as quick as they'd quit working, we would ride up in that area and search for tracks or whatever we'd run into. Then we would take the one-ton pick-up when the equipment was off the road, so we could drive the roads. We would drive the roads at night real slow, looking for tracks crossing the road. Of course, in the daytime, we couldn't drive the roads 'cause they were working on the roads up in there. They had started logging in some areas, and the logging trucks had started coming down from there. We covered as many miles as we could with the amount of time we had. We could only go out so far, and then we had to go back to camp. I mean, we did ride back to camp and use the truck to drive the roads at nighttime.

**Green:** What happened on this particular day?

**Gimlin:** The day we got the film footage, I left early in the morning, and Roger slept in. I just rode out and around. I always got up early, so I rode on out. My horse loosened a shoe, and I came back in to tack the shoe on tighter. About ten, mid-morning or so, I sat around there for a little while, because Roger was gone when I got back. Supposedly, he'd gone down the creek there… ah, Bluff Creek there, and after a while he came back and asked what area I had covered that morning. I told him, and he said, "Why don't we ride up into this area we had ridden into before?" a desolate area down a couple of canyons. There's a creek running through it. So we went ahead and fixed lunch, and he said, "Let's get our gear together so when we ride out, we can stay if we have to and stay a little bit later into the night if we need to." We packed up the packhorse, and it was about midday, perhaps a little bit after noontime, when we went around this bend in the creek bed. There was a fallen tree, and as we came around it, there was this creature standing by the creek. That was when everything started happening. The horses started jumping around, raising the devil and spooking from this creature. Roger… well, his horse was rearing up and jumping around. He slid off him, got his camera out of the saddlebags, and started trying to get pictures of this creature as it was walking away.

The film footage you see [the Patterson film] is what was acquired from that particular sighting in the few seconds we had film to take pictures with… and then Roger ran out of film in the camera. The reason for him running out of film was, as we were riding up there, we just took our time and fooled around. It was in the fall of the year, the maple trees were turning red, and it was kind of pretty, and Roger was taking pictures of me riding up the canyons, pictures of the trees and photographing the surrounding areas. So when this all happened, he didn't have much film left in the camera unfortunately. Of course, some of it was kind of blurry because he was running across the creek to get a better view — a closer view of the creature in a better way and [to] get more pictures of it. When he did run out of film, why, naturally, it was one of those old cameras, and he had to get under a poncho to change film.

We went to catch his horse and the packhorse because I kept my horse under control. I had my horse with me all the time. So we caught his horse, got the new film out of the saddlebags, he got under this old poncho and changed the film around. Then we tried to track the creature on up from where we had last seen it. We didn't have much luck doing it. Then we decided it was getting late in the afternoon. In that area, that time of year, the sun goes down about three thirty or four o'clock. We wanted to get back and take plaster casts of the tracks and then go on into town to see if we had anything on film. We weren't sure from Roger stumbling and falling down on the sandbar and getting up and running… we didn't even have an idea that we had anything on film at that time… in fact, it was doubtful that we did have anything.

**Green:** So you cast the tracks the same day?

**Gimlin:** Yes. In fact, right that afternoon. By the time we got the tracks cast and the different deals that we did to cast the tracks done, it was getting late. It was almost dark by the time we got back down to the truck and got the horses fed and tied up. By the time we got into town at Al Hodgson's store, it was good and dark. I imagine it was about eight thirty or nine o'clock. Then we went on over to… [reflecting]… oh whatever town that was to mail the film up to Al de Atley, Roger's brother-in-law, so he could take it and get it developed to see if there was really anything on the film.

Okay, I'll go back a little bit to the casting of the tracks. I rode the big horse. The horse I was riding was around 1,200 to 1,300 pounds. I rode him alongside the tracks with this new film in the camera. Roger took pictures of how deep the horse's prints were in the soil compared to the creature's tracks. Then I got up on a stump which was approximately three to four feet, you know? We didn't measure it, probably should have. Anyway I jumped off with a high-heel boot as close to the track as we could. Then we took pictures of that to illustrate the depth that my footprint went into the same dirt with a high heel cowboy boot; at that time I weighed 165 pounds. These were all things that we did prior to leaving the scene. It was a good thing we did, because that night when we came back… course, we were pretty excited about just seeing it, and we sat there and talked about it until about twelve thirty or one o'clock in the morning.

Around five thirty a.m. or so it started raining, just a pouring down rain. I told Roger we better get up and do something about the tracks or they'd wash out, and he said, "No. It'll stop raining after a while." I went ahead and got up, put the saddle on my horse, and decided I would ride up there while it was raining really hard and

Roger says, "Ah, it'll quit. Don't ride up there." I said, "No, I'm going to go ahead and ride on up there." I had gotten a couple of cardboard boxes from Mr. Hodgson's to cover these tracks the night before. So when I went outside to get a couple of these boxes that were folded up out there, they were just soggy old pieces of cardboard. I disregarded taking those back up there, so I rode back up to the scene, pulled some bark off some trees, and covered up the tracks the best I could and went back to camp.

By then we decided it wasn't going to quit raining. The little creek that was six or seven feet across was now ten or twelve feet across and four feet deep! We were on the side of the creek that had to be crossed with the truck to get out to the main road. I said, "Well, I'm going to go ahead and cross the creek with the truck and get started out." And of course Roger thought it would stop raining, and he suggested I leave him there and come back and pick him up.

In the meantime, why ah… they had called the track-dog people in Canada, and they were supposed to come down. I think they had also phoned you, Mr. Green, and René Dahinden. I'm not sure when all that happened, but I do remember the people in Canada had been called with the track-dogs to come on down to see if we could track it up on through the mountains from where we last saw it.

**Green:** I think it was the British Columbia Museum that was called, 'cause they were the people who phoned me.

**Gimlin:** Was that it? Oh, I couldn't recall just exactly how that went.

**Green:** A man from the museum had come down with me at the beginning of September, after I was there and told them the tracks were there.

**Gimlin:** Oh, was that it? Okay. Well, I didn't remember just exactly how those sequences happened.

**Green:** Yes, well it was from him I learned of the movie. The call must have gone to the museum.

**Gimlin:** Must have, yeah. Well, Roger didn't do that. I think it was Al Hodgson. I think Roger had talked to him about the calling… well, they had talked about it, but I was not present at the time they did.

**Green:** About how far was it from your camp to where this a…

**Gimlin:** Oh, a calculated guess, I think it was about four miles…

**Green:** That movie that you took, comparing the depths of the tracks, that would be the one you showed at the University of British Columbia?

**Gimlin:** Yes. That is the one shown in British Columbia.

**Green:** Are you aware that movie has been missing almost ever since?

**Gimlin:** Yes, I am aware of that. I asked before Roger passed away, and his reply was that Al de Atley had that somewhere. He didn't tell me exactly where. He [Roger] said Al has the film in his possession somewhere. Of course I asked Al de Atley about it, and he denied having it and denied it ever existed. That seems strange to me because I knew it existed and Roger knew it existed!

**Green:** … and so did all the people at the University of British Columbia!

**Gimlin:** Exactly. See… so why the film disappeared, I'll never know and [will] probably never find out…

**Green:** Sounds almost as if Al lost it…

**Gimlin:** … or sold it. Who knows what happened to it?

**Green:** Well you'd think if it had been sold, it would have shown up…

**Gimlin:** Well you know Al and Roger toured with that film afterward, and it's hard telling what went on in those days, and of course Roger made some deal with American National, which I never did know… I was never allowed to know the exact depth of it or what exactly happened there.

**Green:** But you know René Dahinden and I were the first people to make a deal for the use of the film itself. Al brought to Seattle the film of the creature and a great deal of footage that Roger had taken of the waterfalls and trees and various things like that. The footprint film was supposed to be there, but it wasn't.

**Gimlin:** Was it supposed to be on the same roll of film?

**Green:** Oh no!

**Gimlin:** It was just a different roll of film then?

**Green:** Well, I don't remember now if he brought a lot of little boxes or whether this film had already been spliced…

**Gimlin:** Yeah, see…

**Green:** But anyway, we showed it expecting to find the footprint film, but it wasn't there.

**Gimlin:** Yes, being as I didn't know much about movie cameras or splicing film or any of that sort of thing, anybody could have shown me the film, and I wouldn't have been able to detect a splice, except I knew what was taken [filmed]. We all saw it, you know? Course, the film footage of the creature wasn't that good, but the other film footage was plain. It was taken during sunlight hours, and I thought it was a good film. I don't know what you guys thought about it, but I thought it was a pretty good film.

**Green:** Oh yes, as I remember I only saw it once but it was perfectly clear I thought… [inaudible]

**Gimlin:** Well I saw it at the same time you guys did. I don't really recall everything that happened way back then, you know. Course, there was a lot of speculation at that time, and Roger and Al had big dollar signs in their eyes, you know. They were just going to go here and go there… and well, we did travel a lot with that film. There was a lot of money spent. Course, *Argosy* bought one article at that particular time; I think it was the fall of 1967 *Argosy* bought the article. After that, Al and Roger traveled with the film and promoted it somewhat.

That was about the time I went back to work because I didn't have any income. They just kind of cut me completely out of the thing. It took me forever to kind of… well, even after Roger died, I had to go to court to get any rights at all out of it which… [reflecting]… you know was kind of an odd thing. But between Mrs. Patterson's attorney and her, it was a deal where they did not recognize that I had any interest at all in the film. At one time I was supposed to be one-third partner on everything that happened if there was money coming in, but then that all changed. The film itself… now maybe Al lost it, I really don't know what happened to that film footage where Roger and I took film of the tracks, my boot tracks and the horse's, and so forth…

**Green:** Remember how deep the horse tracks were compared to that of the Sasquatch tracks?

**Gimlin:** The horse tracks were not as deep as the Sasquatch tracks, of course. I just walked the horse through. I walked him as slow as I could, but you figure he was distributing his weight on four feet. The tracks were better than half as deep, but they weren't as deep as the tracks of the creature.

**Green:** But the area of the four hoof prints wouldn't be any greater than two of those footprints, would it?

**Gimlin:** No, no… the hoof print area if you're familiar with sizes of horses' hoof prints, well the horse wore a size one shoe, which is not quite six inches in diameter, probably more like five inches in diameter with a number one shoe on the front feet. The shoes were a little bit smaller on the back feet. They were size ones trimmed down… Of course, I rode the horse too, so there was my extra weight plus the horse's weight plus the saddle and tack and everything I had on him. There was probably a total of about 1,400 pounds.

**Green:** How about when you jumped off the stump?

**Gimlin:** When I jumped off the stump with a high-heel boot in the dirt, the footprint went almost as deep as the creature's footprint. We didn't actually measure. We didn't have a ruler, and we just took pictures of it. Viewing it [the film], you could actually tell better for depth. By looking at it and making a judgment on the sight of it, it wasn't as deep as the creature's footprint. They weren't exactly side by side either. They were probably two or three feet between my track and the creature's track, but there was some distance between them. The soil was practically the same. That soil had all been washed in there from the flood a year prior. There could have been some variation in the soil. We really didn't get into it that deep. It was a thing where we were pretty excited about it all, and there was a time element there to get all these things done before dark.

**Green:** You know when you walked around the tracks, when you took that movie, your boot tracks were there too, weren't they?

**Gimlin:** Yes, right! We walked around it quite a bit, trying to stay out of the tracks as much as possible.

**Green:** But still you would have been close then?

**Gimlin:** Oh yeah. Just walking, we were close, but the boot prints lacked a whole lot going as deep, considerable amount going as deep as the creature's tracks were.

**Green:** Going back now to what happened, when you first saw the creature, how did it come into view?

**Gimlin:** You mean when we first saw it, John?

**Green:** Did you come around a corner, or did you see it from a distance or…?

**Gimlin:** No, it wasn't exactly a corner. We came around a bend. We were riding the creek beds, so when we came around the bend in the creek, this thing was standing alongside the creek — standing upright. We were about sixty to eighty feet away from it when we first saw it. Then, at different times, we were at different distances from it. At one time I was probably as close as sixty feet to it when I rode across the creek and got off my horse. When Roger ran across the creek, the thing immediately started walking away. Then whenever it was that the horses started spooking and throwing fits, the commotion started, and the creature just started walking away.

**Green:** So it was standing when you first saw it?

**Gimlin:** It was standing still, right at the edge of the creek when we first saw it, yes.

**Green:** Right at the edge?

**Gimlin:** Right by the edge of the creek, yes.

**Green:** But fully upright?

**Gimlin:** Fully upright, standing upright, yes.

**Green:** What exactly did the horses do?

**Gimlin:** Well, Roger was in the front, and his horse tried to spin around and come back. I was riding behind him on the big horse leading the packhorse along. My horse was kind of spooky, but not near as bad as Roger's horse. Roger's horse was a spooky little horse. He was a young horse of course. The horse I was riding was an older cow horse, [had] been roped on and used for a lot of things. Roger's horse threw all kinds of fits, and when Roger got off the horse, he ran off, and the packhorse jerked free from me and ran off back down the way we came.

**Green:** Did Roger's horse buck?

**Gimlin:** No, it never did. Just reared and jumped all around. His horse was in front of me, and of course I wasn't looking straight at him all the time. This all happened in a couple heartbeats, you know. It happened fast!

**Green:** But then Roger's horse didn't go down?

**Gimlin:** No. It didn't fall down. Just reared up is all.

**Green:** Because this has been said since [inaudible]… you know that Roger's horse fell down?

**Gimlin:** No, no, his horse never did fall down. No.

**Green:** Okay, that's interesting. So did he get the camera while he was still on the horse?

**Gimlin:** Yes, while he was stepping down off the horse. Umm, a lot of people have asked me about that, and they probably don't realize the agility Roger had. He was a tremendous athlete. Roger had tremendous agility! He had been a rodeo rider, he did gymnastics, and this wasn't a full-size horse Roger was riding either. It was a pony, a small horse.

**Green:** Yeah, I've seen those little horses. He used to haul them in a Volkswagen bus.

**Gimlin:** Yeah, we used to haul two of them in a VW bus. Roger rode them because they were easy to get on and off of because Roger wasn't a very big man. So actually, when he was getting off his horse, he always kept that saddlebag ready. The saddlebag had two flaps on it to keep it buckled down. He kept one buckled and one of them unbuckled so he could get his camera [out] in the event he needed it in a hurry, and this was the case at that particular time.

**Green:** So he practiced getting the camera out of the saddlebags in a hurry?

**Gimlin:** Oh yeah, lots of times. Yes, he did. It was his theory that if he ever had to get it, ah, kept the one buckle on there so it would not bounce out while he was riding and the other one loose so he could get it out in a hurry.

**Green:** Did Roger have a gun at all?

**Gimlin:** Yeah, Roger had a 303 British rifle in his saddle scabbard, and I had a thirty-ought-six rifle in my saddle scabbard.

**Green:** Did you have any expectation that you might see one?

**Gimlin:** No, I surely didn't. I don't think Roger did either! We always carried rifles with us when we went into the mountains — at least I always did, and I'm sure Roger did too.

**Green:** Had you discussed whether you would shoot at one of these creatures if you saw one?

**Gimlin:** Yes, many times. We had talked about it but decided unless it was necessary, we would never shoot. In other words, unless it was violent or attempted to attack us or something in that sense of the word… you know?

**Green:** So, when Roger was off his horse and ran after the creature with the camera, what did you do?

**Gimlin:** Roger said, "Cover me," and pulled the camera out. If they don't understand what that means, well, he didn't have any protection — just the camera in his hand, and in case something were to happen…

What I did was ride across the creek, pull my rifle out of the scabbard, step down off the horse, and just stood there with my rifle. I never raised the rifle like I would shoot or anything like that… just held it in my hand and with the other hand held my horse to keep him from getting away from me.

**Green:** So there was never a gun pointed at the creature?

**Gimlin:** No, never. I didn't point the rifle at the creature.

**Green:** Did you ever feel the creature was acting at all threatening?

**Gimlin:** No. It kept walking away all the time. It turned and looked around, once at Roger and once at me. The first time it turned and looked was the time I rode across the creek. I was off to its right… [reflecting]… behind it, and that was when it made one turn with its head. Then, when Roger relocated himself on a log, steadying the camera at one time, then when he ran to another position to get a better view and a better picture, the creature turned its head a second time. I assume it was looking at Roger. When you view the film, I never could really decide whether it turned to look at me or Roger because all these things happened tremendously fast, and I was trying to hold onto my horse and a rifle at the same time and also keep an eye on the creature and Roger.

**Green:** Do you have much of a mental image now of what you saw as opposed to what you've seen in the movie since that time?

**Gimlin:** I don't think it's changed that much. Yes, I still have a mental image of what really happened that day. There may be a few things I've overlooked or forgotten over the years, but basically the time of the day and how the thing moved and what we did is pretty much still in my mind — pretty exact in my mind because even though we were excited, you never seem to forget those things.

**Green:** When you first saw it, how big did you think it was, Bob?

**Gimlin:** I thought it was about six and a half feet tall, and I would have guessed its weight at 250 to 300 pounds. It did have tremendous muscle bulk. This was an estimated guess at the time, of course. I'm not used to seeing things like that. I was just guessing weight compared to the amount of muscle quarter horses have. It was as big as a quarter horse, naturally, and the height… we were up on our horses at the time we first saw the creature; therefore, it probably didn't look as tall as it really was… Now the horse I was riding was a sixteen-hand horse. One hand is four inches on a horse. My horse was sixteen hands tall, plus my saddle. That would make him approximately sixteen and a half hands high. Now of course, with me sitting up there, you can figure my eye level was about nine feet high, so anything actually less than nine feet, [I'd] be looking down at it.

**Green:** Was it obvious whether it was male or female?

**Gimlin:** Well, it appeared to be a female, but you know, I had never seen one. I had never even seen a track until that day, so I couldn't even make a statement whether it was male or female. But the film indicates that it had mammary glands, so we assumed it was a female.

They had told us the tracks they found in the road were three different sizes. We talked about that at length and discussed it and assumed there was a male, a female, and a younger one, with those three different sized tracks. So, our first assumption was it was a female.

**Green:** What color did it appear to be to you?

**Gimlin:** It was a dark brown, [a] brownish color…

**Green:** Then it wasn't as dark as it looks in the film?

**Gimlin:** No… It was a long ways from being tan, but it wasn't a very dark brown like it shows in the film. It was a lighter brown. Of course it was lighter in different areas of its body too, I suppose. Where the hair was shorter it was lighter or vice versa, it might have been darker where the hair was shorter.

**Green:** Can you remember details on its face?

**Gimlin:** Yes, I can. The face [had] a flat-type nose. The lips… I can't really remember what the lips looked like except it did have lips, and we could see its teeth. The eyes were large eyes — not big, round eyes like a horse's or a cow's but there were large eyes. The hair on its face was short. There wasn't a whole lot of hair around its cheeks and down along the face… The best I can remember is the face didn't have a whole lot of hair on it.

**Green:** What would the skin color be then?

**Gimlin:** It seemed like it was a brownish-color skin… [reflecting deeply]

**Green:** Was it doing anything with its hands?

**Gimlin:** You mean a…

**Green:** Well, in the film they were just swinging…

**Gimlin:** Well, John, that [was] all I ever saw. It never raised its arms or anything to that effect. It just walked with an easy motion away from us and swung its arms like a human being. The best I can remember is the hands were about the same color as the face… [reflecting, with a deep stare of recollections]

**Green:** The bottoms of its feet looked quite light [in color], but that could be sand…

**Gimlin:** I think that is the case. The sand wasn't a white sand. It was kind of a funny-type soil there where the creature walked through, lighter-colored dirt. I think you can remember the color of the soil, John…

**Green:** Oh yeah…

**Gimlin:** It was pretty light-colored soil in there, and [that] might have been why the soles of the feet looked light in the film footage.

**Green:** In the movie, it hasn't quite disappeared when the picture stops because it looks as if it's about to disappear behind a big pile of… well, it looked like a stump or pile of wood of some kind.

**Gimlin:** Yeah, it hadn't disappeared when the film footage… ah, when Roger ran out of film because it traveled on — oh, probably not half again the distance of where he… but another thirty or forty yards. There [were] some trees down in that area, I suppose from the flood and so forth. There were many fallen trees and different things in that area. Then, when the creature did disappear up a little draw, why, I wanted to follow it. Of course Roger didn't want to follow it because he was on foot, and he didn't want to be left there. We thought there was the possibility there were the two others around… We didn't know at the time whether that was one of the ones who had made the tracks up above the scene or not.

Roger was a little bit upset about that, so he wanted to catch his horse and get some more film in the camera. It took quite a while to catch the horse and to catch the packhorse as well and tie them up. Then we rode on in pursuit of the creature. Now see, the way it went… to see if we could see more tracks or… [reflecting again]… I don't know. I thought maybe we could see this creature again. I don't really know why I was thinking that. We never did see it again, but we saw scuffs in the gravel and in the creek bed there that indicated where it had possibly run when it went out of sight. We measured sixty-eight to seventy-two inches in the stride, which was not even close to accurate because it was, as I have said, just scuffs in the gravel. Then we tracked on up the creek bed quite a ways. We saw one wet half of a footprint on a rock as it went up into the mountains, and that was as far as we went with it.

**Green:** So there wasn't sand to show footprints beyond where you saw it?

**Gimlin:** No. It was gravel mostly. There was sand and dirt where it went across the creek, but it never left a footprint in the sand or in the dirt or soil. It did leave a wet mark on the rock in the creek where it went across and went on into the hills from there.

**Green:** Were you ever closer to it than Roger was while he took the pictures?

**Gimlin:** Yeah, I was. When I rode across the creek and got off my horse, I was closer than Roger was with the camera at that time. I rode fairly close to the creature.

**Green:** … and I suppose Roger wouldn't have had much of a look at it because he was looking through the lens of the camera all the time…

**Gimlin:** Well, yes. I feel I had a better look at it. We talked about it like I said. When we got back to the camp that night, we stayed up and talked about that for hours — you know, talked about what each one of us had seen. There [were] things I had seen about the creature that Roger didn't. Of course, he couldn't see it too well, because he was looking through the camera.

**Green:** When you got off the horse, what size did it appear to be then?

**Gimlin:** Well, to be plum honest with you, I didn't even think about sizes at the time it was going away. It was large, but I never gave any thought to how high it was or how heavy it was because it was moving away from me. That was about all that was in my mind at the time — that this creature was no threat to us… and, oh yeah, I was trying to keep my horse under control 'cause, you know, I never had any idea what might happen, and I sure didn't want to be on foot! So I knew I could get back on my horse and maybe if I had to… [pausing reflectively]… well, if I had to, if I had to shoot it and it didn't go down, I could get on my horse and get out of there… and Roger would have to fend for himself [slight grin]. I'm not a coward, but I'll be darned if I was going to stick around if the creature got violent, you know? So I was concentrating on keeping my rifle in my hand and my horse under control… [voice fades off in deep recollection].

**Green:** There is, of course, this widespread opinion that this was some kind of masquerade. Having the film, of course there is a certain amount of blurring and a certain amount of under exposure of the creature itself. You can't see the face, for instance. You had a much better look at it than that. What was your impression?

**Gimlin:** My impression is that there *is* a creature, and I don't feel it was a man in a suit. If it had been a man in a suit, I don't know how they would have gotten him back into that particular area. I have heard this story and thought about it many times. God! At one point, with the film circulating all around and people criticizing, I was almost to the point of not being even sure myself. But I've thought about it all these years, and I'm quite sure it wasn't a man in a suit. I saw the face. I saw the expression on its face. With all the muscles in the arms and legs, I don't know how it could be a man in a suit! Plus, I never had anything to do with a man in a suit, and *if* Roger did, how would he know I wouldn't shoot it? [slight hint of a smile]. In my opinion, that creature was not a man in a suit.

**Green:** Could you see the muscles move when it walked?

**Gimlin:** Yes, I could see the muscles clearly, and that was one of the deciding factors, in my opinion, that this was no man in a suit. The thighs, the buttocks, the arms and shoulders… you could see it move clearly underneath the hair.

**Green:** You have estimated this thing to weigh a great deal less than the horse, yet the footprints were deeper. What explanation could you think of?

**Gimlin:** Well, you asked my estimation when I first saw it.

**Green:** No, no… but…

**Gimlin:** Oh you mean afterward? Well, God, John, there was no way of really knowing. We knew it had to be heavier than it appeared to be when we first saw it. Of course, we thought the horse's weight was distributed on four feet, and I'm not good with the mathematics of such things, but, ah… if you figure 1,400-pound horse distributed on four feet would be about 350 to 400 pounds, so we figured it must have weighed much more than we originally figured. Course, Roger did some research by going over to the zoo in Seattle. He watched the gorillas there and asked how much they weighed and so forth. They had one over there named Bobo. I don't remember his weight exactly, but I do remember he weighed more than it looked like he weighed.

**Green:** Yes, I did the same thing with those same gorillas…

**Gimlin:** Uh-huh…

**Green:** … and there was a female gorilla there that was quite small but was tremendously heavy…

**Gimlin:** Yeah, John, that is what Roger was telling me. I wasn't all that interested at the time, whatever it was, you know? In the end, it probably weighed approximately 500 pounds to make tracks that deep in the dirt. Of course, when it walked, it kicked up a certain amount of dirt from pressure of the toes pushing away.

**Green:** Well it would have to distribute the weight on different parts of the foot when it walks; otherwise, there is no way it could have made a deeper print than the horse.

**Gimlin:** Yes, right.

**Green:** If its feet were put down flat, each foot would have an area as big as three of the horse's feet…

**Gimlin:** Yes.

**Green:** You would have to roll that imprint in some way or another…

**Gimlin:** Yeah, right.

**Green:** So when you saw it, up until that moment, you had never seen a track?

**Gimlin:** Never. Never seen a track at all. That's right.

**Green:** And you weren't at all convinced that there were any such animals to be seen?

**Gimlin:** That is true. I was not convinced that they really existed. You know, I figured Roger must have had a reason. He showed me plaster casts, and I heard different stories from people who had seen them, so I thought, *Well, maybe there is something to this,* but I just didn't believe in them basically… didn't believe it was possible they could exist. Even after we got the film, many people said, "Uh, they don't exist," and still people tell me it's a bunch of malarkey, you know? There will always be a certain amount of people you just can't convince 'less they see one.

**Green:** Well, when you did see it, there wasn't any doubt you were looking at an animal, was there?

**Gimlin:** There is no doubt in my mind at all.

**Green:** Okay. That ought to do it, Bob. Thanks a lot!

**Gimlin:** You're quite welcome, John.

[End of videotaped interview]

The videotaped interview ran more than an hour. This interview may NOT be used, copied or any portions taken out of context for use elsewhere without express permission from John Green and Bob Gimlin. All rights reserved. Uploaded on Bigfoot Encounters website with permission… *Bobbie Short*

© John Green [JG4]

# 13. Bigfoot and Infrasound

Most encounters with Bigfoot talk about the intense fear the observers feel. Usually it is so intense that someone who sees Bigfoot panics to the extent of not being able to think and has not even a remote possibility of staying in the neighborhood of the creature. The question I want to address in this chapter is whether this is normal fear or something else.

Researchers propose that Bigfoot is capable of making what is called infrasound — a special kind of noise that induces uncontrollable fear. I want to explore this possibility by looking at how I handled two encounters with grizzly bears — also pretty scary creatures.

I must say, life in the outdoors is seldom boring. In fact, it seems to always produce memorable experiences — in some cases, the most memorable we have ever faced.

Both grizzly incidents occurred in the 1990s, while I was mountain biking. My next-door neighbor was involved with one, and our oldest son was present for the second. Both of these situations took place along Highway 40 (Kananaskis Trail), which stretches from Longview, British Columbia, north to the Trans Canada Highway. North and south crossing gates do not allow travel on Highway 40 until around June 15, making the date of these happenings relatively easy to remember.

On the first occasion, my neighbor Bob and I were biking in from the south end. There was no traffic on the highway, so it was perfect for a ride. It was at Mist Creek where he and I ran into a traversing grizzly along a cut line that intersects the highway.

Of course we kept our distance from the bear, though Bob did mention that it was the first time he'd ever felt like part of the food chain. We had a chuckle over that, even though the grizzly didn't seem to be paying us much attention, as a food source or otherwise.

We continued our uphill struggle with our bicycles, and three or four minutes passed. Our alarm was raised when we realized the grizzly had circled around and was now semi-upright, standing on its hind legs. It had sniffed us out from approximately 200 feet away, and we were trying desperately to avoid making eye contact with the animal. We finally moved up the highway slowly, trying to warn oncoming cyclists, some of whom were accompanied by children. At that time of year, in mid-June, there were hundreds of riders on the trail. A rather large grizzly population also shares this wilderness stretch — or should I say, they own it.

Our second contact with a grizzly came a few years later, actually on the day that our mother passed away. Brandon, our oldest son, was biking with me from the north side, approximately one mile from the closed north gate. This was also in early June.

As we rode steadily along on the cool mountain morning, cresting a relatively easy hill, Brandon was the first to notice the animal. It was on all fours on the opposite side of the road up ahead, just watching us.

Both of us were closing fast, and Brandon immediately started braking. I followed suit a second or two later, my front brakes squealing loudly since my bike was new. Without any warning whatsoever, the bear rose to attention; apparently, the sound of our brakes reached the animal's ears, spooking it. The thing shot up the hillside and quickly disappeared into the trees and brush. All we had to do at that point was advance slowly, warning bikers just as Bob and I had before, alerting them to the grizzly presence.

Bear encounters are common in this region, and I mention them because it is important to compare this to an encounter with a creature such as a Sasquatch. When you are confronted by a grizzly — or any wild animal — on its own ground at a relatively close distance, you will likely be faced with a sense of fear, uncertainty, and intimidation. In most cases, a bear will offer signs that can be quickly evaluated. This can even provide answers to the creature's level of unpredictability. In the meetings with the grizzlies, it was another day with nature and what she had to offer. Everyone knows that bears can be temperamental, moody creatures.

Bigfoot, on the other hand, stops our thinking. I have faced both of these species, and those meetings had little in common. For starters, the Sasquatch has somewhat of a monster stigma attached to it, which doesn't help. It is a huge creature, seemingly with brains to match, and it is relatively easy to recognize that the beast is far more intelligent than some of the other woodland dwellers. The grizzlies didn't bring tears to my eyes, make my legs tremble, or raise the hair on my body. The bears did not raise my level of nervousness to the point where I felt out of control. Sasquatch was entirely different; there was no comparison to the furry fellow that maneuvers on all fours. Not exactly the prettiest creature of God's creation, the Bigfoot's sheer size and presence strikes an unnerving fear into most who see it.

I can't deny that I felt that fear, but I wonder if there is more to it than that. Could the Sasquatch be influencing its surroundings with something else? This report from the BFRO files may point to one physical possibility, and there may also be others that we can look at in Parts II and III of this book.

> It happened in 1989 on a hunting trip in the middle region of West Virginia. We were on our yearly deer-hunting trip in the remote mountainous area of Randolph County. I was about twenty-four years old and was on leave from the military for the family hunting trip. My family and friends have hunted this area for many years, and I was very comfortable and familiar with the area.
>
> The road back had not been traveled for years and was very washed out and overgrown with brush. It was about seven to eight miles back before we came to the impassable areas of the road, and it was then that we geared up and proceeded on foot. I would estimate we had gone about another two to three miles on foot before we reached the crest of the mountain and decided to find our hunting spots.
>
> The light had just begun to peek over the mountaintop when I cleared my spot and settled in. I had worked up a pretty good sweat on the steady pace up the mountain, so it was not too long after sitting and listening to the first morning light waking up the rest of the forest that I began to nod off to sleep. After going in and out a few times, I decided to get up and move around a little to try to wake myself up.
>
> After about twenty minutes of walking around, I stumbled on a very old wooden tree stand. Although I could tell it had been there for many years, I remember thinking it was in the best spot overlooking the very visible and open woods just under the crest of the hilltop. Not too long after, I ate the apples and

oranges I had brought. After a while, the warm morning sun took its toll on me, and I nodded off again.

A bad smell woke me right up. The forest was completely quiet around me, and all I could think was, *What the hell is that awful smell?* As I became more alert, I could hear the slight rustling below me and what I thought was some faint grunts and whines. I decided it was time to lean over and get a visual on it.

It was about twenty-five feet below me on the slope and directly in front of the stand. It was not aware of my presence above it. It was about five feet tall with long, dark, reddish-brown hair. The hair from its head down its body was of equal length, about two to three inches long. The hair went down its arms and hands as well as its feet. I could barely see fingernails and toenails — not claws, but nails, like a human's.

Most of its hair was tangled and matted in spots, as if it had wallowed on the ground or a tree or something. I watched it smell the orange peels and apple core, then taste them. It looked around at one point, as if to wonder where they may have come from. I wondered how long it would be before it became aware of my presence and what it would do when it did.

Then I heard the rustling coming down from the top of the hill — loud rustling — and I could tell something was coming at a pretty rapid speed. I saw the one below me turn and look in the direction of the noise. It froze for a few seconds and looked almost like a statue.

I could not see at that point what was coming down the hill. I was leaning to my right and looking down. I tried to move my eyes to the left, but my view was blocked by the tree that was holding up my stand and partially by the full-brim hat I was wearing. I kept my eyes moving between the one below me and the direction of the disturbance coming down the hill.

As it moved toward our position, it began to make noises like I have never heard before. I would ordinarily not be able to describe the noise, but I have read where other people have described it as a record being played backward. I would have to say that is a very close description. It is as if it were speaking a language, but nothing like I have ever heard before.

The one below me sprang to its feet and then moved about fifteen to twenty feet to the right of me. It moved very rapidly, kind of between a run and a leap, all on its feet though; it did not use its arms. It then started to bellow back at the one coming down the hill, and it sounded almost like they were arguing. That was the impression it left me with anyway.

It wasn't until the one above me came into clear view that I started to feel very scared. As it came into my immediate area, it moved toward the first one and began to slow to what seemed to be very cautious movements. Its attention seemed to move between the first creature and its surrounding area. I felt at that moment that it was alert to my presence.

The second one was much larger than the first, and it seemed very irritated. The bigger one was covered in very dark hair, almost black. It was very muscular, and its arms were noticeably long. It stood with a slight bend but an upright posture. It had to be about eight to nine feet tall, much larger than a human.

As these two creatures squabbled (communicated?) back and forth, their gestures were extremely humanlike. I was under the impression that the larger of the two was scolding the smaller one.

They moved about forty to fifty feet to the right of me. At that point, the larger one had its back to me. I could make out facial features of the smaller one. It had very humanlike features but a different nose. Hair covered most of its face, but it looked to be thin hair, not like the rest of it.

Then the smaller creature spotted me because it went into a crouched and then squatting position and looked up in my direction. Their chattering began to quiet, and the larger one, with its back still to me, went into a squatting position for a few seconds. The smaller one then began to howl and bellow very loudly. The larger of the two, with its back still toward me, began to howl very loudly also. The larger creature then pushed the smaller one, and the smaller one sprang to its feet and rapidly ran off across the hill to my right. It ran in long, leaping strides and moved very fast, like nothing I had ever seen. I never noticed it to ever look back.

As the smaller one ran, the larger one stood up and slowly turned toward me. It had its arm bent above its forehead, as if it were shading or hiding its eyes. It stood very straight and tall and looked directly at my tree stand.

All the fear from before overcame me again, and I prayed that thing would not try to come up my tree. I thought for an instant that I would yell at it, jerk or jump, and maybe frighten it away, but I could not bring myself to move. I could not even bat an eye. I could feel my legs starting to shake, and I became very hot all over. For an instant, I thought I was going to pass out or become physically ill.

For a brief moment, it looked right at my face. From what I could see, it had very large, humanlike eyes and very large, round nostrils. I could not make out lips because of the hair on its face but I would guess they were thin lips because the hair did not stick out. It did not have much of a protruding mouth or jaw like an ape. It had a fairly flat face like a human's.

It put its arm to its side and began to look around. It swiveled at the hips and looked in every direction. After a quick glance back at me, it then began to walk off in the direction the smaller one had gone. It did not run or act scared at all. It made very long howls as it walked and turned a few times and looked in my direction as it walked away.

I watched it and listened until it became just a black figure moving through the woods. I could hear it howl and bellow for a few more minutes. Then I heard what sounded like something beating a tree or log with a limb or stick or something.

After about thirty minutes, I decided that if it meant to do me harm, it sure had the chance, and it was probably safe to get down out of the tree stand. I made my way back toward my friend that I had left earlier that morning. I never even thought to check the ground for evidence or anything.

After about an hour, I walked up on my friend and could see his blaze orange through the trees. I very carefully made my way in his direction. As I approached him, I could see that he was staring at me. He was sitting against some downed trees, and he did not move a muscle. As I walked closer to him, I smiled and asked him if he had seen anything. He was very pale, and I could tell he was a little scared and puzzled, and then he answered me, though he was not sure what he had seen.

I jokingly said, "You look like you saw a Bigfoot!"

And he jumped to his feet and asked, "Did you see it?"

I nodded to him and then he began to tell me what he saw. Apparently, the larger creature had moved across the hill in front of him, crashing through the trees about forty or fifty yards away. He said at first he thought it was a bear, but after observing it, he could plainly see that it was moving very fast and walking upright, like a man.

I said we should try to track the two creatures, but it really didn't take too much for him to talk me out of it.

This really happened, sixteen years ago in Randolph County, West Virginia. I have never returned to that area of the woods. [BFRO4]

It would seem that the Sasquatch species may have a similar approach to fear as the human species does, if Charles Darwin's *The Expression of the Emotions in Man and Animals* has anything to say about it:

> The frightened man at first stands like a statue, motionless and breathless, or crouches down as if instinctively to escape observation. [CD1]

In the hunter's story, both of the creatures crouched when facing fear and uncertainty. The smaller one even froze like a statue. Let's not forget how I felt when I ran into those two grizzlies. All these are exhibits of fear and general apprehension.

So, does infrasound step it up a notch? The hunter couldn't bring himself to move or even bat an eye. His legs even began to shake. In my case, I couldn't move from the spot. My legs were shaking and my eyes were watering. I experienced none of this when encountering the large grizzlies.

As discussed at the scientific and research level, it might be possible that the Sasquatch shares traits with a few other large animals. Infrasound is a low-pitched sound used to communicate or possibly threaten. A tiger's overawing roar has been known to incapacitate an animal that hears it, humans included. This rumbling bellow holds low-frequency sounds that can be felt but not heard. This low-range sound, also referred to as infrasound, can find its way through dense brush and forest. It can penetrate buildings and travel long distances.

More fuel for the infrasound case is the elephant, another very large creature. Male African elephants have been shown walking silently for more than a mile toward a loudspeaker playing the female elephant's low-frequency estrous call. Standing near to the elephant, faint pulsations can be felt in the air. Could infrasound be the reason that all the creatures go silent when the Sasquatch is around?

Reverting back to the elephant, it may be possible that the mammal can hear messages within a thirty-square-mile area. The calls involve dominance, mating attributes, and other social aspects. Low-frequency infrasound may carry over five miles under good conditions, and clear, dry air and low humidity only assist the process. Infrasound works best in the evening or at night, when temperatures are more stable. When humans hear low-frequency animal vibrations, the infrasound may cause feelings of awe, fear, and helplessness. Does infrasound play a role in making humans feel as if they are being watched?

At the beginning of the 1974 sighting along Tulameen Avenue, both Alan and I watched the creature cross the road and set foot on the gravel. At that time, we felt nothing out of the ordinary. The Sasquatch did not know we were close by. Only when the giant turned around after being yelled at did we experience the feelings of uneasiness and malaise. So, the question remains: Did we feel petrifying fear because the Sasquatch was now paying attention to us or was infrasound involved? Based on the difference between my encounters with Bigfoot and grizzlies, I think infrasound is a distinct possibility.

# 14. Sasquatch and Evolution

Evolution vs. creation is a major debate in and of itself. And just so you know the range of thought out there, I've included a few opinions on what might happen if a Sasquatch is found, be it alive or deceased. Most of the answers in this chapter came to me from evolutionary biologists or those in similar positions, from centers and universities all over the globe, and their input is much appreciated.

> If something like the Sasquatch was found, it could alter our view of human evolution, but it would depend on just what it looked like and where it was. (Richard Klein, California)

> It might provide information on the evolutionary process that led to modern humans, insofar as one more branch could be studied. There were many hominin and primate species. All the hominins, save us, appear to be extinct. Studies of another surviving ape species would provide additional information. Apart from the novelty of finding the elusive creatures, nothing earth shattering would result unless they had cognitive capacities that vastly exceeded [that of] other apes. If that were the case, studies of the biological bases of these capacities would be interesting. Similar studies of low-temperature or locomotor adaptations (any unique derived features) also would be interesting. A live specimen would be best. (Anonymous, Rhode Island)

> I'm not sure exactly what aspects of the evolutionary process you are referring to, but in general, the question that such a finding would raise would be one of trying to determine what selection pressures would have given rise to a creature such as

Sasquatch or Yeti. In other words, what ecological niche was it adapted to? Hope this helps. (Dr. Matt Rossano, Louisiana)

Finding the Sasquatch would create a big headache for evolutionary biologists, especially if it's some form of ape, as one might suppose from its alleged footprints. The great apes originated in Africa, and only the orangutan reached Asia. This is a tropical species, and it would have had difficulty surviving in Siberia and crossing the Beringian Land Bridge with the ancestors of American Indians. If it did so, it would have left a fossil record. So would the Sasquatch itself which, after all, has to exist as a breeding population of several thousand, not as an individual. Could a population of several thousand, living for thousands of years in North America, have done so without leaving a single fossil or other skeletal remains? Hope these thoughts are of help; you're welcome to use the idea.

It's a general problem with the existence of large strange creatures like the Sasquatch, the Yeti, or the Loch Ness Monster: They all have to exist as populations, not as single individuals. So maybe one Loch Ness Monster could escape detection for a time in the deepness of the lake, but 100 of them? The same must be true of Sasquatches, when you come to think about it. Where are Mrs. Sasquatch and her mom and dad and their parents and cousins and aunts and uncles? And how could so many giant apes escape detection in this day and age, leaving so few traces? (Nicholas Wade, New York)

This is a question that often pops up. It is common for people to say that the reality of Sasquatch would have a great impact on human evolution studies: "It will rewrite the textbooks!" I'm a historian, not a biologist, but I don't think it would impact it that much. If Bigfoot is real, it is certainly not a human ancestor. It would be a fascinating species naturally, but it would not overturn anything about human evolutionary history. It is likely, if it exists, a side branch of the hominid evolutionary line. (Brian Regal, New York)

It won't change the evolutionary process, as such, since the details of what happens in the history of evolution are accidents to time and place, not of the process itself. Finding such creatures might change our understanding of the history of primate evolution, assuming that they are primates and not other kinds of animals. Apes occur in Asia and have occurred at much higher latitudes than they presently do, so Yetis would only be an item of curiosity. Primates haven't occurred in North America for thirty million years, and apes have never lived there. If Bigfoot really is an ape, that would be interesting and [would] require an explanation for how it got to be there, but that's all. (Robin Dunbar, United Kingdom)

The straight answer is that it wouldn't do anything at all to "the evolutionary process." That is up and running anyway, whether we (humans) know about this fact or that fact. What it would do is to raise a number of questions about our knowledge and understanding of the living world, [questions] we would need to think about. The scientific method would swing into action. Observations would be made (e.g. of its anatomy, physiology, ecology, nuclear and mitochondrial DNA, behavior.) Testable hypotheses would be proposed to explain the results of these observations, and the observations and hypotheses would be opened to international scrutiny, peer review, comment, and further investigation. And how would it — or could it — change a number of things? The most obvious and immediate question that would be asked is on its phylogenetic relationships. Is it a member of the order primates, one of the other mammalian orders (e.g. Carnivora, family Ursidae) or a new mammalian order? If it is a primate, where does it fit in with regard to the known members of this order, etc., etc.? Only then could we assess the impact of such a discovery on our understanding of the living world. All sorts of issues would subsequently be raised: habitat protection, conservation, ethical issues over welfare, exploitation, etc. (Dr. John M. Deag, United Kingdom)

The information I received merely touches on the issues that might be raised if a Bigfoot were to be caught. As you can see, these scientists generally view it as an unimportant event.

# *15. Bigfoot and the Law*

Over the years, especially in Washington State, legislators have taken an interest in Bigfoot. The purported intent of the laws they have passed was to protect the creature, but you can be sure that the people writing the regulations were well aware of the publicity the regulations brought to their communities.

The first of the laws I found was Bigfoot Ordinance 69-01, written in April 1969 in Skamania County, Washington. An addition was made fifteen years later, Ordinance 1984-2, partially repealing and amending the previous entry. Copies of both ordinances were sent to me in September 2006. Over the years, a fair number of people have mentioned the Bigfoot Ordinances to me, but they were just trying to give further credence to Bigfoot. I wanted to see how this matter really came about.

Skamania County has had several stories of run-ins with the creature — things like the Ape Canyon 1924 incident, as well as the stories surrounding the mysteries of Mt. St. Helens. Mt. Adams, just east of Mt. St. Helens, has its own Bigfoot secrets. Ape Cave and Ape Glacier also have distant association with this creature. Skamania County has been home to this phenomenon for quite some time, but there was also a time when something had to be done about the disorderly rowdies who were causing trouble for everyone in their pursuit of Bigfoot.

For years, the story was building of an enormously tall, dark-haired creature seen on many occasions in Skamania County. Even a few reclusive folks were laying claims to having witnessed a huge bipedal creature walking the roads and woods there. This continued well into the 1960s, the media latching onto encounters from all over the county. Making matters worse was the controversial Patterson/Gimlin encounter of October 1967 in California. Less than eighteen months later in Skamania County, the 1969 Bigfoot Ordinance would be written.

ORDINANCE NO. 69-01

BE IT HEREBY ORDAINED BY THE BOARD OF COUNTY COMMISSIONERS OF SKAMANIA COUNTY:

WHEREAS, there is evidence to indicate the possible existence in Skamania County of a nocturnal primate mammal variously described as an ape-like creature or a sub-species of Homo Sapian; and

WHEREAS, both legend and purported recent sightings and spoor support this possibility, and

WHEREAS, this creature is generally and commonly known as a "Sasquatch", "Yeti","Bigfoot", or "Giant Hairy Ape", and

WHEREAS, publicity attendant upon such real or imagined sightings has resulted in an influx of scientific investigators as well as casual hunters, many armed with lethal weapons, and

WHEREAS, the absence of specific laws covering the taking of specimens encourages laxity in the use of firearms and other deadly devices and poses a clear and present threat to the safety and well-being of persons living or traveling within the boundaries of Skamania County as well as to the creatures themselves,

THEREFORE BE IT RESOLVED that any premeditated, wilful and wanton slaying of any such creature shall be deemed a felony punishable by a fine not to exceed Ten Thousand Dollars ($10,000.00) and/or imprisonment in the county jail for a period not to exceed Five (5) years.

BE IT FURTHER RESOLVED that the situation existing constitutes an emergency and as such this ordinance is effective immediately.

ADOPTED this 1st day of April, 1969.

BOARD OF COMMISSIONERS OF SKAMANIA COUNTY

By Conrad Lundy Jr.
Chairman

APPROVED:

Robert K. Leick
Skamania County Prosecuting Attorney

**Figure 33: Ordinance 1969-01 making it a felony to kill a Bigfoot in Skamania County.**

Investigating along this line, I contacted a very patient and helpful librarian in Vancouver, Washington, who retrieved microfilm of an article from those days. A copy of the written document was later sent through snail mail.

In those days it seemed like Sasquatch was everywhere. The *Skamania County Pioneer News* and the *Columbian* newspaper were but two of the newspapers that reported the stories that were getting around. This would ultimately include the sheriff's office in Stevenson. Heightening the matter, the sheriff collected castings of huge footprints that were located near the town of Carson. I talked with the under-sheriff in October of 2006, but he had no idea where those castings were. He did say, however, that he'd heard stories of Sasquatch encounters from that period, including Don Cox's witnessing of the creature in 1969, just east of Beacon Rock. Clearly, a Sasquatch frenzy of sorts was on the rise.

According to a source in the Columbia Gorge area, whom I corresponded with in 2006, the ordinance and refuge idea may have been done for the reason of safety, more for the hunter rather than the hunted, downplaying the idea of a Sasquatch. Skamania County was being overrun with rambunctious hunters who were crazily determined to kill the Bigfoot and stuff him. The miles of wilderness became extremely hazardous to hikers and campers, as well as other outdoor enthusiasts, the hunters included. According to this helpful source, no one actually got shot, but in her understanding, there were many close calls. She believed the refuge declaration basically eliminated the problem that was becoming a crisis. She would finally state that the refuge and ordinance did not indicate whether or not the officials believed or did not believe in the existence of Bigfoot.

Looking at the updated document from 1984, it is easy to determine that what was a felony in 1969 is now classified as a gross misdemeanor. The fine does not exceed $1,000, with a maximum jail term of one year. Everything is cut in half if this prosecution is deemed a misdemeanor. If they decide you're a nutcase, you just walk.

The one good thing about the law is that if someone broke it, they would not be able to profit from the crime. All those millions from the tabloids and other media would vanish into air — or at least into government coffers — after the perpetrator was convicted.

ORDINANCE NO. 1984-2

PARTIALLY REPEALING AND AMENDING ORDINANCE NO. 1969-01

WHEREAS, evidence continues to accumulate indicating the possible existence within Skamania County of a nocturnal primate mammal variously described as an ape-like creature or a sub-species of Homo Sapiens; and

WHEREAS, legend, purported recent findings, and spoor support this possibility; and

WHEREAS, this creature is generally and commonly known as "Sasquatch", "Yeti", "Bigfoot", or "Giant Hairy Ape", all of which terms may hereinafter be used interchangeably; and

WHEREAS, publicity attendant upon such real or imagined findings and other evidence have resulted in an influx of scientific investigators as well as casual hunters, most of which are armed with lethal weapons; and

WHEREAS, the absence of specific national and state laws restricting the taking of specimens has created a dangerous state of affairs within this county with regard to firearms and other deadly devices used to hunt the Yeti and poses a clear and present danger to the safety and well-being of persons living or traveling within the boundaries of this county as well as to the Giant Hairy Apes themselves; and

WHEREAS, previous County Ordinance No. 1969-01 deemed the slaying of such a creature to be a felony (punishable by 5 years in prison) and may have exceeded the jurisdictional authority of that Board of County Commissioners; now, therefore

BE IT HEREBY ORDAINED BY THE BOARD OF COUNTY COMMISSIONERS OF SKAMANIA COUNTY that that portion of Ordinance No. 1969-01, deeming the slaying of Bigfoot to be a felony and punishable by 5 years in prison, is hereby repealed and in its stead the following sections are enacted:

SECTION 1. Sasquatch Refuge. The Sasquatch, Yeti, Bigfoot, or Giant Hairy Ape are declared to be endangered species of Skamania County and there is hereby created a Sasquatch Refuge, the boundaries of which shall be co-extensive with the boundaries of Skamania County.

**Figure 34: Ordinance 1984-2 changing killing Bigfoot from a felony to a misdemeanor (page 1).**

SECTION 2. Crime - Penalty. From and after the passage of this ordinance the premeditated, wilful, or wanton slaying of Sasquatch shall be unlawful and shall be punishable as follows:

(a) If the actor is found to be guilty of such a crime with malice aforethought, such act shall be deemed a Gross Misdemeanor.

(b) If the act is found to be premeditated and wilful or wanton but without malice aforethought, such act shall be deemed a Misdemeanor.

(c) A gross misdemeanor slaying of Sasquatch shall be punishable by 1 year in the county jail and a $1,000.00 fine, or both.

(d) The slaying of Sasquatch which is deemed a misdemeanor shall be punishable by a $500.00 fine and up to 6 months in the county jail, or both.

SECTION 3. Defense. In the prosecution and trial of any accused Sasquatch killer the fact that the actor is suffering from insane delusions, diminished capacity, or that the act was the product of a diseased mind, shall not be a defense.

SECTION 4. Humanoid/Anthropoid. Should the Skamania County Coroner determine any victim/creature to have been humanoid the Prosecuting Attorney shall persue the case under existing laws pertaining to homicide. Should the coroner determine the victim to have been an anthropoid (ape-like creature) the Prosecuting Attorney shall proceed under the terms of this ordinance.

BE IT FURTHER ORDAINED that the situation existing constitutes an emergency and as such this ordinance shall become effective immediately upon its' passage.

REVIEWED this 2nd day of April, 1984, and set for public hearing on the 16th day of April, 1984, at 10:30 o'clock A m.

BOARD OF COUNTY COMMISSIONERS
Skamania County, Washington

Chairman

Commissioner

Commissioner

ATTEST

County Auditor and Ex-Officio Clerk of the Board

ORDINANCE NO. 1984-2
Page 2 of 3 Pages

**Figure 35: Ordinance 1984-2 changing killing Bigfoot from a felony to a misdemeanor (page 2).**

ORDINANCE NO. 1984-02 IS HEREBY DULY PASSED AND ADOPTED INTO LAW this 16th day of April, 1984.

BOARD OF COUNTY COMMISSIONERS
Skamania County, Washington

Chairman

Commissioner

Commissioner

ATTEST:

County Auditor and Ex-Officio Clerk of the Board

ORDINANCE NO. 1984-2
Page 3 of 3 Pages
Pros. Attny.

**Figure 36: Ordinance 1984-2 changing killing Bigfoot from a felony to a misdemeanor (page 3).**

The real danger might be from Sasquatch itself. Bigfoot isn't like the spotted owl. If the giants exist, I believe they could be pushed into being killers. Considering how human beings are, some idiotic fool would cry foul, even if the Sasquatch were simply trying to protect itself or its young, and it might even happen in a national park or forest. It's better not to kill one.

Another county in Washington also considered the Sasquatch years ago. Although this is construed by some as a Bigfoot protection measure, it has as many holes as Swiss cheese. Whatcom County, just below the Canadian border, passed Resolution 92-043 in 1992, with unanimous approval. It was initially requested by an Al Magnussen, at the Mt. Baker Chamber of Commerce. The resolution was sent to me in the fall of 2006. As for this latest addition to the protection laws, it seemed there was a gray area as well.

When I contacted the Mt. Baker Foothills Chamber of Commerce, a helpful spokesperson from Maple Falls instructed me on how to obtain the information I sought. I wondered why the resolution of 1992 had been put in place. A couple days later, this person helped me find that answer. As she understood it, years earlier the Chamber of Commerce had hosted an annual Bigfoot BBQ in the area. It seemed that the resolution was a ploy to drum up publicity for this event. It was graciously granted by the Whatcom County Council to help with the benefit. I have no idea if the Bigfoot BBQ is still an annual occurrence. What I do hope is that the devoted believers of Sasquatch don't hold these ordinances to heart. Only the Ten Commandments were written in stone.

This trend of Bigfoot legislation continued elsewhere, including the town of Whitehall, New York. The Washington County town signed off on an ordinance quite similar to that proposed in Washington State. The monkey business (and please pardon the expression) was an attempt to boost tourism, as well as to work against the crackpots who didn't know a Sasquatch from a hole in the wall, the narrow-minded extremists running around with loaded slingshots and such.

bigfoot.res 6/9/91

SPONSORED BY: Consent
PROPOSED BY: Harris
INTRODUCTION DATE: 6/9/92

**RESOLUTION NO. 92-043**

**DECLARING WHATCOM COUNTY A SASQUATCH PROTECTION AND REFUGE AREA**

WHEREAS, legend, purported recent findings and spoor suggest that Bigfoot may exist; and

WHEREAS, if such a creature exists, it is inadequately protected and in danger of death or injury;

NOW, THEREFORE, BE IT RESOLVED by the Whatcom County Council that, Whatcom County is hereby declared a Sasquatch protection and refuge area, and all citizens are asked to recognize said status.

BE IT FURTHER RESOLVED, this resolution shall be effective immediately.

APPROVED this 9th day of June, 1991.

ATTEST:

Ramona Reeves, Council Clerk

WHATCOM COUNTY COUNCIL
WHATCOM COUNTY, WASHINGTON

Daniel M. Warner, Chair

APPROVED AS TO FORM:

Civil Deputy Pros. Atty.

**Figure 37: Whatcom County's ordinance from June 1991, protecting Bigfoot (page 1).**

*WHATCOM COUNTY COUNCIL AGENDA BILL* *NO.* 92-247

| CLEARANCES | Initial | Date | Date Received in Council Office: | Agenda date | Assigned to: |
|---|---|---|---|---|---|
| Originator: Council | | | | 6/9/92 | Council/Intro |
| Division Head: | | | | | |
| Dept. Head: | | | | | |
| Prosecutor: | | | | | |
| Purchasing/Budget: | | | | | |
| Executive: | | | | | |

*SUBJECT:*
Resolution declaring Whatcom County a Sasquatch Protection and Refuge Area

*ATTACHMENTS:*
resolution

*SUMMARY STATEMENT:* *Please complete sections of box as appropriate & explain the item below.*

| | |
|---|---|
| Related County contract #: | Should Clerk schedule a hearing? NO / x/ YES / / Requested date: |
| Amount budgeted for this item/project: $ | Is it (or will it be) within budget? YES / / NO / / (Please explain below) |
| Budget line item number(s): | |

This resolution is in response to a request from Al Magnussen, Mt. Baker Chamber of Commerce.

*ORIGINATOR'S RECOMMENDED ACTION:*

*COMMITTEE ACTION TAKEN:*

*COUNCIL ACTION TAKEN:*
6/9/92: Resolution was approved unanimously

*Related File Numbers:* *Ordinance or Resolution Number (this item only):* R92-043

**Figure 38: Whatcom County's ordinance from June 1991, protecting Bigfoot (page 2).**

For our last stop on this tour of Bigfoot laws, we turn our discerning eye to King County in Washington. I ran across a handful of articles that had to do with a Bigfoot blunder that the county council would just as soon forget. The *CBS Evening News*, the American Farm Bureau, the Western Stock Grower's Association, and the *Eastside Week News*, an alternative weekly paper, were just a few of those to print the story on King County placing *Bipedus Giganticus* (Sasquatch) on their County

Wetlands Inventory Species List. These articles ended up on the BFRO and Bigfoot Encounters websites as well. In my communication with researcher Tim Olsen, I was granted clearance to use segments from the article posted on Bigfoot Encounters. I also discussed this disastrous situation with the main character of this story, Jim Baum, who lived in King County.

In 1998, Mr. Baum purchased seventeen acres of property in the Maple Valley area. A year after the purchase, the County Council passed a King County Sensitive Areas Ordinance (SAO). Much of Mr. Baum's land fell under the regulations of the wetlands ordinance. This, in turn, burdened the man with a bevy of legal problems. There were literally hundreds of species of plants, birds, and mammals that called this property home. According to sources, *Bipedus Giganticus* was one tall order on the list. Even without the Bigfoot spoof, the man's land was determined to be a Class 2 Wetland Area. According to those producing the stories, even Baum's dogs running on his own property was illegal, though this is something I never thought to ask the gentleman.

The idea of Sasquatch being added to such a list threw up a storm of contention. It was a bureaucratic nightmare, and neither side really bought it. Two King County officials had this to say of the whole ordeal, according to Tim Olsen, on the Bigfoot Encounters site:

> Even less enthusiastic about preserving Sasquatch habitat in the suburbs is Chris Vance, chair of the King County Growth Management, Housing, and Environment Committee. "I'm a very conservative Republican, but I helped pass our growth management plan here in King County, and I support it," says Vance. "What we're down to today is not debating whether we need wetlands protection or the protection of wildlife; of course we do. Now we're down to discussing the details, and if you look at the details, any reasonable person would argue that having habitat protected for a mythical creature like Sasquatch is stupid!"
>
> The director of the county Department of Development and Environmental Services, Bob Derrick, winces at the prospect of a public guffaw over the County's protection of habitat for Sasquatch. Derrick believes it was someone's joke from a long time ago and says he'd have it removed from the Wetlands Inventory Species List if it were worth the cost of the process to do so. Vance agrees it was probably a prank but says he's seen many other similarly silly administrative antics that illustrate

> what he calls "this bureaucracy's arrogance in dealing with people whose land is being locked up." Vance wonders if the bureaucratic bumble might be humbled if the public gets a glimpse of the County's Bigfoot in its mouth.

After researching these stories of Bigfoot protections, working my way through the media's smoke-and-mirrors tactics and crafty use of sensationalism, I finally managed to straighten some of it out by talking to the man who was at the center of this particular fiasco, Jim Baum. It is a nice feeling to get some truth straight from the horse's mouth, so to speak. The story of the King County Wetlands Inventory Species List continues here, with these words from Mr. Baum:

> I should start by making a couple things very clear. To my knowledge, no one has had their property restricted due to Sasquatch, including me. I also do not believe that Sasquatch exists.
>
> Sasquatch was put on King County's list as a joke and was not taken out in editing. I was doing an interview with the local public radio station and mentioned Sasquatch being on the list because I think it's ridiculous. I did not say then, nor have I ever said, that my property was being restricted due to a Sasquatch listing. I know there have been a number of articles written about this, and some were written inaccurately, even after I told the author their facts were wrong. Once the press got a hold of the story, I used the opportunity to get the County to deal with me and their designation of my farm as a Class 2 Wetland. My battle with King County is not and has never been about Sasquatch. It's about regulatory takings and the way our county deals with making and enforcing such regulations.

In May of 2009, I received an update from King County. All situations related to King County and this story have been presented as I received them, and this last listing is from the county desk in Seattle, Washington. It's a communication back and forth from a very helpful staff member who said, "I did find a reference to Sasquatch as it relates to the SAO: SAI Wetland Wilderness Lookup Table." In other words, the species appeared on a "lookup table," not an endangered species listing or anything similar. The King County staff member went on to say:

| MAMMALS | observed mammal species | *ap* | Aplodontia rufa (Mountain Beaver) |
|---|---|---|---|
| | | *bb* | Ursus americanus (Black Bear) |
| | | *be* | Castoridae (Beaver) |
| | | *bf* | Bipedus giganticus (Sasquatch) |
| | | *bo* | Felis rufus (Bobcat) |
| | | *ct* | Sylvilagus spp. (Cottontail Rabbit) |
| | | *cy* | Canis latrans (Coyote) |
| | | *de* | Odocoileus (Black-tail or Mule deer) |
| | | *el* | Cervus elaphas (Elk) |
| | | *fi* | Martes pennanti (Fisher) |
| | | *jm* | Zapus princeps (Western Jumping Mouse) |
| | | *lw* | Martes trenata (Long-tailed Weasel |
| | | *ma* | Martes americana (Marten) |
| | | *mi* | Martes vison (Mink) |
| | | *ml* | Felis concolor (Mountain Lion) |
| | | *mu* | Ondrata zibethicus (Muskrat) |
| | | *pp* | Erethizon dorsatum (Porcupine) |
| | | *ra* | Procyon lotor (Raccoon) |
| | | *rf* | Vulpes rulpes (Red Fox) |
| | | *ro* | Lutra canadensis (River Otter) |
| | | *ss* | Spilogale gracilis (Spotted Skunk) |
| | | *sw* | Mustela erminea (Short-tailed Weasel) |
| | | *tm* | Scaponus townsendii (Townsend's mole) |

**Figure 39: King County's Sensitive Areas Ordinance, as adopted in 1999, included Sasquatch as one of its listed mammals.**

That being said, the SAO actually does not exist anymore. It was replaced by the CAO (Critical Areas Ordinance) in 2004. I haven't been able to find any reference to a listing for "Bipedus

Giganticus-Sasquatch" or anything similar to that in the new CAO.

What I did find is this following species list in our Comprehensive Plan (which is the County's guiding policy document). There is no mention of Sasquatch here:

> E-487 King County should protect the following native Species of Local Importance, or their habitats, as appropriate. Protection should be accomplished through regulations, incentives, or habitat purchase.
> Species of Local Importance are:
> a. Salmonids — kokanee salmon, sockeye/red salmon, chum salmon, coho/silver salmon, pink salmon, coastal resident/sea run cutthroat, rainbow trout, Dolly Varden, and pygmy whitefish, including juvenile feeding and migration corridors in marine waters;
> b. Native Freshwater Mussels — Western pearlshell mussel, Oregon floater, and western ridge mussel;
> c. Shellfish — Red Urchin, Dungeness crab, Pandalid shrimp, Geoduck clam, and Pacific oyster;
> d. Marine Fish — White sturgeon, Green Sturgeon, Pacific herring, longfin smelt, surfsmelt, lingcod, Pacific sand lance, English sole, and rock sole;
> e. Birds — Western grebe, American bittern, great blue heron, Brant, Harlequin duck, Wood duck, Hooded merganser, Barrow's Goldeneye, Common Goldeneye, Cinnamon teal, Blue-winged teal, Surf scoter, White-winged scoter, Black scoter, osprey, Red-tailed hawk, Sooty grouse, Ruffed grouse, Band-tailed pigeon, Belted kingfisher, Hairy Woodpecker, American three-toed woodpecker, Olivesided Flycatcher, Mountain chickadee, Western Meadowlark, Cassin's Finch, and Purple Finch;
> f. Mammals — Marten, mink, Columbian black-tailed deer, elk in their historic range, mountain goat, Douglas Squirrel, and Townsend Chipmunk;
> g. Amphibians — Red-legged frog; and
> h. Reptiles — Alligator lizard and western fence lizard.

> In short, I am not sure why Sasquatch was listed in the SAO, as the creation of the SAO was many years ago. Either way, however, I do not believe that has carried over into the CAO.
>
> Here is some additional information I was able to find out from DDES staff:
>
> The document in question was created in 1981. Staff listed all reported sightings of different species. They did not conduct an independent verification to determine if the sighting was legitimate. Of course, there are people who do claim to have seen Bigfoot, so that was included in the report.
>
> This animal has never been listed as a protected species in any King County regulations. It is not protected under the CAO, it was not protected under the SAO, and it was not protected under regulations in effect prior to the SAO.

One thing that can be said about all this legislation is that it seems to do some good for protecting Sasquatch. There may be a publicity angle, but there is usually something else, too.

Sasquatch in the world of commerce doesn't fare as well. In a strange way, the creature receives a form of recognition, but it is not taken seriously at most levels. If it isn't some intellectually challenged blonde sitting on a bar patron's lap while wearing a Sasquatch outfit in a beer commercial, then it's things like a Bigfoot trinket shop, specializing in overpriced Troglodyte merchandise. The crafty marketing schemes say little about the actual species running around loose out there. It is all just hoopla.

# 16. Bigfoot Hunters' Equipment

The fall of 2005 gave me the opportunity to take a look behind the scene — to follow up on the Sasquatch subject from a different perspective, actually out looking for the bipedal creature. This took place in the lower mainland of British Columbia, on the west side of Harrison Lake, a few miles north of the Harrison Resort. It was the last week of September, actually a pleasant evening weatherwise. Members of the party included Ken Kristian, Thomas Steenburg, Sebastian Wang, his wife Evelyn, and my son Adrian. Another West Coast Sasquatch individual, Gerry Matthews, couldn't attend. Hopefully, I will meet up with this researcher in the future.

Heading out late afternoon, traveling along the winding road west of Harrison, we happened on a small black bear running in front of the lead vehicle, and we hoped it was a sign of things to come. Mainly, this short expedition of only a few hours was meant to be a get-together of a few minds to sample the technology that each person was trying in the forests. Sebastian Wang, as an example, had an impressive list of cameras and other things he used to search for the elusive giant:

1. Still Camera: 35 mm Canon T-90. Lens: 28 mm, 35-85 mm, 70-210 mm, 100-500 mm, 600 mm reflex, and 2X teleconverter
2. Still Camera: 35 mm Minolta XG-1 and XG-2. Lens: 50 mm, 70-210 mm, and macro lens and tubes
3. Digital Video: Canon Optura Xi. Lens: 1.7 teleconverter. Mic: Canon Shotgun mic
4. Back-up: Video Panasonic S-VHS.
5. IR Lamp: one million candle power spotlight with modified lens (glass stained blue and red)
6. IR Camera with motion detector: Homemade wireless security camera triggered by home-use motion sensors

**Figure 40: Adrian Boulier (on left), Sebastian Wang, Ken Kristian, and Thomas Steenburg on an outing on the west side of Harrison Lake, British Columbia, to test technical equipment.**

7. Parabolic Listening Dish
8. Night Vision (Night Leopard), can be adapted to the Minoltas for still pictures
9. Lights: one million candle power and 10 million candle power

In the Harrison Hot Springs area, we experimented with a number of things that relate to technology and Sasquatch. From our elevated position up from the lake on this Fraser Valley evening, sometimes alone just to contemplate living in British Columbia in the past, I couldn't help but look out into the night and see the lights of Harrison Hot Springs sparkling off in the distance to the south, under colored cloud cover. A guy really had to think about the situation, looking for one or more of the giants in the darkness, while life moved along elsewhere as well. There was a generalized strange feeling to it, a physical sensation I'd felt before. At the Webb Mountain fire lookout that one eventful night, with *something* visiting us for almost two hours, I could see from the east windows the lights of Eureka, Montana, and the silence that accompanied it, the town shrouded in the same darkness we were in again. Such things play on a person's psyche. This also occurred during the 1974 sighting on Tulameen Avenue. There I was, facing a giant creature that had wandered from the wilderness, yet the main area of Princeton sat right across the brown bridge, the town lit up by man's invention.

All this musing went on as I sat on the back of a tailgate in the darkness, studying the lighting of Harrison as I watched and listened for a creature that is continuously shrouded in mystery. Thomas Steenburg ended the late evening by sneaking off unseen, rattling a small tree, bringing everyone to attention after midnight.

I was intrigued that there was such a broad range of equipment for just this one person, so I studied what other research groups and individuals were using to uncover this mystery.

Many organizations use combinations of technology in the wilderness. Some preferred not to reveal what they were using. My goal, however, is to show the odds mounting against the Sasquatch staying ahead of its pursuers. Let's look first at some things that might have worked.

With this undiscovered being, things are rarely what you would expect. There are a wealth of cameras strapped to trees out there in the forests of Canada and the United States, just as one example. The scale is rather large, the growing forest paparazzi visiting the woods, trying to photograph the forest celebrity. We can also add the hundreds upon hundreds of independent researchers out there walking their equipment around on any given day. The numbers are staggering. So far, the success of technology has been about the same as the Bigfoot cage-trap in Oregon, which has failed to capture a biped giant, though the trap did produce good results for catching bears. In essence, both flesh and film have failed. The intelligence of the bear and the bipedal creature are not even in the same ballpark, and it shows.

A writer, Paul Fattig, for the *Mail Tribune, Southern Oregon's News Source*, graciously supplied an article about one trap, for those who have never heard of such a thing:

## BIGFOOT BEWARE

### Volunteers repair damage to the nation's only known Sasquatch trap

**Figure 41: The 1974 Sasquatch trap in the Rogue River-Siskiyou National Forest in Oregon. (photo ©2006 Mario Vaden)**

APPLEGATE LAKE — Dave Enge and Jeff LaLande figure they are following in some mighty big footsteps.

They point to the hefty 12-inch-wide and 2-inch-thick planks that form the ceiling, floor, and four sides. Then there's the heavy expanded metal grate and telephone poles that anchor the 10-foot by 10-foot wooden cage to the ground.

"I don't know how they carried them up here," LaLande observed. "Back in the days when they built this, it was still fairly remote. You had to hike all the way up from the Applegate River at that point."

Perhaps, it went unsaid, the builders of the legendary Bigfoot trap in the Rogue River-Siskiyou National Forest had a little help from a large hairy fellow.

Despite the fort-like strength its 1974 builders apparently felt was necessary to nab the elusive Sasquatch, age has taken its toll. The floor planks have nearly rotted through, and rot has punched a hole through one side.

And a ponderosa pine tree some 2 feet in diameter at the base was uprooted by a storm earlier this year, narrowly missing the trap but taking with it a roughly 10-inch in diameter madrone tree that struck the trap's northwest corner.

"The madrone collapsed part of the roof, which was already heavily deteriorated," explained LaLande. "The roof was no longer doing its job of protecting the planks."

Enge, a retired industrial instrument repairman from Albany, is a volunteer in the U.S. Forest Service's Passport In Time (PIT) program, which enables folks to work on supervised projects during the summer. Although most PIT projects focus on historic or archaeological sites, the Bigfoot trap falls under the program because it is very unusual, LaLande explained.

"Even though this is not historic yet, it is unique in the country," he said, noting it is believed to be the only one in the nation.

In addition to restoring the Bigfoot trap, the PIT crew is putting a new cedar shingle roof on the historic tack room near the Applegate Ranger District office. Besides Enge, the volunteers, all veterans of other PIT projects, include Dana Gaab of North Bend, Marc Herring of Sandy and Charlie Vincent of Myrtle Point.

Located along the Collings Mountain Trail a half mile west of Applegate Lake, the trap was built by the long-defunct Eugene-based North American Wildlife Research Team with a special use permit. The group was attracted to the area after a miner named Perry Lovell found 18-inch humanlike tracks in his garden near the Applegate River. The creature reportedly had a 6-foot stride.

The trap caught no Bigfoot in its six years of operation before the Forest Service bolted it open in 1980 because of safety concerns.

When the trap was built, the Applegate Dam was yet to be built, and the road was on the opposite side of the river, LaLande said.

"They were very serious about it," he said. "It wasn't a joke to them. It was the real deal. They had the Bigfoot fever and wanted to catch one."

"They hung a rotting deer carcass or something up in the back of the trap," he added. "When Bigfoot grabbed it, the trap-door would fall and send an electronic signal down at the cabin."

He was referring to the "watchman's" cabin several hundred feet back down the trail. The moss-covered wood shelter is now settling into the forest duff.

"It seems a bit too close for comfort if you expected Bigfoot to show up," LaLande quipped.

Although nothing was caught except for a couple of bears, LaLande knows there are still believers out there. Moreover, the trap draws hundreds of curious people each year.

"It's known far and wide," he said. "We've even had a French-speaking television crew from Montreal come all the way out here."

Vandals have etched their names in the wood over the years. "Bigfoot 05," reads one. "Free Satch," adds another.

Enge, 63, reared in Coos Bay, had heard tales about Bigfoot as a youngster, but the trap was new to him.

"They must be crazy," he said of his first reaction to learning about it.

But he and the others working on restoring the trap are dead serious about their work. Before they began, forest sawyer Cliff Snavely and a fire crew cleared the trail and bucked up a portion of the pine, cutting seats into the tree, which lies on the south-west side of the trap.

In addition to rebuilding a portion of the frame this week, the PIT crew will put on a new roof, replicating the boards and roofing that had originally been used.

"One of these days, the trap will go the way of all things," LaLande said, referring to the natural decay of wood. "But this will help preserve it."

**Where to find it**

The Bigfoot trap is about 26 miles south of Medford. To reach it, take Highway 238 west to Ruch, then turn left on the Applegate Road to the Applegate Dam. Drive past the dam and the Hart-Tish Park entrance.

> Stop several hundred feet past the park at the Collings Mountain Trailhead on the right. It's marked by a sign, with a footprint insignia on it.
>
> After hiking about half a mile, you will come to a fork in the trail at a dilapidated old shelter. The trap is about 200 feet up the trail on the left. [PF1]

The Oregon cage-trap has gone the way of nature's mobilized forces, the prevailing westerlies putting the finishing touches on it. The Sasquatch environment hasn't been kind to the researchers that are using technological equipment to find this roaming breed of haired giants.

Moving back to cameras, it's a wonder that Sasquatch hasn't been clearly photographed yet. Just try doing the numbers in your head to see what the Sasquatch faces each and every day. We are not talking about hiding a ladybird or beetle. These are massive giants that need a significant number of calories every day.

Below are a number of kind researchers who have allowed me to give an example of what they were using a few years ago to try and trip this creature up. Those individuals mentioned could have things out in the field at any given time, and this is only the tip of the iceberg.

> I do not have the game cam up 24/7, but mainly during the late spring, summer, and fall. (Don Keating, Eastern Ohio Bigfoot Investigation Center)

> At present I have digital game cams in the field that I monitor on a weekly basis. While in the field, I have camcorders, digital, and 35 mm cameras, microphone, and tape recorders. (Diane Stocking, Stocking Hominid Research, Inc.)

> We do have a Stealth Camera in video mode deployed at an investigation site. It has been out there 24/7 since December 2008. This was due to a Bigfoot sighting by a witness in November 2008 on private property. So far we have collected video and picture evidence of an owl, deer, cats, dogs, other birds, other humans, and that's about it at this point. We have had some strange triggers of the camera with no apparent reasons for the activation. (Billy Willard, Director, Sasquatch Watch of Virginia)

> I use six cameras that are always out in the bush… three Bushnell Trail Sentries (each with) 5.0 MP w/ Night Vision and solar panel, one Stealth Cam Epic DAC AVI video, one Leaf

> River IR-7SS 7.0 MP camera, plus a Moultrie 5.0 MP cam. (Bobbie Short, Bigfoot Encounters)
>
> I have done a little of this off and on since 1991. Not doing any surveillance right now, but hope to start again. Used an ordinary camcorder in 1990s, then picked up a Camtracker film camera. Have an X-Cam system, but not yet used it. (Bob Daigle, Michigan Bigfoot Information Center)
>
> I first started deploying sophisticated surveillance cameras in the woods back in 1996, about a year after my Bigfoot sighting. Since then my obsession has been to design, build, and deploy the best possible surveillance system for Bigfoot research. In short, I have developed the most advanced Bigfoot research digital video camera system available today. This system is the result of many years of prototypes and constant funding at my expense. Some of the issues with today's camera systems are ultrasonic noise. I discovered that all electronic cameras and camcorders produce ultrasonic sounds that animals can hear. Wavelengths in the ultraviolet and near-infrared spectrum are viewed differently by animals, so camouflaging cameras can just make them more noticeable. Camera smells like plastic are a dead giveaway, non-out-gassing plastic is available but is never used for game camera applications. To answer your question, yes, I do have a number of units in the woods 24/7/365, but no Bigfoot video yet. (William Dranginis, Virginia Bigfoot Research Organization)

In the technical realm, 2010 was a banner year for discovery. The odds grew greater that the creature would be seen. The trail camera idea was growing faster than the average person could save up the funds to purchase one. There must have been well over two million of these trail-cams in operation. One outdoorsman I spoke with briefly had twenty-three of the contraptions working for him, and I was told others had even more. On the large scale of pictures of animals in the wild, I looked at thousands upon thousands of snapshots; there wasn't one of our overly shy friend among them, of course, but the numbers were staggering nonetheless. Once I eliminated those that were clearly photoshopped (yes, it happens in this hobby as well), I was left scratching my head, asking myself, "How could a giant bipedal creature escape every camera?"

The cameras are highly sophisticated pieces of hardware. For instance, one brand of camera actually has a whistle on it, an attempt to surprise visitors long enough for a snapshot. Other makes of trail-cams have things like early detection sensors and information strips that save data like date, time, moon phase, temperature at the time of the picture. Many are equipped with quick-shot (trigger) options and rapid-fire technology, allowing up to ten photographs with a single triggering of the unit. Panoramic lenses that support a much wider view are options for the trail-cam fan, as well as infrared flash LEDs for no-flash photography.

By now, I'm sure you understand what I'm getting at. When everything is realistically calculated, the Sasquatch creature has, in all probability, little chance of avoiding the technology. Included in with that philosophy are my observations of the two giants — those sightings fueling my skepticism of this being some sort of super creature. While many owners of these trail camera devices are mainly after antlered trophy pics for hunting or things along this line, some do wonder about an elusive upright giant that allegedly frequents the wilderness. This came up many times, usually from behind the scenes. Bears were being blamed for ripping down cameras and swatting them around, something that had been witnessed. After tossing around the idea to others in field-related areas, it was almost unanimous that Bigfoot, if it existed in flesh, could not keep totally secret when it came to this new technology.

Here are some thoughts from people who believe that the lack of evidence suggests Bigfoot can't exist. Bryan Kinkel of BSK Consulting explained the possibilities out there after I had posted the idea of the trail cameras and Sasquatch in the same sentence on the Net. Specializing in small land management, this fellow was not shy. I have appreciated honesty over the years, and this is one of those examples:

> Instead of asking the question of why the animal "cannot be filmed," you need to ask the question in an appropriate scientific manner: "Why has Bigfoot *not been filmed* on one of the millions of trail-cameras in the woods each year?" And the obvious answer is, because it doesn't exist.
>
> In my home state of Tennessee, the wildlife agency receives hundreds of reports of mountain lion sightings every year. Yet, with at least 100,000 trail cameras in the TN woods each year, not a single mountain lion picture. Why? Because they aren't in Tennessee yet — very easy answer.

> For very secretive or nocturnal animals, you will get many trail-cam pictures for every one human sighting. For example, I get many trail-cam pictures of bobcats in my area, yet in twenty-five years of hunting the area, I've seen a grand total of two with my own eyes. Armadillos just recently moved into my area, and I started getting trail-cam pictures of them two years before I saw a live one in the wild. Now if human sighting outnumbers pictures hundreds to zero, the problem is that the animal (Bigfoot) doesn't exist and people are misidentifying other animals.

Another person came into the picture concerning the trail camera issue, two days after Bryan Kinkel. This fellow is a retired police officer from Illinois, who now resides in Oregon. It's interesting to note that in the 1970s, he was on the mailing list for *The Bigfoot News*, a monthly newsletter from researchers in The Dalles, Oregon. (Could this have to do with the Peter Byrne attempt at the Bigfoot in those days?) Highlighting Bryan Kinkel's correspondence, we hear from Jim Gaskins:

> I realize I am stating the obvious, but, unless he has done research of some kind or he was quoting stats he has read someplace, I wonder where he came up with that number. I certainly find it easy to believe there are 100,000 trail-cams in use in Tennessee — in fact, that number could be low. If one in ten persons who buy a hunting license own and use a trail-cam and one million persons buy a TN hunting license, then 100,000 would be correct. But that is simply arbitrary on my part.
>
> In my neck of the woods, I sure talk to a lot of people who use them. The article on my blog about trail-cams was written several years ago. Since then, I have purchased a few and use them extensively. I bet I have a trail-cam in use up to 200 days per year, and I am certainly not alone.

As it turns out, there were five to six of the devices watching each other at any given time. Why? Because they wanted to know who was knocking them down or avoiding them — or they were monitoring, looking for the Big Guy.

Considering how complex this trail camera situation is, odds for and against the Sasquatch, we'll continue on with what Jim Gaskins had to say about his ordeal with the trail-cam hobby, including hunting involvement. This will provide a picture of just what a Sasquatch would be dealing with out there, and these are the specific procedures used by just one outdoor enthusiast. A person can only wonder about the big picture.

> Glen, I spend two to three months per year in the forests of western Oregon. I have done so each year for the past seven years, since I retired. Prior to that, I spent two to four weeks per year in the woods, plus all the weekends I could squeeze in. There are few people, none that I know of, who have spent more time scouting for critters in the coast range, other than myself. I have taken big elk, deer, and dozens of bears.
>
> I am batting nearly 100 percent in helping friends get their first bear, usually on their first trip hunting with me. The only reason I can do that is… scouting research. We hunt bears primarily in the evening. During the day's downtime, while other guys sleep in or sit in camp or drive in circles on logging roads, I am hitting the brush, trails, and skid roads. I use three to four cameras at a time and put them out many weeks prior to the season's opening day. I begin camping for a week to ten days at a time, in my hunt area, weeks and weeks before season opens. By the time spring bear season starts, I know where some are and know their routine.
>
> I have approached elk hunting in a similar way, and to a degree, blacktail hunting as well. If I am not working on a project at home, I am in the woods.
>
> I have gone the long way around to get to a point or two. I often think of the Bigfoot. If I hear a strange sound, I try very hard to determine what caused it. So far, I have no mysteries. I have never seen signs of Bigfoot: footprints or scat. I routinely see bear, deer, and elk tracks and scat. I often see cougar tracks, and the same goes for bobcats. In all the thousands of hours I have spent in the woods, I have never "felt a weird presence," except a couple of times that I feel was perhaps a cougar. I have never smelled a rank odor that I could not eventually identify and put with a cause or owner. The first trail-cam photo I ever got was of a cougar. I have photos of bobcats, cougars, bears, and many other mammals… but none of Bigfoot.
>
> Being a retired cop, in the twenty-seven years on the job, I worked hundreds of criminal cases, including way too many homicides and a never-ending supply of theft, burglary, and fraud cases. Any old-time cop will tell you, "… if it walks like a

duck… " and, well, you know the rest. Every criminal case has similarities to the last one you worked. Evidence is a trail that helps lead to the truth. Evidence points to consistencies in a statement or "story" related about an event, and physical evidence must be consistent and relevant to the scene or event. One piece of evidence should easily link to another to show a trail to the truth. Unfortunately, my stating, "I saw Bigfoot," is not evidence, unless there are other facts to substantiate my statement. If seven people and I all see Bigfoot at the same time, and we are not friends or associates, and we are members in good standing in our communities, and we are sober — that is evidence.

Over the past thirty years, I have met a number of people who have told me stories about seeing a Bigfoot or about hearing or smelling one, but those same types of people tell me about smelling bears, making statements such as, "Those bears smell like a dump, you know. You smell 'em long before you see 'em." The people are generally emotional and come from the same psychological mold. They have no credibility at all. Personally, I have been in the presence or vicinity of hundreds of bears, and I have put my hands on dozens of them. I have never known a bear to have a foul odor. They are no different than any other animal living in the mountains.

Having said all of the above, I am somewhat like you, in that I would like to believe Bigfoot exists. Until there is absolute proof of their existence, I have to remain a skeptic with an open mind. I certainly believe they do not commonly or routinely exist in the areas in which I have scouted, which is basically a couple hundred miles of the west coast, from the ocean to thirty or forty miles inland, in northern and southern Oregon. I have spent quite a bit of time in the mountains of central and eastern Oregon and some in Idaho, and like western Oregon — no Bigfoot signs or encounters.

I truly wish I had the experience you related about your encounters. I really do. I am not a naysayer, but there is a lack of tangible proof. That is the quandary of the Bigfoot research dilemma. I would not publicly say, "I believe," unless I was holding the hand, foot, head, hide, or other proof of its existence in my hand. A photo isn't even close to being enough for me to come out of the Bigfoot closet.

So we have those who say Sasquatch can't exist, but let me add one more story to further complicate the situation. This happened in The Dalles, Oregon, in the 1970s, with researcher Peter Byrne's investigation.

Mr. Byrne did everything in his power to set up a natural-looking observation post on Table Mountain, including a 160-degree angle of view, offering him and the team the opportunity to uncover clues about the legendary creature. The Bigfoot species had made somewhat routine appearances in The Dalles area months and years before, and tracks had been spotted.

As professionally structured as possible, the group outlined the area topographically, marking landmarks that would be identifiable even during the hours of darkness. Equipment was loaned to the research project from the Academy of Applied Science in Boston, including a large night observation device (NOD, 40 mm tube) for light amplification. The NOD, on loan for one month, used starlight as a light source and had a range of up to 5,000 yards. Complementing that apparatus, they also had in their possession two hand-held starlight scopes and a short-range thermal device, on loan for May and June of 1973.

With professionals and volunteers in place, working in shifts, the Bigfoot species did not make one single appearance in their range of view. It was a complete no-show. We had to wonder where the creature went. It couldn't have been the scent of human beings or the equipment, for the gale-force winds supplied on a regular basis from the Columbia Gorge wouldn't allow that. But ultimately, the sneaky creature again left the researchers high and dry.

Forty or so years later, the question still hasn't been answered. If it exists, the creature avoids traps, planted technology, and just about anything else man dreams up or places in its way.

Looking at it from a humorous standpoint, the Sasquatch seems to act as an insider trader on Wall Street, dealing unlawfully with consumer electronics stock. A great amount of moolah is spent on high-tech toys in an effort to locate the creature. The negativity tends to wear down researchers at times and also gives skeptics ammunition to discredit the existence of this hominoid.

But here's my take on the situation. The Sasquatch is unlike any other species. It's very unlikely that you'll see the creature gracing the cover of *National Geographic*. In fact, many people believe the haired creature will be extinct before it is featured.

During my encounters in 1974 and 1985, I believe the creature made critical errors — not to its immediate safety, but the being was caught out in the open, in full view, inside town limits. Our mother came within fifty feet of the cloak-and-dagger giant of the woods. This has shown me that the creature can make mistakes. Many people have seen the giants, but when technology is added to the routine, Bigfoot can't be found. I can't blame critics for turning their noses up at this subject in its entirety. I've spoken with quite a few of them over the years, and practically everyone is packing some kind of camera these days.

So, I'm left with this dilemma. I have seen the creature in the presence of other reliable witnesses, so I'm pretty sure it exists. The trail camera coverage should be more than adequate to have gotten some pictures of a flesh and blood creature by now — unless Bigfoot is supersensitive to some feature of trail cameras that we don't understand and super shy to boot. Bottom line, I believe something else must be part of the mix. We'll look at these possibilities in Parts II and III.

# *17. William Dranginis' Story and More*

Not really that long ago, while taking a stroll through one of the local used bookstores here in Calgary, my wife and I came across a hardcover by Don Hunter and René Dahinden. The Swiss-born Dahinden had personally autographed the copy many years ago. My wife scooped it up and placed it for sale on eBay, through an online business she operates, sure that a keen collector would enjoy it. Before long, the signed copy of the book was sold.

As she packaged it up, I happened to notice William Dranginis' name on the address label she placed on the U.S.-bound box. His name looked awfully familiar. With a little in-house detective work, I soon realized that the world was indeed getting smaller again. I'd had a phone conversation with that individual and exchanged emails. He'd even given me information about the findings of the Arizona fire lookout employee who was doing a continuing study on Bigfoot. It was in West Virginia, though, that William Dranginis met the mysterious giant that would bring folklore to life for him, another person's life changed in a few bats of the eye. Two other witnesses were along with him that day:

## Twelve Seconds of Fame

Unlike many Bigfoot researchers, my interest in the Bigfoot didn't start with movies called *Sasquatch, the Legend of Bigfoot* or *The Abominable Snowman of the Himalayas*. These movies are now considered classics in the Bigfoot field. While growing up in northwest Connecticut, I can't remember if any of these movies ever made it to the local cinema.

My interest in these creatures happened by chance. This encounter occurred in 1995 and lasted approximately twelve seconds. I had purchased a Whites Eagle Spectrum metal detector to search the hills of northern Virginia for Civil War relics. It was a new hobby for me. It got me outdoors, and I found it enjoyable. I learned many things about the life and times during the Civil War. The manual for the detector stated, "It's best to learn the proper use of a detector on your own land. Make a fool of yourself in your own back yard before you start digging up other people's property." I took that saying to heart. Before long, I had potholes all over the place. I did find some Civil War coat buttons, bullets, and even a Confederate stirrup. Later, I found out that my back yard was actually on land that the Confederate Calvary occupied for a short time.

It was a short time after this that I was invited to spend a day metal detecting around some abandoned gold mines located in Culpepper County, Virginia. It was mid-March, and the trees were still barren of leaves. After a fun day of stomping around the woods, we headed back to my friend's house. It was about three thirty p.m. The three of us were walking down a hard-packed logging trail, when all of a sudden my friend stopped and stretched out his arms and said, "Stop!" (I need to add that my friend served three tours of Vietnam as a point man, and at the time of the sighting, he was working as a Special Agent with the U.S. Government. He has since retired.) After stopping, he pointed toward the woods and said, "Follow from my shoulder to the tip of my finger. Seventy-five feet behind that tree is a man!" At that point, he drew his 9 mm pistol that he carried and pointed it at the tree.

I later found out that he had seen this person out of his peripheral vision just before it saw him. Right after eye contact, the person hid behind some trees. Being a Special Agent, he knew the woods were sometimes used by people to grow drugs, and they sometimes stood guard over their area. That was why he raised his pistol. It was soon apparent that this person was not a person at all. Within a few seconds, a large head looked right at us from the side of the tree. It pulled back, and a split second later, this thing started running right in front of us. It ran — and I mean ran — from our left to right in full view, arms swinging, legs outstretched, the hair maybe four to six inches long, flowing as it moved. By this time, both Agents had their weapons drawn.

I have never seen such massive shoulder muscles, the whole body built for speed and agility. I can tell you that I was not scared. I thought it was cool to see something that large — seven feet — navigate the wooded environment that easily and quietly. It continued running and then it used its foot to pivot off a six-inch pine tree. This sighting will always be etched in my mind. It then took a quick left turn and ran away from us at a forty-five-degree angle down a hill, then out of sight. One of the Agents (Frank) and I later talked about what we had seen. He stated that the creature deliberately ran in front of us to draw our attention from what may have been behind it. What it was, we will never know. It could have been the family unit or its mate. But this creature took a big chance by running directly in front of us, making us look 180 degrees away from where we first saw it. I thought about this for a while, and it made sense, because almost all of the Bigfoot sightings I researched stated the creature walked directly away from the witness.

William Dranginis' story reminded me of something that happened to me. While hunting in the Similkameen Valley in the early 1970s, three of us came across a legal buck with a doe, both ruminants practically caught out in the open that morning in a clearing. The male came right toward us, while the female fled the other way. The buck then dropped into a small gully less than a hundred feet directly in front of us and ran for his life. It was a staged procedure on the part of the animal. Sasquatch apparently pulled the same trick. Dranginis went on:

Back to the actual sighting, the second Agent (Jim), who lived across the street, was visibly shaken immediately after the encounter. We could see it in his eyes and by his physical reaction. It was the first time I had witnessed someone in complete denial about what he had just seen. When he said, "It's a bear! Let's get out of here!" the other Agent (Frank) and I looked at each other, then looked at the way the other man was holding his firearm (white knuckles) — so we just kept quiet and left the area. But all the way back to his house, we were all looking over our shoulders.

Two of us went back the next day to look for anything that could help us understand what the creature was. We did locate a great footprint where the creature placed its foot before jumping over a small creek. We also found the pine tree where the bark was pushed to the ground. The damage to the tree confirmed that the creature used it to pivot off of it when it made the turn. It wasn't until the two of us went back to look for evidence that Frank got spooked and wanted to leave immediately. We found a footprint thirteen and a half inches long, and I prepared to make a plaster cast of it. The Agent tapped me on the shoulder and pointed to the woods. "There are two of them out there," I remember him saying. Then I heard it: low whistles, two of them, signaling to each other. Then I heard something moving. That was when the Agent said, "I survived Vietnam on my gut instincts, and my gut says get out of here now — so I'm leaving, and I recommend you do the same." We both left at that point, and my friend never returned. I kept going back to the area with a friend or two, but after a while, I went back by myself.

Frank believes we should leave the creatures alone. He was more disturbed after the sighting than after all his years in Vietnam. Jim was and still is scared to death of the creatures. After the sighting, Jim would let me park my car in his driveway, to go metal detecting, though I was actually setting up cameras and things like that back in the woods. One day he came up to my workplace, fifty miles from his home. He came into the shop and looked around to make sure no one else was there, then shook his finger at me. His eyes were blood red as he said, "Whatever you spooked up back in those woods has been coming down to my property at one in the morning, and my dog is screaming like it was stabbed with a hot poker. My wife and I wake up to this, and I go out to the front porch and use my shotgun and shoot toward where you always park your car, to scare whatever that thing is, to get it off my property — so stay off my property!" He immediately left. I talked to him about a year ago about a job I was working on, and Bigfoot was not mentioned.

I have spent many long hours hiking and studying the land. We have found several other Bigfoot-type footprints, all of them different in size. I have deployed a video surveillance system that would be activated only when an animal or person passes in front of it. I have gotten lots of deer, birds, and all types of other animals, but no Bigfoot.

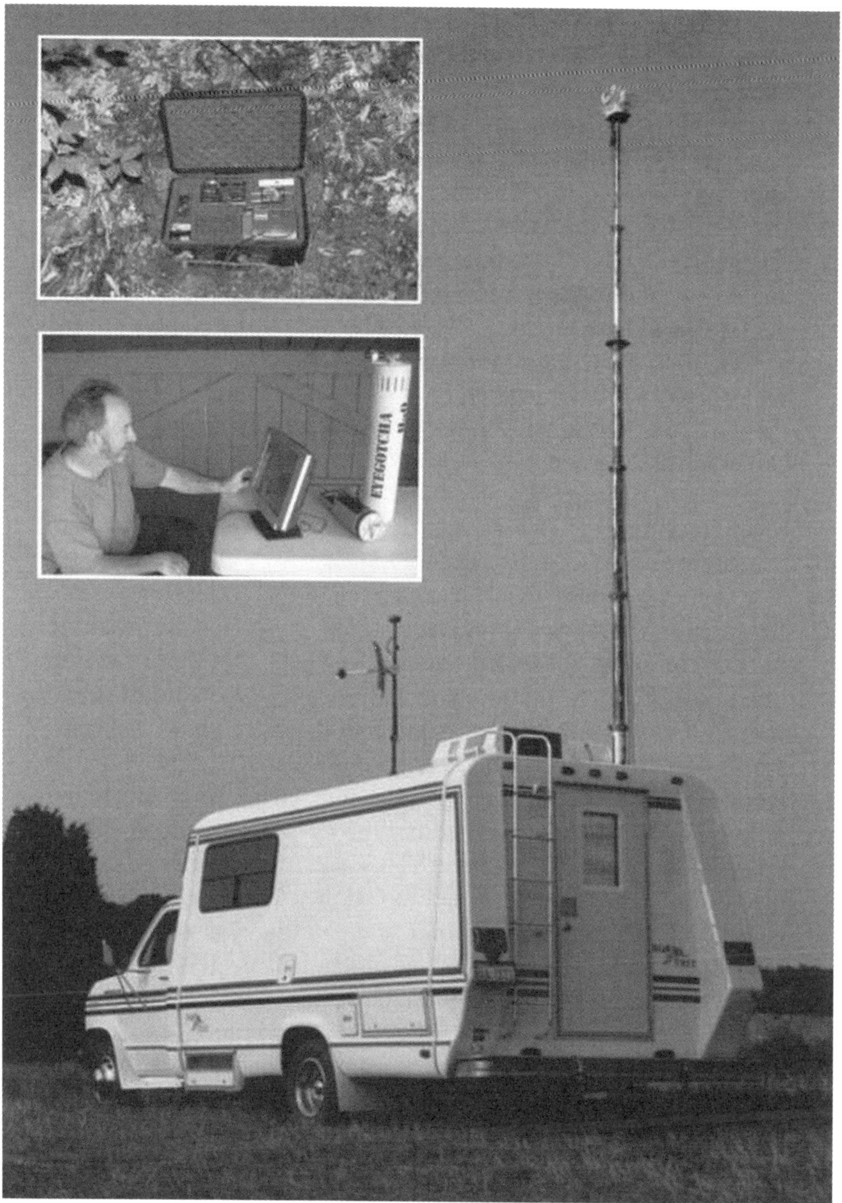


Figure 42: William Dranginis' research vehicle fitted out with camera systems, thermal imaging, video gear, and other surveillance equipment, including the EyeGotcha system he designed. (photos © William Dranginis)

There were a few times when something would approach the camera, which was supported seven feet high in a tree. Most of the activations occurred around one to two a.m. I also had a microphone recording as well. You could hear something approach the camera and tap the housing. Then, a few seconds later, you could hear it walk back into the dense woods.

Researchers from around the world have tried in vain to get a Sasquatch creature on film using some ingenious ideas and sophisticated equipment, to no avail. The reports from researchers worldwide are the same: As soon as we put up cameras in the surveillance area, the sightings stop. I have exchanged emails with former BFRO member Thom Powell a number of times in the past. We both agree that these creatures somehow know that cameras have been deployed in a given research area. Once you put up the cameras, the creatures leave. After you take them down, they seem to come back. It has been my personal quest to investigate why this happens.

My lucky break came in spring of 1998, when one of my field-deployable video surveillance units recorded a deer looking directly into the concealed camera lens. Its ears were moving like it was trying to figure out exactly where some kind of sound was coming from, both ears pointed in the direction of the camera. It was then I knew the deer could hear some kind of sound that the camera was producing. After purchasing some ultrasonic detection equipment, I verified my theory that surveillance cameras produce ultrasonic sound. This was done using scientific means, and I have documented the results. Even in sleep mode, game cameras produce ultrasonic sounds. I have also discovered after more field research that even humans walking in grass, fields, or even in the woods produce large amounts of ultrasonic sound. These sounds are generated by the rubbing of clothing and when you brush up against vegetation. This could be the reason why these creatures have not been successfully videotaped in a controlled surveillance area. Does this mean Bigfoot can hear into the ultrasonic range? I don't know for sure, but I have a hunch they can.

During our visit to the fire lookout at Webb Mountain in 2005, opportunity arose amongst the strange happenings for me to do a little experiment of my own. It happened strictly by accident and had nothing to do with the unusual events that were taking place.

In the mornings that the three deer made appearances at the tower, I wanted to take a few photographs of the animals using my wife's Canon digital camera. I didn't want to scare them off, so I stood on the catwalk to the west side of the lookout, waiting for them, enjoying the breathtaking scenery. And there they were, three of them, walking parallel to me, some 150 feet away, single file, not really paying attention. While they were taking their leisurely stroll, I quietly turned on the camera, with little movement of my index finger and no other body movement. As the digital camera powered up, all three of them stopped immediately, turning their heads toward me and twitching their ears a number of times. It was interesting that the deer had actually acted in such a manner. I decided I'd try something different the next day.

Come the next morning, I was again out on the catwalk, facing the wilderness to the west, the digital Canon in the very same position as the previous morning. The only difference was that the camera was already structured differently. My wife, Rosemarie, had her camera set up so that when I opened the lens cover, it would activate the sound of chirping birds, indicating that the unit was ready. I had moved the lens cover just enough so that all I had to do was nudge it gently to complete the process. The little experiment just needed the invited guest.

When the two does and a buck arrived a short time later, with perfect timing, again in single file on a slow, uphill march, I effortlessly triggered the camera, allowing the birds to sing. The deer didn't seem to notice. They simply kept on walking with their heads lowered, not even hesitating. To them, it was just another fine morning out in the forest and sunshine, with birds chirping away.

I had a chance to discuss these findings with William Dranginis, and he felt the issue could be expanded upon. This could be another avenue researchers could exploit, using a mock form of nature against nature.

Researchers have speculated that during our visit at the Webb Mountain fire lookout the low-battery signal on my wife's cell phone might have raised the curiosity of a strange creature in the woods. Technology may work in a number of directions, but realistically, it only added another dimension to a continuing mystery.

William Dranginis went on with his tale as follows:

> I had the opportunity to have a backstage tour of the National Zoo primate exhibit last year, a one-on-one guided tour

by the curator. Chimps have covered surveillance cameras with straw and rags once cameras were installed. I think there are two reasons why they do this. Maybe they think the lens looks too much like an eye, and they feel uncomfortable with it looking at them. The other possibility is that the camera's electronic or ultrasonic noise irritates them; covering it up helps block the sound. I think both reasons are valid in the case of the chimps.

After speaking with another researcher about the ultrasonic sounds, he went out and purchased an ultrasonic detector to test it out himself. He called a few days later and was mad as hell that the cameras he was using produced lots of ultrasonic sounds. At least someone else has finally verified my claims.

I did have some luck installing a digital snapshot camera the same afternoon, at a property where the owners were installing vinyl siding on an old barn. That night, the camera took two dark images of something about ten feet tall, walking toward the camera and then exiting the viewing area. The image is rather dark, but it does show something about ten feet tall for two frames. The owners of the property told me about the ten-footer, but I really didn't believe them until I saw the images. I believe the creature saw the illumination that was given off by an LED located in the camera housing. Under normal viewing, we could not see the illumination of the LED, since I had placed black tape over the LED, but after the fact, I looked at the camera and was able to see the illumination by using third-generation night-vision equipment. Maybe the creature saw the illumination of the LED and got out of there. One note on the timing of those two snapshots: The building it was mounted to had several people inside, singing in preparation for a Sunday church service. It's quite possible that the singing covered up the ultrasonic sounds emitted by the camera.

The above incident tells me the creatures may be able to see into different wavelengths than humans, but that is just speculation on my part. It also tells me these creatures could be distracted somehow and let their guard down on some occasions. So maybe we need to focus on developing some type of distraction when we deploy a camera recording system. In the future, I will be deploying camera systems that will stay dormant for several months before they are remotely activated. I would hope the

> smells from the camera would dissipate by then, and the creatures would drop their guard of the equipment because it will not emit anything until it's remotely activated. The images taken can also be downloaded remotely, so the site will not be contaminated by the scent of humans.
>
> A Virginia newspaper did a story on "Virginia Bigfoot," and I was interviewed. I was able to relatively control what was written so it didn't make me or other researchers look like fools. That story was one of their bestselling Sunday papers ever. The positive response received by the newspaper made them realize they were onto something. They also found out that they were reaching teenagers — a reader base they had never identified.
>
> One woman was so impressed by the facts presented in the article that she is donating remote land she has owned for almost forty years to Virginia Bigfoot Research so it can be used as a wildlife sanctuary and Bigfoot research study area. The site contains two waterfalls, with a combined drop of over 150 feet. She has also agreed to donate a structure to serve as a base camp and provide shelter for recording equipment. This proved to me that if you state the real facts and not speculation, great things can be accomplished in the field of research.

I asked Mr. Dranginis to sum up his thoughts about Bigfoot. His thoughts are similar to mine.

> I will tell you that these creatures do exist, and they are not dumb apes. They are extremely intelligent and knowledgeable in our human ways. Also, by working in the intelligence community, I can say these creatures have us beat hands down when it comes down to deception. That's why this is such a great cat-and-mouse game.

## Animal Mutilations and the FBI

With the special agents Mr. Dranginis spoke of, I had to wonder about an organization like the FBI and what they might or might not know about Sasquatch. This particular piece involves the animal mutilations of the 1970s, which occurred in a number of U.S. States. Having researched the matter, I feel the Bureau was unaware of what may have happened during their investigative process. It wouldn't have raised an eyebrow, because it was not directly related to the case. The evidence is there, though, on the FBI's Internet site, under the "FOIA Library/Requests — FBIHQ Reading Room — Animal Mutilation Project."

On April 20, 1979, a conference was held in Albuquerque, New Mexico. Law enforcement agencies, news media representatives, and the general public were gathered together on the dire subject of animal mutilations in the United States and the numerous theories that had surfaced. These ideas included satanic cults, predators, extraterrestrial visitors, and some unknown government agency. Many of the animal killings were the result of surgical extraction practices. Body parts were removed but most of the animals' bodies were left behind. Some of the missing animals were never found; that was one of the directions I went in my research. Through it all, something jumped out at me that was worth researching, though it was nothing really associated with who did the initial surgeries.

*Newsweek* magazine for September 30, 1974, mentioned that a few residents reported sighting strange creatures resembling bears and gorillas. At least one farmer claimed that a shiny UFO had landed in a field. At that particular time, the happenings were in Nebraska. I'll leave the Star People theory to a number of New Age investigators who pursue such things. For now, we will focus on the gorilla end of it and the possible reasoning I have about these primate figures being pictured there.

Who really knows what actually became of the slaughtered cattle in a number of states during the seventies? Some questions still remain unanswered. In many cases, after the organ extractions, known animal predators helped themselves to the opened carcasses. That end of it was not always followed up on and was dismissed as a normal part of animal behavior, but there may have been another visitor drawn in for feeding from the dead cattle. Nebraska was the example of this possibility.

Witnesses remembered seeing upright-walking creatures in areas associated with the investigations, animals with a bear and gorilla nature to them. If eyewitness reports are anywhere near correct, we could assume that Sasquatch may have been lured down by the buffet of easy-for-the-taking food. The area held hints of this, and the Bigfoot creature may have made a showing. As in the 1974 *Newsweek* article, there were also at least three documented sightings of the Bigfoot during that year. The creature was seen during autumn in Gage County. It was also encountered on two separate occasions near Oakland, Nebraska, and the giant was seen in Sarpy County in the summer of 1975.

These kinds of things had gone on for many years. During the height of my study, I ran across an author/researcher in 2010 who has had his fair share of mysterious investigative work, both in North America and abroad. Nick Redfern, who now resides in Texas, had this little tidbit about his work in the southern United States:

> The closest I have personally come to a link between Bigfoot and cattle mutilations is in relation to the so-called "Black Helicopter" phenomenon. As many people will be aware, dark and unmarked helicopters are often viewed in the vicinity of cattle mutilation events. This has given rise to the theory that those piloting the helicopters are either (A) monitoring who is doing the mutilations; or (B) are themselves responsible for the killings. I have investigated a number of Bigfoot reports from around Taos and Angel Fire — both in New Mexico — where sightings of Bigfoot-type creatures were made in conjunction with Black Helicopter reports. It was as if the helicopter crews were monitoring Bigfoot activity in the areas. Of course, this is all highly controversial and doesn't explicitly link Bigfoot with mutilations. But, for me at least, the helicopter tie-in with Bigfoot is intriguing, if nothing else.

Horrendous animal mutilation activity has also been reported all over the United States throughout the years. The following areas have also shown reported signs of Sasquatch activity: Dulce, New Mexico; Elbert County, Colorado; Sedona, Arizona; and the Bridgewater Triangle area in southeastern Massachusetts.

In the summer of 2009, I communicated with Norio Hayakawa, who researches a number of things in the Dulce region, and throughout New Mexico:

> I am glad you had a chance to read about the Dulce conference and what took place there.
>
> The Dulce area has been known to be not only of interest among UFO researchers, but also, particularly in recent years, of frequent Bigfoot sightings.
>
> In fact, after talking to so many residents in Dulce, I am convinced that these frequently reported sightings of Bigfoot are as serious as ever.

> Hoyt Velarde, former Police Chief of Dulce, testified to his many sightings of Sasquatch, especially along the Navajo River, and also at his ranch.
>
> He is a member of the BFRO.
>
> There is a UFO researcher here in the Albuquerque area who is a friend of Kewaunee Lapseritis, a nationally known Bigfoot researcher. Mr. Lapseritis definitely says the Bigfoot phenomenon is closely related to UFO phenomenon. I, myself, am not a Bigfoot researcher, but I can say for sure that northwestern New Mexico (including Dulce) is a very significant area.
>
> Thank you so much, for asking about my email. By all means, yes, you can put my email info in your book. I am a very public person. I truly believe in openness and have nothing to hide.

As of December 2009, Bigfoot sightings in the Dulce, New Mexico, area were continuing. I also found the odd personal report attached to the Nebraska circumstances; the creature definitely showed up during the animal mutilations at some point. Anonymity was requested. The people making the requests wanted nothing to do with their names being plastered anywhere. Their immediate areas were investigated by what they called "freaks" equipped with sophisticated gadgetry and strange sounding knowledge.

These stories provide more evidence that the Sasquatch creature may be willing to show itself when nourishment is available. It would only be normal for an animal to follow up on a possible meal, considering its abilities and light-fingered approach. This may be another avenue to pursue when trying to gather more evidence about the creature's existence.

# *18. Bigfoot Rewards*

The story of the search for a physical Bigfoot wouldn't be complete without some mention of the financial incentives that have been offered for proof of Bigfoot or proof that the evidence is fake. Serious money has been offered, but the clever creature still remains at large.

## China Flat Museum's $100,000

Below is an example of just how difficult it may be to pull off the charades of track fixing. The article on Bigfoot Encounters was pointed out to me by Ken Kristian. Author and researcher John Green gave me permission to include the following article:

### $100,000 Reward for BIGFOOT TRACKS

A reward of $100,000 is being offered by the Willow Creek China Flat Museum for anyone who can demonstrate how the Bigfoot tracks that were observed in the Bluff Creek valley in northern California in 1958 and later could have been made by a human or humans.

This offer is genuine. It is not a joke or a publicity stunt.

The money has been arranged for, and the first person or group who can meet the conditions of the offer will receive it. Everyone should understand, however, that the conditions are not easy. The offer is a direct result of recent publicity which has created a perception that the Bluff Creek tracks were just a hoax carried out by a practical joker walking around wearing a large pair of carved wooden feet, but it is not meant as a challenge to the people who originated that story, who may well be perfectly sincere.

The offer also is not a prize for technological achievement, such as being the first to build an effective footprint-stamping machine. It relates entirely to the question of whether the real tracks which brought the Bigfoot phenomenon to public attention could have been made by humans under the real conditions of the times and the places in which they appeared.

The museum has casts of some of the tracks concerned, a few of them copies but mainly originals, available for inspection. It also has some related photographs, and published accounts of what was done and observed in connection with the tracks. There are also people still available for consultation who studied the tracks when they were made.

A formal document setting out the requirements to qualify for the award will take time to prepare, but a successful applicant will have to be able to make flat-footed, humanlike tracks with more than twice the area of human feet and longer-than-human strides which do the following:

Traverse a variety of terrains, including climbing, descending, and crossing steep slopes covered with underbrush;

Show variations of shape and toe position and stride accommodating to the terrain;

Sink into firm ground to far greater depth than human footprints, specifically as much as an inch deep in hard sand where human prints barely penetrate at all;

Leave hard objects in the ground, such as stones, sticking up above the rest of the track.

The applicant will also have to be able to make these tracks under the following conditions, although not all in combination: 1) In the dark, hundreds in a single night; 2) In places where it is impossible to bring any vehicle or other machine or any equipment except what humans or animals could carry; 3) Without doing anything to attract the notice of people a few hundred yards away.

Interested parties may contact the museum president. [JG3]

## Bushnell's $1,000,000

And then, starting in the summer of 2008, there would be much braver contributors to reward the successful. Binocular manufacturer Bushnell, teaming up with *Field & Stream* magazine, offered up to one million smackers to anyone who could produce evidence of the existence of Bigfoot.

There would be few, if any, takers, even though the bounty ran until the middle of December — even though there were a million dollars at stake.

This was a very interesting concept. Provincial or state lotteries or local charities offering up things like million-dollar homes or other extravagant prizes create a frenzy of human activity.

Yet, practically no one was willing to go search for Bigfoot. Why? Was it because most think finding such a creature is an impossible task? Because there'd be no point in chasing a myth, a creature that doesn't exist anyway? Others claim they know but purposely hide the whereabouts of such creatures, for there's more to life than money. At first this couldn't be confirmed, but I've spoken with sincere people who supposedly do such admirable things.

Did a lot of field glasses and magazines get sold in the combined marketing promotion? Who's to say?

## The 1960 Poster

None of this was particularly new, of course, for there were Bigfoot bounties much earlier on. My wife and I found one such poster at a bookstore in Calgary. (The owner wouldn't part with it.) It is dated January 1960 and includes a special seal on it. The gentleman allowed a number of pictures to be taken of the framed item.

**Figure 43: Bigfoot reward poster from 1960. Rewards up to one million dollars have been offered for proof of Bigfoot's existence.**

# *19. Summing Up the Physical Evidence*

Part I is merely a taste of the type of in-depth research being done in the field. So many things are being attempted and experimented with. Still, no researcher thus far has been able to expose the woodland giant. Some lay claim to solving the mystery, but those claims are soon lost by the wayside when the rambunctious individual or clandestine group is unable to provide the evidence needed to process their claim. In the long run, their credibility suffers and the mystery only deepens.

Much of the Sasquatch phenomenon is based on stories, as those in the field have no actual body of the creature to work with. Some stories are too extreme to believe, but I have no idea if even the credible stories are true or not. Some could say this is my case as well, that my sightings of the creatures are just stories. However, within my own thoughts I know what happened. I don't need to fall back on other people's stories to be sure of Bigfoot's existence. Seeing seems to have people like me believing, but in accounts from eyewitnesses, only those who were there know for sure. It is very hard for people who have not had my experiences to know what to think.

A member of the Bigfoot Forums posted an interesting idea about the photography end of things: pictures of the grizzly, and also those ridiculous, out-of-focus, at-a-distance Bigfoot photos. It definitely struck a nerve; a picture is worth at least a thousand words. In a snappy comparison, the member had at least 119 photos there of the *Ursus arctos horribilis*. Above that, there were five relatively blurry pictures of different wooded areas, including what I would consider to be a pin-dot Bigfoot in each of them. The individual's post was right to the point, even circling the supposed creatures in red ink.

These kinds of things coming forward only lit a fire under me at a somewhat spiritual level, for I believe *something* does exist. It wasn't smoke or some strange mist that we saw during my Princeton sightings, though some people thought we were seriously delusional. I found it ironic that these so-called hallucinations vanished like the Sasquatch, never to be seen again. This delusional atmosphere included over thirty years of marriage and three boys brought up well by two loving parents. The truth is, I'm just an average person caught in the middle of something out of the ordinary — and that's somewhat of an understatement.

All this leaves the scientific community divided, the government understandably passive, the media puzzled, and researchers in the trenches scratching their heads. The rest of this book looks at other possibilities. Even the Church is undecided on the issue, which we'll discuss in Part III. Our look at the physical Bigfoot left us with blurry photographs, malfunctioning equipment, romantic and scientific writing, a wealth of sightings, including my own, and anticipation of what's out there — the truth in *whatever form*.

# II. First Nation and Native American Connections

In Part II, I want to tell you about my research into Canadian First Nation and U.S. Native American stories about Sasquatch and the related creatures of the wilderness. I have separated these into legends, Sasquatch on the reservation, and modern stories, but first I want to talk about why these stories are so hard to find. This mostly has to do with the Civilization Regulations as they were enacted and enforced from the 1880s until the 1930s.

Most aboriginal people do not scoff at the potential of such a continuing force of nature as the Sasquatch. Embarrassment, discomfort, and humiliation are the white man's woes concerning the legendary beast. The aboriginals and indigenous look at all of this quite differently. They mainly keep it quiet amongst themselves, because they often honor this great primate in their belief systems, holding Sasquatch as sacred whether it is a physical or supernatural being. Many times, these beliefs are not to be shared, for fear that they might be exploited. It is part of a legitimate ongoing reaction to how they were suppressed for so many years. The legends are clearly illustrated in their beliefs and teachings and, in part, the structuring of their societies throughout the ages. Nevertheless, they are private beliefs of such importance that the people who hold them are not too eager to discuss legends of the Sasquatch.

The beliefs about the Sasquatch come in many varieties. I tried to let the people I talked with see my heartfelt genuineness toward the belief, and I explained my Sasquatch sightings to them in conversation. Some were willing to help me in my quest, though they asked to remain anonymous, which will be respected. In my studies, I found it interesting that the elders sometimes keep younger generations in the dark. They operate under a don't-ask-questions-just-sit-there-and-listen kind of policy.

To make a very long story short, different parts of the Sasquatch and other Native Indian lore are not necessarily equal in nature. Many of their animal transformation legends, comparative tales, and storytellers' fodder come from things of the past — things that have already happened. This may not hold true for the Sasquatch. The giant is still being encountered today, and evidence has continued to slowly trickle in (and I do mean trickle). It is a legend that has not yet been put to rest. Some stories have a lot of detail but many are sketchy and only hint at what is going on. Living and breathing (or at least we hope so), the creature is not yet extinct and is a part of contemporary native culture.

# 20. Treaties and Regulations

To understand the current feelings of Native Americans and First Nations people, we need to look first at their interactions with the white people and the treaties that were made between them. We can start with the controversial subject of the Civilization Regulations of the 1880s to 1936. There would be other agreements and treaties put in place as well, including the Hellgate Treaty of 1855, but for argument's sake, we will jumble them all together and focus on the importance of the Civilization Regulations on the aboriginal peoples of North America, and how the regulations have caused the Sasquatch to be hidden away because of the persecution of these people.

"The Sasquatch will not be practiced out in the open anytime soon." That was a brief but firm statement issued by a tribe member in 2006, in regard to the Wild Man and Wild Woman.

## The Civilization Regulations

The Civilization Regulations, which were in effect from the 1880s to the 1930s, outlawed many religious and spiritual beliefs of the native people of the United States. Canada introduced its own version of the laws, making things such as the Potlatch Dance a misdemeanor; any person even encouraging these celebrations could be jailed. In the United States, especially, many indigenous people were kept away from sacred places. The beliefs were driven underground, sometimes to the point of extinction. The loss of sacred places and spiritual locations destroyed native balance. The losses included lands that held secrets about the Sasquatch.

Of course, the creature was never uncovered by governments or settlers, but it was also lost to aboriginal people who once knew of its existence. With such things as the Civilization Regulations in place, the people became very reluctant to share their beliefs in plain view. These were laws that applied only to native people and their religions and spirituality. Even roaming from government-established reservations brought penalties.

After the people were rounded up and shoved forcefully onto crowded reservations, government policies took a much darker turn, including the absolute banning of native religious beliefs. Some kept the old ways but hid their practices. Also hidden away was the talk of the Giants. Some were dreamers, just trying to keep themselves alive, but others would become intense storytellers. For most, the old beliefs were not a major priority at this particular time. The indigenous people were far too busy fighting for their survival in those drastic conditions.

I spoke with two individuals over time, and they mentioned that the creature, the Biggest Brother, as most called it, moved along with those in that era — certain tribes, of course — at a short, safe distance. The haired giants knew of the pain and suffering, as they saw it first hand. One of the voices that contacted me said this hardened the heart of certain breeds of the creatures, while others remained rather passive, shy, and reclusive.

## Modern Repercussions

One must remember that even today, there is little trust toward government or outside professionals who write about Sasquatch. Many things are taken out of context, and many treaty laws are not being respected by the government. Many are still reluctant to speak, even now.

> We're often pressured to reveal and discuss the why's of our concerns. For some tribes, it's all right to reveal such information. As for our tribes, we are very reluctant to reveal such information and things. (Spokeswoman)

These Regulations remain an explosive political topic, restraining even those who have something to say about the beliefs of such an enthralling creature. Some were willing to hint about such things, wanting to think for themselves while hanging on to their culture, traditions, and heritage. A few became involved, and to them I offer many thanks. There also were those who remained rude and obnoxious, very offensive, even with the simple questions that were introduced. By no means did they feel that a white-skinned fellow should encounter the creature of distant legends, even though some of them claimed to have witnessed the Sasquatch for themselves. The creature of many names was not to be shared.

Of course, focusing on the Sasquatch phenomenon in this case only, is it any wonder at times that the indigenous people turn away from most out-of-reality researchers or those who are utterly intoxicated with creating ridiculous fables involving zippered suits, moneymaking stories, and things that embarrass an incredible mystery? Over time, this is becoming more of a reality: less actual aboriginal involvement and more white man fallacies in the Bigfoot equation. I was actually on the other side of this once, as I gently pressed a group on the subject of Sasquatch. It didn't matter how sincere or courteous I was; I was simply the wrong color to deserve honesty and cooperation when it came to a legend that didn't belong to me. Certain knowledge keepers and those with such understanding were instructed to mislead the everyday world when it came to the very touchy subject of the being that has so eluded us.

Thankfully, they are not all manipulators out there. The Bigfoot shows itself to whomever it pleases, race and creed aside. This has been mentioned by levelheaded indigenous folks, even those of a lower class, according to their own cultures. Fortunately, there is still some decency in the world, even if it comes from a strange creature on a journey, something else that a number of them would hint at or outright say. The messages I received from some of these generous, brave voices were as follows:

> My name is Alex Alvarez, and I am the Cultural Educator for the Poarch Creek Indians. Your question caught me off guard, because it's out of the ordinary; however, we do have such a creature in our history. We don't call it Bigfoot. We call it: Este-cvpko, pronounced "ish-tee jub-koh." It means "tall person." It is said to be very foul smelling and cause confusion when a person crosses its path, in order to protect itself. People have said they become so disoriented that they come out of the woods five to six miles from where they planned on coming out. It is not known to have ever hurt anyone; it just doesn't like the company of humans. Elders have said that if you ever come across it, you must stop and walk backward the entire way back to avoid becoming disoriented. (Alex Alvarez)

Regarding the Sasquatch, I spend some of my time working with remote aboriginal communities in the northern part of [private information]. There are many stories that I hear from very reliable people that all support the existence of a Sasquatch-like entity. The stories are not generally told because of many reasons. The bush holds many secrets. Glen, I prefer that you don't add my commentary in its entirety. The First Nations have not been comfortable about disclosing their observations in public or to a broad public group. It would not be respectful. (Anonymous)

Mr. Boulier, we certainly do have a lot of information concerning what most people call Bigfoot. Please let me share with you our concern when we receive email requests such as yours. It has been our experience now for a number of years that many of the cultural stories and information that our elders and spiritual practitioners have shared with anthropologists, archeologists, and just people in general have been either misrepresented or, in many cases, exploited for personal gain. Because of what I have just stated, I'm hoping you will understand why we are careful with whom we share any information, especially when it comes to the subject of our spiritual beliefs. Mr. Boulier, this is what we are proposing, that you take the time first of all to come and visit and get to know us here at [private information]. In the course of this visit, you may be asked to share with us your intentions for what you will be doing with information that may be shared with you. With respect. (Tribe Spokesman)

We are a people that know of the one you seek, passing down the belief to an upcoming generation. (First Nations Tribal Member)

To the best of my knowledge, our Tribes have never released any information about this topic. Now, as a tribal member, I've heard the so-called Indian theories, as in, "Sasquatch is an Indian name." I've never heard from which tribe. I've heard people speak of it from a tribal sense. There was also a lady in Nez Perce Country near Lapwai who always claimed he'd come and store apples in her shed and sometimes spin her trailer around. But as for official, sanctioned cultural info — never seen it released. Not sure if there is any. Do some families have stories to share? Possibly, but that is their business, and it's something

> I'm not privy to. Non-tribal friends have, through the years, asked me to share my secret knowledge about Bigfoot. It's been fun to shine them on at times. I've had academic friends who were Indian who've shown me dirty jokes and stories made up on the spot to intrusive archeologists — have made it into text-books and presented as tribal lore. (R.M.)
>
> Tribal legends about the Sasquatch... We know of such a creature. They were spoken of long ago. (Tribal Brave)
>
> Many of our ceremonies went underground during that era of genocide attacks from government. Many are still only held within unknown circles of only family knowledge. We are the younger brothers and sisters. (Spokesperson)
>
> Hidden and said for hundreds of years, there has to be truth to the matter. It has been protected, this creature. (Tribal Society Person)

One must remember that there are two sides to every story. And yes, there were so-called "heathen" or "pagan" practices amongst the tribes; the Sun Dance and Ghost Dance were two examples. It would require many pages to expand on both sides of this argument, but that's not why we're here. This is about certain individuals stepping forward, offering what they wish to share about a massive upright creature that has walked in their lands.

# 21. Sasquatch and the Reservation

As I approached the subject of the Sasquatch within the native community, the discussions and communications revealed a pattern. It wasn't about the Bukwas mask, superstition, supernatural beings, scaring children into obedience, or anything like that. It was an up-to-date idea about the upright giant, what it really is. A short note from someone we'll call P.B. particularly caught my attention:

> It is funny you should mention about the Sasquatch, as I was only talking about it the other month to a friend of mine who lives on the Swan Lake First Nations Reservation. This is what she said to me: "We have a Sasquatch living around here and on the Long Plains Reserve too." I have never been lucky to see one. Don't think I want to, but my aunt's granddaughter saw one a few years ago near the lake, not far from where they lived. They drove back fast and looked very sick and pale when they walked into the house. I guess the experience was too much for them. We know they exist, and the people respect them and leave them alone. I hope this helps you on your quest. Blessings.

Considered a higher form in native culture, the Sasquatch is treated with great respect and allowed to run free on reservation lands. They are seldom, if ever, disturbed. So, does the Sasquatch use native land and reservation boundaries to its advantage? What a great place to hide!

All this started one day when I thought about deer knowing when it is hunting season. A number of hunters were interviewed on the yearly event, and it was almost unanimously accepted that game doesn't know. Of course that makes sense, but there is still increased vehicle and human presence, including the sounds of gunfire, and man's deeper push into the wilderness during hunting season. The deer would notice the change. In the case of the bipedal giant, it might notice that it has safe passage in tribal lands. The Bigfoot enter and man does — or should — not.

We know that some species show less fear and anxiety on reservation lands than they do elsewhere. This is true for private property as well. Individuals I spoke with from numerous areas asserted that this being is one of the most intelligent, definitely smarter than the ones chasing it.

I began to look at the numbers, just to see how much real estate the Sasquatch species would have to work with. There are over 550 recognized tribes in the United States, including approximately 275 native land areas, with over 56.2 million acres of land. Canada's contribution is approximately 2,300 reserves scattered around the country, with 600 or more bands present. Interesting to note is the population density, or lack thereof, in the reservations or reserves. The Sasquatch could literally be a small needle in a very large haystack, and a moving, thinking one at that.

As an example, the Little Eagle (Standing Rock Indian Reserve) in South Dakota has just 0.5 persons per square mile on their 2.3 million acres. Of this, 1.4 million acres are tribally owned. Pine Ridge, also in South Dakota, is approximately the size of the state of Connecticut, about 2.7 million acres, with less than 40,000 inhabitants. The Blackfeet Indian Reservation in northwestern Montana has 1.5 million acres with a population under 10,000. Still in Montana, the Fort Peck Reservation is the third largest in the state. Fewer than 10,000 Sioux and Assiniboine reside on two million acres of land,. Another reservation, for the Hupa Indians east of Eureka, California, has a population of less than 5,000 on over 144 square miles. And, a place I've personally visited in British Columbia, the Chehalis Indian Reserve houses approximately fifty-five people per square kilometer. These areas of North America have nothing but space for the Sasquatch to hide, and this is only native reservations and reserves. Crown and government land must also be considered.

Hunters, fishermen, and a host of others sharing this vast land are sighting this creature escaping onto reservation lands. Whether this is coincidental or not is speculation. Just as a deer doesn't know the dates of hunting season, the Sasquatch may not comprehend boundaries, but the creature still may realize that it is safer in a certain area. There are many sightings on the inside, though a majority will never be shared. Only a few reports come out, such as those in the following stories.

On the Onondaga Reservation, a Mohawk gentleman felt that a Sasquatch was headed for a cave that was mostly underground. He believes the cave may connect up with other reservations by channels. In the Southern Ute Indian Reservation of southern Colorado, traditional accounts of the Sasquatch place it in high elevations and remote areas. There are still reports surfacing from the Ute Indians of encountering Sasquatch while hunting on and near the reservation. The tall creature was always reported to be coming or going.

My studies of the elusive Sasquatch haphazardly wandering the millions of acres of reservation land across North America took a slightly different turn, toward South Dakota. The Lakota call the Sasquatch the "Hairy Man" or "Tall Man," and there were many sightings of the creature in the 1970s, related to times of troubles.

My focal point was the Pine Ridge Indian Reservation, due in part to sincere aboriginal interest. It started with a number of sightings years earlier at and around Cherry Creek, South Dakota, a little place that borders the south end of the Cheyenne River Indian Reservation, where the Cheyenne River runs. The Sasquatch was seen scampering in and out of the reservation near Cherry Creek. The reports didn't end there, however, as the animal was also seen on the west side of the reservation, near Faith, South Dakota. The creature roamed in and out of that area as well, in what some purported to be large, zigzagging patterns.

A newspaper editor in the region contacted me and told me that a family of Sasquatch, including adolescents, seemed to be living in the Pine Ridge area. I was told to contact the tribal police on Pine Ridge. The journalist also spoke of sightings recorded at Manderson, just northwest of Wounded Knee.

As news traveled that I was investigating, I was contacted by another newspaper editor, involving Lakota news articles of the past. This conversation led to sightings that had occurred near Kyle, South Dakota, about five miles inside the reservation. The Sasquatch had moved freely back and forth, according to verbal reports and Indian trackers.

The area around Porcupine, a little town less than ten miles from the east boundary, on the Pine Ridge Reservation, didn't escape either. Sasquatch were seen moving through the immediate region. Just down the road, so to speak, on the Rosebud Indian Reservation near Spring Creek, the Sasquatch was doing much the same kind of travel. The western reservation boundary was less than ten miles away. All of this activity took place in South Dakota, and I had to wonder how much of this cross-boundary travel actually goes on in North America. In the case of South Dakota, I wondered if the same creatures were being spotted over and over again or if a large number of them were wandering around.

## North Dakota Stories

Below is an example of North Dakota's involvement with the Sasquatch. It was presented to me by *Grand Forks Herald* columnist, Dorreen Yellow Bird.

### Big Foot in North Dakota? Maybe, Just Maybe

Tales of creatures that disturb our mundane and everyday lives are not uncommon. To claim, however, that you've seen such a creature is to hear snickers or out-loud laughing. Yet, when I heard what happened on the Fort Berthold reservation near New Town, ND, I wondered. It was a sighting of one of the most common of these creatures — Sasquatch or Big Foot.

In one corner of the North Dakota Badlands, at the entrance of the Fort Berthold Reservation, a road runs along the benchlands, then winds down several miles of switchbacks to the bottomland. You have to drive down a steeply curved road. When you get to the bottom, the road splits. The new road continues to a wider, lower bridge.

The old road, which cars no longer can use, now is overgrown with grass and willow. Both roads cross the Little Missouri River, sometimes called the "Muddy Missouri." You have entered the wildly beautiful and rough Badlands.

A few miles east of the new road, the old road crosses the river by an old metal bridge — a bridge that was built when the area was being explored many years ago by white men. It was lost by its builders in a labyrinth of wild, endless, mountainous cliffs and cutoffs. Hence, the old bridge is called "Lost Bridge."

It was there that a man and his son, who live in the area, the other day spotted what they said may have been Big Foot. The creature was walking on the highway that leads to the bridge, the men said.

The time was early evening. As the men watched, the creature dropped immediately down the steep side of the road. It walked in the snow for about half a mile and came back to the road, they told the Tribal Natural Resources Department.

Two men from that department went out to the area to investigate. One of the young men said they did find tracks, but the sun had started to melt them, and there wasn't enough left to provide clear evidence. Still, you could see the outline of five toes in some of the many tracks at the site, the department official said. But the tracks weren't conclusive.

The official didn't know what to make of all this but seemed skeptical that it was, indeed, Big Foot.

Last week, a husband and wife and their children saw a large creature moving very fast across the snowdrifts beyond the back yard, they said. They were beside themselves and called their neighbor. The neighbor said he saw something big moving across the snow too. The dogs, he said, were acting strange and were antsy, not like it was something they usually see.

He and another friend jumped into their four-wheelers and drove to the area. When they got there, they saw a man cross-country skiing. That could have been what the people saw, he said, but there was doubt in his voice. The man was much smaller than what the people said they saw. The skier, for his part, said he hadn't seen anything.

The incident was reported to the police, but the police found nothing significant.

There are other recent stories of sightings, but none as well documented as the two I mentioned above. That includes another sighting west of New Town, near the old S&L Bar.

John Danks, a retired Bureau of Indian Affairs worker and elder rancher in the community, said he'd heard of Bigfoot sightings on the reservation for the last 20 years. He hasn't had such a sighting himself but certainly has heard of them.

When you live in a place where there are stretches of lands where no human has walked and no plow has touched, stories of creatures are not uncommon. As a child, I, too, heard and saw things that certainly were strange.

Our traditional stories tell of beings who live with us but cannot be seen by human beings, so I don't discount the sightings. There are many mysteries that even scientists cannot explain, at least to our satisfaction.

But I am at a wait-and-see stage in this incident. And, after hearing the reports from those reliable people who saw the creatures, I am wondering. [DYB1]

## Tales of Sightings Lend Credence to Bigfoot Myth

On my recent trip to the Bitterroot and Salmon River mountains in Montana and Idaho, I heard some chilling stories about sightings of Bigfoot or Sasquatch. Do these and other stories I've heard about this so-called myth have any credibility?

It seems so. Some of the Nez Perce people made me think there may be truth to the tales of Sasquatch.

It seemed no matter where I went during my trip to Idaho, the Corps of Discovery, Lewis and Clark, had left their mark on that part of the region. The Nez Perce, for example, are the Nimi'ipuu, which means "the real people," but they were given the name "Nez Perce" in 1805 by interpreters of Lewis and Clark. Apparently the interpretation means "pierced nose." (They say this was not common practice among their people.)

When I stayed with my adopted Nez Perce relatives, we spent a lot of time visiting. They are storytellers — tellers of real-life stories. This is one of their Sasquatch accounts:

When Muriel and her father, Allen, were driving to work a few years ago, they came upon an unexpected sight. They were heading for a nearby town some 60 miles west of Kamiah, Idaho, where they live, she said.

This is mountainous country. On a large, mountain-like hill next to the road, Muriel, who was on the passenger side of the car, said she saw a large animal on the hillside. At first she thought it was a cow, she said. It was bending over and suddenly stood up. It looked like a giant, hairy man. It turned its body toward them and looked human. When it saw them, it ran. With only a few strides, it was over this steep hill.

They stopped and walked to the spot where they saw what they assume was Bigfoot or Sasquatch. They found the spot, and it looked as though the creature had been digging roots. There are roots on the reservations that the Nez Perce harvest and use for eating, making mats, and so on.

They measured its footprints on the ground. The prints looked like those of human feet, except much, much bigger.

Muriel covered the same ground over the hill, following the footprints it made in the ground. The beast made it in three or four strides. It took her at least five minutes to cover the same ground.

> There have been many reports of Bigfoot or Sasquatch in that area, but people often don't feel comfortable telling their story because the public doesn't believe them.
>
> A spiritual leader who also was hearing that story said it is true; there are indeed these manlike beasts. He also has seen, heard, and smelled them.
>
> This was on the West Coast, he said, a place where the Sasquatch are frequently seen. He was taken to the place by people who wanted him to see them. They know where the Bigfoot is and keep that home a secret, he said. [DYB2]

It is worth noting that places like this were lost during the upheaval of the Regulations, when lands were confiscated. An American Native Indian, as he requested he be called, mentioned to me that there may have been cases where the Bigfoot moved on as well, threatened by the coming of the settlers and others. This has been spoken of in Native circles and around gatherings. The white man knew little about the presence of such a timid giant, and this knowledge was never shared with the land grabbers and government. I was told more than once that this creature sometimes moved into the areas where the aboriginal people were forced to be. At times, some of these people tried in vain to go back and forth, but they were caught. The Bigfoot was seldom seen by outsiders, and was, of course, never caught.

Dorreen Yellow Bird continues:

> He and his friends waited for the chance to see them. I don't think that at that point, he was convinced Sasquatch was real.
>
> But while he was waiting, he heard noises in the trees, he said. And before he heard them, he could smell them. They smelled awful.
>
> And when they came into view, they were as people had reported: large, hairy beasts with long arms, but not gorillas, he said. The creatures made low, guttural sounds, as if they were talking, but the spiritual leader couldn't understand any of the words. He got a good look.
>
> When these manlike beasts had left, this man and his friends examined the area where they had been. They found footprints that were three times the size of a human's. The footprints were shaped like a human foot, he said. They also didn't report their sightings to anyone. They are best left alone, he said.

I believe there are many things beyond our understanding. I believe my grandmother was right when she told her grandchildren, "It is a fool who thinks they know everything and have seen everything." There are things that are strange to us because we aren't familiar with them, but that doesn't mean they're make-believe.

Perhaps way up there in those dense mountain ranges, these manlike creatures have thrived… or perhaps not. [DYB3]

## Sacred Land

Much, but not all, was lost when the original people were forced onto reservations. I have been told that many of the native tribes and bands were taught to memorize every little detail about the land in which they resided. Those sacred soils held secrets to many things. A few individuals responded to my questions about the sacred land issue:

> I am Northern Arapaho, and this creature is in our legends. I have seen a creature such as this around my neck of the woods. Yes, we remain very tight-lipped on such things usually. (Native Tribe Member)

> I know of the one that walks the mountain — the ways they breathe, being close to them at times — "Uhh-huhhh, uhh-huhhh, uhh-huhhh, uhh-huhhh" — them running swiftly. (Tribal Member)

> I will forward this to one of our Knowledge Keepers, and they will provide direction to you or not, on things of the Sasquatch. (Spokeswoman)

> Glen, Our land was taken; our people were killed in a landslide of systematic genocide. What you people call the "Bigfoot" — this is one of the last animals that actually continues to walk our journey with us, the helper, finding us when we were displaced long ago. This is all I can say to this. (Elder)

# 22. Legends about Sasquatch

There are many legends about the Sasquatch in native cultures. Some are quite strange. Some may hold hidden secrets. Some may even be stories to confuse white investigators of aboriginal culture. Still, they all speak of a belief in the presence of a giant that walks the land with the tribes. That truth is worth documenting.

## The Red Ogre

The Vermilion Bluffs are red-ochre cliffs spoken of by the Interior Salish, the Okanagans. The aboriginal group spent time there digging the ochre deposits for trade throughout the Interior.

With careful perseverance I unearthed a First People's story about the red cliffs. The natives referred to them as *Tsulameen,* meaning "red paint." There were legends galore in that area that something lay hidden there. The stories were repeated among the ancients, but they were spoken of very little by those who received the narratives. Still, something did get out as I scoured the hills of the Coalmont area. I could only scrape the surface.

What I heard about was something called the Red Ogre. During the periods when the deposits of red clay were excavated by the natives of the Similkameen, there came vague talk from a few individuals that a shadowy bipedal visitor hung around at a distance or was seen traveling the area. The upright spirit was spotted from the cliffs as well. The giant was characterized as having a red, clay-like substance clinging to its hair. Some thought the tall giant was carrying the red ochre on its coat, the colors of the Tsulameen bluffs. They were sure an apparition wouldn't attract the colorful clay, or at least they hoped not. I guess what they say about the ochre is true: Don't get the stuff on your clothing.

**Figure 44: The Tulameen River area, as well as the Thompson Plateau, is a rugged, mountainous region in western British Columbia, hiding Bigfoot for at least 125 years, based on eyewitness reports and First Nations people's testimony.**

## Sasquatch and the Raven

Is it time to forge and simulate raven calls for the sake of summoning the Sasquatch? Nature may have two separate species working together to achieve a meal, the unlikely allies of the Sasquatch and the raven. It has already been proven with the wolf and coyote, which both work in unison with bird species.

The raven is an opportunistic bird, levelheaded and intelligent, whether in the wilderness or in captivity. And if the black-feathered scavenger is this clever, just how smart is the Sasquatch? The raven is another creature that shows signs of tool usage. It also shows indications of working with or using the Sasquatch.

The dark bird is able to work in the harshest of conditions, turning things to its favor. The raven has been known to fly ahead of wolves or sometimes coyotes, leading them to prey on the ground. The bird then waits for the sharp-toothed predators to perform the difficult task of dissection, peeling back the layers of flesh; the feathered one can then take advantage of the hard work already done. The raven even uses this technique with other birds, allowing them to do the dirty work in plundering the prey, then swooping in and shrewdly taking control.

Tool users include the raven or crow. A captured Caledonian crow, Betty, was the subject of many studies. She was filmed making hooks from straight wire to get at an out-of-reach food product. Experts feel these ingenious ways can be handed down through other crows or across their generations. The reason I mention these types of things is because they do, in a way, relate to the Sasquatch. Perhaps they have seen enough animals, men, and birds that they've learned a few tricks as well, above and beyond their natural, everyday, amazing capabilities. They must have learned something, for they're always one step ahead of us.

Another example of amazing animal intelligence relates to urban crows. These birds have learned a process to crack the hard-shelled nuts they require for food. An intersection with traffic lights helps this black wonder, as they unbelievably have the smarts to place the nut in the way of road traffic at a red light. The crow then retrieves the little gift upon a second red light. It's quite a complex set of thoughts for a bird, and it can be surmised that the Sasquatch, an even more brilliant creature, knows more than many give them credit for.

It just may be that the raven or crow uses the Sasquatch for the chance at a meal as well. In some reports of Sasquatch encounters, ravens and crows have been present. One such event happened years ago, near Roosevelt Lake, in the Tonto National Forest of Arizona. The individual who sighted the Sasquatch also saw two crows or ravens swooping down near the animal as it walked. In another report that surfaced in Kentucky, a hunter remained on the edge of the forest. Crows began to make a racket, exposing something moving through the bush. Then, a black-haired Sasquatch showed itself. The Georgia mountains supported this as well, as a number of crows were spotted around two Sasquatch. These types of reports are frequent, and the Sasquatch may be using the birds to its advantage, relying on their squawking to give them messages about food and their surroundings. A few members of different aboriginal tribes mentioned that Bigfoot is able to read and decipher the tones and language of these birds. These interactions were watched and witnessed.

So, again, perhaps raven or crow calls would do well to summon the haired creature. I once heard an off-the-wall story of the Sasquatch mimicking the crow. I'd certainly like to hear that, wouldn't you?

## Lakota Legend

I spoke with the Lakota people when investigating the issues of land loss and what some call the Elder Brother (Bigfoot). One Lakota warrior said, "*Esnella, taku-skan-Chiye-tanka. Esnella, taku-skan, Chiye-tanka,*" which means something akin to "a loner, spirit-living force, Big Elder Brother." Many believe the creature is a dimensional-doorway visitor, sent by God (The Great Spirit). They did, however, respect my view on the Sasquatch being of flesh and blood. I explained everything to them with sincerity, including my own encounter with the giants, and they asked me if my brothers and I or my family had been in times of trouble. They informed me that according to Lakota beliefs, the creature often appears during unsettled times.

## Sasquatch as a Comforter

One more story came to me about how Sasquatch was portrayed as a threat, but turned out to be a comforter to a young girl. I don't know whether this should be a legend or a modern story, but here it is for your enjoyment:

> I had a friend once from the Spokane/Yakima/Coeur d'Alene People, and she lived in Yakima, Washington. She was a young girl when this happened. She said she was getting ready to go out to the big festival when the whales run and the salmon are coming into the wheels. She said her mother grabbed her by the arm and told her she was at a particular time when she, as a young girl, shouldn't be around those things. She said her mother told her the Yeti would come and take her away.
>
> My friend spent the rest of the festival days sitting outside their house, listening to the people in the distance. She started crying because she felt she was being left out.
>
> Pretty soon, there was this Yeti standing on the other side of the field, and it made the same crying sound. My friend started making other sounds, and the Yeti came right to where she was and sat there with her, rocking her and holding her. The creature was a female Yeti. Some other people saw what was going on but

didn't make any real comments about it. She was never really afraid of the Yeti, and other people seemed to know why the Yeti had come.

The Yeti stayed with those Yakima people for a few days, and then others came and stopped by the edge of the woods. There were several of them, and they made a sound like someone wailing. The female Yeti ran her hand over the girl's head and held her a few seconds, then walked off to where the others were, making a real long mourning sound, then left.

The little girl was told by her mother later that night that that particular Yeti was the child's own grandmother who'd been taken a long time ago when she was bathing at the river after having lost her child.

## The Giant Named Mosquito

Whitecloud of the Konkow Maidu sent the following story. It's not quite a Bigfoot story, but it does represent the legends of those who live with the First Nations — and are not always welcome.

> Other tribes tell similar stories. I wouldn't want to take credit for an original story. If you just say it is a story that I heard and repeated, that would be good. Bigfoot or Panomaiduem (Bearman) is just another of nature's people. Yes, they are large; they are called giants in our world, and there are several stories about them. One used to live in our area; it was missing a big toe. We, as a tribe, haven't seen his tracks for over seventy years.
>
> Your mom's night terror is common. They have one hell of a scream. It scared me the first time I heard it. I like to tell people who enter our tribal territory to tell us where they leave their camping gear when they hear the scream and run like hell out of our territory. One man thought he would buy a plains-style teepee and live off the land in our area. He told us where he left the teepee, as he was too afraid to go back and get it.
>
> One story common among native people is the story of the giant named Mosquito. One moved in our area and killed and ate our nearby cousins. A man of our tribe decided he couldn't let the giant eat our people, so he set out to track it. He found the giant and watched his shelter for four days and four nights. The giant left his home in the morning, and our man entered his

home. To his surprise, the giant had a son whom he treated very badly. Our man asked where his father's heart was. His son told him his heart was in his heel. Just then, the hide door swung open, and the giant entered. Our man quickly speared the giant in the heart and killed him, but before the giant died, he told our man, "Even though you have killed me, I will always eat your people." Our man, fearing that the giant would come back to life, burned him in his own fire pit. Still worrying that the giant would spring to life from the ashes, he collected the ashes into a large hide and took them to the top of Bald Rock where it is always windy. He shook the hide and spread the ashes on the winds. The ashes turned to mosquitoes. To this day, the giant eats our people.

# 23. Current Information

Although many tribal societies will continue to remain very secretive about many things, including the Sasquatch, word on the creature is filtering out slowly to a waiting world. It is a slow process, as expected, for trust issues still exist. In 1993, the United Nations recognized the cultural voices of the American Indians, declaring that year to be the International Year for the World's Indigenous People. This turnabout comes at a snail's pace, and some tribes and bands are naturally very cautious. Things of the Sasquatch lie tucked away with those like the knowledge keepers. Hopefully, the suppression will subside, making way for winds of change. We can see in the following some of the changes that are coming about.

## Continuing Dance of the Bukwas

During the Potlatch Trials of 1922, among other things that were confiscated, were the masks of the forest creatures known as Bukwas (Wild Man of the Woods) and Dzunukwa (Wild Woman of the Woods). The Potlatch dances and ceremonies were generally hidden from the white populace for many years. Because of increased interest in the old ways, these celebratory events are again taking front stage.

Today's Potlatch usually generates one day and one night of activities. Traditions of the Potlatch include energetic dance, singing, dressing in costumes, and masks — some of them depicting what we call the Sasquatch.

One has to differentiate between reality and the supernatural within the aboriginal culture. There is a fine line between what is and what may be.

**Figure 45: Dzunukwa, a mask of the Wild Woman of the Woods, created by Gilbert Dawson. (photo © The Pathway Gallery)**

After all, much traditional lore accompanies the Bukwas and Dzunukwa: kidnapped children in baskets, sprinkling haunting liquids on the dead, and the Bukwas association with the underworld. But there may also be a factual basis to the dances that have been handed down, something else seen in the midst of the forests of North America. This involves a technique used by the Sasquatch, a safeguarding measure, a kind of habit. This stance is portrayed in the dance of the Bukwas. Situations surrounding the actual creature under these appearances have been witnessed by the average person.

A Kwakwaka'wakw dancer representing the Bukwas character in their beliefs mimics the creature in dance, translating movements taught by the elders, family, etc. One aspect of the dance has the dancer stepping slightly forward with one leg, raising an arm in front of the face, only allowing the eyes to see and be visible. He may duplicate this to imitate possible shyness of the creature if caught out in the open while looking for shellfish on the beaches. After all, the Sasquatch is ordinarily afraid of human beings.

I pursued this much further and communicated with a native gentleman, Buster Wilson. He knew of the dance as a youngster, having witnessed many Potlatches while growing up. This came from his father's side, but also the side of other higher chiefs. He saw the performances and the displaying of the Bukwas mask firsthand.

Speaking freely, he mentioned a dream his brother had about their late father and the Sasquatch. He also discussed the dances involving the forest dweller. These dances are cherished, passed down, and part of everyday life. Buster feels that if you start to see how these creatures think and how the Kwakiutl people receive the dance, then you may be much closer to communicating with the Sasquatch. The folding of an arm in front of their face is something not only spoken of, but also represented in dance. Further exploring the understandings of his people, Buster is interested in how they obtained the design and why they are that way.

Another native gentleman has encountered such things, surprisingly from both sides of the fence. Many years ago as a young boy, he was taught the dance by his grandfather, when he lived near the coastal waters of British Columbia. Out of respect and admiration for an elder, he learned with enthusiasm. He was taught to imitate the Bukwas creature, stepping slightly forward, pulling his arm up in front of his face, and hiding behind the raised extremity. But what mildly troubled the aboriginal British Columbian was that deep down in the back of his mind, he sometimes felt some things were just folklore or tradition. He received a look at the other side of the story years later on the coast.

He and a relative were on a boat, scouting the inlets along a stretch of the mainland, north of Vancouver. Both are members of the Coastal Salish from the Squamish area. At the time of their unexpected encounter, they were running silent, allowing the water's prevailing currents to lead them on their quest. It was getting dark at that particular time, and the duo decided to scan the shoreline with a spotlight on the port side of the craft, something they'd done many times before. Looking for wildlife of any kind, the two fellows trained the floodlight on an upright animal they'd surprised on the beach, as the boat came around a bend. They were astonished to see a creature, almost as black as the coming night, cover most of its face with a huge arm. The two dumbfounded individuals were witnessing the large Bukwas that might have been looking for food during low tide, and the creature was no longer a supernatural spirit to the two of them. The giant crouched down low, observing. In seconds, this Bukwas of legends was heading for the forest with tremendous determination.

With the departure of the legendary beast, after the light from the boat possibly startled and blinded the creature, the one man recalled what his grandfather had nurtured him with — exact teachings about the movement of the Bukwas. "No matter," he said. The creature was now larger than life, and the man found even more interest in the Potlatch festivities — so much so that the native fellow was willing to share his story here.

## Protecting Sasquatch

Separating fact from storytelling, we come to another instance about such a creature. Along the journey, I have been told by the native people that knowledge of the Sasquatch will not be shared because of man's argumentative squabbling about what they're going to do to protect such a creature. On the whole, the aboriginal people would like us all to know that they compare this to waking a person up in the middle of the night and then offering that person a sleeping pill. The Sasquatch is already protected; they protect themselves. I tend to agree with this outlook — they're doing a marvelous job of it. The following example reveals how the Sasquatch is often considered.

In a campground or outdoor recreation scenario, if a grizzly or black bear has made a kill nearby or is just wandering through, a number of things are a surety. The campgrounds will either be closed, or the bear will be specifically dealt with — moved, tranquilized, or whatever measure will neutralize the problem. It must be addressed. It does happen, as I have witnessed such things over the years in Kananaskis Country, Alberta. The bottom falls out of all this if cubs are involved, as I'm sure you understand. Rangers, paperwork, and possible gadgetry can be involved.

Now, as for poor ol' Sasquatch visiting the same campground, wandering through unannounced, after the initial shock by the reporting party, a ranger or equivalent may look into it. This will often involve paperwork, but this is not always the case. The campground will likely not be closed. Sasquatch researchers may or may not be called in, and even if they are, it is likely that some will not take them seriously. Unlike the bear, the Sasquatch is already protected simply because far too many believe it does not exist. The creature seems to have mastered its own protection simply by remaining elusive enough that it's easier to disbelieve Truly, it is as effective as if they had some kind of mind-altering dust to spray on anyone who catches a glimpse of them. The combination of man's head-in-the-clouds, doubting ignorance and the genuine idea that the upright primate does not exist pretty much secures the annals of the Sasquatch. Remember this: If you see a grizzly, people will likely panic and call in for backup, but if you see a Sasquatch, it will be presumed that you are mistaken, a liar, a dreamer, an attention-seeker, hallucinating, just downright crazy — or a whole host of other mental maladies that I need not mention here. Is it any wonder then, why many tribal societies stand firm on keeping their mouths shut, never relinquishing their hold on the truth? They, too, know that the Sasquatch is protected and shielded by human ignorance — perhaps the greatest protection of all.

## Bigfoot as a Spirit Being

One particular woman came forward with concerns about spirituality and the Bigfoot creature. This lady of pure Cherokee descent was quick to warn me about the existence of many imposters, those who pose as important indigenous peoples, or others disguising themselves as full-blooded native individuals. This is rampant, and it is a real sour note for Native Americans. She mentioned that some of this assumed identity nonsense has, of course, trickled down into the ranks of Bigfoot investigative work, supposed sources pulling the wool over the eyes of serious researchers. I heard this from many aboriginal parties, even though they'd likely been warned not to blow anyone's cover. Thank goodness some people are not willing to be manipulated.

The aboriginal woman, a resident of Oklahoma, also had this to tell me:

> Osiyo,
>
> With the reasons of spirituality fresh in my mind, I would very much like to comment on the subject of what I call the "Big Long Man." I call him this because of a story my mother told me some seven or eight times, bless her heart. The real Long Man has to do with the Corn Patch story — nothing to do with the Bigfoot. It is really about the rivers and streams that a spirit being watches over, the Big Long Man.
>
> You have shared that you are a man of Christianity. I have said that my beliefs are more communal. We walk in two different pathways — opposite directions, but ultimately with one overall Creator. But this is not what this is about. We had what was the "Nighthawk Keetoowahs." Those of tradition (holders of Sacred Truths) went underground mostly in the 1800s because of white faith persecution. In Indian country, we had what is known as the "Trail of Tears." Please look this up if you like.
>
> Enough about me. This falls on two people of two different understandings of beliefs, both of us witnessing to what is in white man's terms, Bigfoot. To my recollection, this came from British Columbia. I will speak of it in these terms.
>
> [There is] no way of proving what our souls have seen, but I saw the Bigfoot in California, near sacred land, while living there a decade ago. We have since moved back to Oklahoma.
>
> As you have described your experience, so it was with my sighting of the creature — similarities in size and weight and also motivation to retreat. I have no idea if it is just an animal now or more so. I have only heard stories of the extra talents. It did nothing out of the ordinary that would make one think that maybe this was something else altogether. In the manner it was written, I have no explanation to the message that the Bigfoot's presence plays in my life. Those more learned than I would tell me stories that had me thinking, but that was not what I came across that day in California. The creature I saw seemed to be in deep study of its surroundings, an animal with heightened senses, strangely practicing some kind of art with her hands.

> Even with my presence, the Bigfoot felt its way along in both touch and thought. I could sense this; I posed little threat.
>
> As to our spiritual beliefs, I do not know where exactly this would fit, other than the Bigfoot being a result of the Creator or those that are associated with the Higher Power. As we spoke, you are Christian, and I am Cherokee (native spirituality). If you look into this, our beliefs differ quite a bit. Both of us being truthful in what we saw, the Bigfoot has shown itself to the both of us. Then there are so many others — others with so many other beliefs and standings. There cannot be a hoax so large. I do not believe in hunting the Bigfoot, but Bigfoot hunters have said something similar: "This cannot be a worldwide scheme." When you have seen, you have seen.
>
> You have mentioned the faith issue. We walk in this as well, many on a spiritual journey that they recognize — not as well as I would have liked, the times of a long ago, blending with what is present, making many of us a washed-down version of our distant cultures.
>
> Glen, it seems that the Bigfoot (Long Man) has been here all along. From where originally, that I'm not sure. I only call them as I see them… and you are doing the same.
>
> Mitakuye Oyasin

Another native voice, Huk, had his say briefly, and it is clear by his statements about the Sasquatch that he is aware of one certainty: Things are changing overall, one way or another. Huk had this to tell me:

> The Bigfoot, as you say and call it… they are here now. They are a part of this Breathing Spiritual Energy, all my relations. They're genuine expressions of spiritual nature unconstrained to us.
>
> Seven generations previously, these intelligent dimensional shifters were spoken of — "Mist Weavers" in our here and now. The Bigfoot, as you refer to it, honors capabilities to see through things such as the skinwalkers' disguise. These beings that stick mainly to the forests know much. The Navajo know more about this skinwalker, less on the Bigfoot.
>
> One thing, Glen, which I entirely agree with you on, is the strangeness behind the differences in the geographical climate involving this being. Where we live in the southern United

States, there is more of a mystical tone to the creature that we know. To the north, those indigenous tribes believe this spirit to be more as the flesh of the Earth. Who is right? Can it be both? I think it is so, as I have heard many things. You researchers are not alone in knowing this. Which of these would make more sense? In the north, where would this creature's place of origin be? I have asked myself this before. It exists, but where have they come from on both counts?

This is all I can say about it.

Peace, brother.

D.K., a Native fellow, had the following insights:

I have very limited knowledge of the Sasquatch. I have heard in our parts that there are Sasquatches, Big People, living north of here. I also would mention that I have heard of Little People living nearby in specific areas of the woods. Both the Sasquatch and Little People exist primarily in the spirit world. However, they can manifest themselves into our physical world, seemingly at their own discretion. So the Sasquatch is not an animal like the deer or moose. Both the Sasquatch and Little People are very reclusive and prefer to be left alone. There is a respect for both of these peoples, and also perhaps some amount of fear, in that they are not to be angered or upset. Trespassing into their territories is not a good idea. Perhaps this is why they are not included in pictograph art very often; I don't know if there are pictographs of them or not actually. Also, very few, if any, people have actually seen them in their special condition, so their true appearance is not commonly known.

Personally, I do believe in spirit beings, both good (angels) and bad (demons). But I don't know how, if these particular spirits are either good or completely bad, or what their purpose is in the Creation.

This is the best answer I can give you. Have a good day.

## Bigfoot as a Power Animal

A woman who was willing to touch on the subject, while not afraid of reprisal for her beliefs, did choose to remain anonymous for fear of threats and retaliation. These aboriginal folk feel they lay the only claim to true shaman practices, so many indigenous groups threaten harm to one who speaks up. Their beliefs date back thousands of years, so anything done by anyone else is after the fact. The ancient and traditional practitioner had this to say:

> Because of you witnessing the man/animal many years earlier on in your life, I will speak in regard to the Bigfoot. The word itself is not what my native tongue understands, but to avoid argument, I will use it when necessary.
>
> There are usually three kinds of interceders that assist the shaman, actually leading them. They are the "spirit guide," the "power animal," and the "totem animal." Concerning the human end of it, there is the "traditional shaman" and the "contemporary shaman." In non-ordinary reality, I consider the Bigfoot as my power animal (animal guide), this living being leading me in recovering fragments of a person's soul. Most of us from the ancestral side are quiet within our own community, as there is usual dedication to the tribe only. The word or term "shaman" is so commonly used today that there is much confusion. Many traditionalists actually never heard of [them] or are shown where they are from.
>
> To navigate or negotiate the Other Worlds, the Bigfoot is the one that leads me safely in and out of these principalities; there are unseen dangers there. The shaman is only a vessel during the interaction. The Bigfoot, in my case, is a protector. Each and every power/totem animal has its own brand of special medicine to help in your journey. In this realm, I use the tall helper. In your situation with the Bigfoot, it is something else again — a materialization unique to yourself. The reason? I cannot say at the moment, but I believe your story would hold up under the supporting light from any indigenous campfire. The being comes and goes as it pleases. There is great talk of it being a rider with the Star People.
>
> To each his own.

## Robert Morning Sky

In the fall of 2009, a man by the name of Wallace M. spoke of a native fellow by the name of Robert Morning Sky, as well as the book of man's beginning entitled *The Terra Papers*, which this person held as sacred. The information had initially come from Sky's grandfather and had been passed down to him. There was a possible mention of a huge beast in this mind-lifting material, possibly pertaining to the Bigfoot. After Wallace directed me to this possible source of answers, I checked it out.

Wallace explained the following about the beast that many of us are looking for. He was quite straightforward and downright simple in his judgment of the matter. I couldn't reach Robert Morning Sky at that time, but Wallace provided me with the following findings:

> Glen, on my understanding of Robert's passed-along divulgement of his grandfather's teachings, I believe on page 32, [there] is a referral to the Bigfoot, in simple terms. There is even a picture (drawing) of a man-beast. The creature itself is described as huge, hairy, and black. It obeys commands from a genetic scientist and has well-above-average strength [compared to] any man that has been on planet Earth, and that is saying something. The creature's intelligence would be average or ordinary in comparison with the developed beings around it. The great beast would be considered a worker of some kind. I was intrigued by the picture supplied. It is an end-upon-end being. We have similar beliefs in our tribal ancestry and background. The Bigfoot belongs to family, many generations past.
>
> And a bit screwy with certain parts of R. M. Sky's misinformation on other things like timing, etc., something that the brother admits to, he would come out with "The Eridu Papers." I haven't looked into them yet.

After a few months of trying to contact Robert Morning Sky, the gentleman responded. Via email, I initially asked the man for his opinion on the Sasquatch. His response was similar to others. There was a trust with Robert, as there has been with a few individuals over the years, so when he asked if I would respect his input, I said I would. Having seen the creature myself, I wanted to stick to my guns that it could simply be a phenomenon in itself, but the spiritual options remained, firmly planted in my mind.

The following is from Robert Morning Sky's July 2010 email. Many feel the same way he does, though a great number of individuals are not willing to come forward and say so. After his introduction, Robert will give you an idea of his beliefs on the matter, and he is not alone in this.

Yes, you may quote my reference in your effort. I ask only that the integrity of the statement remain intact. (I mention this only because others have taken my words and given them "spin" in order to make the point that they wanted to make versus what I actually said. I shall trust you to be respectful in your works.) Thank you for thinking of me.

What I am about to suggest to you in regard to the Yeti/Sasquatch question has, to the best of my knowledge, never been revealed before. I must proceed cautiously for reasons that will make themselves known very quickly.

I believe everyone is relatively familiar with the basic principles and practices of shamanism. Most people generally know that the earliest form of shamanism began in the prehistoric and rugged cold lands of Siberia. What is not generally known, and what is always dismissed by the "experts," is that one of the most disciplined practices of shamanism, and certainly perhaps one of the most difficult, is the art of shape-shifting. Believe me, it is easier to leave one's body for travel through this world and to other worlds than it is to remain in one's body and cause it to change shape. It is far, far more difficult! Yet there are those highly skilled and highly disciplined shaman masters who are able to do so.

And so herein lies the secret of the Yeti. In order to travel and endure the freezing peaks and harsh, cold weather of Sacred Peaks and Sacred North Lands (their homelands), master shamans have learned to shape-shift into a form that will allow them to move freely and comfortably through these difficult climates. In this form, they are referred to as Yeti ("Divine One"). When their journey is complete, they merely return to their human form. This is why the Yeti is so elusive and may never be caught. The sighting of a Yeti and the tracks it may leave behind, if they survive the cold winds and snowfalls, would eventually be lost to human footprints leading to a temple. If a Yeti were to be wounded and perhaps even die, the corpse that would be found, if it could be found, would not be that of a large, ape-like creature. It would be that of a poor human being caught outside in the perilous freezing weather. (Shape-shifting would remove any sign of a wound.)

> In a far-too-brief explanation, and one that I offer carefully, you can see why a Yeti or Sasquatch might seek out an individual and why it is so elusive.
>
> The mastery of shamanism is an extraordinary thing, with extraordinary results.
>
> I hope this helps, and good luck on your journey.

## The Names of the Creature

The names the Native American people used for the creature we call Bigfoot tell a lot about them. Author Ella E. Clark, in her book, *Indian Legends of the Pacific Northwest*, lists tribal tales gathered over the years. She first heard some of these while working on a U.S. fire lookout in the Cascade Mountains. The message I am trying to get across here is that words can be coincidence, venturous storytelling, or craftily placed hints at the truth. Melvern, a native from the area of red and orange rock in Arizona and New Mexico, commented on this: "Everything has a spirit, and names mean something — always… always." He agreed that whether the Ts'emekwes (white man's Bigfoot) or the Skookum (supernatural creature) was involved, they were both from the outer reaches. I asked the man what he meant by that, and he said, "Well… you know… " Melvern also said there was evil medicine unified with such spoken legends.

Ella Clark's book contains stories that are very significant in describing something hiding behind a deceptive mask. Many indigenous folks look at it this way, as living spirits waiting to reply. They called for such supernatural beings in dance and shamanist teachings, and up came the broadened *yee naaldlooshii* (Skinwalker), among other things. I discussed this with those more learned than I, and we agreed that if one makes terms commonplace, they will embed themselves into man's consciousness and become an everyday thought. A few examples are listed below, starting with Ella E. Clark's book, *Indian Legends of the Pacific Northwest,* with thanks to University of California Press. We will take a section from the story, "The Valley of Peace in the Olympics, A Seatco Legend":

> But Seatco, Chief of all the Evil Spirits, became angry with the people gathered there. Seatco was a giant who could trample whole tribes under his feet… This demon became angry without

> reason at all the nations gathered in the Valley of Peace… The Indians never went there again…

In "A Nez Perce Legend, The Seven Devil Mountains," we read:

> Seven giant brothers lived in the Blue Mountains. These giant monsters were taller than the tallest pines… Today the mountain peaks are called The Seven Devils. The deep gorge at their feet is known as Hell's Canyon of the Snake River… [EEC1]

Henry Franzoni, in his book, *In the Spirit of Seatco*, offers charts of sightings and encounters. Some of the Pacific Northwest areas are listed below. What's in a name? Coincidences maybe, but who knows? They are compelling all the same.

- Devil's Backbone
- Devil's Cauldron
- Devil's Den
- Devil's Gardens
- Devil's Kitchen
- Devil's Pocket
- Devil's Pulpit
- Devil's Stairway
- Devil's Washbasin [HJF1]

There were many other names that might have a bit to do with our potentially evil, furry friend. An aboriginal fellow by the name of Howie said there are reasons for this. He had spoken with a Big Brother go-between at the base of Devil's Tower, Wyoming, in 2007, as part of a quest for a guardian spirit. The Bigfoot was the messenger, expressing a visual instance where the incoming being (animal) had anthropomorphic (human) attributes. The native fellow had no sense of embarrassment when mentioning this tale to me, as he considered it a privilege to accept a living presence. He had wondered why this same Bigfoot/shaman also referred to itself as a monstrous spirit, likening itself to places of mystery. The supernatural flesh sought the attentiveness of man.

When I mentioned my family's involvement with the wilderness creatures Howie called "the intermediaries," he wanted to know if I had experienced my own vision quest. As I'd mentioned the quest issue before, this individual wasn't the first to ask me such a question. Others told me I could even meet the visitors halfway. This was not something I would choose to do if Bigfoot is truly a representation of darkness.

We'll be looking at more examples of the bewitching that may be in Bigfoot in the Khat Hansen story in the next chapter, and also in Part III of this book.

# 24. Khat Hansen

Khat Hansen is a very courageous, interesting woman who was willing to step out of her comfort zone to tell her Bigfoot tale. This topic wasn't new for her; it was something she'd known all along, and she was willing to voice it to the world, while others chose to remain quiet on the matter. She was sincere, honest, and upfront with her ideas, and I appreciated that. The first thing I heard from her was the legend of the first people:

## The Legend of the Ste'ye'mah (First People)

When Great Spirit created the Earth, He peopled it with the first people, the Ste'ye'mah. They were not like you or me. They were larger, hairier, and could speak to animals with their minds. They were the peacemakers for Great Spirit. When there were problems on this Earth among the animals, they were the ones who settled them. They had the strength to stop the bears and others from physically fighting, by separating them. They could speak any animal language, even communicate with the birds. They could travel with speed faster than the deer; they could outthink the puma in cunning ways. They were the guardians of this place.

After eons of being here and watching, they grew lonely, and Great Spirit heard their calls and made more people. These were different. They were not like the first people. They were smaller, less hairy, and covered themselves. They could not communicate with the animals and ran in fear of them. They made weapons and needed fire to stay warm. They overran the Earth. They were able to multiply like the rabbits and mice, but the bear, wolf,

**Figure 46: Medicine woman, Khat Hansen. (photo © Khat Hansen)**

> puma, etc., could not eat them. Soon, there were too many of them.
>
> The first people called to Great Spirit to help them control the humans, and the Great Spirit explained that they were people and had to learn to control themselves. So the first people asked for another place to live. Great Spirit told them he would not create a new planet for them, but He would give them a doorway to another world without humans so they could come and go without having to share that world with them. In that way, they could still watch over this planet and the animals to keep them in check. This is the legend of the first people.

Khat Hansen graciously allowed me to interview her about her beliefs and interactions with Bigfoot. Khat is not a researcher, per se, but she is a medicine woman and has much to say about the things going on in her life, the phenomenon that has become commonplace for her, even if it remains a mystery to most. The following is Khat's take on the Bigfoot phenomenon:

**Glen Boulier:** Please feel free to introduce yourself.

**Khat Hansen**: I am an American Choctaw Indian soul-eater. I was an archeologist who has since retired from the archeology field after twenty-five years of hard work. I have been trained in my work as a medicine woman since the age of three years.

**GB:** Soul-eater?

**KH:** A soul-eater is simply a fancy name for an empathic healer. It means you come to me, bare your soul, and I will devour its pain and sickness, leaving it clean and clear, taking the darkness and such into mine. I am also an ordained minister who works wholeheartedly with battered women. I also interact on a daily basis with Native American spirit beings, Ste'ye'mah or Bigfoot, Ant People, and Snake People. I have been dealing with these creatures since I was five years old.

**GB:** Who trained and nurtured you for the task of being a medicine woman, and how is a person selected for such duties?

**KH:** I was trained by my grandmother, Olena (Red Wind), and another elder by the name of Dancing Elk for my calling as soul-eater. My path to becoming a soul-eater is a long, strange story. My tribe has interacted with a group of beings called Ant People for as long as we can remember. They tell us when children are to be born who are special and have skills that can be utilized for the good of the tribe. My tribe was without a soul-eater for over thirty-five years. The Ant People arranged for my mother to come from Germany to meet my father, and they foretold that my parents would bear the soul-eater (me.) Lo and behold, after ten years, they came again and told the elder alik'chi (healer) that I would be born early, in seven months — and I was. From the age of three years, they started my training in knowledge of medicine plants, chants, and prayer healing.

**GB:** Because you are coming out to share these things with the world, have you ever been threatened or put down by others who keep or hide this knowledge — like other aboriginal groups?

**KH:** I am threatened constantly, mostly for information. As for being put down, only by those who want to hunt or kill the Ste'ye'mah. As for the aboriginals, never! They know I speak the truth, and many, many tribes welcome me and respect the information I give to the world. They know the Big Men are here, and their own spirit workers have interacted with them, so there is *never* doubt as to whether I speak the truth. I find that the white culture has a problem with receiving my information.

**GB:** Khat, are you assigned to a certain group of these creatures? Are there others that have a specific Bigfoot group to care for?

**KH:** The Bigfoot show themselves to whom they wish. They interact with the ones they choose. I know of four other people in America who have groups such as mine. My friend has interacted with her group for over fifty years now. The Bigfoot initiate contact; they choose who and where and when they will contact.

**GB:** There are so many significant beliefs within the aboriginal communities: the Raven, the Coyote, the Great Bear, the Killer Whale, and many other nature creatures, and all these are shared in museums, dance, totems, with artifacts, and with the world. Why do you think a person receives so much resistance when referring to the Sasquatch? These people are blatantly or ignorantly told no or not to speak of it. Most knowledge is shared and expressed graciously, but this is not true in the case of Bigfoot. Only the surface has been scratched, you could say.

**KH:** It is because the Bigfoot are sacred above all others. They are family. Do you tell of your family secrets? No, unless they say you can. Most people do not have the blessing of the Bigfoot like I do. It is a gift to be able to learn from the Bigfoot. They need a speaker for them in our world, and I have been chosen to do so for the group with whom I interact. They were here before us and will be here after us. They are guardians and watch us and what we do.

**GB:** How about the intellectual structuring of such creatures?

**KH:** Bigfoot intelligence? Think about how wolves, coyotes, and foxes can hear the mice underground and know where and when to dig and pounce to obtain their food in the winter. The same can be said with the chimpanzee, who utilizes sticks and rocks for tools. They have developed a society that has taken researchers years to understand. The same is true with the Bigfoot.

They are in tune with the elements and forces of the natural world that we humans have long since forgotten. By becoming civilized and moving into overcrowded cities and towns, we have lost the ability to listen with our souls. We do not hear what the world around us is trying to tell us. We cannot hear the voice with which the Earth speaks. The Bigfoot are in tune with that voice and have total comprehension of what it is she is telling them. They have developed gifts over the centuries that we can only barely understand. One of these is the ability to *mindspeak*. They have the ability to read humans and their intent from up to four miles away. I cannot explain how they do it or how it works, but they know of you before they ever allow you to see them or come into contact with them. The Bigfoot have the ability to adjust their muscles and forms to exceed speeds of fifty miles per hour when they run. They can travel great distances in a few hours by means of shifting and adjusting their forms and finding a place that has certain magnetic frequencies (a portal). Using this, they travel from one world/realm to another. They have learned to ultimately camouflage their bodies by learning how to bend light around themselves, thus making themselves appear to be invisible.

Many people ask me: Can the Bigfoot communicate, and what do they sound like? I have explained that when they mindspeak, it is with pictures and a fleeting voice that is like an echo. When they verbalize their voices, it sounds gravelly and deep.

When they imitate animal calls and voices, they are exact; the only way you will know it is a Bigfoot and not the animal in question is at the end of the whistle or call. As you stand there with your head cocked and listening, you will get a small chill and realize that it has a human quality to it. *That* is how you know it is Bigfoot. It is the ability that all humans seem to have when we hear a voice or noise and know that it is human generated.

Several researchers have learned over the years that we can communicate with the Bigfoot by leaving them chalk or charcoal. They use a primitive type of drawing, similar to that of a three-year-old child, but they do get their points across. When you find these drawings, you instinctively know a human-type creature drew them. I have shown them to children, and they always ask me the name of the child who drew them.

**GB:** While interacting and communicating with the Bigfoot, is there a special creature amongst the bunch, one of them that stands out in favor?

**KH:** Myself and Ki'ho'sa, whom I've been interacting with since I was five years old. I have known him for what seems like forever. He is not an animal, nor is he human. He is something else altogether. I have watched him vanish before my eyes and reappear 100 feet away. I have witnessed superhuman strength that would put ten men

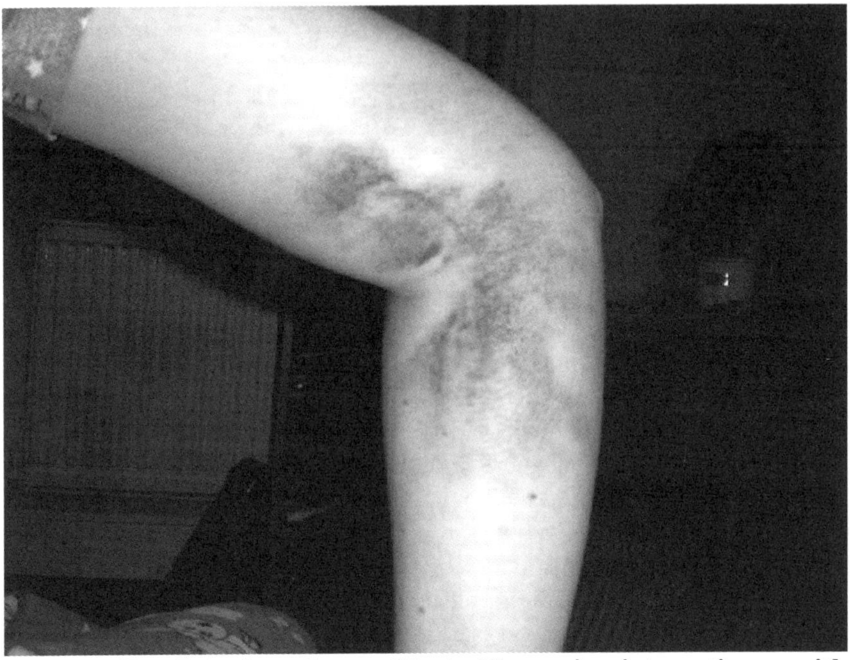

**Figure 47: Injuries from Khat Hansen's interactions with Ste'ye'mah. (photo © Khat Hansen)**

to shame. He has incredible mental abilities. I have watched him use these to kill six antelope from almost a mile away. He is the most awe-inspiring creature I have ever met. I am in amazement of his abilities every day — and in fear of him. To live with something that can take over your mind if it wants to is a horrible thought. Many times, I have run from them.

**GB:** You have been injured occasionally during your encounters with these creatures. What were the circumstances?

**KH:** There are too many to list here, but running away, annoying them, infringing on territory, not waiting my turn, not wanting to share with me, angering them, not obeying some sets of rules, etc.

I have several photos of the injuries. Over the years, I have been injured due to: being pushed over small cliffs and logs; being picked up and literally thrown; being footballed (they put their head down and tackle me); being bitten twice and slapped in the face with hands, rocks, and branches; being slammed down on my butt too many times to count; and being bowled over from behind as I am running away, about twenty or thirty times now.

**GB:** If an actual specimen (Bigfoot) were found alive or deceased, how would this change things, or how would it be addressed?

**KH:** Well, I would not be surprised as they are mortal like you and me. I would, however, seriously doubt that it would be in a good state of preservation, as it would take quite a while for the wound to manifest and become terminal. They are made of a much more densely packed atom than we are. I liken it to atoms that make up a rock; they move slower, so it takes more to break the rock. They can be killed, and I have seen them do it to each other, but the strength it took to do it and the length of the battle was amazing. This is why it does not seem to affect them when they are shot; it really does, but it just takes a while for the wounds to manifest.

As for what would change, it would be awful. Humanity would actually have a model to go after, hold up, and actively look for its flaws and ways to kill it. And humanity just does not have the ability to keep anything under protection or safe from other humans. So, in the end, it would be a death sentence to the Bigfoot.

**GB:** Khat, it has been said that there were five copies made of the original Patterson/Gimlin film — the famous short film of a female Bigfoot at Bluff Creek, California, in October of 1967. The person you knew, Jon-Erik Beckjord, was one of the five who had a copy. Was the film believed to be actual footage, not a hoax?

**KH:** It was as real as real gets. Jon went to his grave with the copy; he would not part with it. He used to make an ornery joke that he would sell it for a million dollars because he knew no one in the Bigfoot world would pay that kind of money.

I just did an interview with Dave Paulides, and he had stills from one copy of the film and was actually happy with me being able to tell him what was what, answering questions he's had for a while. It made me happy to vindicate Jon for once and to corroborate what they thought they knew.

**GB:** And, continuing on with Ki'ho'sa?

**KH:** He has shown up in the town I moved to. I thought I was safe with people, cars, and animals around me. How wrong I was. I know he shifts in and out of our dimension with ease. I have watched them run, and when they choose to do it, it is unbelievable how fast they can cover ground.

**GB:** I've also seen the Sasquatch run, albeit more simply, during the encounter in 1985.

**KH:** If they wanted to, they could outrun us [even if we were] in a vehicle, driving at a realistic speed. I know it is amazing, but just stop and realize that these beings are flesh and blood like us, only different. They exist alongside us and always have. They come and go from our world to theirs, which is just next to ours. I have said before that they can be wounded; it just takes a while for it to manifest in our time. For the same reason, they age differently. They age much more slowly, and reports come in again and again about a Bigfoot looking the same over the years because it's the same one.

**GB:** You are very informed.

**KH:** Remember, I did not choose these creatures; they chose me for some reason. I have hated that since day one, when I first met Ki'. I wished and wished for him to leave me alone, but he has a reason for showing himself and his tribe to me, and I must learn from him what it is.

**GB:** And about such a group?

**KH:** I don't mind talking about the family and group dynamics of the Ste'ye'mah. I have been asked quite a lot about their habits, tastes, tempers, etc. So, after twenty-five years of constant research with my group, I will share some of what I have discovered.

The group I was originally introduced to consisted of twelve creatures: two children, three adolescents, and seven adults. There are always more females than males. I have only seen two females pregnant at the same time, and this is a rarity in itself. I noticed over the years that the Ste'ye'mah care for the babies as a group. By this, I mean the mother is the primary caretaker, but she is helped by all. The males are not like humans. They tend to ignore the babies unless they are directly placed in their care. I have seen the females walk over and hand a baby to a male. They pretty much just hold it until the female can relieve them of their burden. When the babies start to wander and toddle, the males become more active in caring for and protecting them. As the little one reaches five to seven years, the Ste'ye'mah tend to ignore them, letting them wander off and find their own way. It is very disturbing to watch as a youngster leaves the group and no one follows it or watches over it. As far as I can tell, the adults will go look for them after an allotted time. I think this is where I first bumped into Ki'ho'sa, while he was looking for his son. Once the toddler is brought back, it will repeatedly wander off again and again. It is as if the older ones do not care to instill the lesson, "Stay put."

As for lessons being taught, the Ste'ye'mah are very aggressive when it comes to hitting or grabbing. I have watched the males grab a toddler and hold it by the ankle above their head while snarling at it, only to literally drop it on the ground, right on its head. They think nothing of smacking the youngsters with hands or sticks. They push them onto their butts with such force that sometimes you can actually hear the air come out in a whoosh from the toddler's lungs when they hit. I was concerned about the mortality of their young at first, but I've learned over the years that it is not their discipline or watching abilities that are the reason for the decline in their birth rate. It is something else. I have watched them bring female after female into the group, trying to infuse it with new blood, yet there have been only seven births into this group over the years. I have seen the young die of malnourishment and colic. I have never seen them die due to mistreatment or abandonment by the group. I have tried to ask where the babies are, but I only get the head thought, *No more*. It is very disheartening.

**GB:** Is it possible to continuously track or follow the Bigfoot?

**KH:** Yes, it is possible to track them to a certain degree, but come winter, they leave. I have never really tried to follow them, but from what I gather, they wait at a specific portal area and go somewhere else. They do not trek across country. This theory always makes me smile. When I asked them about this theory, Ki'ho'sa grew impatient with the thought of hiking or trekking. He got very agitated and led me to an X that marked the nearest portal, then began shoving sticks through it. He sent the thought, *I go here*.

**GB:** Would these portals be anything similar to what the courageous Gorman family supposedly faced at what is now known as the infamous Skinwalker Ranch in the Uinta Basin badlands of Utah? There is also a ranch in Colorado that reports paranormal activity, mirroring the Utah spread in strange happenings. These types of creatures (Bigfoot) were seen many times around these ranches, for whatever reason.

**KH:** Yes, you are right in your assumptions. They are portals. They have a movement of air around them and feelings that something just isn't right. The Bigfoot travel through them to get from their realm to ours and back again.

**GB:** Can humans also travel through these portals?

**KH:** Geronimo was a master of using what is available to us here on this planet, as are the Bigfoot. Portals are everywhere. My grandmother and another elder showed them to me when I was a child. Elder Red Wind knew how to use them to walk in silence, to travel from one place to another. I am afraid of them, so I have never tried it.

**GB:** When the creatures die, where do their bodies go? I've been told more than once that they are taken off the planet somehow.

**KH:** Bigfoot bodies are taken home. This is how they answer that question.

**GB:** I still find it fascinating that one or more indigenous groups, even today, think of the creature as a Big Elder Brother, while another band or tribe thinks of it as the Evil Cannibal Spirit.

**KH:** I would tend to believe it of the Red Ste'ye'mah, as they are the most aggressive, and the natives of the Northwest and my own tribe do have stories of them. I have said before, they are not the Harry that the Hendersons encountered. Also, I am always on my guard against Wild Woman. She kills just for the joy of it.

**GB:** Who and how bad are the Red Ste'ye'mah?

**KH:** Glen, the Red Ste'ye'mah are just a more aggressive type of Bigfoot. They are known throughout Indian culture as eaters of men, attackers, stalkers, killers, etc. I am not happy that Ki'ho'sa brought one into this group. I was absolutely shocked when I saw her for the first time. They are terrible, evil beings.

**GB:** Could you tell me a little more about Wild Woman. Clearly you have your guard up concerning her.

**KH:** Wild Woman is apparently my archenemy. I did not set out for it to be this way. I personally think it is her nature, as I watch her with the group and see how antagonistic she is toward them, fighting at the drop of a hat, killing animals, etc. Wild Woman got her name because that is the way she acts. She stands up on hills at sunrise, whooping, getting into garbage, pooping in driveways, etc. She has no couth and is as animalistic as you can get. I am amazed sometimes that they (the group) have not chased her off yet.

**GB:** Over twenty-two persons have gone missing over time in the Pitt Lake region of British Columbia. After negligence, including possible everyday predator attacks and even a cult operating in the area, the Sasquatch has taken the blame for at least a few of the missing. Tracks and the creature have been sighted in this remote and rugged area. Strangely, not even clothing is found.

**KH:** I have said many, many times that I do feel the Ste'ye'mah are actually responsible for a large number of the missing persons cases in the wild, especially when the missing are the type of people who are knowledgeable about hiking and understand the woods, etc. For these people to never, ever be seen again is kind of eerie, especially when you start going back and looking in that area to see just how many Bigfoot sightings there have been. I do have firsthand knowledge that the males will go after a woman, especially if she has red or blonde hair.

**GB:** Have you ever heard of a killing zone?

**KH:** In my photos, look at the sheep skulls on trees, in trees, on the ground, etc., due to the hostile group in Utah. I was just speaking on the subject of Bigfoot breaking necks as the method of choice in killing animals. I have bighorn sheep here, and when they kill them, it is very interesting to watch my neighbor, a veterinarian, try to explain this to ranchers. They *know* what is going on, but he just refuses to believe.

This is why they bring their sick or dying animals to me to leave up canyon for the Bigfoot. Tell the gentleman in Texas to be careful. This is a warning to all creatures, human and non, to stay out of this area. When they do not hide, it is because they are aggressive.

These creatures kill all types of sheep and coyote and occasionally cows, horses, dogs, and small animals. I am tired of the media dummying down the Bigfoot. It has only been since about the 1970s and 1980s that Bigfoot has been construed as a nice, sweet creature. Indians have never considered them this way. Certain ones are cannibals. It was pointed out to me that there are no known cases of them attacking humans recently, to which I replied, "That is not true."

**GB:** Do the Bigfoot creatures possess the knowledge to use primitive tools of their making or otherwise?

**KH:** The only tools I have ever seen them use are rocks and sticks: rocks to break or stun something and sticks used to beat on things. Sometimes when the males are feeling aggressive, they will swing a big stick around.

**GB:** Is it possible that the Bigfoot used fire in the past, and would they dare use it now, with all the advanced technology capable of finding the source of open fires? One of the reasons I ask is because I had a report come in that mentions a fire tower worker tracking down a nearby fire on foot, only to find three of the creatures at the unauthorized small burn in the middle of nowhere. He returned later and saw tracks left by the creatures, the only remaining clue.

**KH:** Glen, I have never ever known them to make fire. They will play with it, however. They will pull out sticks or put them in the fire, and when the stick is burning, they like to wave it around. They are not the greatest tool users. Sometimes they use rocks or sticks to get what they want, but that is it. Fire is very interesting to them.

I want to tell you something, and I hope you will not be offended. I got a flash when I read your email. It was of a solitary man/hiker, sitting by the fire. I think the Ste'ye'mah took him. I do not know where you stand on the Bigfoot subject, but they are not of the *Harry and the Hendersons* variety. They will take solitary hikers or women and use them for their own purposes. I do not want to elaborate here, so use your imagination. Your most terrible imaginings are probably correct when it comes to their behavior. They were *playing* with the fire, my friend. I feel horrible for that hiker. This story is very upsetting to me, and I am sick to my stomach because I know what they did. I try to keep my group fed so they will not resort to stealing people. I am truly sorry that I cannot help you with more info.

[Khat Hansen had the suspicion that whoever had started and initiated the fire was now missing. Concerning the fire idea itself, everyone I have talked to over the years about it seems to agree that while the Bigfoot creature cannot create fire, the giants can and very well may exploit an unattended fire of some kind. In many documented instances, the curious creatures have watched fire in use.]

**GB:** There is this thing about the Bigfoot and clothing. First Nations spoke of this in the Hedley, British Columbia, area, the odd Sasquatch creature having arranged a garment on themselves, or possibly hanging from them, all twisted up. Pioneer Susan Allison also heard stories about the Big Men wearing manmade clothing in a hippie/Woodstock sort of way. I was kindheartedly told pretty much the same thing about the Similkameen Valley, British Columbia.

**KH:** I have been asked a few times about Bigfoot and clothing. I have known since the age of five or six that they do mimic humans. I can remember the creatures stealing clothes off the clothesline, and on occasion I would see one or two with the odd clothing, usually not using it properly, but with it draped over their shoulders or arms, etc. Sometimes they would use them for nesting material, and other times they would just wave it around frantically. I never really understood it. As I became older and then finally a mother, I watched my older girls give blankets and shirts and my best towels to them. They always dragged them in the mud, etc., then carried them off. Sometimes we would find the items in the forest, high up a tree. I never really used to understand this either. Now, looking back, I realize that it is not for me to understand. I just have to accept that the Ste'ye'mah were curious about these things and what we do with them. I recall my children showing the female how to drape a towel around her shoulders. Then, for about a week or two after, she would show up with the towel in tow, sit down, and drape it across her shoulders, as if to say, *"See? I can do it!"* I have not given them towels or blankets or clothing in over ten years now. I only have a couple of reports of the Bigfoot wearing clothing like we do. I am almost 100 percent sure they are mimicking us, especially when you read the accounts.

**GB:** Would the average person or researcher capturing, exposing, or uncovering such a creature start an environmental war?

**KH:** There is *never* this issue, my friend. They will never capture this being, for the Earth does not wish it to occur. Can you imagine the awesome power that is the Earth? Imagine that working against the capture of this being. Everything on this Earth would be turned into a subterfuge against such a capturing. It would not be violent, as it does not have to be. The Earth has all of the powers at her disposal to stop such a thing.

**GB:** And what about some of the possible big players in such a phenomenon? A number of extremists want to market the creature, to put them on display like a pheasant under glass — not as a scientific venture but as a business undertaking, investment, or enterprise.

**KH:** I have an issue with insincere and deceptive people. I am not this way, so I do not have the knowledge to deal with them. I am approached by people who are more savvy or business smart than I — people who have been dealing with the business of Bigfoot, some of them for decades. I myself have just dealt with the Bigfoot on a personal level. I have never thought of them as a business commodity before, but apparently they are.

Every day, I am approached by people who want a piece of the information I have to impart. Some, if not most, of these people do not have honorable intentions. They are willing to use me to get whatever it is they want or feel they need. I have spent nights crying myself sick, trying to understand their motives. It is not in me to understand them I guess. They come to me, trying to woo me or sway me with promises of great wealth and fame. In reality, I am poor and was raised this way. I have no desire for great wealth; I was always taught that you cannot miss what you've never had. These wealthy people seem to feel they can take whatever they want from me and that I am not intelligent enough to ascertain their true intent. They try to sway me with their sweet words and influence. When I am not as forthcoming with information or do not show the proper amount of enthusiasm that they feel I should, they become petulant and angry. It is then that I see the true side of them, the side they hide from me, trying to convince me that they are worthy of the information.

The truth of the matter is, my first and foremost concern is the welfare of the Ste'ye'mah. It always has been and always will be. I stand alone when it comes to speaking for them and keeping them safe. I alone am responsible for Ki'ho'sa. I made him and his group a promise years ago that I will do whatever it takes to make sure they are well guarded. I take this vow very seriously. Just because I will answer questions or give advice, that does not mean I will sell the creatures themselves to the highest bidder. I am disgusted with people's intentions where the Bigfoot are concerned. Individuals come to me and expect me to know who other searchers are for the Bigfoot, but I neither know nor care. I am not a so-called Bigfooter. I am a woman who was given the gift of friendship to the Bigfoot. I have no interest in hunting them or finding and capturing them. I interact with them on almost a daily basis because I have a form of love for them. It is called friendship.

I am not a researcher, per se, so my records are not as uniform and informative as others wish them to be. I never set out to research and study them. It is just for my own private journals that I write down the interactions. I find it interesting that there are at least four others besides myself who interact with the Bigfoot, yet I am willing to bet the wealthy people who want to find the Bigfoot do not know these individuals. They have not kept it secret. They have spoken out as well. It is just simply the fact that the famous people have decided I am to be the one they show interest in, which leads me to this assumption: They must think me a complete idiot, without the capability to see through their sweet talk and lies. On the contrary, I *can* see through it. It just takes me a little bit longer, because I believe others to be incapable of such deceptiveness; I believe them to be honorable and loving, as I am.

As I've said before, I am my brother's keeper, human and Ste'ye'mah, it would seem. I will try to lead all down the right path by example. If you have a clean, guilt-free heart, you will have a happy soul.

**GB:** Khat, there have been numerous Bigfoot expeditions over the years in search of these giants, but nothing substantial or earthshaking in terms of a find. What could be happening?

**KH:** Well, I can only give my personal opinion. From what I gather about these beings, they have always walked with one foot in our world and one in another realm. This enables them to have different abilities than humans. I believe they have evolved certain capabilities that allow them to literally hide in plain sight by bending light or wrapping light around themselves, so as to appear invisible, even when they are literally right in front of us. They have also honed their psychic and psychokinetic energies to the point where they can sense another's approach and are able to use infrasound to confuse, frighten, and annoy another being (such as a human) to the point where we will leave them alone. They can appear to be two places at once or look like a tree stump. I KNOW for a fact that they can smell the guns and gunpowder, batteries, and camera film from literally hundreds of yards away. My people believe you will never find a Bigfoot footprint unless the Bigfoot *wants* you to.

**GB:** Rewards and high-money payouts are offered for capturing such a creature on film or in person. Are you interested in such things?

**KH:** I would and do adamantly refuse to take any money for the knowledge I have about these beings. I have even been asked to put a PayPal button on my website so people can donate to my group, but I will not. Thank you, but no thanks. I hate the fact that people are trying to make a buck off of something that is our brother. How sickening!

[We stopped the interview here because her answers had given me a lot to think about. I wanted to do more research before asking her more questions. When we resumed, I asked her about where her research is going and about some of the people I had discovered in my research].

**GB:** Concerning coming times, who is the man known as Standing Elk? Also, who are the Sihan Tanka? And, Khat, have you heard of the Sasquatchitan?

**KH:** I will answer the best I can, but I am not familiar with all native tribal beliefs. The God we worship is called Wakan Tanka and is recognized as the dominant role played by the supernatural in the lives of men. I am not familiar with Sasquatchitan. Standing Elk is one who spoke when he was not chosen to speak. I will have to think on this question further so that I may speak with honor and truth.

[We paused the interview again while Khat thought about what she would be able to say. Miss Hansen was as surprised as I was about this relatively new angle on the creature, the new day (Star Knowledge/Nations) Bigfoot. She provided me with links for information on Standing Elk and we shared links about Sasquatchitan. When either of these is used as search terms on the Web, it will pull up a wealth of information. Both can be investigated further by looking into star knowledge or star nations. The available information touches on a number of issues, but we are focused mainly on the Bigfoot situation.]

**GB:** I will be writing about the out-and-out idea of the strange creature. I have seen them, and you are dealing with them. What do you think about the topics we've just researched?

**KH:** Glen, after carefully reading the Sasquatchitan information, I cannot agree to any of this. This is not the type of being I have interacted with for over forty years now. My group is intelligent, yes; emotional, yes; rational, somewhat. By this, I mean they communicate with mindspeak and sign language. They do not put thoughts into this elegant of a format. I am sorry, but I must decline comment on this subject, as it is something I am definitely unfamiliar with. I am sorry, my friend. I just do not wish to offend another person or their beliefs.

**GB:** Khat, the last while, I have been busy researching the not-so-new idea of the Bigfoot and the paranormal (UFO). These two topics collide at times. What's your take on this? I'm also concerned about the possibility of the abduction scenario and how widespread it is becoming. Also, are you an ordained minister?

**KH:** The Ste'ye'mah and extraterrestrials (ETs) are not connected like you would think. Ki' explained this to me a long time ago. ETs use the Ste'ye'mah as an incentive; they scare the humans with them. Do the Ste'ye'mah want to do this? NO! The Greys have superior mind skills and draw the Bigfoot to them when they want to use them. They cannot resist them and have no power to stop them, so they end up like slaves, doing whatever the ETs want.

Yes, I am an ordained minister, and an abductee by the Ants and Snakes. I know firsthand of which you speak. There have been instances in my lifetime when I have seen Ki'ho'sa or Wild Woman standing across the creek, approximately 200 feet away, watching as I am led to the Ants. I have screamed at them mentally and physically, asking and begging them to intercept these beings. I always get the same answers: *Cannot stop*, puzzlement as to why they cannot stop them, and puzzlement as to why I am scared. That is all I get from them, both during and after. I must admit that the Ants and Snakes have never, ever used Ki' or his group to physically carry or drag me. The Bigfoot just watch while it occurs. They are not fearful of them, just leery. I feel horrible for all abductees; while I know what's going on, due to my people's history, most of them have no idea. The Ants are here from a place that exists alongside of us, but it is not space. They are here because we are like cattle, pets, etc. to them. Please tell your clients that they need to pray in the name of almighty God; believe it or not, it does work! I rebuked the Ants and told them they could not enter my home, and they have not entered in six years now. Instead, they lure me outside. Still, in some ways, the prayers hold them. I pray constantly when I interact with them. I almost wonder if they are the spirits the Bible talks of.

**GB:** I often refer to Bigfoot espionage. What would be so important that spies, plants, infiltrators, and the like would be involved? What could be behind such madness as spying on the Bigfoot subject? Surely it isn't as if this is the end of the world. Have you dealt with this as well?

**KH:** Glen, they are afraid that if the world finds out the Ste'ye'mah are anything more than a dumb ape, laws will be enacted to protect them. Picture what it would mean to upset an entire world of people, to make them aware that, living alongside of them unnoticed and totally hidden, there exist beings who can/could/would kill them if they choose. These beings even live in some of our parks and on the fringes of our suburbs. They walk into yards and garages, go through garbage, and even eat outdoor pets. Now, add to this fear that these beings can make themselves invisible at will and can also thought-blast you to scare, harm, or even make you forget. Can you see the big picture, where this might go? Humans would begin to question all of their moral beliefs and even the authorities, wondering how long they have known about them, etc., etc., etc.

As I interviewed Khat Hansen, I discovered that there had been many attempts to assassinate the woman's character. I wasn't the least bit surprised to hear of Khat's struggles. In Khat's case, a false Facebook page was created, using her personal photos and her actual birth name, meddling with her identity. Even her website, *Bigfoot and Creatures,* was not immune; it was shut down by hackers with major experience, unstoppable even by the cyber police. This cruel activity even tried to reach my laptop. In the end, I was very grateful that she was willing to share her story with me.

# 25. Star Nations

A new area of Sasquatch beliefs relates to the Star Nations. A growing percentage of indigenous people throughout the world harbor a belief system about an off-planet creature that moves back and forth from dimension to dimension. The following excerpts will enlighten you on the Star Nations aspect of Bigfoot.

> But then, what is it to "be" in this universe? One only knows so much, and I think everything has an unknown dimension all around it and within it that can be called "spiritual." The world is much more mysterious than we can even begin to imagine. (Steven Streufert)

> I sometimes think those beings on Earth that are closest to nature are aware of the positive ETs or have some communications with them, but I've never heard of this directly. It is only my own thought. (Toraya Ayres)

> The Star Messenger you are hearing about is the Bigfoot. When the Earth is right, they will show themselves in a different way than we have been accustomed to. (Aboriginal Woman)

> Bigfoot, or Sihan Tanka in Lakota, is an Earth guardian. I will email you the message from the *11:11 Book: A Message from the Bigfoot Nation*. (Lelie)

> I am of Navajo descent. Some many years ago, my granny spoke of a drawer full of things involving our Indian culture, including a nearby Indian town next to us that had numerous visits from Bigfoot. During these stays, the Bigfoot would mainly crouch or remain in a seated position, grooming the small

community for knowledge, it would seem. Braves scattered around and throughout this town would hunt and battle this stranger, hitting the beast with a number of arrows, the Bigfoot walking off into the woods and vanishing. It would return again and again repeatedly. The best Navajo warriors could not locate the tall stranger, and there was no blood trail to follow. This was claimed to be bad medicine.

There were other yarns of a mysterious visitor vanishing when followed. Other Indians ran away from it because of Bigfoot's formidable appearance. I myself have never seen one. I think there was mention of these things on the Internet somewhere. (Rodney)

If Bigfoot is a reality, then I believe it would be one of this dimension's earthly origins, somewhat different than that of the Celestials. (Lynn)

The two most likely explanations, in order of probability are: (1) They are descendants of Lemuria, or, better yet, survivors from Lemuria, and they go to and fro to the inner Earth, using deep Earth caves, where they go in the winter; or, (2) they are descendants of extraterrestrials who were stranded on Earth a long time ago. Nope, they will not find them. They make themselves known only to earthlings they can trust. We have some in the mountains here (Ouachita, West Arkansas).

Glen, the more mentally rigid and timid Sasquatch researchers steer clear of any high strangeness aspects to Sasquatch. There is a connection between Sasquatch and UFOs and other non-human entities. There are many good books and articles about this connection. There is an implicit connection between UFOs, aliens, and Sasquatch. Sasquatch-type creatures have been sighted all over the world, and I believe at least some of the Sasquatch/large hairy creatures have some kind of metaphysical capability. Certainly many indigenous peoples around the world, especially in North America, believe there is a metaphysical or inter-dimensional facet to some of these entities. (Jimmy)

The Sasquatch is indeed a unique critter. It travels around by way of energetic planetary ley lines. Wherever these ley lines intersect on our globe, there will be a doorway, a portal the

> Sasquatch uses to phase itself somewhere else. The natural, multidimensional awareness of the species makes them impossible to physically catch, because they can merely phase away to wherever they choose along the connected ley lines. As an example, the Washington and British Columbia Sasquatch are of the same family that migrates along the latitude ley lines. Websites show where these lines are located on the planet, and I'll bet if someone were to compare Sasquatch sightings and the ley line locations, they would find amazing correlations (just as I did). The Church, as well as many other cultures, try to dowse and build upon these ley line intersections in an attempt to supposedly tap into the power source. I am not convinced that the Bigfoot is from another planet. I am more convinced that they are an alien from a slightly different dimensional frequency and phase in and out of our reality, just as a human can step into the various levels of subconscious brain activity: alpha, beta, theta, spirit walking, astral, etc. Next time you go hunting, take an expert dowser with you, and I guarantee you'll see the tracks end at one of these energetic ley line crossovers. Happy hunting. (David, "The Oracle" Pilz, White Star)

The responses haven't all been positive. I've received my share of threats over the years as I've continued to delve into this topic. If there was nothing to all of this, there would be no reason for such threats to occur. Below are a few of the remarks I've heard from aboriginals in one area I was in:

> Nope. We don't discuss "him."
>
> We call him Muupitz. We don't talk about him, and we bloody well don't go looking for him.
>
> Not supposed to talk about him. Leave him alone.
>
> Be careful when you open your trailer door. You just might get pulled out and shredded to pieces.

Clearly, these people feel that the Bigfoot Brother is to be protected at all costs. It actually seems to strike a supernatural fear into some and causes division. It was perfectly acceptable to talk about Coyote, Raven, and the Great Bear, but for some strange reason, Bigfoot is in a league all his own. The aboriginal people were more than happy to tell me about their background, culture, and ancestry, but the creature that roams the forest or the cosmos as Bigfoot was a topic many people thought should be left alone.

Happily, there were many others willing to talk about Sasquatch. This shift in willingness to talk seems to have something to do with the critical times we are living in, something to do with the current Earth phase, before the mankind-induced desecration of our planet.

I received more word on the subject from a spiritual judge, of sorts, an intermediary for an indigenous voice that had information on the creature, which many believe to be a staple of the new era. I communicated quite a bit with this kindhearted spokeswoman, Janet Lightstone, an apprentice to a Native American elder. My initial question was, "Where does Bigfoot fit into today's scheme of things?" She did not initially know the answer but offered to check with Maria Yraceburu, an Apache holy one and a descendant of Nochaydelklinne, Apache dreamer and prophet. Maria teaches the Quero Apache Tlish Diyan tradition. This is the answer I received:

> In general, I believe Bigfoot is a guardian, of sorts, for the giant forest, nothing to be feared. I would also say Bigfoot lives between dimensions; that is why it cannot be found when looked for. But this is just speculation. I don't know if there are more of them or where they are primarily active. Maybe it is just a reminder that there is much more to this Earth than can be explained by reason. I feel it's something to be in awe of and not to be feared. Bigfoot: guardian, protector. There are certain animals in the world that are here to maintain things — Bigfoot, whales, dolphins, and hummingbirds, just to name a few. I know one Bigfoot beat up a guy who was pounding on his wife, then stood guard while a cousin of mine got the woman out of the house and to a safe place. From this story and what I know about guardians, I would say Bigfoot is a helper and protector. If you are in alignment with the universal forces of love, you have a friend; if you are not, you will have trouble. Guardians maintain Earth's energy and balance. She (Earth) needs a lot of them since we are constantly bringing her out of balance. Some other mystical guardians are dragons — very big forces in the Earth's ley lines, rivers, mountains, and oceans. Fairies also work with plants and animals. Bigfoot is one of these but gets a lot of attention since he manifests in physical reality, which is very rare for

dragons and fairies. People who choose to demonize these guardians are most likely the ones who do not value the Earth and seek to control her. You and your mother have been very blessed to have a sighting of this awesome power!

Where does a person begin, when there is such a broad range of opinions on the Sasquatch creature? I saw a haired giant over thirty-nine years ago, and I do not associate what I saw with a hairy woodsman with extraterrestrial roots. I hold my spirituality above everything else. I don't feel Sasquatch has anything to do with the end of the world, even though there is tremendous fighting and bickering going on at every turn with chest pounding and histrionics.

A long, focused look at all things Bigfoot-related makes it clear that there is a pattern of something extremely different. It is far more than some shy giant full of curiosity, sidestepping through the bush. A number of the tribes I talked to seemed to believe it is a friendly creature with one foot in this reality and the other in another existence. Undeniably, the Star Nations secret has grown over time, and the taboo creature has some place in an evolving process, particularly as it is connected with the extraterrestrial or as a creature of dimensional doorways.

As I warmed up to the possibility of Bigfoot being something even more strangely different than I originally assumed, a few teasers stirred my curiosity further:

> Me-ya-when, Mr. Boulier. I am in receipt of an email that you sent to our tribal chairwoman. We are Desert Cahuilla from here in the Coachella Valley, and we, too, have spiritual beings who live among us and protect us and provide guidance. I will not begin to pretend to know what the understandings of the people in Sasquatch's realm know to be real.
>
> I wish you the best in your quest for Native knowledge. (Mary)

> My personal opinion (and I am no expert) is that the Bigfoot is not an "outsider." I think creatures like this (and Nessie) are species that are almost extinct and have not been properly cataloged. An alien experiment gone awry, perhaps. As for an actual extraterrestrial, no, I don't think so. (Mintaka)

> Yes, I have heard about this and I believe they are extraterrestrial in nature; however, I am no expert on this matter. Actu-

> ally, I have always considered Sasquatch to be highly intelligent. That is my perspective. I have had many experiences with extraterrestrial beings, but not Sasquatch. I have never felt fear from the stories about Sasquatch. How wonderful that you have had these experiences. No doubt Sasquatch is communicating with you, or you would not have had these experiences. (Virginia)
>
> Yeah, even though I am known around the world as a UFO/paranormal researcher, I have spent a lot of time on Bigfoot. I know a lot about the subject. And yes, it is right, Bigfoot is somehow directly connected with UFOs, aliens, and the Star People. A common thread runs through the whole scenario. Bigfoot is an interdimensional entity, very often connected to aliens and UFOs, etc. They probably have an intelligence that is far more sophisticated than ours but in a different way that would be hard for us to understand. You live in the right place to study them. (Tom Dongo)
>
> Star knowledge is not fresh, but now has a birth in the new man. I am only beginning to know this myself; numerous things coming together in signs. An awakening is taking place. The Bigfoot is, in part, a diversified piece of the dawning of fulfilled teachings that the indigenous have understood throughout [history]. This traipsing creature has its given place in the primary realm but also a secondary domain. Have you ever seen anything so elusive? Something quick-witted and rational, then clumsy on the other hand? Contrary to what Bigfoot hunters wish to believe, they, as us, are being led along by a secure leash. The extraterrestrial is the illusionist of the open air, while the Bigfoot is the magician of the forest venture. If Bigfoot researchers only understood that they are being watched extensively from what you might call an outdoor balcony, they would go about their work differently. (Sidney)

Gayle Highpine, an indigenous Kootenai who has visited many North American reservations over the years, has heard both sides of the story about this mysterious creature, the flesh-and-blood beliefs as well as its potential to be from the stars. A number of medicine men and other aboriginal people have shared their knowledge with the writer, and I would like to thank them and Ms. Highpine for her contribution to the subject. The following excerpts come from Gayle's writings about Bigfoot in "The Track Record" #18, 1992:

> Here in the Northwest, and west of the Rockies generally, Indian people regard Bigfoot with great respect. He is seen as a special kind of being because of his obvious close relationship with humans. Some elders regard him as standing on the border between animal- and human-style consciousness, which gives him a special kind of power. (It is not that Bigfoot's relationship makes him superior to other animals; in Indian culture, unlike Western culture, animals are not regarded as inferior to humans, but rather as elder brothers and teachers of humans.) But tribal cultures everywhere are based on relationship and kinship; the closer the kinship, the stronger the bond. Many Indian elders in the Northwest refuse to eat bear meat because of the bear's similarity to humans, and Bigfoot is obviously much more similar to humans than the bear. As beings who blend the natural knowledge of animals with something of the distinctive type of consciousness called intelligence that humans have, Bigfoot is regarded as a special type of being.
>
> But, special being as he is, I have never heard anyone from a Northwestern tribe suggest that Bigfoot is anything other than a physical being, living in the same physical dimensions as humans and other animals. However, among many Indians elsewhere in North America — as widely separated as the Hopi, the Sioux, the Iroquois, and the North Athabascan — Bigfoot is seen more as a sort of supernatural or spirit being whose appearance to humans is always meant to convey some kind of message.
>
> The Lakota, or western Sioux, call Bigfoot Chiye-tanka (Chiha-tanka in Dakota or eastern Sioux); chiye means "elder brother" and tanka means "great" or "big." In English, though, the Sioux usually call him the Big Man. In his book, *The Spirit of Crazy Horse* (Viking 1980), a nonfiction account of the events dramatized by the excellent recent movie *Thunderheart*, author Peter Matthiessen recorded some comments about Bigfoot made by traditional Sioux people and some members of other Indian nations. Joe Flying By, a Hunkpapa Lakota, told Matthiessen, "I think the Big Man is a kind of husband of Unk-ksa, the Earth, who is wise in the way of anything with its own natural wisdom. Sometimes we say this one is a kind of reptile from the ancient

times who can take a big, hairy form; I also think he can change into a coyote. Some of the people who saw him did not respect what they were seeing, and they are already gone."

"There is your Big Man standing there, ever waiting, ever present, like the coming of a new day," Oglala Lakota Medicine Man Pete Catches told Matthiessen. "He is both spirit and real being, but he can also glide through the forest like a moose with big antlers, as though the trees aren't there… I know him as my brother… I want him to touch me, just a touch, a blessing, something I could bring home to my sons and grandchildren, that I was there, that I approached him, and he touched me."

Ray Owen, son of a Dakota spiritual leader from Prairie Island Reservation in Minnesota, told a reporter from the *Red Wing Republican Eagle*, "They exist in another dimension from us but can appear in this dimension whenever they have a reason to. See, it's like there are many levels, many dimensions. When our time in this one is finished, we move on to the next, but the Big Man can go between. The Big Man comes from God. He's our big brother, kind of looks out for us. Two years ago, we were going downhill, really self-destructive. We needed a sign to put us back on track, and that was why the Big Man appeared."

Ralph Gray Wolf, a visiting Athapaskan Indian from Alaska, told the reporter, "In our way of beliefs, they make appearances at troubled times, [to help troubled Indian communities] get more in tune with Mother Earth." Bigfoot brings "signs or messages that there is a need to change, a need to cleanse" (*Red Wing Republican Eagle*, "Giant Footprints Signal a Time to Seek Change," July 23, 1988.)

Matthiessen reported similar views among the Turtle Mountain Ojibway in North Dakota, that Bigfoot — whom they call Rugaru — "appears in symptoms of danger or psychic disruption to the community."

Hopi elders say the increasing appearances of Bigfoot are not only a message or warning to the individuals or communities to whom he appears, but to humankind at large. As Matthiessen puts it, they see Bigfoot as "a messenger who appears in evil times as a warning from the Creator that man's disrespect for His sacred instructions has upset the harmony and balance of

> existence." To the Hopi, the Big Hairy Man is just one form that the messenger can take.
>
> The Iroquois (Six Nations Confederacy) of the Northeast — although they live in close proximity to the eastern Algonquian tribes with their Windigo legends — view Bigfoot much in the same way the Hopi do, as a messenger from the Creator [who is] trying to warn humans to change their ways or face disaster. However, mentioned among Iroquois much more often than Bigfoot are the Little People, who are said to inhabit the Adirondack Mountains. Some present-day Iroquois assert that the Little People are still there, just not seen as often because the Iroquois don't spend as much time hunting up in the mountains as they used to. Many Iroquois seem to regard both Bigfoot and the Little People as spiritual or interdimensional beings who can enter or leave our physical dimension as they please and choose to whom they present themselves, always for a reason.
>
> The existence of Bigfoot is taken for granted throughout native North America, and so are his powerful psychic abilities. I can't count the number of times I've heard elder Indian people say that Bigfoot knows when humans are searching for him, that he chooses when and to whom to make an appearance, and that his psychic powers account for his ability to elude the white man's efforts to capture him or hunt him down. In Indian culture, the entire natural world — the animals, the plants, the rivers, and the stars — are seen as family, and Bigfoot is seen as one of our close relatives, the Great Elder Brother.
>
> Keep tromping across British Columbia, reserves, and logging towns, and you'll probably collect a ton of stories. [GH1]

As I was reviewing Ms. Highpine's piece, I received another word or two from different sources in response to my question about the new ways Sasquatch is showing up in the world. Years earlier, it had been nothing more than big footprints left in a field. Now there were other manifestations. One such anonymous source answered:

> Who can say what is going on for sure? People are seeing countless things now relating to what has been around for thousands of years. My voice is nothing. When it comes to speaking about the Star People, I can only share what is hidden to most,

> what I've heard myself. Yes, the Yeti, the Sasquatch, and Bigfoot (including all the Indian names given) are all the same type of being — and are connected with the people of the Milky Way Galaxy, maybe more. Exactly what their standing job is, I surely have no idea. Maybe they are watchers of some sort, or maybe they are the keepers of information and will tell us when we are ready. Some tribal people say we come from the stars. Maybe they are remnants of our home world.
>
> I'm sorry I cannot offer a more conclusive answer for you. Maybe someday we will know for certain, but for now, I like to believe they are here to remind us of the diversity in creation and the spark of the divine in all.

Due to space constraints, I cannot include here all the different tribes, bands, and reservations — with their chiefs, elders, medicine people, and leaders — who believe the creature comes from the stars. However, I will include a note taken from the pages of Richard Boylan, pertaining to the Star People. It also carries with it aboriginal thought, at least in part, through the writings of this scientist, doctor, and researcher. Star Knowledge Conferences have been going on for years now, hosting quite an array of beliefs and teachings from all walks of life. Richard Boylan explains:

> 1996 — For ten days in June, the Yankton Sioux reservation on the windswept high plains of South Dakota was a gathering place for indigenous tribal leaders from around the globe and hundreds of Native and Euro-American listeners. The occasion was the Star Knowledge Conference, convoked by Lakota (Sioux) spiritual leader Standing Elk in response to a vision. The vision showed that Native American spiritual knowledge about the Star Nations was to be shared. This Conference also fulfilled ancient Hopi and Lakota prophecies. Spiritual shamans from the Plains Tribes (Lakota, Oglala, Dakota, and Blackfoot) were joined by spokespersons from the East (Iroquois, Oneida, Seneca, and Choctaw) and Southwest (Hopi, Yaqui, and Mayan) tribes. They came because they had seen signs that had been predicted by ancient prophecies. These signs signified to them that the time had come to speak openly about their most closely held oral traditions. These traditions include their origin from the stars, the influence of Star People visitors on the formation of

their culture and their spiritual beliefs and ceremonies, and the imminent return of the Star Nations.

Kewaunee Lapseritis, MS, fascinated the crowd with his film, photos, and personal encounter accounts with the intelligent, telepathic, psychic, compassionate resident Star Visitor races known as the Sasquatch and the Old Ones.

Puerto Rican Jose Fernandez, of mixed Indian and Spanish ancestry, spoke from the cultural perspective of his deeply Catholic island. He spoke in Spanish, with translation provided by UFO investigator Giorgio Piacenza. Fernandez talked as an experiencer who has been asked to represent a star group, the Council of Twenty-Two. He spoke of an elliptical craft from Venus that took him up into a spaceship where the Council was. The following year, he was contacted by a star being from Mars, who was accompanied by a Bigfoot.

Eldon H. was another representative who had much to convey on this highly controversial subject, the works of the Star People and the Bigfoot. The man from the New Mexico did not beat around the bush, sugarcoat things, or accept some watered-down version of what is quickly becoming, as he called it, "a stand in the sand." Eldon had this to say:

> A few hard-luck years ago, while growing up, my family and I were on one of our highs, vacationing in the Tahoe Basin area, a good time including a pinch of California, the Desolation Wilderness in El Dorado County, if you want to look this area up in your research. Our enjoyment of this journey was tracing roots to where ancestors crossed the Sierras, making their way out to the West. With help from my father and granddad, we located a few signs along the trail that pointed to those long ago, making their way across the land. It was hard to grasp the hardships that others had; those poor people. Imagine moving a covered wagon only a few hundred feet on cursed ground, an entire day taken up by pilgrims in your household caravan, slaving away.
>
> Sorry for beginning what is a long original story shown and told to me, but another family of outlandish souls obviously ruled in their environment, the Bigfoot family.
>
> Around the Carson Trail (Nevada), to my surprise, an extinct giant sloth walked on two legs; this was uncovered in the early

1900s. [I checked this out and confirmed it, beginning at the Carson City Convention and Visitors Bureau.] The three Bigfoot we saw were spotted in California, somewhere around the area known as Emigrant Gap, way up on the California Trail. People may be more familiar with the Truckee area. Nevertheless, the trio we came upon on our summer break were all rich brown in color, and traveling what we considered eastward. On a casual rush, they made a beeline for what would result in better cover, a thickness of forest to their left. The lead changed hands a number of times between two of the hominoid/apes. Their motion and direction was that of knowing what exactly they wanted to do. They never staggered like other animals I've seen. They mysteriously moved in unison, never talking or communicating, but each in complete rhythm with the awareness of the other. I had never seen anything like it; that was extraordinarily different. It did rate up there, however, with what a well-situated researcher said later on about such creatures, for the entire world to hear. As far as I was concerned, this reflected on his organization. The brash guy stated plainly that these animals know if they hurt humans, more humans will come. They're careful not to injure you because they want you to depart under your own steam. The researcher was full of himself, also stating that these animals throw rocks, big and small, but if you get hit, it will be one of the smaller stones that strike you, since it wouldn't be a good idea to kill people. Do you know what kind of brain an animal would have to possess to make such deductions? What would happen if the damn things weren't that good of shots? They must get old as well and can't see straight — at least a few of them. Enough of this foolishness!

Let's be serious about this subject if that is at all possible. I am of mixed blood, but I still do not like what I am seeing or being witness to: wasteful ways and flights-of-fancy teachings. There are hundreds, if not thousands of frauds, impersonators, and cigar-store Indians that are of little value to society. Everyone is a Wisdomkeeper these days, or what may amount to one in hearsay. That is a large moccasin to fill. People get upset with me when I call a fraud a fraud. There are many who are into Bigfoot simply because they know Bigfoot can make them a few dollars down the road. If these imposters knew anything about anything, they wouldn't hide behind the Red Man's blood, whether they are of the lineage or not. Supernatural things happen to superstitious people.

I thought about this as well, going over our witness of such a sight in California. There is something distinctively odd about these ape/people, something I still can't put a finger on. Seeing them really only added to the predicament that is the Bigfoot, at least for me. These animals were rushing along to some secret locale; we could just sense this. The secret is still alive and well. While researchers eat their own afterbirth, this gentle animal continues to be effective and operative against man. Star Knowledge qualities beginning to take the forefront on things. You won't track that which can't be tracked. This cannot be followed up on, the animal/being pursued to destination. You've heard similar things, and I have as well in the mix.

Rounding out the idea of the Bigfoot creature being somehow involved or associated with the extraterrestrial, we will flash back to another who has spoken of this sort of thing, Red Elk, the Native American medicine man. He has received threats in the past for his beliefs, just as others have, but while others have choked about such things and kept quiet, he has relayed forbidden information to a waiting world, including on the taboo topic of the Sasquatch.

I must credit Rick Martin, an investigative journalist, and his wife Gail Cortright for this information about Red Elk, for presenting articles of various natures (a few quite controversial) in the early 2000s. While I didn't have the opportunity to speak with the owner and editor of *Spectrum Magazine*, formerly published in Tehachapi, California, and now out of business (to the best of my understanding), I must express my gratitude to them for interviewing Red Elk about his thoughts on who and what the Sasquatch is. They asked, and he delivered, in a taped session, as follows:

**Gail Cortright:** Does Bigfoot exist?

**Red Elk:** Yes! Our original Earth (human) beings. We are DNAed into our shape form (advanced) stage via people from other planets out of Bigfoot stock. Adam and Eve were the first successfully DNAed human beings. Bigfoot are our living ancestors. Why aren't they often seen? Because these brothers have evolved in abilities that go different from our own. They are masters at stealth/invisibility. They are alive. They are still here. Honey, we have not taken so long to evolve. If you want to see those who are on the evolution path, go talk to Sasquatch. They are our original people.

**GC:** I remember you saying that on the *Art Bell Show*.

**RE:** Adam and Eve were the first evolved through DNA, of them, Sasquatch.

**GC:** So we've evolved from Bigfoot?

**RE:** No, no, no. We were Bigfoot. They modernized us — different brains, different bodies, and everything else. [RM1]

The Medicine Man Red Elk had more to say about the creature that is Sasquatch, including talk about an Unholy Four, outsiders who are fighting over possession of the human race. This is noted in the man's booklet, *The Agendas*. The four include the Reptilians, the Bee People (Greys), the Gargoyle Race, and Sasquatch.

# 26. Seven Sacred Teachings, Kitch-Sabe

Within aboriginal spirituality lies what are known as the Seven Sacred Teachings. An aboriginal producer in Canada, Lisa Meeches, hosts a website, *The Sharing Circle*, which shares knowledge of this and other things. I uncovered many references to these teachings among the Calgary Board of Education program, including a children's book by author Dave Courchene, Jr. (*The Seven Teachings*), and specialized artwork on the *Murals of Winnipeg* website. The *Murals of Winnipeg* site had this to say:

> Our mural design this year is a theme of helping others. Because this building is occupied by Project Neecheewam, we put in a lot of aboriginal content and customs like The Seven Sacred Teachings. The inclusion of The Seven Sacred Teachings came about as a result of being suggested by one of the kids. Each of the teachings corresponds to the animal with it. For instance, Truth is the Turtle. Six of the seven animals have been incorporated into the design. We left out the Kitch-Sabe, as we were unsure of its form. We had conflicting versions.

David Bouchard is a Metis writer from British Columbia who wrote the book *I Am Raven.* I asked him about the possibility of the Sasquatch giant being the same as the Kitch-Sabe, to which he offered this very positive reply:

> Absolutely! He is one and the same by most views. There might be some who would argue not, but Bigfoot is the Kitch-Sabe! When we wrote the book, Joseph and I thought twice about using him as opposed to a representation that was milder. This we talked about at great length, in hopes of being true to

belief, yet accessible to the widest range of audience. Hope this makes sense. Miigwech… and good luck.

Again from the *The Sharing Circle* website, former Supervising Producer Kim Bell gave me the go-ahead to use the references available to explain what these teachings are all about and what they represent:

## The Seven Sacred Teachings

The traditional concepts of respect and sharing that form the foundation of the aboriginal way of life are built around The Seven Natural Laws, or Sacred Teachings. Each teaching honors one of the basic virtues intrinsic to a full and healthy life. Each law is embodied by an animal to underscore the point that all actions and decisions made by man are manifest on a physical plain. The animal world taught man how to live close to the Earth, and the connection that has been established between the animal world and that of man has instilled a respect for all life in those who follow the traditional aboriginal way. They are:

- Love – Eagle
- Respect – Buffalo
- Courage – Bear
- Honesty – Sabe
- Wisdom – Beaver
- Humility – Wolf
- Truth – Turtle

Long ago, there was a giant called Kitch-Sabe, who walked among the people to remind them to be honest to the laws of the Creator and honest to each other. The highest honor that could be bestowed upon an individual was the saying, "There walks an honest man. He can be trusted." To be truly honest was to keep the promises one made to the Creator, to others, and to oneself. The elders would say, "Never try to be someone else; live true to your spirit, be honest to yourself, and accept who you are the way the Creator made you."

Ronnie Beaver puts it this way:

Sabe is a spirit, and he is a part of God's creation, just like you and me… non-native people call him Sasquatch or Bigfoot… he was the first to walk on Planet Earth, long before human creation… Sabe works for other animal spirits and native people in search of herbal medicines… this is the reason why he earned the right to teach others about honesty. Sabe would never lie about where the medicines are located.

Again and again, things seemed to fall into place in this particular vein of my research. No sooner had I discovered this information, than another individual who'd encountered some strange things came forward to communicate with me. The woman was kind enough to share her story with me, as she had before, in other avenues. The significance behind this unusual tale is that it involves the idea of the creature (Kitch-Sabe), researcher Dr. Richard Boylan, and the inkling of the Star Being presence. Susan MacLeod Browning has been called White Star Woman by a First Nations elder, as stated on her website, *Healing Quest*. Her dealings with possible Bigfoot-like creatures are explained as follows:

## Night of the Sasquatch: August 15, 2005, 11:00 P.M.

I remember that night well. My dear friend Barry had just passed away the previous afternoon, and the next night, I made a fire in my tipi for him. I took down my medicine bundle and my drum as I sung his spirit a song. I missed Barry so much already. It was a nice, bright, starlit night, and the fire was comforting, as I felt that Barry was there too.

Then I heard a grunt and another grunt, then something brushed the skin of my tipi. I looked out across the pond that looked upon my house; I didn't see anything. Then another loud snort/grunt, and now the tipi skin shook. My first thought was that it was a bear!

So I put more wood on the fire and put some long sticks in to catch them on fire so I could go out with a burning torch. I sat still for some time and heard nothing. Good, I thought. The bear is gone.

I gathered up my things and got ready to leave. I was not ten feet from my tipi when I heard a noise. I turned toward the Miskwaaziibi (Red River), the river ran behind the tipi. There, on the riverbank, in the moonlight, I could make out the shadows of four to five beings. Some stood seven to eight feet or taller, and others were shorter. Then I noticed the eyes. They were reflective, like an animal's eyes in the lights. Some were red, some green, some yellow. I knew this was not a bear family, yet similar to standing bear-man. The fur was very long and shaggy, and the shoulders were sloped. Some had long arms; others stocky.

I then went back to my tipi, as it was closer than my home. I left all my things there and just took my drum and my bundle. I decided I would drum my way up; I thought making a noise would scare them off. I got out and glanced over. They were still all there, only they had moved down some on the riverbank, toward the big swamp. I made my way to the house, my heart just racing. I could still see some of them by the river. I went inside to tell the others of my encounter, but when I got to my back door, the first one to greet me was my daughter. "Mom, you better get in here. Something is going on!" She seemed very frightened and very serious.

My sons were also in quite a state, and my little guy Matty was crying, "There are black things all through the house."

"Yeah," Robert said. "These black things are all over, and they are really fast."

I immediately lit my sage and purified the house. Instant calm was back. The kids were really shook up, and now I really wondered, What was the connection with the shaggy creatures? Were they there to tell me something was wrong in my house? This was so much to handle!

They did get my attention, so I ventured up to the garage, where my partner, Mel, was looking out the windows. As soon as I got to the garage, he spoke really excitedly, so much I had to calm him by yelling back! All he could say for some time was, "What were you doing in the tipi?" He seemed very frightened, searching for answers, as was I. "All these black things have been around — shadows, you know, very quick." I felt his fear.

I was getting really tired and so overwhelmed again. We decided to light some sweetgrass, and Mel went through the garage with it. I just wanted to tell someone what I had seen. The kids were so upset! Black things?

I just felt I needed to get away to collect my thoughts, so I stood out in the middle of our gravel country road, Edwina Drive. It was around eleven p.m., and no one was on the road; yet even if a truck had come, I would not have moved, as I was looking up into the heavens, praying for answers. I called Mel, as I noticed three stars, moving at a same pace that the other stars in the sky were not! The formation then inverted itself but kept on moving in the same southern direction, as if to get my attention. Then the three stars shone; orange-yellow lights became very clear, and I realized I was looking at a massive — I mean massive! — flat blue-black ship. I felt I was looking under the great hull of a ship. It was majestic. It went very slowly, like a blimp, just puttering along, then disappeared over the tree line. Now, I knew what we saw, but how could I explain it?

Seeing that was much like a trauma to me. It has taken a long time to write this, three years, and I will say it was a trauma to see all of it. Did I see the Sasquatch? And if I did, I do think the Sasquatch is much like the hairy things out of *Star Wars* or *Harry and the Hendersons*. It really does look like a walking bear-man. I really think this is why all these sightings are just footprints and hair, but never a body or any evidence. I know what it is to see such a thing and have no proof, as the next day I went around my tipi, and nothing, yet they were there. I had heard them and felt them brush my tipi, and I saw their eyes. I do believe the craft was a connection, and is to me, obvious. They are some sort of travelers and have a ride home! Or is this home?

As for the black things flying through my home and garage, I have no idea — some sort of energy, very quick, but thank goodness for the sage and sweetgrass!

That night, my little ones slept well. I still had not told anyone the full story of my experience and would not for some time. This is another experience I will never forget — never.

Since this encounter, I have been contacted by a Dr. Boylan. I hope to meet with him this year. Also Jack "Kewaunee" Lapseritis, MS, who wrote a great book called *The Psychic Sasquatch*. He called me from Duvall, Washington, and asked to view my surrounding property. Both have studied the Sasquatch for over forty years! As well, I was just interviewed on a radio show by producer Tom Biscardi. Seeing this amazing being or family has me absolutely believing in the elders' stories.

A while ago, I was called to facilitate at a conference up in northern Canada. There I met a wonderful man, Leading Earth Man Dave Courchene, Jr. He said the Sasquatch represents hon-

> esty: "To be honest with yourself is to live in the spirit of how you were created. Never lie or gossip about each other. The more honest you are, the bigger you become as a person." Well said!
>
> I was told to send them kindness and love, as they can read our thoughts. I now feel honored our brother came to join me in my grief and brought the family. As well, when you see him, it must be an honor; they don't show themselves too much to anyone. I believe... send him/her your kind thoughts.
>
> Blessings... Miigwech.

In a final email with Susan MacLeod Browning, I told her that my interests had changed over the years concerning the Sasquatch phenomenon. Something about the creature exists in a mysterious realm. The questions that lingered were, "What are we witnessing? Who or what is this mysterious giant?" In Susan MacLeod Browning's response, it became clear that she had wondered about such things as well.

I studied her account, as well as what others had to say about it. There was something shady about it, though this statement is not meant to take anything away from the woman's generously detailed story. I will let Susan MacLeod Browning finish the conversation about this creature being a representative of one of the Seven Sacred Beliefs of the aboriginals. This has surfaced in a few tribes, as well as within Anishinabe culture.

> I still feel such a bonding or something from that night that I cannot explain. The sightings, etc., have continued. To read your account of your encounters and type this, my heart is racing! We are coming from the spirit of this creature, honesty. Thank you truly... Miigwech

# 27. Summing Up the Legends

Part II has included mysterious and contradictory legends, as the stories of a flesh-and-blood creature expand to include those of an off-planet or spiritual nature. These can be unsettling in our present-day culture. Is the old-school belief in a physical Bigfoot now really a thing of the past — becoming outside the norm? One would think so, with the scales tipping from the weight of uncertainty.

New information and strange teachings are now being shared and beginning to take center stage. The topic has gone from everyday scientific research to highly controversial acknowledgement of other possibilities. Has a flesh-and-sinew Sasquatch given way to a flesh and see-through beast? Or maybe it's a universal creature that rides shotgun for a Higher Power—whichever that might be. We'll continue looking at the possibilities in Part III.

# III. Bigfoot and the Spirit World

All I have seen teaches me to trust the Creator for all I have not seen.

— *Ralph Waldo Emerson*

In Part III, I want to look at other ways that events involving Sasquatch might be explained. The large number of sightings combined with no reliable physical evidence is a real problem for everybody.

I think René Dahinden spoke very well for the physical side years ago, "I'm not interested in Sasquatch in his mind. I want Sasquatch in the bush!" His hope was to find the creature where it roamed in the wilderness areas of North America. But what if it doesn't, at least not as a flesh-and-blood creature? I have a stake in this, since my family and I fit somehow into this phenomenon. I must admit, I harbor an ounce or two of doubt. My evangelical background naturally raises my guard in such situations, and this questioning spirit is warranted by my belief in the Gospel, even though "religion" seems to be a dirty word these days.

To the best of my ability, I have explained what my family has experienced over the years, as well as many other encounters with the Sasquatch beyond my own. I've again and again been asked this question in a variety of ways. A number of sincere individuals want to know if there might be any other explanation to the eyewitness sightings — even a slim chance of us having seen something other than a Bigfoot, if we saw anything at all. We are sure we saw a Bigfoot and not some other animal, but there may be another way to look at what happened.

Being as informative as possible and sticking to what I always thought was feasible in regard to the Sasquatch phenomenon, I want to now look into a seldom-traveled pathway for answers to this profound mystery. It is an extremely sensitive issue, of course, but it is part of a thorough examination from every possible angle.

This part finishes the threefold outlook on the Sasquatch. We have viewed the creature as an animal, and we've looked at the spiritual side as reflected in the Native American culture. Now we continue with a look at the spiritual from a Western perspective including a biblical perspective.

A part of me would have preferred to continue to sit back and watch the pitched battles from the sidelines. That part wanted to focus just on my past encounters with the creature. In the end, I decided this part of the story needed to be written, too.

This discussion is not an easy one, because there are so many different viewpoints on the subject. One example is a high-spirited Algonquian woman who contacted me during my research. It seemed word was getting out about my work, and various questions — most of them serious — were being asked about the creature. It was as if I was delving into a place few dared to tread, and my perseverance was most certainly not considered a virtue in this case.

The aboriginal Algonquian was a bold woman and was willing to talk, but I had some difficulty with the choppy sentence structure and unusual character of this multilingual matron. Her spirit and mine did not seem to operate on the same plane of consciousness. Long-standing elders backed her ways, as she proudly declared, all of them with the same umbrella of beliefs. But I am the type of person who does not back lineage when they do things that trample the human race, including misleading people. There is no ancestry aspect here, and I offer my own heritage as an example. We were given a brain to reason and think, and there is a right way and wrong way in everything in life.

I realized that there were two spiritual forces at work with the woman. First, she tried to persuade me that this creature is some kind of higher power. I denied this immediately, certain that the creatures are not even at demigod status. The high-minded woman stated that if we would just let go of the reins and allow the Sasquatch (my terminology) to take control in every aspect of our lives involving them, they would show themselves to us, to communicate with our minds. She didn't speak clearly on how this would be done, but I didn't think for a moment that it involved sitting quietly in a wooden rocking chair in the deep forest with my eyes closed, waiting for the creatures to show up and serenade me. I wondered who had put her up to such an idea, or what final result she was trying to achieve in our conversation. I could tell then that we weren't going to get along so well, but I could sense in the woman's sincerity that she was certainly not up to any kind of prank. She truly believed what she was telling me.

Others offered different viewpoints. I contacted Jeff Meldrum for his insights into the systematic and scientific side of exposing the giant biped as a flesh-and-blood creature. He was very understanding when I mentioned in my email that there might be a spiritual side to the phenomenon, the side I was specifically researching at the time. He offered me no humorous condemnation and didn't accuse me of Sasquatch blasphemy. His was only a professional stance, which I could appreciate. Many try to uphold such things, and you can't blame them — Sasquatch in the flesh. That being said, we need to consider the other possibilities, too.

There are many things we could look at outside of the purely scientific realm — things that science says can't exist. We'll start by taking a look at a few of them. Then we'll move on to other ideas that are frankly spiritual — places where I think the truth will really be found. To keep things balanced, I will present other spiritual views besides my own. As always, I will let you know what I think while telling you about the other points of view. That said, let's continue.

# 28. Bigfoot and Cars that Cease to Run

Occasionally, automobile engine and headlight interruption occur in the presence of the Bigfoot. Two such stories happened in Red Lake, Minnesota, in 2005 during a time when many Bigfoot sightings were being reported.

I spoke with two indigenous people from the area, both of whom wish to remain anonymous, even from each other. Perhaps these indigenous folks were members of some tribal council, or perhaps it was their own paranoia in a community already troubled, but as soon as they shared their stories with me, they ceased contact. This was by no means the first time for this to happen in my research on this project.

Both are native Red Lake Nation people, Ojibway, who live within the boundaries of Thorhult to the north and Little Rock to the south. Both of them encountered Bigfoot's interference with technology. While it is not a common occurrence among those who report Bigfoot sightings, it is interesting to ponder.

Both individuals refer to the Sasquatch as the Bagwajiwininiwag. (How's that for a mouthful?) They have heard of legends involving the Puk-Wudj'ies, the Little Folk of the Forest. Stories and sightings of these shortened versions of Bigfoot are few and far between, though — nothing compared to the reports of the large creature that roams through North America, Red Lake included.

The first Red Man (as he requested to be called) had only a little to say about the topic. He was told by relatives in Minnesota that their truck had literally conked out when strange lights seemingly hovered at about forty to fifty feet above them; shortly thereafter, the whatever-it-was took off. A tall, grayish, older, humanlike Bigfoot was encountered only a moment later, but the haired creature quickly vacated the area. He does not believe the giant was flushed out of the trees by the UFO; rather, it seemed to cohere with what was going on behind it. The animal was not frightened and was in no particular rush, nothing like a deer trying to flee a forest fire or pursuing hunters. The Red Man's kin assured him that the creature did not once look back toward the obscure lighting that was on the move.

They listened for another vehicle once they exited their own, only to hear a slight hum coming from the direction of the lights. It was around dusk, and they were a few miles from civilization. The witnesses were utterly baffled, even more so when the headlights on their vehicle just seemed to cut off for no reason. The three family members were not able to start the truck until the Bigfoot was out of sight. That episode brought Bigfoot to life for the three, along with new questions. What was the spooky light that moved aimlessly through the woods? What was that creature? And what silenced the Dodge, which had been running just fine before that? Throughout their ordeal, they felt a little lightheaded but still were able to function fully. The three wrote this side effect off as shock. Bigfoot just walked off, as always, but the Bagwajiwininiwag was no longer a fairytale or legend. For the Red Lake residents who experienced that, he became very real that evening. They never did figure out what produced the odd illumination, so the hovering object remains unidentified.

Party number two's tale is spellbinding. The rumor mill had stories circulating around the hundreds of thousands of acres that make up the Red Lake reservation. UFO and Bigfoot sightings were common, Bigfoot the more common encounter of the two, and no one associated one with the other. In the Ojibway belief system, while Bigfoot was a thing of legend, extraterrestrials were not, though the men I spoke with said a lot has changed over the years, and much of the new generation has forgotten much of the old culture. While the leaders can explain away the Bigfoot visitor, they cannot substantially pass off the space travelers. In the second man's tale, the two subjects were separated by only minutes.

Just west of Red Lake (the actual location remained concealed), four occupants were out for a day of riding dirt bikes. Since they only had two bikes, two were left behind in the truck to wait their turn. That afternoon, while they were waiting, a glare came across their windshield. The startled driver brought the vehicle to an abrupt stop. The passenger exited the vehicle instantly and witnessed what he thought was a cylindrical object in the sky. The bikers were not far away and quickly showed up on the scene. Then, everything happened seemingly in an instant: The truck stalled, and the bikes lost power. From what they recall, a moment or two passed before their stunned silence was interrupted by a heavy rustling and commotion coming from the nearby bush. Three of the four men caught a glimpse of a hurrying, upright animal making its way through the scattered timber. The fourth man was still looking for the object in the sky. After discussing it later, the three determined they had, indeed, witnessed the Bagwajiwininiwag of Ojibway legend. Between them, four Ojibway had seen two mysterious oddities, an unidentified flying object and an identified moving haired object.

Not until later that day would they comment on their dying vehicles, for each thought the others had simply turned off the ignition. As they realized that was not the case, and that all vehicles had shut down within seconds of each other without human intervention, it seemed very strange. They joked amongst themselves that they should start servicing their machinery properly, blaming clogged and choked gas filters, but they knew the truth did not lie in mechanical failure.

The spokesman who told me this story made it clear that he and his friends do not wish to come off looking like a bunch of drunken Paiutes. Unemployment and uncertainty are common in their area of the world, and that is not a risk they were willing to take.

Another interesting note on whether or not the Bigfoot creature might have a hand or two in upsetting motorized technology came from U.S. researcher, Dr. Richard Boylan, Ph.D.:

> The Sasquatch are telepathic and have a variety of psychic abilities. I would imagine these include telekinesis; thus [they are] able to affect things like machines from a distance. In addition, they have advanced technology, including antigravity craft, so a relatively simple device like one which would suppress the car's electrical system from firing would be within their capabilities.

Claims of *Chariots of the Gods* and Bigfoot using the same playing field are more common than one might think: the phenomena seem to appear in close proximity oftentimes, either by coincidence or planning of some kind. One UFOlogist stated that this notion of the two working together is no different than a few pro-flesh Bigfoot researchers believing that we originally came from tree-climbers some 1.8 million years ago (evolution). Truly, which is a more bizarre theory of the two? Bigfoot is too complex to pass off as a normal defecating primate. He states that while the creature may not come from the stars, per se, it does come from somewhere very out of the ordinary. The researcher also said, "You and your younger brother at Latitude N 49° 27' 28" Longitude W 120° 30' 38" (Princeton) would alarm an undisclosed species that is yet to be fully acknowledged." Flip the same coin over to present day, when there are thousands of intelligent human beings with credentials out the ying-yang, and we are still just barely allowed to toy with a haired animal who has the cunning of many different animal classifications. When this type of story is included in the mix, we move into deep paranormal areas. If we think we can explain everything about Bigfoot by saying it's a physical animal, we are just fooling ourselves.

# 29. Disappearing Footprints

In this chapter I want to look at three instances where tracks disappeared with no place for Bigfoot to go, at least in the physical world. All of these instances defied ordinary explanations since they were winter occurrences, making the tracks and then the disappearance easier to see.

I'd heard of this type of thing before, footsteps stopping abruptly and a creature vanishing into thin air. Seth Evanoff's story of a happening near Kalispell, Montana, is one example. Other researchers have told their stories, as well. Three of my own investigative follow-ups sparked my curiosity, and again it all evolved into a mystery. Two of these three witnesses saw a strange, upright creature in the beginning, and the third followed what seemed to be a fresh trail, though he saw no sign of the creature.

Let's start with the fresh trail story, the tale of a hunter and his buddy on a hunt in Washington State Region 5, part of the southwest area of the Evergreen State. A man (whom we shall refer to by the initials LH), along with his friend, had just come into their second clearing of the early morning. There was recent snow ahead of them, still untouched except for tracks that looked as fresh and crisp as the morning. LH discussed with his hunting partner that these prints were new, as the snow was still caving in around the edges. The prints were left in the shadows of the eastern mountains, the sun was not over them yet, and temperatures were still quite low. The hunters were interested in the oversized footsteps for two very distinct reasons. LH estimated that the tracks were eighteen inches long, based on a measurement he took against his rifle. Later, a tape measure confirmed that his estimates were almost correct; the tracks were in the seventeen-inch range, perhaps a little smaller. Beyond the size, the other intriguing thing about the tracks was that the footsteps were quite straight, as if a huge man had made them. The span between each step was approximately five feet. He said he was sorry that he hadn't measured to somehow confirm everything.

They followed the tracks for curiosity's sake.

Out in the open, the whole thing went sour when the prints simply vanished. LH recalled that he and his buddy had looked to the sky, dumbfounded. They felt uneasy, but shrugged it off to the strangeness of the setting. They looked in every direction, trying to fit the puzzle together, and finally focused on backtracking maneuvers that might explain the stoppage. There was no evidence whatsoever that anything around the trail had been disturbed, and neither of them could come up with any feasible possibilities.

As they stood and thought about it, the experienced hunters looked for a jumping-off point from the last two or three tracks. All prints were mostly the same distance apart and the depths in the same range, so clearly the creature hadn't made a run for it. They moved away from the final steps, assuming that perhaps a freak wind burst covered the remainder of the tracks over, but they found no evidence to support such assumptions. The nearest tree had to be twenty-five yards away. They checked the treed area just for the hell of it. For both of them, it was the damnedest thing they'd ever come across. Paranoid or not, the hunters felt as though they were being watched from nearby in an easterly direction, where the morning shadows were still being cast.

When I asked LH how many tracks there were that day, he told me there were somewhere around seventy-five. Clearly, the animal had headed west. Unfortunately, the hunters' investigations contaminated the site, and LH admitted that at the time their interests were not on preserving the integrity of the scene. They were somewhat bewildered by the whole thing and, in the end, LH left me with the following:

> Glen, there was no way in a million years that any kind of forest creature reversed almost seventy-five exactly placed footsteps. It didn't and doesn't happen, my friend. Do you know what kind of intelligence it would take to escape something like that?

The second case also took place in Washington State, on a dairy farm in Whatcom County. The farm owner responded when a small part of his herd began to make a racket. There was something in the immediate area, inside the property boundaries. It wasn't the first time the herd had been disturbed, and the farmer suspected some kind of natural predator was making its rounds, which was usually the cause for such commotion. Within a couple minutes, the farmer left the house with a double-barrel shotgun in hand and two dogs at his side, only to encounter a creature that resembled a man more than a wild animal. The fully haired man kept a suspicious eye on the excited hounds, and the farmer was amazed to see that his dogs were in the early stages of some strange, tranquilized state. They were barking strangely and had their tails tucked between their legs. Before he could think of raising the shotgun, the giant creature was running for available cover, behind a barn to his right. The farmer could tell the brute wasn't stupid; going behind the barn was the only option to get out of the line of fire.

The confused farmer gave chase through almost three inches of new snow. When he found himself on the other side of the barn, there was no giant, but the creature had left a set of tracks in its wake, leading away from the barn to the far side of the property, a fence less than fifty yards away. The nearby woods were unquestionably the creature's goal. It was easy to follow the tracks, since the few cows hadn't trampled this area of the barnyard.

The dairy farmer was at the fence in less than two minutes. The dogs were sniffing all over the place, but they wouldn't go over or through the fence. The man could see the tracks on the other side of the fence, picking up where they left off on his side. The damn thing just nonchalantly kept walking, without any hesitation.

While the hounds should have known the direction the animal had taken, the man led the way. After he squeezed his large frame through the wire fence, he saw tracks leading straight as an arrow from there, directly away from the fence. The farm operator could see the shuffling he'd left in the snow behind him, but the creature hadn't even broken stride going over the top.

A grove of trees were a stone's throw away, but the hasty, firm tracks ended approximately twenty yards from the fence, quite a ways from woodland. He managed to keep his dogs in tow with a strong hand on their collars, but he couldn't manage to find an explanation for how the elusive animal could have just disappeared into thin air. He was certain the creature couldn't have turned in its own tracks or backtracked over the wire hurdle. It simply did not seem possible. When I discussed this with him, I mentioned that the creatures are presumed to have an uncanny ability for side movement. At first the poor guy thought I was mocking him, and he said there wasn't even a leaf on the top of the snowfall there that day. There was no landing spot to either side or straight ahead toward the woods. And to beat it all, the dogs didn't pick up on the creature's scent. Both canines were confused and did not pay attention to his commands when he shouted, "Find!" — a word his trusted hounds usually responded well to.

Of course, there are other stories where people attempt to explain the odd disappearance of the creatures and their tracks. These chases took place, though, on more difficult terrain and surfaces speckled with trees, rock, and thick brush — all within easy reach of a creature like the Sasquatch. Areas such as creeks and rivers were also discussed, and it wasn't as simple as going up or down the stream.

The third episode of these strange disappearing acts occurred in Idaho, in Bonner County. A fisherman/tracker by the initials of BL was ice fishing by himself atop a new snowfall, though there wasn't much in the way of accumulation. The hole, already open when he got there, was on the south end of the lake. His outerwear was mostly white, enabling him to blend in well with the winter surroundings; he even shyly admitted that he felt white was his lucky color, so he wore it while he fished year-round, and he never missed. When I asked him if he was about to tell me a fish story, he told me he had a much better story than that.

He was not moving around when a large, ape-like creature strolled onto the lake in a commanding fashion. BL was actually facing the large, dark brown giant when it showed up. He didn't dare raise his head out of his parka, but he had to raise a curious eyebrow, keeping a watchful eye on the creature and hoping the monstrous thing wouldn't pick up on him sitting there, "waiting to get ate," as he put it.

The walking giant moved off rapidly, away from the ice fisherman, then disappeared around a bend in the lake. BL thought it was rather odd to see a Bigfoot out in the open like that, in broad daylight. For one thing, there was no way a man could walk that fast. He had to see more, so he slowly and carefully got up from his hunched-over position, leaving the fish to their own devices momentarily.

As long as he was out in the open, BL wasn't nervous. He moved to the strange tracks and followed them immediately. The outdoorsman rounded the bend in the lake within a matter of minutes. He followed the tracks, which seemed to be in single file, wavering very little from side to side. There was no creature positioned anywhere as BL looked down across the lake. He walked farther, assuming the animal must have headed for shore. The man was starting to think that the heavyset beast might have fallen through the ice, which tended to thin out near the edge of the lake, but he later changed his mind, realizing that the creature was so tall that even if it had broken through, it still would have been five or more feet above the ice.

Oddly interested and closing in on what he thought would be a few huge holes in the ice where the Bigfoot had fallen through and then waded a distance to dry land, he realized, much to his confusion, that the snowy footprints were gone — absolutely nowhere to be found. BL estimated the animal's weight to be between 600 and 700 pounds, and he went on to say that there was no way the thing could have pole-vaulted or long-jumped to the banks of that lake from the last of those tracks he'd followed; it was way too far to even be considered. The final tracks didn't support evidence of a fanciful flight of escape, as there was no drag, no stutter, and no hopscotch-looking steps.

He stood on that unmarked bank that day, looking back out on the lake, and the idea of the whole thing sent a shiver through him that had nothing to do with the freezing temperatures. BL even checked around to see if the creature had drowned, looking for a point of entry through the ice. The ice fisherman searched for a mound of snow that might have hidden the creature, but he found no such thing. It was as if the creature simply vanished. BL was sure it couldn't have been a hoax, especially since there was nowhere for a hoaxer to jump ship. The man was perplexed by the disappearance, and he now had to consider the Bigfoot, something he'd never put any stock in before.

An aboriginal chap from British Columbia was quite interested when he heard these stories, and had this to say:

> Seeing one of these nature creatures is to be given a gift by the Creator. My sister and an accompanying companion saw them drink from a swift-moving creek. I've seen the tracks but have never seen the Sasquatch. [They are] able to transform their main anatomy into anything they desire, [so] they can never be caught.
>
> In these times, my people are connecting with all resources, and the understanding now taking place. A transformational structuring into the spirit world occurs during our days of ceremonies. This I can tell you.

Another person with interest in such things, Dr. Richard J. Boylan, had this to add:

> When Sasquatch (Bigfoot) tracks suddenly seem to discontinue or "disappear into thin air," as you quaintly put it, it is a matter of the Sasquatch choosing to use psychic abilities to transport himself to another location (i.e., to teleport to a nearby underground location where his family group lives).

Attempting to make a little more sense of the three individual stories of disappearance, I wanted an honest opinion about what might be going on. Each tale couldn't simply be written off as something that was explainable as a normal occurrence. I asked a tracker from the UK. The considerate woman, Rhoda McGivern, offered me much feedback via email:

> I really can't be sure of an explanation unless I saw the tracks for myself. It is entirely likely that there is an explanation other than the paranormal, but without seeing the tracks, it would be difficult to say what it was. Unusual that it happened on three separate occasions though. I can see why you are perplexed. I don't suppose any photographs were taken of the scenes. I may be able to decipher something from a picture. Give me a couple days to do some research and have a think about it, and I will see if anything comes to mind. Any other information you can give me on each individual situation would be very helpful, if you have the time…
>
> Hi, Glen. Sorry to take so long in getting back to you. I have had a good think and consulted some of my tracker friends as well. Without seeing the tracks, none of us can come up with practical ideas as to why the creature would have just vanished. We have some thoughts on paranormal explanations for this, but I am not sure this is any good to you as I suspect you are after a physical explanation only. One of my friends has a contact who runs tracking courses in Washington and may be able to help you further. Would you like me to pass your details on to him?…
>
> I am happy to help whenever I can. The only other explanation my friends and I thought may be a possibility was a spiritual one. There is talk of these creatures and others being able to walk between this world and the spiritual world. It is said that when they walk in the spirit plane, they leave no tracks, so on the occasions when the tracks vanished, it could have been that the creatures moved to the spirit world.

**Figure 48: Tracker Rhoda McGivern with Ju'Hoansi San Bushmen in the Kalahari Desert of Namibia. (photo © Rhoda McGivern)**

Tom Brown Jr. apparently talks of personally having a similar experience when doing a vision quest in his book, *The Journey*. While in a trance, he walked from one location to another and left no tracks allegedly, as by being in the trance, he had moved to the spirit plane. Might be worth following up on if you haven't already. Anyway, I wish I could help you more with this.

Given the opportunity to investigate a similar sighting and then disappearance of both creatures and tracks, I would love to be able to get to the sites and look at the depth in tracks. I am sure that if any physical, logical reason for the disappearances had occurred, this would be readable in the resulting tracks, and we might be one step closer to solving the mystery. Even if this was a way to eliminate the physical possibilities, leaving no other option but the spiritual, this would be very interesting indeed.

Perhaps one day I will be lucky enough to have the opportunity to investigate further.

What the Sasquatch doesn't do when tracked is make mistakes, paranormal or not. Aware of this, I talked briefly with another individual concerning the tracking issue, Walter Muma from Ontario. Our discussion centered on the comparison of what a Sasquatch creature may do to avoid man versus what a human being may do in situations when they are lost in the wilderness.

> A lost person typically goes into shock as they become aware of their situation. It causes them to do irrational things, such as drop canteens of water or remove coats in cold weather. Tom Brown Jr. tells of a hunter he'd tracked who, in his panic, had crossed the Garden State Parkway, then only a two-lane road, not even knowing it. According to tracker Tom Brown Jr., all alleged Sasquatch tracks he ever examined, whether viewed live by him or in photographs, were fake.

Similar statements have been made by BFRO. A small handful of individuals have asked me about the prevalence of paranormal-based reports on the BFRO site and suggested that the Internet group might have had some idea about the extraterrestrial angle. I wanted to hear it straight from the horse's mouth, so to speak, so a BFRO representative, Mike Aragona of New Jersey, cleared the BFRO stance up quickly for me:

> The BFRO believes Sasquatch is a flesh-and-blood animal and that there is nothing paranormal or extraterrestrial about the species. My personal feeling, based on my own research and encounters, is that the misunderstood and elusive behavior of this primate tend to cause people to associate it with the above mentioned; in reality, this animal does things we have yet to understand and comprehend, things we will only begin to understand and learn from once one is proven to exist, captured, and studied, although it is not the goal of the BFRO to capture one of the creatures.

Yet we are still faced with the evidence of this chapter, as well as the other evidence presented earlier. It is, most definitely, an interesting concept to ponder, the Sasquatch being all-knowing while mankind is most certainly not. This could be quite significant, particularly when you consider that there could be some sort of paranormal intervention aiding Sasquatch.

A Bigfoot enthusiast from Washington had this to say:

> Glen, I think you may be on to something very important with the Bigfoot outline. I know of one individual who has seen the dimensional animal before. Less than eighteen months later, they reported seeing a UFO, a cylindrical something, in the mountains of central Oregon, around the range of Three-Fingered Jack, between Mts. Jefferson and Washington. The Bigfoot sighting was close to Porcupine Rock. Similarly by comparison, Henry Franzoni, a researcher, has encountered both in his studies, the Bigfoot and an oblong craft, found in the general vicinity of each other. This kind of thing sure doesn't help the cause for average or normal research methods, but it does go in the direction of your work. As for the findings, there are others, you know.

Bless his heart, René Dahinden would roll over in his grave if he knew what he'd face in today's Bigfoot environment.

# 30. Thomas Hues

Thomas Hues' information definitely falls into the realm of spirituality. Both Thomas and I have dibs on finding or maintaining a theological connection. I knew this going into the interview, after reviewing an article written by author/columnist Candace Talmadge, a three-part series in which Hues mentioned that the Sasquatch can help man with his spirituality. Being fair, I offered my opinion on what I thought was happening when Thomas and I talked. Our interview and chat session lasted for well over two hours and, at one point, I asked Thomas about the possibilities of the Bigfoot question being infiltrated or tampered with by supernatural forces — in whole or in part.

We weren't in that frame of mind long, and I felt Thomas was slightly nervous going down that road. I understood, for I used to be nervous asking that question and inquiring along those lines, but now I know the question is valid. The Sasquatch — or something — *is* relaying information.

Thomas mentioned a number of things relating to his ongoing witnessing of the Sasquatch that he has befriended. The man is a Texan of Irish, Welsh, and Cherokee ancestry, and our conversation was as delightful as it was informative.

**Glen Boulier:** Thomas, how did you happen to get your calling on the subject of Sasquatch or the Bigfoot creature? And how did they come about finding you?

**Thomas Hues**: Oh, it was a moment where my life was in a total shambles, and I was sitting outside of my office… umm, and I-I closed my eyes and said, "I don't know who's listening, but I'm ready to go. So, if you guys want me to stay in this sagging skin suit, you're going to have to give me a reason to get up every day." That was when I was compelled toward studying the hairy folks, as I call them. And I didn't just study them here. I studied them in Australia as well, with the Yowie. And I began to discern behavior patterns, based on the people who were encountering them.

**GB:** Why would it be me? Why would it be you or the others encountering and witnessing these things?

**TH**: I don't have exact reasons. I spoke with a Cree elder on a Blog Talk Radio (BTR) show back in April last year, and I asked him, "Why am I having these encounters with the Sasquatch People?" And he said, "What tribe are you, my brother?" And I said, "I'm part Cherokee." He said the answer was simple: "They see in you what you don't see in yourself, and they're simply calling you home."

**GB:** The things we have addressed in the past, have these things been going on for some time?

**TH**: And it grows. My people, the Indians, they have sayings about, uh, planting seeds and letting them grow. So, the seeds have been planted long ago, and they're slowly growing. This is what's going on. Dr. Melba Ketchum has done BTR shows, and her evidence and findings are going through peer review at this time, but she finds the Sasquatch People to be between .4 and .5 percent different than us. That's only half a percent, so they are a type of people. It's almost like going to a different continent and discovering new people and having to go through learning all the etiquette and protocol to interact with them. That's basically what it is like. I know through my own experiences, I've had to learn a lot of things. One of the first things I learned was, I don't ask what their name is. I ask, "What do I call you?" That's the appropriate way to ask the question.

**GB:** Do the Sasquatch People have special ways in using nature around them to help them with health concerns?

**TH**: Yes. They know what herbs and things to use out there in the woods to take care of certain, you know, ailments of the body.

**GB:** In the past, we, as a family, have just received what I call, flashes or fragments of this phenomenon. Others are much more extensively involved, it would seem.

**TH**: That's happening more and more, and I'll be completely honest with you, Glen. As much experience as I've had — which isn't very much, in my opinion — there are people out there who make me look like a Tinker Toy.

**GB:** Things have seemed to come about concerning these creatures and spirituality. Some say the Sasquatch have been sent. Do you have any idea where these creatures come from?

**TH**: Uh, the soul or the spirit. It's what's in their body. It's the same kind we have, so when we get out of these sagging — what I call skin suits — we're all the same life form. We're all beings of light. So there's a commonality between them and us right there. We share the same life form. Even though our physical bodies are different, our soul is the same. There are people on the planet right now. They may not be aware of it, or they may be aware of it, and being quiet about it, but they've lived as a Sasquatch in a past life, in another lifetime, so they're bringing that knowledge forward in ways that people can't understand or don't see. Where does that knowledge come from? Well, it's coming from the hairy folks.

**GB:** What about the extraterrestrial/UFO/Bigfoot connection?

**TH**: When I mind-spoke with the female I interact with, I asked her about that. She gets on spaceships or has encounters with off-worlders, and her answer was very swift: "You're not ready for that knowledge."

**GB:** You've heard of the infrasound issue, as well as projection. Is what the aboriginal/indigenous people say correct?

**TH**: Yes.

**GB:** They've also told me, especially from the British Columbia area, of something called putting the power on an individual. Do these creatures have that capability?

**TH**: Yes, and I would say the infrasound theory is nothing more than a theory. But I know for a fact that they can reach right into your mind and trigger certain synapses within your brain, causing fear.

**GB:** Do you have any idea how Bigfoot is staying away from our technology or from the individuals putting it out there?

**TH**: I do. Actually, I know that very well. Again, I go back to how we're focused on the left side of the mind, and they are not. When their children start to show abilities of the mind, they don't tell them, "That's not real. That's your imagination." In fact, they do the opposite. They foster those abilities and help that child develop those abilities so they know how to survive when they become an adult and can add to the tribe or the clan they are a part of at that point. All of them know the trick. They learn it at some point; it's a learned behavior, a learned trick. They reach into the human brain and simply say, "You can't see me." A lot of times you'll hear people say the Sasquatch disappeared right in front of them. That's one of two things: They're either sliding into another dimension, which is right here on this planet, or they're just doing the simple trick of reaching into your mind and saying, "You can't see me." At that point, you can no longer see the reflective light off their bodies, so they seemingly disappear, even though they might still be twenty feet from you. You can't see them anymore because they have put that suggestion in your brain.

**GB:** Thomas, still on that, what about the thousands upon thousands of trail cameras out there? How is such a creature escaping detection?

**TH**: You know, you're out there in their home environment. When you go out to set up a game camera, for example, they know what it is because they're reading in your mind what the thing does. They don't know what it is in the sense that they look at photographs or work with that equipment, but they know what it does, so they know to avoid it. They know to turn the camera, cover it up with deadfall, or whatever the case may be. They know it's out there, and they stay away from it.

**GB:** There is the question of tracking and the disappearance of those footprints. Have you heard of such things?

**TH**: Yeah.

**GB:** A lot of people are guessing, but where did those creatures go?

**TH**: Well, you have to understand frequencies and how they operate. Our body resonates at a certain frequency, and that frequency is coming up. It's elevating right along with the planet. That's why time seems shorter right now. The days seem to go by in a big hurry, compared to what they did just two years ago. The scientific community has shown that the harmonic resonance of this planet that we live on was eight cycles per second, eight hertz, in other words. Now, in 2011, the harmonic resonance of this planet is thirteen cycles per second; we've increased five cycles per second in vibration. That's why days seem shorter, why time seems to go faster — because it is, in a sense. But your physical resonance, or frequency, is important to understand. They've had hundreds of thousands of years to learn this on their own. That's why they know how to raise the vibrational frequency of their own bodies and slip into another dimension right here on this planet.

**GB:** Would you have any doubt, living with such mysterious creatures?

**TH**: I wish I was physically able to go out there and live with them. I'd be gone in a heartbeat.

**GB:** What about the hostility of such a species as the Sasquatch? Are they ultimately dangerous?

**TH:** What I can tell you is that if you walk into the wrong area and you don't take the [warning] signs they give you, they're going to take you out. There are a lot of clans out there who are all about protecting their way of life, and they don't take any chances. There's a place in the northern territory, just above British Columbia, called the Nahanni Valley, nicknamed "Headless Valley." A lot of people went in there to look for gold between 1921-1922, and twelve were found headless on the outskirts of that valley. The people who live in that valley absolutely protect their way of life. They don't take any chances, and I would not go in there myself.

**GB:** Native folks pointed out the Nahanni Valley to me, an area of mystery they told me. Not trying to make legends bigger than life, they toned it down to the land of the Bear-dog and Sasquatch, as huge footprints were found around the areas of a few missing persons. One way or the other, the region is infested with evil spirits.

We've talked about British Columbia's Pitt Lake area, north of Vancouver. Also the possible killing zones of the Bigfoot, and how the forest giants could operate at times.

**TH**: That's right. I've said this to people who would hunt them: It's not the one in your gun sight you need to worry about. It's the two or three coming up from your side or behind you who are going to take your ass out. They're not going to let you kill one of their family members.

**GB:** A little change of pace, Thomas. Are they handy with food?

**TH**: Yeah. They know how to do the same things that the Indians used to do. They know how to cut strips of meat and lay it on a rock or wooden rack they've made. They dry it out into a type of jerky.

Somebody else you may want to get in touch with is Arla Williams. She's in Oklahoma, around sixty years old, and she's been seeing the hairy folks since she was seven years old. Like I say, when you're talking to me, understand that I'm a Cracker Jack toy compared to some of these people who've been experiencing 'em just about their whole lives.

**GB:** And other things?

**TH**: Glen, you should have seen how much flak I took when I mentioned on a BTR show one night that hairy folks use the trains to ride on. They actually get running real good and grab a train car and get on it. They use trains to travel across the country. There's nobody patrolling anymore.

**GB:** And the final results today, Thomas?

**TH**: You know, if you ever get the chance to come down here in the States, Glen, a good place to go would be the Kiamichi Mountains in Oklahoma. There're probably a dozen clans or tribes who live in the Kiamichi Mountains. That's eastern Oklahoma, Indian territory. Once you begin to accept and realize that these are intelligent life forms just like we are — in fact, more intelligent in certain ways — then you can look at them as your brothers and sisters. There are reservations in Oklahoma, and when they have a ceremony or a dance around the thunder-drums, the hairy folks come out of the woods and join them.

Thomas Hues and I discussed many other things, and there was even the mention of the Sasquatch helping humankind pick ourselves up after the supposed December 21, 2012, deadline. As we know by now, it was not the end of the world. If anything, Earth's inhabitants are going through a spiritual consciousness transformation, and we've already heard that the Sasquatch is a player for some in this. Therefore, let this be your warning on a very complex subject: Be careful about what lures you out to the woods.

# 31. Bigfoot Telepathy

Bigfoot's use of telepathy is another reason to think that Sasquatch is more than a physical animal. Many people I've discussed earlier talked about the confusion Bigfoot causes. We looked at the possibility of infrasound. It could be a case of telepathy instead. David Cleaver had this to say about his experiences with Bigfoot telepathic communications:

> One thing I have clearly noticed or felt is the mind screw, for lack of a better word. These creatures have an amazing ability to mess with your mind/thoughts in a telepathic way. On the receiving end, people are just not acclimated to receive information in this way, thus creating fear, confusion, and other strange feelings within your mind. It has happened to me enough that I am now ready to read their mental transmissions and not freak out — like learning a new language. If you are not mentally prepared for their mind games, you can get stupid real quick and imagine all kinds of crazy stuff.
>
> One very important aspect of Bigfoot research is to consider their telepathic abilities. Of course, this is only my opinion and is based on many years of observing and interacting with wildlife, as well as my experiences studying Bigfoot.
>
> We humans have a highly developed ability to communicate verbally, but we are lacking in other forms of physical communication, including posturing, physical movement, and telepathy or ESP. It has been proven that human babies have higher ESP capabilities, until they start to develop language skills and lose these abilities. Most of us have experienced our own ESP capabilities throughout our lives in various subtle ways, so we know

it's there, but most can't understand how to use it; it would be like learning another language that nobody knows how to teach.

Bigfoot, on the other hand, has a highly developed telepathic ability. So many times, when people have had encounters with these creatures, strange things have happened in their minds: feelings of being watched, feelings of dread and extreme fear, forgetting that you have a camera or other device on your person, unable to fire a weapon, and just plain being scared and stupid. Attention to detail at times is hard to maintain, and clear thought goes out the window. Part of this fear is simply the unknown, as our minds are not used to receiving information in such a manner. When these thoughts suddenly appear in your head, you wonder how they got there at an almost subconscious level, and this alone can create fear and panic.

I have had about six occasions where I've felt like a Bigfoot was invading my mind, and the first time this happened, it put me in a blind panic. This was during my original sighting back in July 1969. Since taking up the quest several years ago, I became aware of this phenomenon and have at least learned to recognize that it is happening to me and to just relax mentally. I also believe they can read our intentions to a certain degree, so care must also be taken not to give your thoughts or intentions away. I try to stay mentally positive, think about my wife and kids, or old girlfriends — whatever it takes. If you are out looking for Bigfoot, and with a specific agenda, good luck! You won't likely find him. I could have explained in detail the six incidents when this all happened to me, but it would end up too long.

# 32. Remote Viewing

Remote viewing is a difficult topic for me, and I won't confuse you with the spiritual end of it, except to say that many have agreed with me that it bears a striking resemblance to astral projection and out-of-body experiences.

The U.S. and Russian governments have used controlled remote viewing, which is rather self-explanatory. Similar to this is something called grid travel. The phrase itself was coined in 1974 by parapsychologists Russell Targ and Harold Puthoff. On the whole, remote viewing consists of gathering information on targets from a distance, by a probing viewer. In other words, it is like being able to see what is on the other side of a hill or in the next room. Normal senses do not qualify in the procedure, but a successful remote viewer can describe certain details, sometimes drawing them out. Remote viewing is generally considered, at best, a pseudoscience.

Christophe Brunski, though, sees it differently, as he described in *The Anomalist*:

> Over time, we, as industrialized humans, have eroded this innate potential, and we further grow away from it when we dismiss our occasional moments of deep, accurate intuition as mere chance. It is said that some of the isolated populations most virgin to modern society, such as the aborigines in the most remote parts of Australia, may have retained all of their original remote viewing skills. The possibility exists as long as there are still indigenous peoples on the Earth who live with little or no corruption of their original ways. Serious research into this topic, however, is practically non-extant.

Webber, a flamboyant spokesman of the indigenous, explained their beliefs about remote viewing as it applied to Apache life:

> Ask the Apache. They will tell and instruct you on nature working closely with the Red Man, something most have forgotten. Kensah, among other Apache references to the creature on stroll, blends in with the forces of the mountains, streams, and elements. There exists a great spirit of the land, not foreign to those who know him. The artist Geronimo knew him and achieved the power that the Hairy Man also possesses. Bred with this power, they elude man when they wish. In one minute, you may sit with them; the next minute, they are gone. Kensah draws off everything that is original. They can feel you around, on the outside of their thick skin. Hard to explain — many would not understand. But another thing though: I have read where Geronimo and other Indian hunters would spend an hour or so moving on deer that were nourishing, many times in the open field. Not to be seen, the braves would be extremely patient, crawling along with tumbleweeds or brush in front of them. This could take quite some time, especially in the heat, but they endured. Kensah has this supernatural patience, but with greater awareness.

The Arizonian Apache knew of the legendary Geronimo and what may have made him a ghost of the Western frontier. Webber also knew of the Bigfoot creature, an artist in its own right, with mankind as its guinea pig.

Some remote viewers and agencies were happy to share their opinion on the Sasquatch creature with me. Some even wanted big bucks to sort out the question of Bigfoot. The first remote viewer I corresponded with is a thought-provoking individual, a professionally trained viewer and a member of Ed Dame's Matrix Intelligence Agency RV team. Jordan explains:

> Can remote viewing be used to determine whether this creature exists outside of myth/legend? Yes, this is a very easy job for remote viewers. Even beginners would be able to handle a project of this nature. One approach would be to take a written account of your sighting(s) and target the creatures in your experience. This provides us with a jump-off point for determining exactly what you saw.

> Can remote viewing be used to track down the creature? Technically, yes, but locating a creature who is on the move is a very difficult task, and even more so if they are in a homogeneous environment (mountains, forests, etc.). Recent proprietary developments allow for locating things down to plus-or-minus thirty meters using a GPS-like technique; however, this assumes that the target is stationary.

The remaining remote viewers I spoke with generously provided the following answers about their craft and how it might pertain to Bigfoot:

> Assuming that Bigfoot is a biological creature (and I think there is enough information to confirm this), the question is, Which Bigfoot would you want to locate? — similar to: Which person should I locate? There are many possible people, and you need to identify an individual or family of Sasquatch. Yes, you can use remote viewing to discover Bigfoot either by dowsing a location or remote viewing landmarks. I have heard that they have nesting places or live in caves, so they could be located. What would you do if you located one? I would say leave it alone except to take photos and video, making sure you have landmarks such as trees and rocks to estimate their size. I don't think searching for them would lead to their extinction, as there seem to be many around the world, particularly in North America, including Canada. Hopefully, when discovered, they will be put on the Endangered Species List and protected! (Angela T. Smith)

> Okay to study — yes, maybe to find. A little harder but not impossible. Let me expand on these answers. Remote viewing, as one of its prerequisites, should really only be used on targets that have sufficient feedback information to check this against, the psychic information to assess accuracy. So yes, a remote viewer could describe in great detail the physical details, habits, lifestyle, and even what a Bigfoot thinks. The problem we fall down on a little is that there doesn't exist solid feedback to assess these claims, but it could still be helpful. Please bear in mind that a remote viewer also always works projects blind. This means they have no information on the project upfront, so you can be assured if they do describe the actual project at hand, the info is actual psychic data, because the remote viewer has no

information. Finding things is hard with remote viewing. I know this because I've spent the last two years working missing person's cases for the police. The reason why is that remote viewing is a process that describes things in great detail. Part of this process is that we try to not name things. I may get great, descriptive data of a location and generate great sketches, but actually naming a location is hard. This may be a problem when searching, as my description of, for example, "a densely wooded mountain range" may not help pin down an exact location. That said, we can help narrow down areas, and if someone can match our sketches to actual locations then it does help. So yes, it is possible remote viewing can help in many ways, but remote viewing is not 100 percent accurate and does need to be used properly with other information sources — not instead of. (Daz Smith)

Remote viewing to study the Bigfoot? Yes, of course, but you have a lot of questions. What exactly do you want to study about these beings? To locate them is another question. Yes, this can be done, but it would take a few sessions, although this may be achieved quicker by dowsing a map after you have made up a target pool of questions, not all of which will apply to the Sasquatch. A remote viewing session can give you a description of the nearest or largest structure (e.g., a building), but then again, they could still be some distance from this, so another two targets would be needed for triangulation of said target (Bigfoot). Should we leave them alone? This is another good question along the ethics guidelines, but I am sure, seeing as they have survived all this time, they will, even if we wish to study them, survive into the future. So, in my opinion, I doubt it would lead to their demise. I have seen a map of sightings in a particular area of, I think, the southern part of the U.S., where multiple sightings have occurred. Not sure if these hunting cameras have been set up or not, but that would be one way to start. Also, I have heard that one remote viewer has done sessions on them, and they appear to come up as an off-planet type of being. His reference had them as a type of slider, and they appear to only have a limited time here before they move on, or so I was informed. So a short answer to long questions: These beings can be remote viewed in a session(s). If you have any photos, I would be quite interested; it could also be used in remote viewing as target reference material. This could validate the photo or not, once a session has been done on it. Hope this all helps. Let us know. (Rick H.)

Stephen A. Schwartz's reply sums up how several remote viewers seem to feel about the idea of a legendary creature like the Bigfoot still existing today, and whether or not remote viewing can be used to find them or if it might be used against them:

> It could be done, but I wouldn't do it, and would not recommend you do it either. If they ever locate this creature, they will either kill or incarcerate it. I want no part of either.

Georgia researcher Leigh Culver spoke of remote viewing as well, and he linked me to approximately eleven clips on the phenomenon and similar things, including the U.S. government's processes and protocol regarding the matter. The government really has no interest in Bigfoot; they are far more interested in military use of psychics.

Leigh Culver spent more time discussing some of the things he and others are dealing with at a much closer range than many do out there. This is his baby, and he may write a book about it in the future, though certain issues remain confidential at this time. As a member of the Society of Primitive Technology, International Society of Professional Trackers, and a founding member of the Georgia Tracker's Alliance, Leigh has trained numerous individuals in applied remote viewing. He has experience on five continents in places like the arctic, desert, jungle, and high-altitude mountains. He has also trained with the Soviets on their soil on a number of cases. Remote/special operations, medical support, and search-and-rescue operations are his specialties.

Leigh explained a Florida visit where the creatures showed up unexpectedly:

> In brief, here is the gist of it. We were in central Florida, teaching our Bigfoot tracking course to some Bigfoot investigators in November of 2009. We had just finished teaching the night tracking exercise. We were sitting around a campfire at a campground, just talking; the campground had previous Bigfoot activity. While sitting and talking, we all started hearing woodknocks coming from the forest — not too far away. We kept hearing them, so Allan decided to go check them out. He initially

walked up to the tree line, then later entered. He was gone a while.

After some time, JT stood up, and put on his pack and said, "I'll be on Channel 3." I then did the same, as did Craig. We headed in and found Allan, then divided up into two teams and headed deeper into the environment. The Florida folks didn't quite know what to think, having never seen how we operated before. They were not sure what to do, so they remained at the campfire.

Long story short, for two hours we experienced a prolonged encounter with possibly four Sasquatches, up close and personal. We heard enough wood-knocks to know without a doubt that the sound was not wood-on-wood knocking. We heard up-close-and-personal chatter, whistles, and bipedal movement all around us. JT got boxed in for a time by two of them. Initially, when the bunch of us went in, the initial howl/scream/moan was a bit threatening, but after that, JT, Craig, and I started projecting good intentions, as well as returning whistles. We attempted to become very interactive with them. The finale occurred when one of them got within about ten feet of us, behind a large bush that we could see through, and knocked loudly. It was as if one of these creatures had counted coup on us just to show us s/he could. All four of us were together when this happened, and it materialized just as we were starting to be surrounded. Allan and I were closest to this knock. We all jumped back. After this, we all took defensive positioning to cover our zone, not unlike a wagon train. I continued to face where the knock came from. Suddenly I heard a sound, like I was about to be rushed or charged, only to continue to see nothing. I mustered up a bit of courage and walked around the bush, speaking softly, only to find nothing there. There is no way to convey what all happened that night: too much happened. The high strangeness part is that even though we had a full moon with fairly good visibility, most of the time we never saw them — not even when one was standing virtually right in front of us. (There is a radio show available for the details at http://www.blogtalkradio.com/bigfoottonightshow/2011/09/19/special-guest-leigh-culver.)

I want to add that these men have stayed alive over the years, especially in dangerous foreign countries and treacherous areas of the world because they know what is going on around them at any given time, never letting anyone get close enough to do them harm, bodily or otherwise. Yet here these creatures were, right on their doorstep, one of them alone large enough to take on three grown men. Researcher Leigh Culver continued:

> Below is an edited version of the email I sent back to the Florida folks. It basically described what we learned from this encounter:
>
> We know there were three, possibly four Bigfoot operating in the immediate environment. We know that at least two of the Bigfoot were probably seven to eight feet tall, based on track size and stride. We know, based upon the pitch and straddle, that the Bigfoot are probably adolescents and haven't bulked up as of yet. We know by the stride that they were being very stealthy and careful in their movements. We know that in at least one location, a Bigfoot had crawled to his/her location of observation. We know there were several locations where the Bigfoot stood watching us for some time by their foot shuffling while standing in place.

To validate that the forest dweller is a breathing, acting reality, I must mention that this same movement has been seen by me and catalogued by others, a shuffling of the large feet. In the 1985 encounter, both Richard and I watched the creature shuffle on the hillside with a nervous appearance; I have never forgotten that vivid detail. A few years ago, Oregon researcher Todd Neiss contacted me via email to confirm that Bigfoot did such a thing. Another researcher followed, then another. It was a comforting thought, as it indicated that the being is more likely flesh-and-blood than a spiritual manifestation. Even so, I also firmly believe it has some spiritual influence, shuffling or not.

Culver continued on the issue of the foot shuffling and wood-knocking:

> This is information we got from track and sign interpretation. Keep in mind that Visual Tracking Level 1 is all about seeing a sign and following it. The more advanced tracking levels are all about interpretation and making sense of it all. So, just from the track and sign from Sunday, an incredible amount of information was gleaned.

We know Bigfoot are not doing wood-knocking but making the knocking sound by some other means. This is important information. There was not a dry, non-rotten piece of knockable wood in those woods, especially, for the number of knocks we heard; we heard so many knocks that I lost count at twenty. I'm not talking about individual knocks but salvos of knocks. The number of knocks per salvo ranged from five to three at a time. The five knocks were extremely rapid, and in my opinion would be difficult to do with a stick against a tree. The knocking sounds remained extremely consistent in quality, pitch, and tone. In my opinion, the knocks are most likely hand-clapping or possibly, jaw/tongue-popping-like vocalizations, not unlike the sound a bear can sometimes make but on a louder scale.

We know that the Bigfoot, once they realized we were not going to act fearful nor in a threatening manner, decided to interact with us. I would whistle, and one would whistle back. I would whistle, and one would knock back. This went on for quite some time. We heard knocks, whistles, chatter, and in one area, bipedal movement. The bipedal movement was in an area where one or more Bigfoot were attempting to get close to us for observation. I maintained the whistling so the Bigfoot would always know where we were. In other words, we lured them in closer, and we did it in a manner that put the situation under their control and their terms. Our research has consistently demonstrated that if we interact with them and let them know where we are, they will just about always come close to where we are for observation. The key here is that your intention must be totally non-threatening. Our experience demonstrated that when you split up, they will try to get you back together as a group, the same way they did with JT in trying to box him in. They will also use rock-throwing, etc.

Most importantly, we learned that a Bigfoot can get within ten feet of you and knock loudly without you being able to physically see or hear him/her, even in bright moonlight and on noisy, leafy groundcover! It is one thing for a Bigfoot to creep up on you when you are in a tent or non-focused on the surrounding environment; it is entirely another for one to do it when you are being extremely vigilant. From where Allan, JT, Craig, and I were standing, it would have been virtually impossible for a creature who is approximately 7.5 to 8.5 feet tall, weighing approximately 670 to 770 pounds, to creep up without being observed or heard. As you all know, we had a full moon and virtually 360-degree visibility in the woods due to light debris cover. Add to this fact that three of the four of us come from spec-op/tactical backgrounds, and we get very hyper-vigilant when we go into the woods. The fact that this Bigfoot could do this is very significant.

I could easily write ten pages regarding what JT, Craig, Allan, and I learned from that experience. The truth is, so much went on during this event that it is almost impossible to recount all that did happen. On our drive home, JT, Craig, and I tried to put it all in perspective, especially regarding the timing and sequence of all of the events. The sequence is also very important. If I hadn't lightened my pack for the tracking course, which broke my personal protocol, and if I had been actually wearing my jacket rather than just a long-sleeved shirt, I would not have come out of the woods and would have stayed out there all night. I'm sure JT, Craig, and Allan were of the same perspective.

Normally when it comes to knocking and whistling, our protocol is to not knock back so the Bigfoot will not associate such behavior with us. This situation was different. The Bigfoot knew where we were at every step once we entered the woods, and they also came to know that we were trying to interact with them in a non-threatening way; hence their change in behavior.

My opinion on the whole event is that there were two to three, possibly younger Bigfoot near the camp, probably wanting to raid a dumpster. We were sitting around the camp, and they wanted us to leave; hence the first knocks we heard. The rapid-fire five knocks we later heard, I think, were from an older Bigfoot trying to call the younger ones back in. Once they realized we were not a threat and that we were trying to communicate with them (which I'm sure no human in that area has ever done before), they got interested in us in a different way. This is all conjecture, but it is plausible to me, based upon the whole experience of that night, accompanied with the track and sign seen the following morning.

Remember, no one knows everything about these creatures. We think we know a lot about them, but the truth is, we know very little about them. Most of the Bigfoot beliefs we hold true and dear are largely anecdotal at best. A research team must be willing to think outside the box and attempt new ideas and concepts.

# 33. UFO Connection

The standard viewpoint on a connection between UFOs and Bigfoot is that it is nonsense. Researchers say Bigfoot is a flesh-and-blood creature and UFOs are a fantasy. Over the years, some researchers have changed their outlook on the UFO situation. In this book I give the reader the background of a possible flesh-and-blood creature, something that would make things much simpler, even in my case. However, with the critical information coming in, a different explanation seems to be required. Sasquatch phenomena have occurred that have led some to accept the possibility of an off-planet connection. As we saw, the aboriginal community is divided on the issue of where the Sasquatch live, whether underground, on the surface, above the ground, or in some other dimension. Certainly if this is difficult for them to discern, it is even more so for average souls looking for answers. Here are some others who have thoughts on the connection between UFOs and Sasquatch.

During my extended talks with David Cleaver (which were discussed earlier), I asked a couple of questions about his UFO experience and the UFO/Bigfoot situation. Here are his thoughts:

> I did have a UFO encounter one time, with three of my best friends. It lasted forty-five minutes. We watched the craft in a low orbit, making extreme maneuvers, and at amazing speed. We figured it was going from satellite to satellite, as it stopped frequently. The event ended when the object shot back into space at a mind-blowing speed and looked like a shooting star in reverse, leaving a trail. But the most amazing thing was what happened a split second after it shot off. Something from Earth shot at it with

> some type of greenish laser beam and just missed it! Wow! It was one of the more amazing things I have ever seen!
>
> Well, after thinking hard and applying logical thought to the question of Bigfoot vs. Aliens, the key word here is need. Who needs who? I would think the Bigfoot would be protected by the aliens, as they were the original breeding stock for the human race experiment and are needed to continue the experiment. Also, the Bible makes reference to the "giants on Earth," and I have always thought that document was a teaser to so much history. Yeah, I know. I stayed up thinking about that one, but it's the only thing that makes sense, unless they eat them, which I doubt.
>
> Still, I am not really onboard for the UFO/alien connection. However, as explained in the previous email, I did offer what my take on it would be if I had to give a possible reason for it. It's just that any Bigfooters that have gone down that road have suffered a loss in their credibility. The same is true for paranormal explanations. I have discussed the paranormal aspect concerning Bigfoot with some of my buddies, but am just not there. With my encounters, nothing that has happened would persuade me otherwise. I am just not comfortable with explaining a mystery with a bigger mystery.

David has had an interesting life, full of surprises, and when asked for more details about his UFO encounter, he had this to report:

> This happened in the fall of 1974 and was a memorable oddity. My best buddy and I were driving too fast down dirt country roads, definitely out in the middle of nowhere. We ended up off the road over a small cliff, wedged between two trees. Yup, we were very lucky to be alive. Anyway, we knew we were close to our other friend's multi-thousand-acre working ranch, which had a radio tower with a strobe light on top, back on the "south forty," as we used to call it. We located the tower in the distance and took off through the woods. This was around two a.m. We got lost and turned around, disoriented, but finally emerged into a small clearing, and there sat a perfect thirty-some-foot diameter circle. In the circle were two machines the likes of which I have never seen before or since. One was about dishwasher size and the other about half that size. Both of these contraptions were

> some kind of polished metal, with no seams, screw, bolts, or welds anywhere. The panel on top had no buttons, dials, or anything to be messed with. It had several small screens with multicolored lights. Thinking about it now, I would guess it was a touch-screen, but we didn't touch it, as it was on and making a low humming noise. If that wasn't weird enough, the markings — or hieroglyphs, for lack of a better word — were in several places, made of the same metal in raised relief, again with no seams. The letters had no attachment points and appeared to be part of the machine.
>
> This totally freaked us out, and we left post haste. I still wonder what in the heck that equipment was, what it was for, and what in the hell it was doing in the middle of nowhere.
>
> I am still best buddies with that friend, and we have talked about this shared experience many times over the years. To this day, neither of us has ever seen anything like it, and it truly falls in the realm of science fiction… just weird!

And that's David's viewpoint, yet another voice to some of the growing uncertainties facing us. There are also many authors who have exposed the truth or hinted at it in one way or another — actually far too many to mention here. The UFO thing means something, yet nothing particularly good, at least from my perspective. I interviewed a small number of carefully screened abductees. Something had happened to these people, and a distinct fear lingered. It was as if they were cursed. The least I could do for them was to keep them under the cloak of anonymity. These were some of the luckier ones, as they could still reason like many of us. Others can no longer really express their concerns, objections, and abhorrence of what ails them. These poor souls are the lost voices, inhabitants of mental institutions.

Thousands of individuals are influenced by the UFO phenomenon. In some cases, the presence leads its host like a dog, as if it is man's best friend. In others, it inflicts injuries and performs cruel experiments on human beings the way human beings do on lesser creatures. Believe it or not, this exact sort of thing is on the Sasquatch cutting edge: real-life dangers await those who dare to wander to the outer boundaries. Do not open your mind to this craving. When one travels this route, the mind is often altered. The New Age Sasquatch waits for you there.

Other things seemed to add up when it came to paranormal teachings and Bigfoot inclusion in the flying saucer continuum. Stephen Yulish was well grounded in the Gospel, and he wrote many articles on the subject of extraterrestrials. I highlighted the idea that the Sasquatch question could be contaminated by weaving all of these things together. Yulish had the following to say about the evolving alien argument. He also offered this opinion on the direction I was taking on the investigation:

> Several people have expressed to me their bewilderment over me writing articles for *UFO Digest*. While most of my articles do discuss UFOs, they rightly say that my articles overwhelmingly tend to end up discussing the Bible. That is a fair assessment, because I sincerely believe that extraterrestrials are not aliens from another planet or galaxy, but are, instead, fallen angels here to undertake a diabolical plan that is more sinister than any alien invasion.
>
> Glen, your insights and spiritual concerns seem well founded to me. Keep up the good work.

Another truth-seeker out there, Thomas Minderle, Tom of Montalk.net, is an individual who combines UFO thoughts with demonic aspects of the problem. He also recognized that things are changing in Bigfoot research in a dramatic fashion and had this to say:

> I am in complete agreement that the Sasquatch is not just a sophisticated bipedal, gorilla-like animal native to certain mountains and woods. There is a supernatural component to them. No corpse has ever been recovered. And, like you said, footprints disappear into thin air.
>
> Three possibilities come to my mind: 1) They are mere projections or illusions created by nonhuman trickster entities (the "ultraterrestrials" hypothesized by John Keel in *The Mothman Prophecies*); 2) They are actual physical beings but have developed the ability to dematerialize, teleport, become invisible, etc. (like chameleons changing color, but on a much more sophisticated level); or 3) They are physical, but not native to Earth and under the ownership and direction of other entities that use them, move them, and disappear them as needed.
>
> The third possibility is supported by abduction/UFO accounts, where the Sasquatch has been seen during some abductions, manhandling abductees. For instance, someone gets abducted while going for a walk in the woods; they get paralyzed by some force field, and then a Sasquatch carries them into a

craft where other beings like reptilians, mantis, or greys await to carry out the finer details of the abduction. As far as the Sasquatch goes, if physical beings like ourselves can be teleported into and out of alien crafts, then aliens (whoever they may be) could do likewise with physical servants in their keep. No abduction account, to my knowledge, has ever portrayed Sasquatch in a position of authority. They are always lower-class servants, used mainly for brute physical tasks.

Now, in my own experience, there is a definite difference between demons and aliens, although it appears to me that negative aliens (including those pretending to be good guys) are either possessed by demons or ultimately work in their service. The difference is that demons are more spirit-like, non-physical, non-technological, opportunistic, like sharks feeding on a person and trying to possess them; whereas true aliens tend to be more patient, strategic, and far more likely to use actual technology, whose reason for operation you can sleuth out; whereas trickster/demonic entities rarely do that, and if they do, it's strictly sham props psychically projected that don't have any substance to them or logic to their operation.

But for all practical purposes, negative aliens and demons are both bad news, and both operate along the lines of spiritual warfare when ensnaring and manipulating their targets. Spiritual warfare works against both of them as well, but that doesn't mean aliens and demons are identical, in my view — more like demons have both feet in the non-physical realms, and aliens have one foot there and one foot in the physical. Thus, with both sharing operation/presence in the nonphysical, spiritual warfare is used by, and can be used against, both of them.

In fact, that is the great secret being hidden in the alien/UFO phenomenon: It has a spiritual/demonic component and spiritual methods can be used to combat them, because they're not 100 percent 3D physical beings like us. I'd say aliens are amphibious, some mostly like us, and some mostly like demons, some perhaps even resembling angels, and everything in between. It's a spectrum, not a black and white thing. After all, even with people you have a spectrum: Some are more angelic/Christ-like, others are more demonic in their predatory ways, and everything in between.

The UFO/Bigfoot relationship definitely has researchers split, and it will likely continue to do so. It's hard to find a compromise.

Over the years, native Pennsylvanian Stan Gordon took part in the UFO investigative process, including the search for strange creatures. Stan had quite a dossier with over forty-five years of investigation. He's documented reports galore about a large, haired, bipedal giant seen in the vicinity of UFO cases. He had this to say:

> It is good hearing from you. I am well aware of the Bigfoot issues you are describing. When I investigated the massive 1973-74 wave of Bigfoot and UFO cases here in Pennsylvania, many similar events turned up. There were cases of disappearing footprints and even a case of a woman shooting a creature at very close range; it vanished right in front of her. I also investigated some of the best-documented incidents at that time, where UFOs and Bigfoot were seen at the same time and place. What direct connection, if any, between the two anomalies is still open for speculation?
>
> Over the years, I have investigated multitudes of Bigfoot and UFO cases in this state. There may well be more to the Bigfoot phenomena than many researchers may want to believe. I have two new books which I hope to have in print during the next few months. The second book, *Silent Invasion: The PA UFO-Bigfoot Casebook*, focuses on the events of 1973 and 1974. Please keep me updated with your findings.

To demonstrate that there really is a danger in investigating strange happenings, I found out that there have been over 200 deaths in association with UFO research since the late 1940s, many falling into the suspicious deaths category. The Bigfoot issue, either by itself or tied into the UFO phenomenon, doesn't seem to share this cruel fate, as these researchers seem relatively intact and lead normal lives. A couple from the UFO group spoke of the government being interested in the extraterrestrial work. The Bigfoot, on the other hand, poses no real risk to national security, threat to facilities, or extreme radical behavior by followers. UFO cults such as the one led by Billy Meier are a prime example of demon possession and spiritual forces intervention. On the casual end of things, general fibbing is among the list of *faux pas*. Over the last few years, the kinds of things we see in paranormal intervention have also been seen in the Sasquatch area.

# 34. Other Voices

Many other people have spoken of Bigfoot, offering ideas beyond the idea that they are physical creatures. In this chapter I want to share some of those views with you.

One point that needs to be made is that there is more going on than some creature in the woods. UFOs and spiritual mediums are playing their part, too. What I found was that there was certainly intelligence behind everything, but it was not the expected form of intelligence. Messages began coming in from various regions of the world and from numerous individuals who had no connection whatsoever to each other. The UFO contactees received identical communications, similar to the way channeling mediums and other practitioners of black arts and techniques do. These were not swindling fortunetellers and con artists who were only interested in making a profit. I say this because I believe satanic forces work through these kinds of spiritualists in an attempt to pawn off falsehoods as truths, burying flea market gypsies in a quagmire of confusion. They have no idea they are being used. The more naïve and gullible man becomes, the braver these fallen spirits get.

Some spiritual mediums claim they can channel the spirit of the Sasquatch, a creature who can give wisdom and direction. Some shamans use soul retrieval techniques, though this is not a new art at all. Now, once the laughing by some dies down, we are left with present dangers displayed by the occult. It isn't a lie; spirits are indeed waiting and ready to be communicated with. That's a given, and the Sasquatch phenomenon is a new tool on the market. The reason I mention the contemporary medicine men or women is because, at times, they do include the typical American Bigfoot as the target, since the creature resides on the plane needed for gathering the information.

## Star People

We looked at the Star People from a Native American perspective. Here is what is said about them from a white perspective. A very well known paranormal researcher, Kewaunee Lapseritis, wrote in his book, *The Psychic Sasquatch*, of the teachings of the spirits of agnosticism. Of course the man wouldn't know this, because of the craftiness in giving mankind the falsehoods needed to further those planted many centuries ago. The well-educated individual would ask a Sasquatch, "What about the likes of Adam and Eve?" The creature would respond, "I know nothing about Adam and Eve." The Sasquatch would say, "If you want to find out about them, you'll have to wait and ask the Star People. They are the ones who brought them."

A woman who escaped a UFO European sect, even though she feared vengeful retaliatory measures, wanted it known that the Bigfoot were spoken of within the specialized circle. The woman also talked about the sect's connection with a Star Person, a female extraterrestrial entity named Semjase. The human chronicler wished to remain anonymous when she told me what the Star Person said.

> Mr. Boulier, a pleasure to meet your acquaintance. Involvement with a "stem" of the gathering over a number of months, and not to dull you with all the documented details and also forgeries that have made their rounds, there was mention, however, of the ET Semjase invoking change to religious order on this planet standing alone in the crux. The other worlds offered no such thing. She had spoken with a renowned Earth world contactee. The man was told that under the Universal Laws of Creation, the original Ten Commandments were now overturned, an interplanetary substitution or wholeness put in place to complete instruction. Man had evolved.
>
> A long while after my departure, I have heard numerous similarities to a creature's existence from a number of channels that weren't a part of our interrelations.
>
> From a human standpoint, a gentle-minded Stan Johnson did memoirs of his life with such creatures. He wrote, "Sasquatch are both interdimensional and psychic. They know our intentions, and they can slip into an invisible state. They work with ETs and serve as their scouts."

If you key *paranormal Sasquatch* and *paranormal Bigfoot* into your browser, you will turn up an interesting bit of information. At the time when I last performed these searches, they returned a combined total of 6,210,000 results. Filter through them at your leisure, and you could receive an extensive paranormal education that you never could have gotten fifteen years ago.

These are some of the changes happening with the UFO/Sasquatch idea in modern-day thinking. The statements and teachings are very plain in their meaning — plain and dangerous. It would make the Star People, literally, gods.

## Joan Ocean

Researcher extraordinaire Joan Ocean has a master's of science in counseling psychology. She is a psychologist, shaman, and scientist, and a woman with many talents. Her specialty involves whales and dolphins, and she has been in the spotlight in certain circles for many years. She is one who you could say has met the Sasquatch halfway, as she claims the creatures have communicated with her at different levels. The Sasquatch refer to her as "Water Woman." Change and enlightenment are continuous processes, and the list of researchers in various fields following the Sasquatch is constantly growing. The holistic Sasquatch seems to be openly exposing itself to the world — to anyone who will listen attentively.

In her research based in the Hawaiian Islands, Joan has effectively communicated with whales and dolphins, and she is regarded as an authority on dolphin tel-empathic communication. She has started to apply similar techniques to the more mysterious Sasquatch. Below are excerpts from her involvement with the creature that discuss its connection with the Star Nations. There is more information about the creature on her website at www.joanocean.com.

> On many occasions, we have noticed that our Sasquatch friends appear see-through and seemingly vanish instantaneously. The Ancient Ones can dematerialize. They are able to move freely between our three-dimensional, linear reality, and their world, which exists outside our conventional laws of physics, in the expanded world of quantum physics. In the physical world we know, they make shelters, forage for food, walk long distances, eat, sleep, defecate, communicate, and make loud

growling sounds. In their extra-dimensional world, life is different. Their bodies are of a different frequency; therefore, their needs are not the same as when in a three-dimensional, physical environment.

In their own words, they have confirmed that they use the refined frequencies available to them to travel to distant places; they call it dream-walking. They do, however, have limitations with respect to distance and location. For example, they told me they cannot dream-walk to Hawaii from the mainland; it is too far away. The particular group of Wise Ones that I have been introduced to can explain what they have communicated to me in writing.

We settle into a deep meditation for contact, proceeding with the help of a medicine woman, to enter the portal. We experience the swirling energy, starting at our feet and slowly moving up, enveloping our bodies. At some point, as each of us is ready, we leave the physical realm and travel with two Wise Ones through the Sometime Place into their alternate reality. There we meet with the medicine woman, and she is happy to welcome us. I ask to see the future of earthling and Sasquatch contact. I then experience a round room with many Ancient Ones, Sasquatch, and Earth people, all of whom appear gentle and wise. We are learning many things from these advanced Sasquatch people: how to live in splendor in their forests and fourth-dimensional homes. They know about all the life forms in the woods. Every growing herb in the forest has a different nourishing and healing characteristic. We are even learning about herbs for dream-walking, dematerializing, shape-shifting, spirit-enhancing, voice- and sound-projecting, and entering other realities. They seem to recommend mind-enhancing herbs for out-of-body experiences as a preparation for entering the invisible worlds.

We had two very powerful weeks in the forest with our friends, the Wise Ones and their cousins the Sasquatch in April of 2008. Some of the interactions stretch believability, in that the messages we receive come to us via unusual, shamanistic revelations using animals, trees, bouncing lights, visions, and of course telepathy. These messages are transmitted anytime of day or night.

It is understood that following (uncovering) these hidden facts will lead to a greater understanding of the Sasquatch/Wise Ones civilization, in preparation for sharing their extraordinary culture with the human race, and that it would bring to light some of the hidden truths about the origins of humans and our relationship to each other and to other Star Nations.

Sitting around the fire looking into the woods, I see two large trees standing alongside each other, twelve feet apart. In the dark they look like pillars of a doorway. Between them appears an entry to another world. I am reminded of points of contact that open to our world from other dimensions. It relates to a fundamental knowledge of the Earth's subtle energies — what the Hopi call Sipapuni, a place for accessing spaces unimaginable to most people. The Native American people of the Northwest believe Sasquatch can pass from one world to another. They apparently know how to access the portals beyond what we think of as normal space-time parameters. This is linked to their understanding of natural subtle energies in and around the Earth. (And even now, in the new science, the existence of other dimensions of space is understood as mathematically and theoretically possible, and more people continue to explore these realms.)

## Spirit of Seatco

While addressing this subject at the paranormal level, I happened upon Bobbie Short's Bigfoot Encounters website once again. Researcher Henry Franzoni's book, *In the Spirit of Seatco,* covers much about what may actually be going on, though some would suggest Franzoni pushes the envelope. The author addresses Native ideals and spirituality, things within their belief system.

Researcher and author Thom Powell published a book review of Franzoni's controversial work on the Bigfoot Encounters website. Alicia, a thoughtful individual I connected with through the Bigfoot Forums, linked me to Mr. Powell's email address. I had the chance to contact Thom about our joint findings as researchers, regarding these changes. The following is an excerpt from Mr. Powell's March 2009 Bigfoot Encounters book review of Mr. Franzoni's book:

> … the book Henry has written is immensely important. In it, Henry posits a bona fide scientific theory for what is behind the

Sasquatch phenomenon, and he invokes multiple lines of evidence to support his unified explanation for most, if not all, of the puzzling observations and experiences that are sometimes reported in association with the Sasquatch phenomenon.

Most books on the Bigfoot subject attempt to explain the phenomenon as a race or species of animals, and they do so by ignoring or denying the more mysterious and contradictory aspects of these enigmatic beings. A few books, like mine, acknowledge the mysterious aspects of the subject but utterly fail to explain them because the author (for example, moi) lacks the depth and breadth in their scientific background that might enable them to make sense of the more vexing aspects of the Sasquatch beings.

Despite his disdain for much of that which passes for "Bigfoot research," Henry establishes his street credibility in this realm. He then does one better by shining considerable light on Native American perspectives. Some Indians may be horrified to learn that Henry provides more Indian information on the Sasquatch than has ever before been handed over to us prying palefaces. Henry draws deeply from his secret well of professional and personal contacts in various North American tribes. Then, Henry assimilates information from his equally deep scientific background. He manifests an understanding of a broad array of relevant scientific principles, especially general physics and electrical engineering, to explain and unify virtually all the loose ends that frazzle the minds of those of us who struggle to fathom the true nature of the Sasquatch phenomenon.

Here is an example: Most authors offhandedly dismiss such notions as the "disappearing Bigfoots" for fear of relegating their work to the pile of new age baloney books. Though my book, *The Locals*, acknowledges the reality of such ideas as "disappearing Bigfoots," I, in no way, offer an explanation for this strange matter. I do identify this particular mystery as essentially an energy problem: Where and how could such beings possibly get the energy to perform such energy-intensive feats?

Henry has the answer. He provides a theoretical solution to this energy problem by stitching together a few complex scientific principles, sighting report data, and place name data. No one else on Earth could have done this, because no one else anywhere ever could do this. Henry's combination of field experience, broad-spectrum scientific knowledge, and access to Native American culture has no match; nor does his keen insight that interprets the data and formulates the appropriate interpretation.

Which brings me to the one thing about Henry Franzoni's book I like best and one thing I like the least. I really like the fact that Henry's book makes my book, *The Locals*, look timid. I like that because the most common criticism of my book is that it goes too far in giving serious consideration to the so-called paranormal possibilities surrounding the Bigfoot phenomenon. Those who hold that view of my book would do well to avoid all contact with *In the Spirit of Seatco*. Henry's book vindicates my position by going not just light-years, but parsecs farther in his serious treatment of the oft-pooh-poohed paranormal possibilities. It gets me off the hook, but at a certain cost: it also renders my book obsolete.

Which brings me to the thing I like least about Henry's book: It's the last word on the subject. Not only does it render previous Bigfoot books obsolete, but it may also eliminate the need for any future books on the subject. What bothers me is just that, that it's the last book on the Sasquatch subject that one will ever need to buy. Damn! I like buying Bigfoot books. I like going camping and searching for Bigfoot.

*In the Spirit of Seatco* is more dense with information and profound in its conclusions than any other book that has ever been written on this subject and likely any other book that will ever be written. That's what bothers me. After Henry's book, there's nothing left to say. There is no more searching for tracks, hair samples, or Bigfoot hideouts — no more sighting reports to study. Henry's book gives us the only answers we'll ever get. It's over. Time to get a new hobby. Bigfoot mystery: Case closed. [TP1]

## John Keel

In his book *Jadoo*, John Keel explained mysteries he was trying to uncover in the Far East. One such find had the author traveling to meet with Sherpa Tensing Norgay, of Everest fame. The expert climber spoke of the Abominable Snowman (Yeti) with John Keel in the 1950s, and it was in India's Sikkim State, nestled nicely in the Himalayas, where Keel was shown huge tracks of what was believed to be a Yeti. He also heard the shriek of the supposed monstrous beast.

There was much more to John Keel than a discussion of Yetis, though. His research, like mine, led down many strange pathways.

In my initial email to Thom Powell, I asked for his ideas regarding the spiritual aspects of Sasquatch, and I wanted to know what he'd experienced in the field or heard through the grapevine. I also shared my findings and what was materializing on my end. Truly, it wasn't pretty. His reply to me was as follows:

> Your message was most interesting and indeed profound. Further, I have no argument with anything you say. In fact, I think you are on the right track. I might suggest you look for a copy of *The Mothman Prophecies* by John Keel, which will elucidate you into the nature of beings and phenomena we define as "paranormal."
>
> It is true that a few more researchers are coming around to more spiritual interpretations of the phenomenon, but I still think you will find that your point of view will not sell a large number of copies because it is so "unscientific." But one of John Keel's ideas is that you find what you are looking for in paranormal investigations. Since most folks who pursue it are scientifically minded, they find scientific things, but those with a spiritual or paranormal view find support for their inclinations in their investigations.

I did not know much about author John Keel at the time. I had heard of the thought-provoking *The Mothman Prophecies*, but I'd never really been interested enough to know who had written it or why. When I took the time to learn about the flamboyant thinker and writer, I uncovered Mr. Keel's material on UFO/extraterrestrial existence, twists and turns that fueled the controversy of satanic forces and their continued heated barrage on mankind.

Keel had his own uncertainties, and much criticism came his way, but he was onto the answer. After my deliberation on the paranormal Bigfoot issue with Thom Powell, I received the following from him:

> In my view, the various views do begin to morph together, and the Sasquatch phenomenon also begins to blend with other phenomenon such as UFOs, especially after one begins to sus-

pect that it does. Classic John Keel. Also, according to Keel, a paranormal phenomenon also has one other bizarre aspect to it: The phenomenon changes in response to your studying it. They begin to know that you are studying them, and they begin to alternately throw you some crumbs and throw up roadblocks. You are correct about one thing: They will not be found. But you can let them find you, if you dare. It sounds like you already have. It may be that they are checking out gardens, as I have seen a fair amount of that, but it may also be that they are checking you out. I regret that I may be putting a chill on your spine, but it must be considered, don't you think?

Nor do I have any problem with talk of demons and the like. Personally, I see biblical descriptions of angels and demons as referencing the real but vexing phenomena that seemed to originate from above (angels aka space-based UFOs) and the phenomena from "below," meaning the terrestrial- and sub-terrestrial-based Sasquatch (demon, mountain devil) phenomena. The two interact, though not always amicably. Some say the Sasquatch are subservient to the space based beings. Others say they are one and the same.

Since you are spiritually inclined, you might even try communicating, through prayer, with the subjects of your inquiry. I think it can be done, although anything you get from such an avenue will only make your writings more unscientific and marginalized. In any case, you may find that you have to struggle to find a publisher, in which case I would strongly encourage you, as I encouraged Henry, to self-publish. He was very happy with that course of action because he retained total control of his material, distribution, and, of course, monetary return.

Meanwhile, keep talking to the indigenous people if they will open up to you. That is quite a trove of information. This isn't the best time to do things outdoors, but also work some of your areas with an eye toward leaving little signals to the forest people or whatever they are. Soon, you will start finding the subtle sticks and stones and feathers and other things they leave for you to find. They may have already entered your world and have been dialoging with you in ways you may or may not be aware of. As John Keel says, communication is possible, and if you have been studying them, they most certainly know who you are and where you live.

And finally, you might want to make careful note of the precise places where these tracks abruptly ended. These locations may represent places where some kind of portal or something sometimes opens. Look for other indications of strange events at these locations, specifically weird behavior of compasses and other indications of magnetic anomaly, as well as other strange events in the immediate vicinity, including mound structures, groundwater, and geologic oddity. This field of study is wide open, but it seems to require substantial departure from established scientific method if progress is to be made in understanding it. You have to formulate your own hunches and see if any of it correlates with the findings and hunches of others. Very unscientific, to be sure, but you are way out on the scientific fringe already. In truth, you can always back up and test an idea or two scientifically at a later date. First, you have to assemble a paradigm that provides hooks in the right places for you to hang the findings of your fieldwork upon, and that need not be an utterly scientific process. Follow your hunches, assemble a picture, and then scientifically test it at some later date, once your picture has taken a coherent shape.

That's about the best help I can offer. Not sure what else I can give you that you can use for your tome, but if any of this seems useful, it's all yours. I hope this helps more than it serves to add confusion.

Researcher Thom Powell spoke of confusion in his final comments. I couldn't agree more. In his book, *UFOs: Operation Trojan Horse,* Keel initially supported the UFO phenomenon. This changed over the course of a year, as evidence came in otherwise that supported the idea of something else at work here.

The war raged on as I gathered information on the subject of supposed extraterrestrial presence, never mind including the Bigfoot creature at first. I promised myself that I wouldn't get involved in these written battles, these wars of words, these forum fiascos or even death threats or anything else that lacks constructiveness. There was too much floating around to even put a dent into it. It didn't take long for me to realize in my research that there have to be reports of at least 10,000 alien species, everything from reptilians to short trolls waiting on the outer rim. The list was growing, and Bigfoot had become a major addition to that catalog. There are nearly as many opinions as alien species! One night, I bellied up to my computer and typed "UFO-Bigfoot Cases" on the Web. The number of stories that came up under this topic was nearly unimaginable. These battles cannot be won or resolutions reached, so really, I am just another voice, telling you of the things that cross my desk. Some of the UFO faithful call this "disinformation," but no matter what you call it, the debate rages on and likely will for a long time to come.

John Keel passed away in July of 2009, but I ran across an old friend of his, researcher and author Loren Coleman. Mr. Colman gave me permission to use segments and tidbits about *The Mothman Prophecies* author. He also stipulated that a disclaimer should be in place, since quoting someone does not necessarily mean the cited author agrees with one's theories or conclusions. I understood completely; when it comes to the Bigfoot/UFO issue, it's every researcher for him- or herself. Let me state clearly that Loren does not agree with my interpretation of Bigfoot evidence. Loren had the following to say about Keel's situation:

> I certainly do not feel, as you seem to, that John Keel had any novel insight into the reality of any phenomena he wrote about — and my passage, in many ways, was written to show that he distanced himself from the mainstream thinking evident in ufology.

That said, Loren wrote the following about Keel on the *Cryptomundo* website:

> It was Keel's second book, *UFOs: Operation Trojan Horse* (1970), that alerted the general public that many aspects of contemporary UFO reports, including humanoid encounters, often paralleled certain ancient folklore and religious encounters. Keel also argued that there is a direct relationship between UFOs and elemental phenomena. Keel informed me often that he did not consider himself a ufologist, but a demonologist.
>
> "Ufology is just another name for demonology," John Keel told me.
>
> As Keel himself wrote, "I abandoned the extraterrestrial hypothesis in 1967, when my own field investigators disclosed an astonishing overlap between psychic phenomena and UFOs. The objects and apparitions do not necessarily originate on

> another planet and may not even exist as permanent constructions of matter." [JAK1]
>
> In *UFOs: Operation Trojan Horse* (1970), Keel argued that a non-human or spiritual intelligence source has staged whole events over a long period of time in order to propagate and reinforce certain erroneous belief systems (mirroring Vallée.) Keel conjectured that ultimately all anomalies, such as fairies, 1897 mystery airships, 1930s phantom aeroplanes, mystery helicopters, creatures, poltergeists, balls of light, and UFOs are a cover for the real phenomenon. [LCJK1]

I also consulted with another American researcher and author, Jerome (Jerry) Clark, about John Keel's changing outlook on the extraterrestrial hypothesis, and he kindly responded. According to Clark's book, *The UFO Encyclopedia, Volume 1: UFOs in the 1980s,* John Keel was

> … a radical theorist who believes that UFOs are "ultraterrestrial" rather than extraterrestrial. By that he means they are shape-changing phenomena from another order of existence. These ultraterrestrials are basically hostile to, or at least contemptuous of, human beings and manipulate them in various ways for example by staging "miracles" which inspire unfounded religious beliefs. Ultraterrestrials and their minions may manifest as monsters, space people, ghosts, and other paranormal entities. [JC1]

## Nick Redfern

Author and investigator Nick Redfern had the following to say about the paranormal aspects. While he is a British writer, he is also a Texan. Nick has gotten his hands dirty on a quest to solve many of the mysteries of our planet. He has researched thousands of documents formerly labeled "Classified" by the Royal Air Force in England. The investigator's list of published books on controversial matters is extensive, and he had this to say about Bigfoot:

> Like a lot of people within cryptozoology, I first got deeply interested in the subject as a teenager, although I had visited Loch Ness with my parents when I was about five years old. Certainly, Bigfoot was one of those crypto-creatures that really

fascinated me. As a kid, things were very much black and white: Bigfoot was just an unclassified type of ape, or maybe a surviving relic population of the presumed-extinct giant ape known as *Gigantopithecus*. However, as time progressed, as I uncovered more data, and as I spoke to more and more witnesses, I came to believe that something stranger was afoot. Bigfoot wasn't just elusive; Bigfoot was too elusive. I spoke with people who had been tracking Bigfoot prints in the snow, and they would just stop — as if the creature had vanished into thin air. I interviewed several people who said they saw Bigfoot while driving their cars late at night in the woods; and as the creature — or creatures — got near to them, the engines and headlamps of their vehicles would fail. Others felt Bigfoot possessed skills and senses that far exceeded those of the human race, such as infrasound, possibly to warn off people. There are numerous reports of people trying to shoot Bigfoot, and even of the bullets hitting the creatures, always with no lasting effect. I have investigated a lot of Bigfoot reports in Britain, where I'm originally from; but clearly Britain is way too small and densely populated to support thriving colonies of seven-foot-tall apes. Still, people do see them in Britain, very often near ancient stone circles, interestingly enough. So, my view today is that Bigfoot is far more or paradoxically far less than a flesh-and-blood animal. People have varying degrees of opinion as to what the paranormal may be, but I firmly believe Bigfoot is indeed a paranormal entity rather than simply an unknown giant ape. I've come across quite a few high-strangeness cases involving Bigfoot and even cases where the creatures seemed flat and one-dimensional — like a shadow in the shape of a giant ape.

## Church of Scientology

I checked also with the Church of Scientology. A member of the U.S. branch contacted me in 2010. I had made it a practice to place my name on the World Wide Web at almost every level of society, as mentioned before, to gather what I could on the Sasquatch phenomenon. Once I had the opportunity to sift through the feedback I received, I was able to find out what some of the existing beliefs are.

Scientology believes that a true member will be an Operating Thetan, an exceptional spiritual being with the universe as his or her oyster. My input into this was that man was, again, a cosmos astronaut destined for bigger and better things and the Bigfoot is merely a tagalong who periodically helps, an intervenient. I found that not everyone knows or believes this. After the discussion with the free associate, I contacted the Church of Scientology and asked them about the Bigfoot. The answer, which came from someone who merely signed it with C., was very short:

> Thanks for asking. I am sorry, but I can't give you any information on this. I am sure he fits in somewhere. Might have to do some investigation somewhere else!

My initial contact had told me this is how my research from this end would end up.

In the world of Bigfoot, many researchers are becoming frustrated. Researcher Autumn Williams was a prime example of this, throwing in the Sasquatch towel. The feisty woman laid it on the line with her 2010 book, *Enoch: A Bigfoot Story*, but frustration continues to rear its ugly face, and "Any day now… any day now… " has been echoing out of the woods for years. Desperation is lurking behind many a tree.

# 35. Hairy Man Pictograph

For those who haven't heard about the Hairy Man pictographs, we'll start off by identifying them. The colorful artworks are on the eastern side of California, a formation called Painted Rock, also referred to as CA-Tul-19. In this area, the Yokut People (possibly the medicine man or a shaman) sketched drawings of a Bigfoot family. There are two Painted Rock locations, but this particular one is situated up from Porterville, on the Tule River Indian Reservation.

I wondered if the pictographs at Painted Rock might have represented the giant bears that practically owned the area. I also had to consider that the artists who were drawing them might not possess sound minds. Let's take a closer look at this, as I've got this placed in the "spiritual" section for good reason.

Over what I would consider to be a short period of time, information began to filter in to me about the Tule River Painted Rock above and beyond Porterville, California. Some of the informants had been to the location, and others had not, but the consensus was that the pictographs were drawings of *Ursus arctos horribilis* (the dreaded and unpredictable grizzly). Following is what some of these individuals had to say:

> I was warned as a child and told as an adult — never to visit the Painted Rock sites at night or during the darkness, because spirits reside there. Never did hear about this Hairy Man. (Native Joe)

> It has nothing to do with Bigfoot. The pictographs are found in what was Yokut territory in California. I don't believe the Yokut Tribe had any mythological figures that could be considered Bigfoot, though I am no expert on this. The figures are

**Figure 49: The Painted Rock known as CA-Tul-19 may show a family of Bigfoot creatures depicted by the Yokut People. This drawing was done by Garrick Mallery. [GM1]**

> probably bears or other animals. Many California tribes had a bear shaman cult. (Jon Harmon)

A third short note on this controversial subject was from author David S. Whitley, who has gone toe-to-toe with others on a number of issues. His books include, *Cave Paintings and the Human Spirit*, *The Rock Art of California*, and *Introduction to Rock Art Research.*

> The figure is a grizzly. The modern myth about Bigfoot was introduced into the region in the 1970s by a white schoolteacher (I think it was) who moved down from northern California and wrote a short, popular book with that theme.

Carl Bjork is a retired forest ranger/law enforcement/battalion chief, with thirty-two years of service in California. In the 1970s and 1980s, back when we faced Sasquatch coming from the woods, Mr. Bjork was busy helping to develop crime scene investigation techniques and serial criminal profiling. He had something interesting to say about our area of study:

> At the Carrizo Plain Painted Rock, there are similar pictographs that look like the Hairy Man paintings at the Tule River site. I will send you a couple photos. The Carrizo paintings are Chumash, cousins to the Yokuts. The Chumash tell that the motifs are grizzly bear clan symbols, not Hairy Man.
>
> The Yokut live mostly on the east side of the valley, at the base of the Sierra Mountains. When the first Spanish came into the area, they reported hundreds of grizzly bears living in the valley, usually near the ponds and marshes that covered the valley floor, before the building of the dams. So it would be not unusual to find pictographs depicting something that looks like a bear or Bigfoot. You will find that most bedrock mortars are located high on top of large boulders and rock outcroppings; bears were a constant danger, so they needed a high place to watch for bears. If I were to hunt for Bigfoot, I would look for ancient evidence over in the Coast Range that runs between the valley and the coast. Not many folks live in the Coast Range, except in the Bay Area.
>
> I have found evidence of what we call giants in the Great Basin area. Folks have told me there have been found skeletal remains of people who were seven to ten feet tall. Also, there are many Paiute and Hopi stories regarding these giants.
>
> I am not into the shamanism thing nor New Age, but I know that rock art sites do have a spiritual connection to something — not sure what it is, but it is there. Many Native American elders have shared much with me regarding the spiritual connection.

When I investigated the sacred land issues, I also posed a general question as to why the Sasquatch was seldom represented in pictograph drawings and rock art throughout North America. A creature so secretive and respected was rarely portrayed on rock. The aboriginal people I spoke with found this fascinating when they thought about it, especially since the Sasquatch was exhibited in the totem and mask carvings, among other things. I asked them if it would have been customary to certain tribes and not to others. Those I spoke with agreed rather wholeheartedly that that was likely the case. It simply depended upon whether an artist wanted the story told in that particular region, and this was based on a variety of priorities. A certain indigenous chief and a native woman had this to add:

> Good question. I have never seen a pictograph or native drawing of the Sasquatch among us, nor has anyone ever talked about it. My grannies used to talk about seeing the Sasquatch many times. Even they never drew pictures of or about them. I will ask more people and let you know. (Aboriginal Chief)

> As far as I know, there is no rock art of the Bigfoot. There are, however, tribal legends about them. Mostly, I hear of the Pitch Woman around here. She was a very large creature who lived in the woods. (Native Woman)

It seems most likely that the pictographs are simple renditions of the bear family, but it's always best to look at both sides of the story.

Researcher Kathy Moskowitz Strain, a feisty woman on a mission, continuously suggested the reality of the Hairy Man in the Tule River region. At a young age, she became interested in the giants and later made a career of working as a forest archaeologist in the Stanislaus National Forest, after receiving her Bachelor of Arts degree in anthropology in 1990. She added a Master of Arts in behavioral sciences, but academic experience aside, Kathy did not take a suit-and-tie approach. She focused instead on prehistoric human ecology.

I touched base with her on Brian Brown's Bigfoot Forums. I informed Kathy that when everything was said and done, I would look at the subject from a spiritual perspective — adding a little something strange into the mix. If those colorful drawings were a souvenir of the Yokut people, a legacy of their knowledge of the monstrous bears that shared the wilderness, that would be a natural way to look at it. If, however, Kathy Moskowitz Strain and Tule tribal elders' reasoning were correct, evidence of Sasquatch is, in fact, written in stone.

One of the first things Kathy mentioned about the Painted Rock pictographs was that she'd also heard about bears. In one case, that involved a shaman dressed up in a bear costume, thus explaining the theory of the *Ursus arctos horribilis*.

As we communicated back and forth a few times, I realized that ultimately it was possible that everyone who was out playing in the dirt or those who were researching from their armchairs were being duped one way or another. I also told Kathy that someone would have to prove me wrong. I was putting all my money on the phenomenon being tampered with by things we couldn't control. I'd spotted the giants years earlier, and decades of carrying those questions around without any verifiable answers meant I had no shame.

The following is what researcher Kathy Moskowitz Strain had to say when I asked her about the people I'd encountered in the Tule area. I was sure that talking with the knowledgeable researcher would prevent me from being tricked by others out to pull my leg, or worse. I would encourage all of you to seek out her writings where you can, as you will likely find them as enlightening as I have.

> Oh, yes, tribal politics are sometimes more messy than the Democrats versus the Republicans. Tribal people don't always share the same beliefs or ideas, and there is often a lot of conflict between older and younger tribal generations. My info came from the tribal elders (who were in their seventies) who were adamant that the pictographs are Bigfoot. That was in 1992, long before the casino came around. The Tule River story, *Bigfoot, The Hairy Man*, was published by Johnstone in 1975. I think the safest view is knowing what the tribe itself promotes.
>
> I know that the tribe believes Bigfoot is both flesh/blood and spiritual. I wrote a short article about those beliefs, but it hasn't been published yet, so I think I'm restricted from sharing it. But in general, there is a lot about the spiritual aspects of Bigfoot that tribal people have shared with me. Still, my own personal belief is that Bigfoot is flesh and blood.

It is possible that Kathy Moskowitz Strain could be right in her assumption, something she wholeheartedly believes in. The woman has done her homework, studied it close at hand, and has done a marvelous job of putting a number of facts together concerning Hairy Man. Nevertheless, the issue of bears just kept popping up as I explored the Painted Rock pictographs story. Both sides have legitimate arguments.

Let's say that the drawings on the rock were placed there by the Native American Yokut hundreds of years ago. I'm not concerned about when it occurred as much as how it was accomplished. It is documented in historical accounts that the Native Americans in the Tule River area in the past have had their say. Now it's my turn to consider if these drawings are, indeed, of the elusive Bigfoot.

Many Native Americans agree with me on one point: The beasts of the field, fowl of the air, and waters teeming with living creatures, were created first by a Creator. The Christian scriptures speak of the same, but things do tend to divide there, as man and woman are created next by God, personally and on His own. Genesis specifically states that man and woman were to rule over all the creatures that moved along the ground — so important a premise that it is mentioned twice within three verses (Genesis 1:26-28). This conflicts with the following information on creation beliefs of the Yokut in regard to the Bigfoot animal/creature.

In the Yokut story Hairy Man is thought to have helped in the creation of both male and female human substance, and is also held responsible for mankind walking upright. The Yokut people on a whole believe they are in existence today because the Bigfoot creature achieved special powers to create. Taking this one step further, one of the Yokut creation stories suggested that the mythological coyote and the Hairy Man had squared off in a race: Mankind was the prize for the victor.

I've been told that the Bigfoot possesses a spiritual nature, some sort of religious structure. The thought of a flesh-and-blood Bigfoot with supernatural powers seemed to be what deceptive spiritual forces wanted us to believe. And let's not forget that man was given the responsibility of exercising authority over every living creature. Bigfoot would have no power over mankind and would never be in a position to religiously instruct the human race; I've heard about the supernatural helpers of the Yokut, Bigfoot notwithstanding. To the average person, this should send up a number of red flags, as there seems to be too much reliance on the Sasquatch creatures giving out knowledge, guidance, and spirituality.

Now, with the Internet being what it is, information crisscrosses the planet at lightning speed. The Yokut (Bigfoot as partial aide to the Creator) tale fell on the desk of a certain Jewish rabbi from New York City, and the well-informed fellow was willing to comment on a couple of issues concerning giants. He did, however, request to remain anonymous, as he has no time for ridicule.

> How you came about reaching me is as strange as this topic, Bigfoot. Reading creation accounts of the American Indians at my leisure, my letter to you, however, will focus strictly on something in comparison to the North American Bigfoot. I know enough that I have heard that the native people use the sacred circle and medicine wheel. I am not ignorant to the facts. In our Torah and Talmud, we also host giants such as the Leviathan, and the Ziz Bird. There are also Jews in India, Nepal, and Tibet who hold stories in the tradition similar to yours. In ways that

you've described the Bigfoot outline, Rabbi Loeb (a Kabbalist scholar) of Prague created what is the Golem — a creature, I suppose, with proportions very similar. If I'm correct, Rabbi Loeb used the four elements of earth, fire, water, and wind in his formula. The Native Americans also use these four to their purpose, whichever it is.

The problem I have with the story is that Jews are forbidden from creating life of any kind. The Jewish people, native populace of the Americas, as well as this Bigfoot, do not breathe life into something becoming a life form. It is told that Rabbi Judah Loeb received divine intervention in response to his persistence and spiritual requests, this to rescue the Jewish people from persecution in the 1600s. There is so much more to the story, its rituals, and moral parameters.

I don't know what to make of this Bigfoot, but I know I have questions for the native people. (If they were created by this Hairy Man and are the chosen ones, who, then, completed the process for others? The other helpers of God? This would make the Bigfoot part of the Supreme Power. Then shouldn't he be open to all?)

The creation stories are fascinating, but we still need to look at the details of the Tule River Painted Rock pictographs, as well as who the painters were.

Most believe it was the shaman or medicine man who made the drawings at Painted Rock. Not just anyone was allowed to roam in and mark their territory. Spiritual battles took place amongst these shamanic medicine men, and evil thoughts were part of that process. Nevertheless, that is not our main focus here. Could the artists in the Hairy Man drawings be credible, or could they have been susceptible to ever-present satanic forces? After all, there have been many questionable practices among groups such as the Yokut. One thing is for certain: The Hairy Man drawings are significant in some way.

The Yokut were in contact with the spirit world through trance and hallucinatory episodes, and that also included the use of the naturally occurring *Datura stramonium* (Jimson weed), as well other mind-altering substances. The Yokut (and a few other tribes, as well) utilized a rain doctor or weather shaman. Putting Bigfoot aside for just a second here, didn't Satan, in the story of Job, use a mighty wind to help kill members of Job's family (Job 1:19)? And just previous to that, fire fell from the sky, burning up his servants and sheep (Job 1:16). Satan accomplished his goals then, and he has also done so via the idea of the weather medicine men of the Yokut. The similarities in means are enough to make me think that the Yokut were demonically influenced while applying paint to create the Hairy Man pictographs on the rock. These men already worked closely with the spirit world and could have been easily manipulated to further a phenomenon in later years, when opportunity presented itself.

Taking this another step further, Alfred L. Kroeber, an anthropologist and author, was considered an expert in the field of cultural anthropology. In his *Handbook of the Indians of California*, the man speaks of the Yokut in a variety of ways, and of great intrigue is their background with the supernatural. A number of authors have written about the Yokut, but Kroeber specifically pointed out spiritual things about them. Either the shamans (medicine men) were magicians working the fable scam, or they were actually calling on the spirits, as they claimed. If they were just everyday storytellers, their credibility would have been zero, attributed to wishful thinking and plain old scare tactics. But members of the aboriginal community tell me these individuals *are* given insight and guidance into the spirit world. I tend to believe this, knowing such "principalities and powers" work continuously, feverishly. I have to wonder, though, what the painters believed. Some information from Kroeber's *Handbook of the Indians of California* might shed some light:

> Supernatural power, beings, or things are called by all the Yokuts "tipni" or "chipni." … In some usages, the term clearly refers to beings, monsters, or spirits. In other connections, it is said that a man, say a shaman, is "tipni," or possibly that he has "tipni." In the above prayer to the seven gods, the word seems to mean "with supernatural power"; but a translation "by supernatural ones" is also possible. Altogether, it is clear that "tipni" is used indifferently as a noun and as an adjective; and that it is employed, according to circumstance, to denote spirits, supernatural or monstrous beings of any sort, men who possess spiritual or magical power, and, if indications are not deceiving the essence or power or quality itself… (p. 512)
>
> SOURCE OF THE SHAMAN'S POWER. The northern California idea of shamanistic power is bound up with the notion of control over small, animate, disease-bearing objects, these material "pains" having many of the faculties of spirits… The

> Yokut shaman owns a spirit. This may be a monster or an animal that turns into a man, or possibly a permanently disembodied spirit. It is certainly most often one of the two former. It may be met in actuality, dreamt of, or both. But it is a being, with an independent existence, and with a defined relation between it and the medicine man; not a little noxious thing, a sort of animated fetish or amulet, that he swallows and keeps inside his body. (p. 513)
>
> Shamanistic power among the Yokut comes both unsought and to men desirous of acquiring it. It is most commonly derived from animals or monsters inhabiting the water or from their appearances in dreams after their haunts have been frequented… (p. 514) [ALK1]

If we do not accept the explanation of the bear shaman, we are then faced with the option of spirits at work at Painted Rock, assisting the hands of the aboriginal presence there many years ago. Were the Yokut of sound mind? If so, there are really only two possibilities: They were either under the influence of the drugs of their day, or they were receiving supernatural help.

Researcher Kathy Moskowitz Strain could very well be right in suggesting that these inspired paintings depict a Bigfoot family at Tule. But again, we are faced with the question: Who and what is the Bigfoot?

# 36. Evil Cain — Maybe Evil Bigfoot

We continue here with yet another piece of the puzzle, pointing to more evidence for what may really be going on. A figure in the early years of the Mormon Church had an unusual encounter in the 1800s. The setting for this unsettling rendezvous was a backcountry road in Tennessee, where David W. Patten claimed to walk and converse with the evil Cain. Although beliefs differ among various religious denominations, it could be said that talk of Bigfoot has remained somewhat of a neutral ground. D.W. Patten's supposed Bigfoot story isn't the only one that LDS pioneers have been a part of, but it could be the strangest. The Mormon Church itself would prefer that this embarrassing story disappear into the winds of time, as it ultimately poses a threat to our perception of the mental stability and credibility of a man who was quite influential, one of the Quorum of the Twelve Apostles in the Church of Jesus Christ of Latter-day Saints.

The story was documented long ago and is still spoken of periodically around Mormon campfires and on a few college campuses, primarily in Utah. David Warren Patten was accompanied by a dark stranger. While some confused souls have purported that this description would lend itself to the belief that he was speaking with an African-American, it is best to cast that unlikely idea aside.

From the pages of Lycurgus A. Wilson's *The Life of David W. Patten* (*Salt Lake City Desert News*, 1900), we can learn much about Patten's story, part of which is included below. It has also been published in Spencer W. Kimball's *Miracle of Forgiveness:*

> Dear Brother: In relation to the subject of the visit of Cain to Brother David W. Patten in the State of Tennessee, about which

you wrote to me, I will say that, according to the best of my recollection, it was in the month of September, 1835.

It was in the evening, just twilight, when Brother Patten rode up to my father's house, alighted from his mule, and came into the house. The family immediately observed that his countenance was quite changed. My mother, having first noticed his changed appearance, said, "Brother Patten, are you sick?" He replied that he was not but had just met with a very remarkable personage who had represented himself as Cain, who murdered his brother Abel. He went on to tell the circumstances, as near as I can recall, in the following language:

"As I was riding along the road on my mule, I suddenly noticed a very strange person walking beside me. He walked along beside me for about two miles. His head was about even with my shoulders as I sat in my saddle. He wore no clothing, but was covered with hair. His skin was very dark. I asked him where he dwelt, and he replied that he had no home — that he was a wanderer in the Earth and traveled to and fro. He said he was a very miserable creature, that he had earnestly sought death during his sojourn upon the Earth, but that he could not die, and his mission was to destroy the souls of men. About the time he expressed himself thus, I rebuked him in the name of the Lord Jesus Christ and by virtue of the Holy Priesthood and commanded him to go hence, and he immediately departed out of my sight. When he left me, I found myself near your house."

There was much conversation about the circumstances between Brother Patten and my family, which I don't recall, but the above is, in substance, his statement to us at the time. The date, to the best of my recollection, is correct, but it may possibly have been in the spring of 1836; but I feel quite positive that the former date is right.

Hoping the above all be satisfactory to you and answers your purpose, I am with the kindest regards, as ever.

Your friend and Brother,
A. O. Smoot [LAW1]

Clearly, this is interesting, but as I continued to research the idea of Cain, I came across a fellow by the name of Shane Lester. An established writer, Mr. Lester has published three books, including the *Clan of Cain: The Genesis of Bigfoot*. The author, who holds a bachelor's and a master's degree in professional writing, both earned at Utah State University, had this to tell me:

> First off, good luck with your writing project.
>
> My interest in the subject began in 1998, when I found the story of David Patten, a Mormon leader at the time, who lived in the 1830s and had an encounter that seemed Bigfoot like. That set me off to find a connection to the occult or some spiritual connection. I have talked with numerous people to understand their feelings during an encounter. I have only found a few experiences that seem to suggest an evil presence. The one that comes to mind is an encounter by a Native American in Utah. The result was a great feeling of doom or spiritual evil during the encounter with Bigfoot. In talking with other researchers, I find that they seem to shy away from the connection.
>
> I would wonder about your experiences. Other than awe and fear, was there a feeling of evil?
>
> Of course my book, *Clan of Cain*, takes the fictional position that Bigfoot is cursed, a descendant of Cain. As such, there should be a lot of evil spiritual influence during an encounter. Maybe fear is the most recognizable feeling. Fear and hope (good and evil) cannot exist at the same time.
>
> Maybe we have found the connection, even if it is not overtly stated. The fact that nobody has found any real, hard evidence seems to put the creature into the realm of the metaphysical. Who knows?

In case you're wondering, it's safe to say that Mormon frontiersman David W. Patten had all his marbles. As far as anyone knows, the man had a good head on his shoulders and no drinking problem or anything else that might lead one to question his reliability. If all that and more is true, let's focus our attention on the question: Cain.

It is really quite impossible that David Patten addressed the first murderer on the road that evening in Tennessee, and while it may be obvious, I'll tell you why: Cain was mortal and did not live forever. Yes, it was true that no one could take his life, as the evil firstborn of Eve had a mark placed on him personally by Yahweh, but God did not say that Cain was immune from dying of natural causes or that God couldn't ultimately just remove him. And, for the sake of argument, even if Cain had lasted hundreds and hundreds of years and lived to a ripe old age, he still wouldn't have escaped the flood that righteous Noah had to contend with, since only Noah and his descendants were allowed to enter the cypress-wood ark.

The Nephilim were on the Earth in those days as well, and we could say that they, too, went down without the ship. Let's face it: Cain did not cling to a loose board on the hull as a stowaway, buy a boarding ticket, or bribe someone to avoid drowning. Since we can pretty much dismiss the unbelievable notion that David W. Patten encountered the biblical Cain or the ghost of Cain on that Tennessee trail, just who did the Mormon fellow hold that conversation with? It couldn't possibly have been the ordinary flesh-and-fur Bigfoot of our day, could it? The creatures supposedly have a language, but it is not believed to include English or anything remotely similar. Many have come to me, however, about the mind-thought issue. The problem is, once we step outside the ring, the subject of Bigfoot begins to move off to the wild blue yonder.

As we ponder a real-life Bigfoot rubbing shoulders with a Mormon in Tennessee, things get even stranger when we consider what the creature allegedly said. First of all, Lucifer is a creature who cannot die. The beast of Patten's story spoke of that as well, claiming it could not perish, even though it had tried. It was also quite uncanny that the male stranger was admittedly on a mission to destroy mankind — not just physically, but particularly our souls. Also interesting is David Patten's report that the visitor was stuck with "wandering *in* the Earth and traveling to and fro." Is it mere coincidence that in the Old Testament, in the Book of Job, God asks Satan, "Where have you come from?" and the devil replies, "From roaming *through* the Earth and going back and forth *in* it"? The verbiage in both of these examples is strikingly similar. It would seem that Satan can take a shortcut, as is expected of his nature, but what about the strange creature who conversed with D. W. Patten? Was it a wanderer *in* the Earth as well?

An author who has looked seriously into the subject of a Cain/Bigfoot connection based on Mormon folklore is Matthew Bowman. I happened upon Mr. Bowman during my research, and at the start of our conversation, I filled the author in on what we had encountered at Princeton, including a little history of what else had gone on there in the Similkameen Valley. In all fairness to the possibilities of Bigfoot, he had the following to say about where we may be these days with the phenomenon:

> Sounds fascinating. I've attached a copy of my article, in which I trace sort of the opposite trajectory that you lay out here; that is, I argue that the ways in which Mormons have talked about this creature reverses the movement from scientific analysis to the supernatural that you're coming to. David Patten said the creature he encountered called itself "Cain," spoke to him, and exhibited malevolent intelligence. More recently, however, Mormon stories have made the creature more animalistic, less intelligent, and certainly less demonic. Equating what David Patten saw with what Bigfoot has been, I argue in the paper, a way to strip it of those qualities and make it more a creature of the animal world. Hope the article is useful to you…

Matthew Bowman's article in the *Journal of Mormon History* (*JOMH*, Volume 33), was an investigation into many things about the Latter Day Saints, the use of Cain as the result of evil, and how the name itself and his character were used throughout time. It was commonplace that when certain strange events took place, referrals mostly went in that direction by either the witnesses present or those who would give spiritual explanations for the confrontations. In essence, Cain has become somewhat of a scapegoat. Evangelical beliefs would blame the manifestations on Satan or his horde.

Below are sections from Matthew Bowman's *JOMH* article, describing the dark, haired, unclothed creature in Mormon stories:

> One story from the 1970s tells of "two boys from the Bear River Valley who had just received their mission calls… While they were riding, they saw a big, hairy creature. It spooked their horses… They went to their stake president… He then told them it was Cain." Another story, collected in 1998, describes a giant "Cain-beast which chased two elders to their car." (p. 70)
>
> Here is a representative modern story, collected in 1997: "A group of Boy Scouts was on a camping trip when they heard strange noises. It was Cain, who chased them through the woods and into a cabin. They locked the door, but Cain tried to climb through the chimney… The boys prayed, then got the idea to light a fire in the fireplace. The boy who lit the fire saw a big, hairy man's face in the fireplace right before it went up in flames. Later, they saw Cain running across the field yelping in pain." (pp. 77-78) [MB1]

In his informative article, Matthew Bowman's emphasis is on the creature Cain/Bigfoot being less of a demonic, supernatural beast. He seems to take the direction that the being is just another wild animal, living in the wilderness as animals do. The Bigfoot-like Cain of Mormon religious theology is being replaced by a mysterious haired forest dweller that is still being encountered today.

Bowman goes on to say:

> Another collected in the same year (1998) tells of Cain stalking an old man's farmhouse late at night. It emphasizes Cain's monstrousness, since "two horses… died in the night from heart attacks because they were so afraid." For his part, Cain reacts like any other predator, fleeing when the panicked animals awaken the farmer. In another story, the teller's grandfather looked out his window late at night and "saw a big, huge, hairy man looking in at him." The grandfather immediately closed the blinds. Reopening them a few moments later, he "saw a huge, hairy beast running across his fields. He believed this man to be Bigfoot." Interestingly, the teller introduced the story as his "grandfather's experience with Bigfoot/Cain," but the text itself does not. (p. 78)
>
> Other recent tales further this transition by deemphasizing or distorting older theological issues connected to Cain. One 1998 story rejects the traditional curse entirely, instead explaining that Bigfoot was an "Indian spirit that turns into a hairy Cain-like creature." (p. 79)
>
> A 1997 story provides us with a fascinating retelling of David Patten's encounter with Cain that demonstrates what the Cain cycle has turned into. The teller announces that he read this story in Kimball's *Miracle of Forgiveness* but goes on to tell a very different account: "During the early days of the Church in New York state, a brother was riding his horse through a thicket of wood when he came across an extremely tall, frighteningly hairy creature roaming through the trees. This monster-like form stopped the man and told him that he was Cain… Because of this spotting, many members of the Church believe that Cain is Bigfoot." While this story and Patten's affirm several similar details about Cain (height and hairiness), the modern version replaces Patten's description of dark skin with "frighteningly" and "mon-

> ster-like." In addition, this story omits Cain's description of his diabolic mission and Patten's exorcism. (pp. 79-80) [MB2]

In the age of change, even in the evangelical ranks, fewer and fewer recognize the theology on the deceptive manifestations of spirit forces that burden the human race. As humankind evolves, so the enemy presents itself, continuing to make things transpire to its advantage. What worked in the last century may be adjusted today, making sure that the influence persists.

We have heard that in most cases, Mormon believers are transforming their thought. Many believe the idea of Cain as Bigfoot is something from the past, although many still understand Cain to be ever present.

Now if these and other stories are true, is it the Bigfoot that is taking credit for making contact with influential Mormon individuals? When it comes to Bigfoot, all explanations seem strange, including the idea that the Bigfoot creature has to flee in the name of the Lord. If these individuals were not just Mormon storytellers, then why in every situation would the creatures leave immediately? It's not like they could understand plain English or gather the meaning behind evil being cast aside. Other than mankind, there is not another species that could comprehend such a thing. There really is no way around it: These particular haired creatures must be placed in the category of the supernatural.

In my attempts to ratify my findings, I came across a short story in one of the LDS Church History Libraries in Utah. This piece could also be found on the Internet, and I've located a slightly different version at times, perhaps a little sensationalized. Below is what was sent to me from a library staff member:

> Thank you for contacting the Church History Library. We have in our collection a copy of a typescript. The author of the typescript is unknown. It is alleged to be an experience, in about 1919, of E. Wesley Smith, who was president of the Hawaiian Mission at that time. The author states the experience was told to him by President Smith in July 1948.
>
> It says President Smith was sitting in his living room when the front door banged open. He saw "an unusually tall man come through the door. He was tall enough that he had to stoop to enter. His eyes were very protuberant and rather wild looking, his fingernails were thick and long, and he presented a rather

> unkempt appearance, and wore no clothing at all." Nothing was said about hair. President Smith was frightened, and he commanded the person to leave in the name of the Lord Jesus Christ, which he did. A moment or two later, President Smith looked out the door and saw no one.

When I began to question how the creature came to be in the Hawaiian Islands, a person or two explained that the Bigfoot had accomplished this by telepathic means, projection, and other applied techniques. It seems the species is presumed to be capable of anything. Joan Ocean dealt with this type of Sasquatch in the Hawaiian area at the paranormal level many times. A measured footprint of almost three feet had supposedly been found in pineapple fields in the earlier years around Helemano, Oahu. That would be one big Cain!

I checked Bigfoot sites on the Web, just to see if sightings came from the islands. Not to my surprise, the BFRO had absolutely none; the state of Hawaii was actually blacked out. It wasn't much better at Bigfoot Encounters, which had one heading that read "No Modern-Day Accounts of Sasquatch-Like Beings in Hawaii." Other sites had similar findings. So whom did E. Wesley Smith rebuke the night before a temple was to be dedicated? If we remove Cain from that equation, whose face was projected in the flames in the fireplace in the Boy Scout story? It couldn't have been Cain or Bigfoot. Cain is no more, and the Bigfoot creature isn't about to fit down that or any other chimney. So, the question becomes: What are we left with? Everything taken into account, we must assume that satanic powers were involved. Otherwise, we're facing an English-speaking, soul-seeking, flame-retardant, immortal, God-fearing creature that fits the bodily identity of what many individuals out there are looking for.

Allow me to say again: The odds are against it.

# 37. Bigfoot and the Devil

How can a creature such as Bigfoot make such an impact on the world and still remain practically invisible? The being seems to have a contract with luck and good fortune. Photographers of every variety, with all of their technological wonders, have failed to capture it, save for a few blurry shots and the highly controversial Patterson/Gimlin footage. Hunters haven't been able to shoot it, or at least not recover it afterward. The best of trackers have failed to track the giant, in spite off its huge brush-breaking size and the big feet that leave sizable tracks behind. Drivers have claimed they've hit them, but no one has ever proven they have. Scientists can't monitor it or agree on it. And governments can't admit it exists, unless tourism is on the agenda.

The Sasquatch mocks man to the greatest extent, and, when all is said and done, the human feuds that ensue over the matter are unbelievable, sometimes to the point of sadly humorous. Also, I have another interesting question: Why is it that Sasquatch has so often failed to pick up on hunters lurking in their tree stands, yet they have no problem making a joke out of every picture-taking device in the woods, highly technical devices that have been meticulously placed by knowledgeable electronic professionals? Is there a difference between flesh and mechanisms?

There also seems to be a rash of poorly timed camera malfunctions: the last picture on a roll, or an SD card being full, and so on. Truly, it almost seems criminal at times, and we have to wonder if something is up. In the end, it seems like the Sasquatch is having the last laugh — and the joke is on us and our fancy equipment and petty bickering.

If something is up, there would be such a critical line drawn in the sand — things of a supernatural substance involved here. Because I chose to research and write about this prickly topic, many have thought me to be fixated on the Sasquatch. One specialized person from First Nations thought so, and even a family member of mine figured the same. But when all things are said and done, I will close this chapter of my life — walk away from the focus that is Sasquatch. My goal with this project was to give readers informative ideas on what is happening within the Bigfoot phenomena. As we've alluded to already, there are so many circus sideshow claims and scammers out there that it is nearly impossible to count them anymore. Some seek to turn the whole thing into fortune and glory for themselves, and they are more than happy to make a buck or bask in the limelight. *They* are the extremists. I am simply someone who saw something rare and unique and would like answers as to what it was. Even when it touches my soul and beliefs. Before this, very few people even knew about me out there you could say. This is where my research has led me. We are almost at a standstill — a dead-end. There will be nothing but peculiar things occurring now within this subject. Hoaxes aside. So as a friendly warning, get ready. Because things are going to get bizarre.

I will hint at scriptural things in this section because of the numerous strange happenings surfacing on a rather regular basis these days. I do not want this to be viewed as any kind of philosophizing-religious tutorage. But in saying that, something is mysteriously prying at the door.

An adversary is very real today, and I raised a question with a number of church pastors and the Christian Research Institute of Canada. Truth be told, the UFO experience carries many dangerous similarities to this phenomenon. At times, the two are actually related. This aspect is growing. Many purport that if there are two such species, human and aliens, God would not allow us to clash. In records of these supposed abductions, Christ is never mentioned from the alien perspective. I will not fill these pages with pastors' and theologians' viewpoints on UFOs, but I will say many are aware of these ideas, and I have had several conversations with many to that end. It is only pertinent to mention here because of the similarities to the Sasquatch phenomena. Perhaps the same puppet master is at play in both cases, pulling the strings and taking great humor in watching human beings dance around the issues.

My sightings of Sasquatch challenged my spirituality, and the other mysterious situations I learned of over the years only added to the questions. It wasn't about being a religious zealot. It was about being a pragmatic realist regarding tough issues that required an answer. Circumstances given to the Sasquatch subject, we were now way past the idea of the giants being the Nephilim of the Bible. A diabolical plan is in the works. For me, this only furthers the need to discover the Sasquatch, if it truly exists. As an example, I'd hate to think about what we saw that morning in April and October. Let's not even think about the basement.

Sasquatch is not just on the skyline anymore, but is also over the horizon. When one realizes what is possible, it becomes evident that the idea of Sasquatch is being tampered with, and branching off mysteriously into a number of different directions.

To find out the opinions of other experts in religious matters, I contacted a number of pastors from different denominations for their opinions on the subject of Sasquatch and spirituality, a growing topic. This wasn't your average, run-of-the-mill shoptalk. And please have an open mind. It is an intense subject with many parts.

Some of the answers I received are shown below, confirming that many truly believe there is a chance that the Sasquatch phenomenon could be tinkered with, arranged, or even staged to a point. Spiritual forces could play this role.

> I would guess that an evil spirit could masquerade as anything they want, and especially to people who really want to be masqueraded to. (Pastor TB)

> Our secretary passed your email on to me. You ask some interesting and serious questions. My response? Anything is possible. Satan can and does use many means of "distraction," playing on people's fears, doubts, and wishes. (Pastor Trent)

> Interesting question. I have two points that may be helpful. First, I can think of nowhere in the Bible where angels and demons are strictly relegated to simply spiritual — that is, nonphysical existence. It is clear that the laws of physics do not apply to them as they do [to] us, and [it] seems to imply an existence that is nonphysical, but it does not state it explicitly.
>
> Second, there is at least one text where angelic beings take on the nature of men (Genesis 18 and following.). There are three "men" in Genesis 18:2: one is the Lord, and the other two are described as angels (Genesis 19:15). So, if it is possible for angels to take the form of men (doing things like eating, walking, pulling a man through a door, and striking a mob with blindness), it is logical to assume it is possible for a demon to do so as well. But it would be unusual. (Pastor Aaron)

There is no Biblical reason to believe that the Sasquatch does not exist, unless it is assumed the Sasquatch is some type of missing evolutionary link or of a humanlike quality that contains a soul. Those two criteria missing, there isn't a Biblical mandate to believe that all existing God-made creatures are found (as we find new species yearly). I would state that it is possible for Satan and his demonic forces to create many lies that can be spiritual, visual, audible, or even physical. I believe most so-called "alien encounters" fit into this category. Satan is a master at deception and illusion. (Pastor Jordan)

We already know that thousands of years ago, creatures in North America, such as elk and bison, grew a lot bigger than they do today. I think it is entirely possible that a highly intelligent, reclusive, officially undiscovered species of great ape (or whatever) could be living in the wilderness areas of North America, and, for whatever reason, they still grow to the same large size that everything else did. Maybe they were even larger back then. And if they were never very numerous to begin with, then they never left fossils of themselves that we have discovered.

However, if the Sasquatch is not a real creature, then I think it is entirely possible that demonic/satanic influences could be at work. Why some people are more susceptible to such things, I have no idea. I think scripture strongly indicates that the angelic realm can affect the physical world. For instance, in the case of demon possession, the spiritual realm acts through physical (i.e. human) agents. Whether or not they can directly affect the physical world, I'm not sure. I would tend to say [they can], since they can affect human beings in their physical bodies. I'm trying to think of specific instances in scripture but don't really have an answer, except for maybe the angel of the Lord that killed the firstborn in Egypt and destroyed the Assyrian army besieging Jerusalem. Those instances may refer to God Himself and not any lesser created being. No, wait… what about the two angels that visited Abraham (along with the Lord) and Lot in Genesis 18 and 19? They ate with Abraham. Presumably, they observed the customs of hospitality when they ate with Abraham (i.e. washed their hands/feet before they ate). Presumably, they left tracks in the dust as they walked down to Sodom. They ate with Lot and his family. They struck the men of Sodom with blindness (the spiritual realm directly acting upon the physical). They led Lot, his wife, and his daughters out of Sodom by the hand.

I think we also need to remember that "weird" things happen occasionally. In the rest of the world, they are still viewed as [being] caused by spirits. It's just our scientific culture that tends to discount anything other than naturalistic explanations. I think the truth is somewhere in between. Some things attributed to the spirit world have naturalistic explanations, but some things that people try to explain away by natural causes are, in fact, caused by the spirit world.

I think you are correct. There very well could be an elusive species of creature lurking in the wilderness areas of western North America. However, if Sasquatch does not exist, then I believe the best explanation is what you have suggested: some sort of satanic/demonic deception. In which case, Glen, I would caution you to be very careful. If you already know of people who have been led into the occult through their research, then take pains to guard yourself against such deceptions. If you become convinced that a spiritual realm explanation is the best one, then I would think it wisest to leave well enough alone.

May God bless you in your research and search for answers in these perplexing matters. Again, be careful and put on the full armor of God. (Senior Pastor Ron)

One thing the Bible makes clear is that "Satan masquerades as an angel of light" and "his servants masquerade as servants of righteousness" (II Corinthians 11:14-15). I believe Satan is capable of meddling with the phenomenon you describe, but his usual way of working is to masquerade as something good and wholesome — even as a pure and holy angel. He attempts to deceive people by using human agents who appear to be righteous and holy but are not. That's why we need to be on guard against Satan's deception each and every day. There are many things in this world that remain unexplained mysteries, the Sasquatch being one of them. Some of these mysteries will never be solved by our human understanding and investigation. Perhaps, for some reason, God wants them to remain hidden. (Pastor Rick)

**Figure 50: Doré's woodcut showing Jacob wrestling with an angel. (photo © Bob and Susan Whitehead)**

Can Satan transmute himself into creatures? Indeed the experience in the Garden of Eden, the experience of Moses in Egypt, and Christ and the demoniac's exorcism into swine would indeed grant sufficient power to Satan to do this. Even the disputed passage in Genesis about the sons of God cohabiting with the sons of men adds additional scriptural warrant. The incarnation of demonic beings is always presented in scripture as a satanic means to cast doubt on the Word of God; to destroy the seed of Abraham and His offspring (Christ and the Church). Lastly, the most common incarnation of evil that the Church can expect, is "angels of light" — "wolves in sheep's clothing." The goal of this strategy is to lead men and women away from the truth. (Pastor Jim)

Demons, as fallen angels, apparently retain great powers, such as the manipulation and restructuring of matter, as well as the ability to influence or control human consciousness and experiences through classic possession by direct psychic implantation of a set of experiences. (Curt Wagner, Ph.D.)

Is it possible that the Sasquatch is a tool to lead thousands away from the truth? Several others who contacted me had much to say about this:

> The answer to the question is rather simple, yet complex in its outworking. You most likely labeled it for what it is in your opening comment: demonic. However, in saying that, there could be a very real possibility of a chemical imbalance occurring with the individual in question. If indeed this is the case, they should be seen by a specialist. The individual could also be suffering from what I term "overexposure." This is a mild form of psychosis that occurs when one is overexposed to extraterrestrial influences (or any similar influence). If they read a lot about extraterrestrial visitations, watch too many movies, or listen to too many people discuss extraterrestrial activity, they could become overly exposed and open themselves to becoming psychotic. If it is demonic, then the individual must want to seek out deliverance from the Church (those people in the Church schooled on helping people escape demonic influences). Counseling is also available. (Pastor S.D.)

> I agree — very similar to the UFO situation, which is definitely demonic and not from outer space. I've never thought of Bigfoot in this light, but thanks to your email, it makes sense that it is satanic. (Pastor H.S.)

> Greetings. I appreciate you taking the time to investigate this issue.
>
> Although I have heard of these sightings since I was young, I have never encountered such a creature. While I suppose a creature like this may exist, there is not a tremendous amount of evidence to verify it, so I remain skeptical. Is it possible that Satan could/would present an image like this? Certainly he has, within his limited power, the ability to do such things. Why? I'm not sure. If his purpose was to distract people away from faith in Jesus Christ, then perhaps. Indeed, Satan's priority is to draw people away from faith in the Savior. If he can do that, he will take as many people to Hades with him as possible. (Pastor Jeff)

> Thanks for the emailed question about Sasquatch. I believe the UFO phenomenon may be demonic, but I've never thought about the Sasquatch appearances as demonic. However, in thinking about your comments, I do feel that you are on the right track. The devil is the great deceiver, and scripture teaches that he can take on many forms, such as, of course, the serpent — but he can even appear as an angel of light. So, yes, I think this may be part of his strategy to convince people that we are here by evolution and not by the direct creation of God, as scripture clearly teaches. (Pastor Mel)

> Congratulations! You have asked me a question I have never encountered in fifteen years of ministry. I can't think of anything even close. Hmm… I have no definitive answer for you but would like to reframe the question.
>
> There is a very human tendency among the faithful to fear that which we cannot explain. Could Sasquatch be an occult phenomenon, or could Satan be responsible? Sure, I suppose that is possible. But we must resist the urge to categorize anything outside the realm of the ordinary as potentially evil. So much is beyond our grasp and experience. I believe you have many other alternatives, including a slew of unknowable possibilities of which we cannot even begin to conceive. Your research sounds fascinating and unique. I pray for success in your tireless search for truth. (Pastor Corey)

> Satan will use almost anything to divert people's attention away from knowing Christ personally, including truth of the Gospel. Certainly evolutionary beliefs are one of the main factors in keeping people blinded. This creature, whatever it is, is another example of mankind trying to find a link to that. I would count in such things as the Loch Ness Monster in this category. So, would I conclude that is directly satanic? Probably not. Would I say Satan is using it to keep them blinded? Certainly. (Pastor Roger)

A handful of the pastors who responded to me named Darwin's evolutionary theories, as well as the missing link principle, as possible motives, and I began to see a pattern taking shape in their replies. They appeared to be consistent and in agreement on a great number of ideas. Each of these individuals felt the Sasquatch creature, a reality or not, could be used as a steppingstone for satanic forces, linking the entire phenomenon to the idea of an evolutionary process rather than the biblical doctrine of creationism. The enemy knows *all* the angles to alter the direction of man. We believe in one way or another, that a few parts of the Sasquatch experience have been infiltrated by those angels who were tossed from heaven in the Great Rebellion.

The Sasquatch conundrum spans a range from the depths of native shamanism to the sophisticated levels of scientific study, where evolution is a player, throwing confusion into an extremely sensitive subject. Every one of these things can be capitalized on by deceptive spirits.

Whether Bigfoot is God's creation or the devil's is one important topic to consider further. For a closer look, we continue with responses from more men and women of the cloth:

> I have no doubt that Satan is capable of producing such phenomena. The Bible is quite clear about his considerable power. However, the vast majority of Satan's labor and influence in the world is designed to distract people from the things that really matter and get them to focus on things that really do not matter at all. It seems to me that spending so much time on something like this plays right into the devil's hands. I would encourage you to chalk it up to a mystery. (Pastor Carl)

> Any animal that actually exists in flesh-and-blood form is a creation of God (Ephesians 3:9, Colossians 1:16, Revelation 4:11.) It's possible that Satan could have created some kind of mirage or other image in order to fool people. (Jeff, Staff)

> I have heard many stories concerning this creature in my life. I have some background myself in two different ways. First, when I was twelve years old, I and several school buddies made a Bigfoot shoe attachment that we used to leave tracks in various sites where we grew up. Not all that nice, but at the time we believed it was funny — even funnier when nobody noticed that the Bigfoot had two right feet! Also, while hunting here in Oregon when I was sixteen years of age, I saw what I thought was a large brown bear marking a tree. When we waited for it to leave, it walked away on two legs for about fifty yards, then ducked into the tree line. We measured the tree he was at, and it stood about eight to ten feet tall. I still don't know what that was. Now that I've shared those two stories with you, I don't

personally have any evidence that it is of satanic origins at all. I have not heard of all of the stories nor the experiences you have had, but I do believe that the possibility of a North American ape is very plausible. However, I will say this: There are many things that can be given to satanic origins. We have only to look for the earmarks of such things in this world. These include fear, wonderment, mystery, and an uncanny ability to mesmerize people with an obsession over it. We see this in both UFOs and ghosts. Could the Bigfoot sightings be satanic? I suppose so, but as I have said, I have no evidence at this point. (Clyde)

The bottom line is that Satan was cast down to Earth after being kicked out of heaven. Using my reason, I would deduce the creature as supernatural and not flesh and blood. Man's technology has grown very much in a short span of our history. In my opinion, as someone who has my own biblical worldview, I would say it is most likely a demon or spiritual being. (Pastor Leon)

Some had longer responses, like this one from Roger:

Could it be a trick of Satan's? I suppose it could, since he can appear as an "angel of light."

In working with native people for the last thirty-some years — and in that venture having talked to a couple of Navajo ex-medicine men, converted to Christ, and the things they've experienced in the spiritual realm (under Satan's domain), like shape-shifting, changing into an animal and roaming the desert, etc. — I suppose Satan could indeed impersonate a Bigfoot creature. ([Of] course, how do you impersonate a creature that may not actually exist?)

I know there're possibilities that are more locally known through occult practices — black arts and those kind of things (voodoo, etc.) — that seek to invent and animate creatures to induce fear in the locals. There have always been stories/accounts of those kinds of things.

I know even in Native medicine practices, especially those of the evil intentions, sometimes even animals, like birds, seem to be able to be directed in participating in curses. Owls, according to the medicine men I've talked to, can be sent to another person's house to warn them of impending death, or at least to scare them into thinking they're going to die. Again, not sure how that might apply to the Bigfoot, but maybe it does.

Not having studied Bigfoot stuff that much, I don't know if supposed sightings tend to be in particular localized geographical areas or just randomly anywhere. With the Navajos, shape-shifting always seems to happen in their territories where medicine men are practicing. Never hear of it anywhere else.

I know this: If these things are of Satan or not, you can't let yourself obsess over them. Whether Satan is directly the cause or not, he sure knows how to capitalize on such things to get people to obsess in interest or fear and, in doing so, divert attention away from Christ and our Heavenly Father.

Pastor Alex had this to say:

First, I have no idea what limits the variety of manifestations a demon may or may not take. So, is it possible that a demon might appear as a Sasquatch? Yes, I suppose it is. I think of stories I've heard from my First Nations friends who tell of the witch doctor changing shapes. If true, it's certainly demonic.

Second, whenever discussing demons, remember that their only power over a believer is through the use of a lie. They seek to re-enslave by substituting the truth for a lie, and through the lie (their native language), they control and entrap.

Third, if a demon manifests itself, he does so because it serves as an advantage to his cause; again, that is to enslave us. Either his appearing will fill us with fear (which is powerful for enslavement), or it will distract us and lead us away from our life with God.

If you were to have asked me if this creature is a real animal, I would have answered that it seems unlikely, but there is a remote possibility that an elusive Sasquatch might still go undetected; but again, this seems quite unlikely. Eyewitness accounts, of course, contribute to the possibility that this creature exists, but false accounts discredit the idea as well.

There were, of course, a few pastors or leaders who hoped this subject would necessitate a flesh-and-blood creature to satisfy us all. We must remember that Satan can still prey on the phenomenon, including getting into the head of such a creature and warning them of man, with a hint of demonic influence thrown in. If the timberland giant is a living, breathing species, one of the reasons for its elusiveness could be just that: satanic presence convincing it that it must avoid us at all costs. This would allow the phenomenon to continue as the mystery it has always been, and it would continue to be a vicious circle. An old Chinese proverb asks, "What's the smartest animal in the world?" The answer? "The one that hasn't been discovered by man." This is something to think about for sure.

That said, let's look at some of the further responses from clergy and church representatives who tend to concur:

> Hey, Glen. We have lots of stories about Skookum among our people. I know some very reliable people who have seen them — even some relations — so I believe they are out there. As to your question, "Could it be Satan?" maybe, but I really doubt it. You would think he's got more destructive things to do than to run around as one of these creatures. Those are my thoughts. (Corey)

> Beelzesquatch? I suppose if demons can inhabit a herd of pigs (as clearly happened in the Gospels), it's not too big a stretch to think they could inhabit a freakish beast in the woods. (Pastor Dave)

> Here is my point of view, though you will get different ones from other pastors. The Lord your God, the Lord is One; only God can create. And whatever God creates is good "in the beginning," whether it is a flesh-and-blood creature or a creature of the spirit world. Anything God creates may be distorted or misused, or may, like humans, choose death over life.
>
> In this time in human history, we might even interpret our encounters with such creatures as a warning about how much of the Earth we are using for ourselves, encroaching on the wilderness with all our machinery and destructive ways. Peace. (Reverend Arty)

It is wise to consider the question: What has the creature actually done? Others have suggested similar notions. A few teachers wanted to look at the situation of the Sasquatch more closely, seeking information to arouse their guard. I even contacted Billy Graham's office for an expert opinion. A spokeswoman there told me that the Sasquatch and similar topics are not Mr. Graham's given specialty in Christianity and that it would be best to work with local pastors. Clearly, this was a very touchy subject.

A pastor from Florida, all too familiar with fallen foe working feverishly to inflict harm and deceit on mankind at every opportunity, had something to say about the issue of spirit activity as it might pertain to the Bigfoot. There is substantial work being done to free supposed alien abductees from the hold placed on them, as well as education available on what to look for. The phenomenon of Sasquatch may be headed in this direction, if the paranormal outlook shows up more. Putting it kindly, there are some pretty mixed-up people out there. Below is Pastor Chris Ward's response to the questions I posed on these matters:

> Have you read the Book of Jasher? The Nephilim mingled the seed of men and animals to provoke God.
>
> Satan cannot create life from scratch, but then again, I cannot make toast without bread. Satan is a master of DNA. In Genesis 3:15 the whole argument of seed came up, and God put enmity between Satan's seed and Eve's seed.
>
> In Genesis 6:4 there is evidence that the Watchers shape-shifted and came down to the daughters of men and cohabitated with them and produced the Giants. These Watchers are the Star People of the Hopi.
>
> In the Book of Daniel (5:18-21), the king of Babylon is changed into a lycanthrope (werewolf). If he can be changed from a man to a werewolf, why can't a fallen angel change from an angel-spirit to a man or Bigfoot?
>
> The Book of Jude verifies this, in that the angels left their first estate (rank)…
>
> Also in the Book of Daniel (2:43), "… they will mingle with the seed of men."
>
> The Bible is replete with examples of shape-shifting. Did the angel step into the fire and go up with the smoke? If that is not shape-shifting, I don't know what is.
>
> In the Book of Acts (8:40), Phillip is "transported" to Azotus, but Phillip was found at Azotus: and passing through he preached in all the cities, till he came to Caesarea. Is that multi-dimensional enough for you?
>
> Tell me when to stop…

Our Bigfoot friend has also gathered some attention from the cosmopolitan Catholic community, but it seems they are more interested in what is outside of earth than what may be hidden on it. The Catholic emissary had the following to say:

> Seeing that there is flourishing interest among the masses concerning the beliefs of "extraterrestrial life," there is talk of the Church addressing this in the future. To what is the greatest extent of it, I do not know.
>
> For the creature in North America, the one you call the Bigfoot animal, this race of humanlike giants has been mentioned along with the ET through conversations had about the subject of New Age. On the Roman Catholic Vatican Website, there is mention of the "NA." (Just what they're hearing — keeping parishioners informed.) I've often wondered why Vatican City has its own observatory, including another… at another disclosed location, monitoring the stars, I think. Amongst their pages sits documents of the following: "Religious Implications from the Possibility of Ancient Martian Life."
>
> Now, Glen, on your topical subject, the Bigfoot has seen a place in discussion over some time — not something of everyday chatter, but still in the minds of a few believers amongst the masses. I hope this addresses your research — quite a subject for everyday church.

Continuing from this viewpoint of things, there was a second voice that commented briefly about the topic:

> I think the recent conference on astrobiology at the Pontifical Academy of Sciences shows that the Catholic Church is in the process of "gathering contemporary wisdom" on the question of extraterrestrial life. It has been doing this for a good while, even millennia! There was a *Time* article, which could have been written today rather than in 1955, along this line. (Chris Corbally)

Of course, many pastors had never heard of such things before, and they were shocked to find out. For their close scrutiny, I told them about different sites on the World Wide Web to bring them up to speed on some of the things that were actually going on — not because I am a cyber junkie, but because I wanted to lend a helping hand in alerting those who teach the truth to others. To say the least, they were astounded. Stiff, hard suits in Georgia freezers and the like never came into it, all that fakery and forgery of those trying to make a buck by exploiting the Sasquatch, hoping to profit from furthering the lies. There was no time for the foolishness, so I only sought to show them certainties.

Others, besides religious leaders, also had things to say about the connection between Bigfoot and the occult. One, whom we'll simply refer to as John, stepped forward to share what he and the locals in a southwestern area thought about such things:

> I am intrigued by your question. I have had an interest in Bigfoot for some time. I, of course, live on the reservation, in a culture that believes in the skinwalkers. Having lived here for a long time, I know skinwalkers are demonic and very real as a result, but as a believer, I do not fear them, for I know God is greater, and the devil belongs under one's feet. The battle has been won, and that is that.
>
> With Bigfoot, I believe some sightings could be demonic, especially in areas where the culture believes and has the shape-shifters. The devil will give you what you fear most. But I also believe there is good scientific evidence that a large North American ape or gorilla exists, especially in the area where you are. It is the perfect habitat.
>
> But having said that, until one is found dead or alive, Bigfoot will be nothing more than a good topic of discussions and such! But I don't think trying to discover the truth is ever a waste. The world was once thought to be flat until someone decided to go take a look. I think anything can be of the devil, depending on what you do with it. The question is, is what you are looking for or doing interfering with your relationship with God? If the answer is yes, then it is a distraction from what our eyes are truly supposed to be on.
>
> Thanks for writing. I enjoyed the question. I really did.

In her book, *Know Thine Enemy*, Connie A. Huft, a Christian paranormal researcher, talks about some of the deceptive practices unseen spirits use to manipulate mankind, something I've seen many times, and documented over the years. Connie has seen the good and bad of life, having escaped the art of witchcraft and the occult to see the light of things, claiming that the Ancient of Days (God) freed her. She is another voice among many. We'll end this chapter with what Connie had to say:

You have had some incredible experiences. Not surprisingly, when I talk to others who have experienced a Bigfoot, they seem to have a recurring affinity to it.

I am interested in your research, especially with the Churches and the UFO/BF connection. Intriguing! Not sure if you have been to my website and seen my article on Bigfoot or my fellow brother in the Lord, Robert, who is a Christian Bigfoot witness. He just started a forum and has been a serious researcher for years, but he has left the field because of the same things you have stated.

If you have any research or a website or blog, please let me know, I will link it to my site. These creatures, demonic or hybrids, are definitely an entrapment issue for many; their very nature has the stench of Satan all over it. Another intriguing question: Why would the Lord allow us to be a witness to such a creature? I would love to explore that one.

Thanks for contacting me. I look forward to what you have to bring to the table. Would love it if Christians would start coming together with real answers for today's seekers!

# 38. Flesh and Blood Believers Respond

We have spent many pages in Part III looking at the spiritual possibilities of Sasquatch. I thought it would only be fair to speak with a number of long-time pro flesh-and-blood researchers, to see if any of their beliefs had changed in light of all the new ideas that had been presented since they started their research.

> It is a mystery what Bigfoot is; however, I don't feel one can get to the bottom of such a phenomenon by invoking otherworldly powers alone. The natural explanation still needs to be thoroughly pursued. Some native tribes swear by the latter, while some entertain the former. Perhaps just mentioning the fact that both theories exist is enough.

In writing this, Terry Melanson paid heed to all the possibilities that are out there. He obviously felt the crunch of so much research — and from so many different schools of thought. Ultimately, nothing has been proven yet. Can battling factions live together in a truce on the subject of Sasquatch? It's hard to see how it could come about.

The Sasquatch phenomenon has come from a variety of sources. Of course there were the early stories, which I really knew nothing about, as they occurred during my teen years. These are the tales held by the old hands, the first to come forward, breaking ground with great determination. I have now investigated all sides of what the Sasquatch might entail: flesh, spirit, or even extraterrestrial, and I believe what I saw was the flesh part. All things considered, the flesh Sasquatch would be the easiest to expose to the world, but even then, even with the tangible, it is a long shot.

Mike Aragona, of the BFRO, spoke of this species being an undiscovered creature yet to be fully realized. Daniel Perez, researcher and founder of the Center for Bigfoot Studies, has been working on the mystery since the late 1970s, storing what is known of the Bigfoot with a neatly kept arrangement of files. He is also editor/publisher of *The Bigfoot Times Newsletter* and had this to say:

> As for my belief in Bigfoot, it is somewhat akin to a belief in Santa Claus. I think the term is misleading. They don't ask astrophysicists or astronomers if they believe in black holes. Rather, the question should be, How do you feel about the evidence for Bigfoot, largely based on eyewitness testimony? Having studied the mystery for over two decades, I am certain there is a species living in the flesh and blood here in North America. Based on my own informal studies, I strongly suspect the population is very small; therefore, sightings and such might be few and far between. Because of that, there is a magical, mystical quality to the whole mystery, but until a body is collected, anyone can say anything on the subject matter, and no one can tell them different.

German-born Wolf-Henrich (Henner) Faurenbach, a researcher with numerous credentials to his name, offered his opinion as well:

> My opinion is that anything spiritual or paranormal is in the observer's mind and has not a thing to do with a Sasquatch, any more than you would expect a paranormal bear or squirrel or chicken. I suspect that the fear or shock induced by a close encounter with such a creature can warp your perception in unpredictable ways, and pursuing these misrepresentations, especially in misguided print, is doing a disfavor to the public, who is generally scientifically naïve, if not illiterate, and will resort to any outlandish explanation before knuckling down and doing some laborious, real research. Even though I have had fairly close encounters myself, I have found nothing at all that requires resorting to supernatural explanations. I also had friends tracking footprints for close to eighteen miles without the Sasquatch taking flight or any other absurdities. There is always an explanation, even in newly fallen snow! You simply have to refuse irrational explanations as coming from irrational minds! The latter explanation is far more realistic than that the laws of the universe get suspended momentarily and temporarily for the benefit of just a couple Sasquatch hunters!

Although Sali Sheppard-Wolford has experienced a few mysterious things in her lifetime other than Bigfoot, she was kind enough to write about her experiences in *Valley of the Skookum.* In the area known as the Carbon River Valley of Washington, she and her family were visited by the giants starting somewhere around 1977. In the summer of 2010, the author's daughter, Autumn Williams, penned her own book, *Enoch: A Bigfoot Story*, a work that created waves of controversy.

I had the opportunity to correspond with Sali via email to discuss her sightings. It was of special interest to me, since my family had also seen multiple sightings. I learned the following from this remarkable author:

> In my opinion, Sasquatch are a type of early man of some sort, certainly not an ape. The two my daughter and I saw on the trail behind our cabin seemed as stunned to see us as we were to see them. None of us moved until the adult male cocked his head and looked down at my fur coat. I could almost hear him ask, "What kind of animal are you?" They are much more intelligent than most people believe. I think Sasquatch have honed abilities that most humans have forgotten how to use. How else could they have eluded humans for so long? I think they can sense a person's intent and whether they pose a threat or not, long before they're near.
>
> Most long-term witnesses seem to be women and/or children who live on the fringe of society, and the sightings usually happen when the menfolk are gone. I think there's a reason for this. Men are normally the hunters, while women are the gatherers. Men go into the forest for a reason. They dress in clothes to make themselves blend in, are usually armed, and sneak around. Women normally dress in bright colors and do what they usually do: pick flowers, play with the kids, or just hike.

Sali's mention of the male Skookum cocking his head struck me right away. As the Sasquatch tilted its head in the 1974 sighting at Princeton, I felt the same sort of scrutiny being cast upon me, as if the creature wanted to know who or what I was. I also recalled a similar event in the story of the man and woman who were biking the KVR in 2007, so I quickly contacted them again. Sure enough, the couple told me they felt the same way. That Sasquatch had also cocked its head in surprise, as if to determine who they were and what they were up to.

www.theborneopost.com FRIDAY, JUNE 13, 2008

# 'Bigfoot' was here!

Villagers have no explanation for giant footprints but businessman says proof is in the pudding

By Gaing Kunding, Raymond Tan and Conny Banji

DARO: Villagers here are reeling from the shock of discovering two extra large footprints near the fence of a nearby orchard.

They probably resembled those mentioned many times in foreign reports in claims of sightings of the mysterious 'Bigfoot'.

The shocker has been spreading like wildfire in Daro district for the past few days and among those drawn to the phenomenon was local businessman Tan Soon Kuang.

(According to Wikipedia, Bigfoot is one of the more famous creatures in cryptozoology, and, like many cryptids around the world, there is a fierce debate as to whether the Bigfoot species exists or not. Cryptozoologist John Willison Green has postulated that Bigfoot is a worldwide phenomenon.)

Yesterday, Tan, 42, e-mailed the images of the mysterious creature's footprints. He said he personally went to the village (which he refused to name out of respect for the wishes of the locals) to check on the truth of the story.

"The truth is in the photographs that I have taken with my camera," he told The Borneo Post in a telephone interview yesterday.

According to him, each footprint measures 47 inches from heel to toe and 17 inches sideways "clearly too gigantic for any normal human being".

Asked when and how he went to the village and took the photos, Tan answered: "I went there last Wednesday, June 11 after I heard about the news.

"I drove about five minutes from Daro town to the village. Then, I walked on foot along a footpath for quite a few minutes to the place where I met many villagers who were gathered there.

"Then some villagers pointed to the big footprints. I was shocked to see them and excited as I took those photographs."

On his conversation with the villagers, he said: "When I asked the villagers the first time they discovered the two big footprints, they told me it was June 9.

"They also told me they now recall that before they came across the footprints, the villagers had, a few months ago felt uncomfortable and sick as if there was something 'unclean' in the air.

"They said they decided to look for a 'bomoh' (medicine man) who told them to go to an area, dig a small hole, then build a fence around it.

The bomoh further told them to make offerings outside the area fenced.

• See Page 3, Col. 1

SHOCKING FIND: Picture shows a group of boys gathering around the right footprint which measures 47 inches by 17 inches and (right) a girl points to the two big footprints circled in yellow. The distance between the left footprint (foreground) and right footprint speaks volume of the size of 'Bigfoot'. — Photos courtesy of Tan Soon Kuang

## Income tax exemption in 2009 Budget?

PUTRAJAYA: Personal income tax exemption or reduction to lighten the people's burden following the fuel price hike and food supply crisis was among the proposals put forward during the 2009 Budget consultation yesterday.

Second Finance Minister Tan Sri Nor Mohamed Yakcop said the proposal was made by several Barisan Nasional (BN) Members of Parliament during the consultation between the BN Backbenchers Club and Prime Minister Datuk Seri Abdullah Ahmad Badawi, who is also Finance Minister, at the Finance Ministry here.

"We will include this point as a proposal and see whether it will be implemented in this budget," he told reporters after the consultation.

According to records, personal income tax exemption and reduction to one or two per cent had been implemented on 91,000 tax payers in the 2002 Budget.

Nor Mohamed said at the moment, only one million of the 10.5 income earners in Malaysia paid tax. He said those who were single and earning less than RM2,950 monthly needed not pay income tax, while those married and with children were also not required to pay the tax if they earned less than RM3,200 monthly.

"Out of one million tax payers, only 38,000 pay at a high quantum of 28 per cent."

Nor Mohamed said income tax contributed about RM10 billion out of the estimated national income of RM147 billion this year.

He said the 2009 Budget would also focus on improving the transportation system, including the government buying buses for use not only in Kuala Lumpur and Penang but also in other areas, besides providing incentives to public transport operators. Prior to this, the government had announced its plan to buy 100 buses including 30 in the next few months for the purpose. — Bernama

**Figure 51: Bigfoot stories are not confined to North America, as we can see in this newspaper article about large footprints that were found in Borneo. (photos © Ahua 101)**

The following researchers have years of experience tied to their names, and all of them are sound believers in the theory of a strange creature walking about in the forest.

> As to what I think the Bigfoot are, flesh, blood, and bone and tissue. In other words, they are absolutely 100 percent physical. A few people (for example, the late Jon Beckjord and Henry Franzoni) have preached wild and completely unsupported theories about the Bigfoot being other than this, with, among other fanciful physical capabilities, the ability to appear and disappear at will, etc. To these theories, I adamantly do not contribute. As to what they are, my theory (or speculation if you like) is that they are a primitive hominid form, as opposed to humanoid. Contributing strongly to this are, among other things, the upright (very human) bipedal gait, the whites of the eyes (again, a singularly human characteristic), and the oddly human, non-ape face.
>
> A few prominent Bigfooters might well also believe this hominid theory, but, desperate to make a find, they have deliberately expounded the ape theory in the hope that someone will shoot one. Among those who have participated in this are John Green, the late Krantz, Titmus, Dahinden.
>
> Time, and a find will tell. My personal hope, which began when I worked with Tom Slick in the sixties, was and still is solidly aligned with his great desire: communication with them. (Peter Byrne)

> I don't agree at all that reports of supernatural phenomena associated with Sasquatch are increasing. They have always been there, and they are puzzling, but they are a small percentage, and unless I someday experience something of the sort, I will continue to ignore them.
>
> I'm not taking a position as to the reality of things supernatural or extraterrestrial; they are simply outside the range of phenomena I consider it possible for me to deal with.
>
> There is the physical evidence of huge, extremely heavy footprints that humans have been unable to duplicate, plus a film that likewise defies duplication, plus a massive body of testimony for the existence of a large, upright, hair-covered species of ordinary animals reported in locations suitable to provide them with food and concealment and seldom elsewhere. That's

what I am investigating, and the fact that the scientific world chooses to ignore that evidence, plus the lack of any physical remains, constitutes enough mysteries for me without trying to explain anything via additional mysteries that lack such evidence. (John Green)

What is a Sasquatch? Since interest in the Sasquatch took hold in the non-native communities in Canada and in the United States, where the creature is commonly referred to as Bigfoot, most often the question asked after the obvious, "Does it really exist?" is "If they are out there, what are they?"

To the First Nations going as far as man has been on the North American continent, the answer simply was that they are hairy people who live far back in the mountains with various abilities, powers, and behavior traits, as various as the First Nations themselves. When the white man first started to take an interest in this subject in the late nineteenth and early twentieth centuries, the Sasquatch was simply an Indian legend that fit into the same category as old European legends like dragons, fairies, vampires, and werewolves — stories to be told to misbehaving children to get them to behave, etc.

It wasn't until the 1950s, when pioneer researchers such as Joe Dunn, John Green, and René Dahinden actually started looking into reported encounters of a strange, upright-walking, hair-covered creature that another possibility started to take root. When listening to First Nations describe a creature covered in long hair, it was assumed for the longest time that the long hair was only on the head. It wasn't long after these men started to look into the whole matter that they realized the hair description really referred to hair all over the entire body.

Suddenly, people were describing a more ape-like creature than a large human with extremely long head hair. At this time, a theory was put forth that perhaps the Sasquatch legend had been based upon a very real but rare animal that had existed in the wilderness area of North America.

This theory suddenly brought the Sasquatch legend away from the realm of mythology and placed it in a possible realm of zoology; however, since the creature's existence has not been proven in the world of zoology and just sits in the realm of cryptozoology as reported but unconfirmed animals, it will remain so until hard physical evidence is one day brought forward for the academic community to study and confirm. Once that happens, the Sasquatch could be declared a new species; of course, that would bring an entire new series of questions and studies and open a whole new can of worms for the scientific and political world to sort out.

Researchers in this field of study have proposed that Sasquatch is closer to human than to ape. Many well-respected researchers have supported this theory, and I have to admit to my mind that perhaps one day they may be proven to be right. But as of right now, and since I began to research the Sasquatch question, I think this creature, when proven to exist, will turn out to be a more ape-like creature, possibly the *Gigantopithecus blacki* line, which is simply continuing to this day. Of course, in reality, the ape or human debate is really a moot point, since humans are apes in the eyes of science. We are all primates. "Hominoids" is used to describe living creatures and now extinct creatures which seemed to more resemble modern man than, say, the gorilla or chimpanzee. To me, until the hard physical evidence is found, what they are and where they came from and what their future holds is rather irrelevant.

There are those who say the Sasquatch is paranormal or extraterrestrial in origin. I dismiss such explanations as modern-day mythology. The Sasquatch, if it exists, is a creature of flesh and blood, probably rather rare, living in the deep woods. It has a very elusive nature, only on occasion wandering near people, going about its own activities, possessing keen animal senses such as hearing, smell, and good night vision.

They are shy and elusive and want nothing to do with the modern world of human existence. They simply go about living their lives in the deep woods, searching for food and to procreate and avoid physical injury, yielding the ground to the first intruder, human or large animal. I think if they were aggressive, by now we would know about them. Of course, all this is simply a theory, and it will remain so until the Sasquatch has been proven to exist. Human-like or ape-like, the Sasquatch is the last great mystery of the North American frontier. I hope it will be confirmed during my lifetime as a living, breathing creature of flesh and blood. That is the only possibility that makes sense to me. If not, then it is mythology. (Thomas Steenburg)

**Figure 52: Statue of a Yowie in Caloundra, Australia, showing a relative of Bigfoot, or Bigfoot by another name. (photo © Melanie Cook)**

> Oh, Glen, what a disputatious subject we've chosen to be a part of! I guess seeing it with disbelieving eyes does help with a person making one's choice, and many of us little people have witnessed what I would like to believe, and I hope it is flesh. This is where I stand on the issue of Bigfoot. Being a Pacific Northwest girl, that's me. You are brave in drawing attention to other possible solutions that have come forward. You will get caught in the middle of a shit-storm, to put it politely: I can guarantee you that. But to my understanding, and from our conversation on the phone, this, to you, isn't about winning or losing. It's about what is taking place.
>
> You ask a lot of questions and take nothing for granted; this whole forest giant thing is in no particular person's back pocket. As the Cult of Flesh Sasquatch is always stirred up, is it any wonder that this other research belief (Star something-or-other) thrives? I've viewed the likes of J. Ocean's and J. K. Lapseritis's pages on the Web. They, and others like them, are sometimes very professional in what they believe, and it shows; they are extremely confident.
>
> I think I'll stay as an independent though, believing in flesh/earth-bound. The other camp will have a harder time delivering the truth, more on their plate. It is just too hard to prove — a proof of purchase. All this is very entertaining, but damaging to the public. (Michelle S., Tracker)

Another professional tracker voiced his concerns about this subject. I came to know him through communication about a little problem I'd faced while doing follow-up research work at Montana's Big Creek Baldy Fire Lookout in September of 2009. North of the tower, I was looking for clues to a giant creature's presence and also testing my own tracking skills, following a buck and doe who had eaten from one spot for over two hours. After I descended fifty-two stairs and reached ground level, the deer made their exit, and I attempted to track their northward movement.

After roaming approximately 100 yards from the tower, I saw the male watching me through the trees. That was the last time I saw either of them, though I continued to make my way slowly north on that lazy, sunny afternoon.

Out in a small opening, facing north, I took a look around and had a feeling something was behind me to the south. When I turned to see what it was, I noticed that part of the landscape was screened by rock and low-lying, hilly terrain. I immediately started back, following what I thought were my previous footsteps. The hiking trail was rather primitive, and parts of it were marked by rocks stacked upon each other to indicate the trail. After I walked back about fifty feet, I realized I might have possibly been followed, because there was a steaming pile of greenish-looking scat sitting in the middle of the trail. Long story short, I sent a photograph of that smelly remnant to six expert trackers, and I was told it was likely a coyote or a small cat checking out the situation.

One of the responding individuals took quite an interest in my remarks about the mysterious disappearing Sasquatch steps and the vanishing of this creature. Conor, the tracker, and his colleagues were greatly embarrassed at their failed attempts to put closure on the issue, as they were expert trackers with skills that had been handed down for generations.

Conor mentioned the Shadow Wolves, trackers so gifted that they were called upon to help stop contraband from entering the United States via the Arizona/Mexico border, particularly on the Tohono O'odham Indian Nation grounds. The Native American trackers come from backgrounds such as the Navajo, Chickasaw, Sioux, Kiowa, Lakota, Pima, Blackfeet, Omaha, and others. Conor mentioned their various backgrounds to point out the vast array of skills they brought to the table. The Shadow Wolves were mentioned in *Smithsonian Magazine*, as well as on the Internet, dubbed to be "possibly the world's best trackers" and said to use "time-honored techniques."

Conor fit the profile of a professional tracker, as he'd learned secrets in the manner of his clan. The heritage of his background was supplemented with modern-day technology, blending as one. He and others with similar upbringings apply these skills to their efforts to uncover a mystery. He spoke about the ill-fated Pacific Northwest expedition of the late fifties and early sixties, as well as other things that made up the Bigfoot belief system. Conor's group operated quite secretly, mostly in California and Washington, often way out in the boonies in northern California national forests such as Klamath, Modoc, and Shasta. In Washington, it was the national forests of Gifford Pinchot, Snoqualmie, and the national parks such as Olympic and the North Cascades. It was a take-no-prisoners approach, and they would tolerate no foolishness like that which seemed to hover over the Roger Patterson film. The small group was dead set on digging away at the dirt until they found something.

Conor stated right off the bat that he didn't want to brag. He did mention some of the ways he and his group did their investigative tracking of Bigfoot, hoping to give the public an idea of what they were up against. He was not initially a firm believer in Bigfoot; he simply wanted to expose the truth. Conor and his companions figured there was no way the phenomenon could withstand their microscopic approach, and they were out to prove it one way or another. The tracker explained:

> Glen, my membership into this would take all my knowledge and training as an experienced tracker. I will give you a few of the outdoor clichés that are involved with such an art.
>
> Disturbed ant piles and bees festered at the ground are examples of soil scatter and the basics. This would also apply to a spider web being tampered with. An ordinary person can look out at the forest or desert and see nothing unusual. Trackers who utilize "the old ways" can tell of other things when evidence is present. One of these things is called "shining." On your average day, mostly everything sees a period that is lusterless. As an example, an animal walking on grass presses it down. Using what is referred to as "side-heading," a tracker will see the shiny prints as sunlight catches them — the daylight accounts. Keep the tracks between you and the sun. The forest can give off a story in itself to the tracker who is patient and well taught. Disturbed dew in the morning is also another measure. We have tracked the Bigfoot under these conditions, when normal prints become scarce, the creature altering moisture on the vegetation. Also in your findings, don't just see the tracks, but feel them with your hand. There are signs there also.
>
> There is a substantial difference between the last-generation tracker and the newer breed. The previous hunter-gatherers had to know everything about their surroundings and all aspects of the animals and wildlife that lived there. If you didn't have the skills, you and your family could starve. Many trackers of our day do not have these pressures, and this waters down their aggressiveness to learn. The ancient ways are not being followed or reflected. These points that I am explaining have had to do with attempts made at finding the Bigfoot at our level of understanding. Over a number of years, this breed has never been seen

> by the members. In my opinion, it may be time to have a world hunt — not to kill, but to recover. We should take a collection of the world's best trackers and possibly do two things: First, allow the professional ranks to hunt for their own versions of the creature — a loosely monitored, timed event because of the situations with borders and politics; Second, the better way to document such a scientific tracking pursuit is to have the worldly tracking teams either working together or in contest (sponsored). I say go international or global because of the talents in tracking out there, passed down through the generations — everything they know… at work. It could be a complete blitz on the Bigfoot. The Chinese have their Yeren, Chinese Wildman, and in India, the Mande Barung. The Barmanou is another forest man, said to live in Afghanistan and Pakistan, and the Amomongo is associated with the Philippines. Australia is yet another place of a strange and upright creature, and the Sherpas of Nepal and Tibet call it The Wild Man of the Snow. These countries have excellent and versatile trackers with abilities that could be utilized in trying to recover this creature.
>
> Another exceptional group of trackers would be the Africans. It is a little different environment at the moment, but with their skills and know-how, they could quite easily adapt to the confines of North American terrain. They, too, could teach us a thing or two. We must remember again that these hunter/trackers do so for a living and survival. Many of these people do not have "hobby" in their word stock. After explaining the rules to them, you would have a great ally working with you — many gathered minds focusing on one of the greatest mysteries challenging man. We've tried to solve this on our teachings and beliefs but have come up short, the whole idea of it is an embarrassment at best. We could not close on this creature by any means, angle, fundamental training, and upbringing. The dog's nose was also used extensively. Swallowing my pride, and looking at this realistically, it may be time to go at this on a much larger scale. It is man versus nature. It isn't at the top of my list of things to do, but it will take a combination of minds and skills to try this. I wish anyone luck when attempting this.

Several others were contacted, many of whom might have had the ingenuity and resourcefulness to work on such a project, but they did not wish to go on any public record, not even under anonymity. These professional trackers knew all about the details of the mystery that had included the forests and wilderness, but they wanted to wait it out until the scales tipped one way or the other. Then, and only then, would they take a stand. I cannot blame them for not wanting to tarnish their reputations. I have written about what we have seen, as well as the possibilities of what may be occurring, but not everyone wishes to be so open.

In my investigative practices, trying to leave no stone unturned, I spoke with some shamanic trackers, medicine men, on the tracking issue. There was a lot of talk and a lot of human experience involving opening and recognizing nature in the raw. The credentials were sometimes staggering — what they knew, what they could do, and how they could do it. Still, no Sasquatch was tracked to its ultimate destination. Sadly, the most common responses I got consisted of skirting the issue. I heard, "There would have to be a major reason to track such a creature," or, "We'd best leave them alone," or, "You should not look for this animal with improper intentions." It was reminiscent of the Bigfoot organizations stating, "We could photograph and film them, but there is no need to." In my opinion, there would either be evidence to the physical Sasquatch or not, and we are still waiting to answer the question.

# 39. Conclusions

I want to start my summary by expressing my appreciation for everyone who contributed in any way to what you've read in these pages. It all began as a family observation that piqued my interest. Then many came forward with their observations and wisdom — from those who believe the forest giants are flesh-and-blood (a regular species that has yet to be discovered), to those who believe it has paranormal aspects — forcing my research to extend to the outer reaches.

On this journey, I have experienced the best and worst of people. I have met some great people with heart, caring, honesty, self-sacrifice, and determination — the best of what mankind has to offer. The personification known as Mother Nature has been unkind many times to the weary researcher. I have seen people helping other people under all sorts of conditions. If anything, these are the sorts of positive things that the Sasquatch mystery has done, giving the opportunity for people to help one another. Many have shared their knowledge, never holding back, even in the face of ridicule and threats. Even though an area like the online *Bigfoot Forums* can be harsh at times, I have still witnessed individuals or researchers who have come to the aid of others, even helping outside the field. When it is all said and done, it is not always about the creature itself. The interactions will always rest in a person's soul. Some are lost along the way, when their calling brings their investigation to an end. Even then their contributions live on.

I wish to thank all of those who gave their time, effort, hearts, and stories here; this book is a reality only because of them. Some of the personal stories were new at the time they were presented, and only because of years of investigation have we even gotten this far. Without the experiences and stories of others, research will never fully be complete. Even the stories readers may have heard before are part of the bigger picture, and the inclusion of them here is most appreciated.

If I have learned anything about Sasquatch in this quest, it is that there are no boundaries in the scope of beliefs.

The mystery has taken many turns over the years, with many pathways leading to dead-ends and others becoming more and more mysterious with each passing day. The thing of it all is this: Contrary to what many hope and think, the question of Bigfoot is nowhere close to being resolved.

My personal observations placed it in the woodlands, where I saw it for myself more than once. Mainstream researchers and investigators say it is an undiscovered species in the forest. Indigenous folks place it in the wilderness, but in the form of a spirit creature with powers beyond those of a physical animal. Paranormal researchers look to UFO connections or associations with the demonic, but, even so, when they find the Sasquatch, they find it in wilderness settings. Whatever it may be, everyone seems to agree that Bigfoot lives in the wild places.

I saw what appeared to be a physical creature, but countless hours researching the phenomenon and talking to the experts in several fields leads me to think that there could be some paranormal or demonic influence. When we put together the thousands of sightings with the fact that no conclusive evidence has ever been found, the conclusion that there is more to Sasquatch than a big, hairy biped acting on its own in the wilderness seems like the most reasonable conclusion.

About the entire mystery, we can only hope this woodland creature is, at least to a large degree, of flesh and bone. If it isn't, a person like retired logger Bob Mervin was injured for life for nothing — a human mistake made on his part, possibly involving satanic forces that are ever present and always patiently waiting for an opportunity. As strange and fiendish as it may sound, if this was the case, then Bob would never have killed anything, as the entire thing could have been diabolically staged by an unearthly presence.

Khat Hansen is another example of possible physical injury by what is supposed to be a creature of flesh, blood, and sinew. David Cleaver has also bodily collided with and touched this legendary giant. And as well, if this is all staged by supernatural beings from another realm, what did happen to Roger Patterson and Bob Gimlin at Bluff Creek in October 1967? They didn't brush up against the creature, but Patterson did film something standing in a dry creek bed. That something walked off, caught on film, changing the idea of Bigfoot forever.

Rumors still come out of the Princeton, British Columbia, area, where this all started for me. Stories are still told of visits of a hairy, tall one who comes down from the mountains periodically, its presence challenging man's beliefs about the nature of things, leading new generations into the mystery.

Which way will the scales fall? I have mentioned my end of it, but I am not the type of person you will usually see at the symposiums, hosted gatherings, or inched into the occult following. As a matter of fact, once I have voiced my knowledge of what my eyes have seen, I will then take a less aggressive approach to the whole idea of it. My information is now shared with the general public.

For those who carry the baton in the race, the best of luck to you, for it will be a major uphill struggle. The topic of Sasquatch will get stranger and stranger, I'm afraid.

I would like to mention something that came into my possession near the end of my writings, very coincidental and fitting indeed, from a person who has been saddened and hardened by this phenomenon, an anonymous Bigfoot enthusiast:

> I'm sorry, but I am no longer involved in the Bigfoot community anymore. There's too much in-fighting, bickering, and strife where there shouldn't be, despite a common interest or belief in these creatures. We should all be working toward a common goal: the official acceptance of these creatures. But everyone seems to be in it for themselves, whether they are glory hounds, wanting to make big bucks off of Bigfoot, or for other silly reasons. I have distanced myself from the Bigfoot community for these reasons. Best of luck to you in your search.

I have found this unbelievably saddening and disheartening, and I've heard so many others throughout the years… and there are still others I've seen for myself. I've witnessed them, just as I've witnessed the legend — and I still don't have any definite answers for them or for myself.

Ultimately, it will be up to you to consider these ideas and decide what you believe about the Sasquatch controversy. A rather large majority of the public disagrees with me about these sightings, and I've learned that there are thousands of individuals out there who have pondered Bigfoot and have their own ideas and opinions. So many times I've been told that we, as a family, must have simply misidentified some creatures of the wilderness, but that's nothing more than a broken record.

I've witnessed a legend. I've spent the last few years of my life trying to uncover what that legend is. It may become flesh and blood for a time when it is sighted. That explains what I saw. But there are so many observations of things that don't fit in the physical world that I'm sure there is a spirit component, too.

Then we ask, what kind of spirit is it? Maybe it is evil and deceiving man. Maybe it is good with the job of protecting Native tribes and nature. It could be somewhere in between with each Sasquatch making its own choices. I am not sure. There is evidence for all three possibilities. Research can continue.

For this book, though, we are finished. You've seen the range of evidence. Now you can make the decision about what all of this means to you.

The best to everyone — all creatures great and small… and hairy!

# References

Bigfoot Field Researchers Organization (BFRO). www.BFRO.net

Bowman, Matthew. 2007. *Journal of Mormon History, Volume 33.*

Byrne, Peter. 1976. *The Search for Big Foot — Monster, Myth or Man?* Pocket Books.

Clark, Ella E. 2003. *Indian Legends of the Pacific Northwest.* University of California Press.

Clark, Jerome. 1990. UFO's: in the 1980s. *The UFO Encyclopedia, Vol. I.* Apogee Books.

Coil-Suchy, Linda. 2009. *Who's Watching You?* Hancock House Publishers.

Coleman, Loren. John A. Keel Has Died. Cryptomundo. http://www.cryptomundo.com/cryptozoo-news/keel-obit

Crowe, Ray. The International Bigfoot Society. http://bigfootology.com/?page_id=811

Currie, Laurie. 1970. Sasquatch on Film Here. *The Similkameen Spotlight.*

Darwin, Charles. 1872. *The Expression of the Emotions in Man and Animals.* John Murray (publisher).

Franzoni, Henry J. 2009. *In the Spirit of Seatco.* Ste Ye Hah Publishing.

Green, John. 1992. John Green Interview with Bob Gimlin. Bigfoot Encounters. http://www.bigfootencounters.com.

Green, John. Reward Article. Bigfoot Encounters. http://www.bigfootencounters.com

Green, John. Sasquatch Database. http://www.sasquatchdatabase.com

Highpine, Gayle. 1992. *The Track Record #18.*

Huft, Connie A. 2009. *Know Thine Enemy.* Highway.

Keel, John A. 1957. *Jadoo.* J. Messner.

Keel, John A. 1970. *UFO's: Operation Trojan Horse.* Putnam.

Kroeber, Alfred L. 1925. *Handbook of the Indians of California.* Washington, DC: Bureau of American Ethnology Bulletin No. 78.

Lapseritis, Jack "Kewaunee". 1998. *The Psychic Sasquatch and their UFO Connection*. Blue Water Publishing.

Mallery, Garrick. 1886. *Pictographs of the North American Indians: A Preliminary Paper.* U.S. Gov Printing Office.

Marcot, Bruce G. ... *around the world, they call it Sasquatch, Forest Man, Yeti, Bigfoot, Matdngdng.*

Martin, Rick and Cortright, Gail. 2000. *The Spectrum Magazine*. March 2000.

Matthews, Gerry and Kristian, Ken. West Coast Sasquatch. http://www.westcoast-sasquatch.com

Matthiessen, Peter. 1980. *In the Spirit of Crazy Horse.* Viking.

Morgan, Robert W. 2008. *Bigfoot Observer's Field Manual.* Pine Winds Press.

Ormsby, Margaret A. 1976. *A Pioneer Gentlewoman in British Columbia: The Recollections of Susan Allison*. University of British Columbia Press.

Palmroth, Bill. 1992. See No Sasquatch. *Oregon Fish & Wildlife Journal.* Winter 1992 Edition.

Powell, Thom. Review of *In the Spirit of Seatco.* Bigfoot Encounters. http://www.bigfootencounters.com.

Pyle, Robert Michael. 1997. *Where Bigfoot Walks: Crossing the Dark Divide.* Houghton Mifflin Harcourt.

Robinson, Harry. Edited by Wendy Wickwire. 1989. *Write It on Your Heart: The Epic World of an Okanagan Storyteller*. Talonbooks.

Sheppard Wolford, Sali. *Valley of the Skookum: Four Years of Encounters with Bigfoot.* Pine Winds Press.

Short, Bobbie. Bigfoot Encounters. http://www.bigfootencounters.com.

Wilson, Lycurgus A. 1900. *The Life of David W. Patten.* Salt Lake City: Desert News.

Yellow Bird, Dorreen. 2004. Big Foot in North Dakota? Maybe, Just Maybe. *The Grand Forks Herald.*

Yellow Bird, Dorreen. 2004. Tales of Sightings Lend Credence to Bigfoot Myth. *The Grand Forks Herald.*

# Index

## About the Author

Glen Boulier was born in Eastern Canada (Summerside, Prince Edward Island) in 1955, and grew up mainly in Princeton, British Columbia. He has been married for 35 years to a wonderful German girl (Rosemarie), and they have three grown boys. He spends his time writing, is an avid amateur photographer, and enjoys camping, biking, and especially loves renting the U.S. fire towers in the Western United States. Glen and his family reside in Calgary, Alberta. They have a six-pound watchdog, Snuggles.

Please feel free to meet the author on Facebook, or visit his photography page at Glen Boulier Photography on the World Wide Web.